Lady Justice

Edinburgh Studies in Law, Justice and the Visual

Series editors Peter Goodrich, Director of Law and Humanities, Benjamin N. Cardozo School of Law, New York
Desmond Manderson, Director of the Centre for Law Arts and the Humanities, Australian National University

With an editorial board comprising leading figures in interdisciplinary approaches to visual culture, this series grapples with the burgeoning fields of optical representation, depictive practices and aesthetic critiques of law. Moving beyond narrowly textual resources, *Law, Justice and the Visual* explores the ocular, plastic and artistic, breaking new ground in expanding the sense and sensibility of the juridical. The series warmly invites innovative scholarly contributions on topics as precise as the typography of law, and as broad as the history of images of *Justitia* or theories of retinal justice. Working with both renowned and emerging scholars from around the world, we seek to apprehend the imaginal of law, its visual discourses, and the technologies and theories that subtend the social appearances and political performances of justice, both throughout history and in our contemporary world.

Editorial board
Mieke Bal (University of Amsterdam, cultural theorist and video artist)
Chiara Bottici (The New School, Department of Philosophy)
Christian Delage (Université Paris VIII, Département d'Histoire)
Lucy Finch-Maddock (University of Sussex School of Law)
Adam Gearey (Birkbeck School of Law)
Piyel Haldar (Birkbeck School of Law)
Paolo Heritier (Università degli Studi di Torino, Dipartimento di Giurisprudenza)
Linda Mulcahy (Oxford University, Centre for Socio-Legal Studies)
Lynda Nead (University of London, Birkbeck College, Art History)
Richard Sherwin (New York Law School)
Jessica Silbey (Northeastern University School of Law)
Igor Stramignoni (London School of Economics, Department of Law)
Marco Wan (University of Hong Kong, Faculty of Law 香港大学法学院）
Patricia Williams (Northeastern University School of Law)
Alison Young (University of Melbourne, School of Social and Political Sciences)
Carey Young (Slade School of Fine Art, University College London and visual artist)

Titles in the series include:

Lady Justice: An Anatomy of Allegory
Valérie Hayaert

Visit the **Edinburgh Studies in Law, Justice and the Visual** website at https://edinburgh universitypress.com/series-edinburgh-studies-in-law-justice-and-the-visual

Lady Justice

An Anatomy of Allegory

Valérie Hayaert

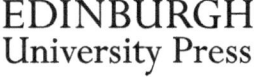
EDINBURGH
University Press

Edinburgh University Press is one of the leading university presses in the UK. We publish academic books and journals in our selected subject areas across the humanities and social sciences, combining cutting-edge scholarship with high editorial and production values to produce academic works of lasting importance. For more information visit our website: edinburghuniversitypress.com

Grateful acknowledgement is made to the sources listed in the List of Figures for permission to reproduce material previously published elsewhere. Every effort has been made to trace the copyright holders, but if any have been inadvertently overlooked, the publisher will be pleased to make the necessary arrangements at the first opportunity.

Edinburgh University Press Ltd
13 Infirmary Street
Edinburgh, EH1 1LT

First published in hardback by Edinburgh University Press 2023

Typeset in Warnock Pro
by Biblichor Ltd, Scotland

A CIP record for this book is available from the British Library

ISBN 978 1 4744 8748 1 (hardback)
ISBN 978 1 4744 8749 8 (paperback)
ISBN 978 1 4744 8750 4 (webready PDF)
ISBN 978 1 4744 8751 1 (epub)

This book benefited from a research fellowship at the Käte Hamburger Center for Advanced Study in the Humanities 'Law as Culture'.

This work was partly supported by the Le Studium, Loire Valley Institute for Advanced Studies, Orléans & Tours, France under Marie Skłodowska-Curie Actions, grant agreement 665790, European Commission.

This research was supported by the EUTOPIA Science and Innovation Fellowship Programme and funded by the European Union Horizon 2020 programme under the Marie Skłodowska-Curie grant agreement No 945380.

For Dana Hayaert (1973–2022)

Contents

Figures

Acknowledgements

I would first like to express my deep gratitude to Peter Goodrich, *Bonus Dives Imaginosus*, for his patient, generous and tactful replies to my naïve enquiries about law and the psychoanalytical roots of legal science. He has read numerous drafts of this text with characteristic wit, care and acumen and arranged for me to deliver parts of Chapters 6 and 7 as lectures to audiences in New York. It also gives me great pleasure to record my gratitude to Desmond Manderson, who accompanied this process of committing to writing in English, insisted on the virtues of lucid prose and added insights to the creative venture itself, including the freedom to disagree and to interpret differently. Both enthusiastically welcomed this study in the new series launched by Edinburgh University Press, *Edinburgh Studies in Law, Justice and the Visual*, and made a radical commitment to co-thinking and building otherwise the relationships between Law and visual regimes. What marks off new ventures from going over old ground is finding myself plunged into a language which is not my own. Writing in English (in contrast to Globish) can also be the threshold of imagination. Thanks to both of them, the final version of this book is better than I could have hoped.

Faced with the magnitude of the field of enquiry, Antoine Garapon has been a major source of encouragement and inspiration, providing invaluable counterpoints and lively discussions on some of the knottier problems of symbolic practices. Alain Berthoz and Daniel Bennequin introduced me to the necessity of tackling the fertile ground of spatial geometries of the gaze. Over the past few years, I have counted on the support and encouragement of a number of friends. Fabienne Verdier urged me to be bold when my spirits flagged. Samuel Mareel and his staff as the Buysleyden Museum in Mechelen gave me the benefit of their collective wisdom. Ian Maclean, Robert Jacob, Anne Tessier-Ensminger, Robert Carvais, Michel Jeanneret, Subha Mukherji, Vanessa Selbach, Yann Sordet, Werner Gephart, Maria Eichhorn, Carolin Behrmann, Gianmaria Ajani, Peter Schneck, Olivier Jouanjan, Olivier Beaud, Greta Olson, Jeanne Gaakeer, Anne-Marie Bonnet, Aïda Kazarian, William Barton, Gary Watt, Jean-Michel Massing, Mara Wade, Hans Brandhorst, Christian-Nils Robert, Bob Darnton, Olivier Christin, Natalie Zemon Davis, Julie Peters, Gretty Mirdal, Nicolas Lyon-Caen, Stefano Marrano, Damien Scalia, Jean Lassègue, Rodolfo Savelli, François Ost, Alain Wijffels, Xavier Rousseaux, Georges Martyn, Vanessa Paumen, Manfred Sellink, Xavier Prévost, Géraldine Cazals, Catherine Kessedjian, Nathalie Goedert, Ninon Maillard, Giovanni Rossi, Maksymilian Del Mar, Simon Stern, Carey Young, Harold Epineuse, Sophie Gabillet, Denis Salas, Etienne Madranges, Sylvie Humbert, Valentino Cattelan and Shirin Naef have all in various ways accompanied the fulfilment of this *peregrinatio academica*.

I was able to carry out this project thanks to the exceptional working conditions provided by the Paris Institute of Advanced Studies, the Käte Hamburger Kolleg 'Law as Culture' of the University of Bonn, Le Studium, the Loire Valley Institute of Advanced Studies and the Criminal Justice Centre of the University of Warwick. I received generous grants (MSCA and EUTOPIA SIF) which permitted me to pursue research in Belgium, Switzerland, Italy, Germany, France and the United Kingdom. I hope that this book goes some way to paying the enormous debt I owe to these institutions and to the digital collections that have made this research possible.

During its long gestation, this book has seen changes in the nature of collecting data which also need to be acknowledged. In 2013, the Rijksmuseum in Amsterdam launched Rijksstudio, a revolutionary online presentation of 125,000 works in the collection, totalling 690 gigabytes, offering ultra-high-resolution images of works, both famous and less well known, for free download and copyright-free manipulation. The distinctive feature of Rijksstudio is a focus on the image as it believes in the strength of the images themselves, which are used to create an engaging online aesthetic experience. Scholarly writing on Law, Justice and the Visual is often scarcely illustrated, much written in abstract or conceptual form, far away from the materiality of images.

My aim in writing this book has been to reflect on the concept of the aura of Lady Justice's avatar, to use Walter Benjamin's term (1968). The digitally reproduced artwork may serve as an enticement to reassert the uniqueness of a visit to a real-word museum. This is especially important when we remember that courthouses are not museums and that most of the artworks contained in their precincts are inaccessible.

I have always wanted to ensure that *Lady Justice: An Anatomy of Allegory* would be a beautiful object, visually appealing and lavishly printed. I owe a special debt to Peter Goodrich and the editorial team of Edinburgh University Press, who fulfilled my desire. I began to write this book in Bonn; most of it was composed in Tours and Paris and I finished it in Warwick. I would like to thank Sarah Foyle, Laura Williamson, Helena Heald, Judith Mackenzie and Eliza Wright for their patience, continuous advice and meticulous care through the production phase of this book. My greatest debt is to Alexandre Vanautgaerden. We have shared together the pleasures of researching, writing and debating Art and Humanities, a rich family life filled with funny and feisty art visits, repeated trips to archives, conferences and courthouses, and the arrival of Swann, who knows more about Lady Justice than any other seven-year-old little girl, despite having to bear with the obsessions of her parents. She constantly reminds me that there is more to life than writing books.

Introduction

This study aims at dismembering the allegorical figure of Lady Justice, organ by organ, limb by limb, as I believe the allegorical medium can be an effective tool for the exposure of affective justice. As an attempt to imagine some of the multifarious responses of those who originally encountered her bodily presence, it gives a central place to the physiological substrate of judicial ethics, locating it within the history of gestures and postures as they are shared by judges, litigants and citizens across the whole social body. Beyond the conventional objects of art historians, setting aside styles and schools, Lady Justice may be seen as law's conscience, an archetype of the judge's daimon, and an affective, numinous address to his consciousness.

In rendering the history of Lady Justice as a chapter of political and judicial anatomy, this study claims to unearth some of the elementary structures on which European visual regimes are based. Justice cannot be only reduced to an extrinsic and formal iconological notion. She belongs closely to the effects of ambiguous rituals, where decorous images can easily be subjected to bold inversions. Images of *Justitia* aim at clarifying the antagonistic essence of justice by embodying its innermost struggles.

This book is born out of an investigation into judicial symbolism in ancient courts of justice, from the perspective of the *longue durée*. Cicero (*De officiis* 3.17) famously claimed, 'we have no solid and express effigy of true law and genuine justice; but we can enjoy shadows and images to represent them' ('Nos veri juris germanæque justitiæ solidam et expressam effigiem nullam tenemus: umbra et imaginibus utimur').[1] Unable to access the perfect image of genuine justice, in the shape of an effigy, we are left with faint representations (images), the shadows of law and its eternal good. Cicero highlights the essentially paradoxical nature of images of Justice: these imperfect representations are but models interposed between justice and its transient material depictions in earthly embodiments. These symbolic expressions are nothing more than obscure images of the thing they wish to define. Their similitude, agreement or conformity to eternal justice is always questionable. Technically speaking, crafting images of Justice depends on the ability to draw a general outline, limiting the size and proportions of the figure to be represented, whether rendered on a wall, paper, canvas or in the three-dimensional space of statuary.

Justice, therefore, emerges from a double dialectics: that between the divine and the human, and that between the ideal and the terrestrial, the theophanic character of the unfathomable and the earthly embodiment of its avatars. Because the concept of Justice has long been embodied in the shape of a female allegory, it is also always a mixture of physiology and language, as well as a mixture of how Justice as an institution intended to present herself and how viewers have actually interpreted her.

If the mere goal of painting Justice is sometimes paradoxically described as impossible, it means that there is a symbolic context to be addressed, that the multiple and inconstant gestures and physical allegories of *Justitia* will be investigated as key elements of the allegorical process. My purpose is to offer a study of the many physical allegories of Lady Justice, to discuss their iconography, so as to show that from the late medieval age until modern times, the ascent and ebbing away of the figure of Lady Justice can be thought as more ubiquitous and sophisticated than it may at first appear.

The present book is therefore founded on five premises:

1. I wish to introduce a novel approach to the study of the history of representations of Justice as material and visual expressions of Justice that have an independent life and aesthetic of their own that should be understood from the disparate perspectives of the context and viewers of such imagery.
2. This means taking seriously the plurality of meanings intended by the artists who produce such imagery and the variety of viewers who would see these meanings.

3. The symbolic, artistic and institutional contexts in which such imagery appeared deserve close scrutiny.
4. Close viewing of a changing and plural imagery requires close attention to gesture, body parts, movement, symbolic context and accompanying virtues.
5. The gestural allegories depicted in the images of *Justitia* also play an important role in relation to law, both as a mechanism of ethical constraint upon legal action and a mode of rendering law's presence in everyday life, thus mediating between strict law and a social sense of justice.

Types, emblems and symbolic reductions of the notion of Justice are often approached through iconographic or stylistic study alone. In reducing images to illustrations of texts, iconographers fail to seize the essence of the artistic phenomenon, which cannot delimit the expressive possibilities of images through discourse. The allegories of Justice studied here will be perceived, read and valued through an understanding of the artist's intention, the materiality of the artwork and the disposition of its viewers. Hans Belting established that medieval art cannot be reduced to an allegorical exegesis that subordinates meaning and motive to rational reduction.[2] In keeping with this protocol, what images of Justice teach us are the collective ways in which significance was created and conveyed. Images of Justice are not trivial instruments of didacticism: their deontological function brings to the fore novel ways of understanding their role in judicial contexts and raises crucial images of reception. David Freedberg has notably addressed the range of responses triggered by the power of images, drawing on Wolfgang Brückner's *Bildnis und Brauch*.[3] Lawyers had recourse to various forensic rhetorical modes at work in the representation of the juridical, and these tropes flesh out an entirely new spectrum of possibilities.

Periodisation

The period under scrutiny, 1450–1850, with some incursions into contemporary art in the Epilogue, is particularly revealing: humanists have constantly questioned the meaning of pictorial images produced throughout Europe. Given the conceptual framework outlined above, too strict a periodisation would have acted as a deterrent to gauging the persistence of enduring *pathos formulae*, the products of a conjunction of variable schemes and their dissemination. Allegorical schemes are not easily reduceable to a firm chronology as their seriality only allows glimpses into mutable chronological lines. The mass production of allegorical forms during the period under examination intensifies antique schemes and iconographical patterns. Allegories of Justice always appear in the European visual field as images of the living body, and this compositional element is still valid today, though it is challenged by aniconic or iconophobic gestures. In a sense the very nature of allegoresis, blurring the difference between representation and symbolisation, is perhaps more easily understandable if we use the anatomical structure of the body as a tool of investigation: a distinctive feature of European cultures is the embodiment of Justice in a female allegory, and this will be the object of the ensuing study.

Terminus ante quem: 1515

An important dialogue on how to depict *Justitia* (*De Justitia pingenda*) is to be found in the Mantuan humanist Battista Fiera's treatise on the challenge of painting the allegory of Justice. This fictitious dialogue, set around 1488–90 and published in 1515, opposes Momus, a personification since antiquity of carping criticism, to Mantegna, who had been commissioned to paint an image of Justice for the Chapel of Pope Innocent VIII. Mantegna appears in Fiera's dialogue as a ghost (he had been dead for nine years by then; Fiera was one of the witnesses to his will on 1 March 1504).[4] Momus criticises each of the iconographical proposals by consistently pointing out their paradoxical gestures and conflicting attributes. For him, some of the artistic choices made are absurdities. Whether divine or human, the malevolent Momus brings an ironic and satirical tone to the task of producing the appropriate allegory of Justice. Momus' philosophical criticism tends to view the very possibility of an image of Justice with disfavour. Allegories of Justice trying to represent the unrepresentable are nothing but foolish attempts and expressions of vanity. Momus describes the presumptuousness of those who believe it is possible to paint images of Justice, a spiritual notion, which, according to the most radical theologians, should transcend all iconic mediation. Momus' viewpoint will accompany us all the way to the end of the book. His commonsensical remarks regularly underline the challenges of allegorical creation. This dialogue is a key entry point into our investigation as it addresses the question of intentionality. Are images of Justice to be considered *acheiropoieta* ('made without hand'), that is, without the intervention of any human agency? If *Justitia* is indeed a goddess, the subject of genuine adoration, how do artists acknowledge her miraculous incarnation and translate it into a form, a figure or hieroglyphic presence?

Giving a body to the allegory of human justice entails engaging with sensible compromise, a necessary descent towards materiality. Any attempt at representation should thus be carefully scrutinised. An adequate image of *Justicia* (human justice, as opposed to divine justice) will be accepted only if it becomes a mediator between high and low, visible and invisible, divine and human. The dialogue between Momus and Mantegna highlights the core problem of visualising a paradoxical notion, as it reveals the manifold reactions of potential viewers according to their perceptual habits. Iconophobic theologians will not agree to aesthetic communion unless they find in the allegory of Justice a useful figurative concession. At any rate, Momus claims, the law of Justice was imprinted on the human mind, in order that evil men would have no excuse for ignoring it. But if Justice is imprinted deep in the human mind, why should anyone want to figure it at all? After listing many of the ambiguous attributes or gestures of Dame Justice, Momus, through a process of Socratic questioning, sees the challenge as a conundrum:

Mantegna – [A Carmelite theologian] maintained that Justice cannot be depicted at all.

Momus – And there he is certainly right. If all these different opinions of philosophers were so, I also agree with him. For how can you represent Justice both with one eye and many eyes; and how can you depict her one-handed, and yet measuring, at the same time weighing and simultaneously brandishing a sword? – unless of course, they are all raving mad. Clearly, the thing can't be done.[5]

Momus' ever-watchful eye preserves us from hermeneutic dogmatism. Bluntly exposing conflicting discourses about how to represent Justice, Momus anthologises the various interpretative paths and the relativism of a wide range of visual patterns. Against too high a conception of divine justice, Momus' prosaic approach brings us back to the enigmas of any image, inevitably subject to a series of fluctuating perceptions. An adequate image of Justice should be able to address shifting audiences, but also local parameters and temporal circumstances. To be effective, judicial imagery also requires translation into the sensibility specific to each local culture.

Justitia and her siblings: the four cardinal virtues

In his discussion of the humanist tradition of art criticism, Michael Baxandall reports a minor skirmish between Lorenzo Valla and the canon lawyer, poet and scholar Antonio Panormita (Antonio Beccadelli, 1394–1471) about the verses they were both asked to produce to accompany the four virtues (Justice, Charity or Liberality, Prudence and Temperance or possibly Fortitude), which were to adorn a portrait of King Alfonso V of Aragon in armour and on horseback, to be painted in Castel Capuano, Naples. In 1436, the new Aragonese ruler of Naples had decided to rebuild Castel Capuano, originally a defensive outpost of the city, as a residential palace. The Gran Sala of the royal residence was adorned with tapestries, and the royal throne, worked in gold and silk, would occupy the centre of the room.[6] Both contenders composed verses for each virtue, but not in the same order and not from the same viewpoint. The equestrian portrait of King Alfonso was to be flanked by the four virtues, two above and two below. Numerous representations of the prince as equestrian figure would appear with inscriptions recalling the pun on *equus* and *æquus*. Panormita's verses are addressed directly to the king, whereas Lorenzo Valla chooses to have each virtue speak for herself.[7] In Valla's judgement, Panormita's verses are a banal praise of the addressee. Instead, Valla shows multiple viewing parameters and emphasises the necessity of presenting new visual formulas. His critique of Panormita's conservatism echoes many of the problems we will address in this book:

Antonio made his verses such that the speaker must be either the beholder – which is absurd – or the Virtues themselves; and yet if it *is* the Virtues speaking for themselves, they are not speaking about themselves. I, on the other hand, made the verses such that the Virtues are plainly speaking to each other about themselves, and also such that they can be put in the same order as the painter wants to put their figures. Antonio's cannot begin – as they should – with Prudence.[8]

Justitia's avatars: an art of gestural ethics

To explore the paradoxes of effective judicial symbolism, this study questions various aspects of the ways in which Lady Justice has been used to depict human justice and divine justice, crime and punishment, guilt and innocence, visually over the course of several centuries. Instead of seeing allegory as a straightforward vehicle for a noble ideal, the various examples analysed here investigate the art of gestural ethics, a form of symbolic expression which is constantly negotiated and is essentially self-contradictory. Of particular importance is the fact that these symbols, as we will see, were most often produced within judicial contexts.

Series of popular allegories, mediated through designs produced in large quantity, will help to show how moralising allegories were widely used in the North and South Lowlands throughout the opening decades of the fifteenth century. Silver-stained white glass roundels with grisaille, for example, encompassed a great variety of topics, and depictions of allegorical judgment scenes were not uncommon. They were made of unleaded glass painted in matte, vitreous paint, and tinted with fired silver oxide to produce translucent yellow, gold or copper shades.[9] They were usually commissioned for domestic (well-to-do burgher castles), civic or professional settings. In the Lowlands, they served in judicial contexts as *exempla justitiæ*.[10] Secular panels would often represent themes where judgment was dispensed, such as the stories of Zaleucus of Locria, the Judgment of Solomon, the Judgment of Susanna, or the Judgment of Cambyses. These topics were adapted to small-scale formats in judicial contexts such as tribunals and city halls, but also in civic buildings such as town and guild houses. By the end of the Middle

Ages, a large market in small-scale stained glass was destined predominantly for such secular uses. Images of Justice naturally played an important role in this burgeoning new style, at least north of the Alps. Ideally suited to new forms of civic architecture (private office, secret chamber, *otium* room), the scale of the roundels was especially well adapted to thematic series, and their subject matter provided an ideal medium for ethical reflection.

Lady Justice's polyonomy

Renaissance syncretism crafted different types of allegories of Justice rewritten and reinterpreted from antique sources. The polyonomy of Greek divinities (Astræa, Dike, Nemesis) is a starting point: Lady Justice often unites several avatars that were already conflated by the ancients. A clear illustration of this phenomenon is the case of Nemesis, who acts not only as the goddess of measure and restraint but also as a figure of Tychè, the power of fortune that rules each individual's destiny. The etymology of Nemesis derives from *nemein* 'to impart, to distribute',[11] and the action verb is helpful to highlight how and why the goddess performs the law. Nemesis and nomos are linked by their etymology. Represented as holding a cubit-rule and a bridle, Nemesis stands as the final cause, imparting to each individual her measure of efficacy and strength. Straton reports in the *Greek Anthology*, that Nemesis' motto was 'nothing beyond due measure' (*meden yper to metron*).[12] But Pliny (*Natural History* 1.15) remarks that even if 'there is at Rome an image of the Goddess on the Capitol', he wonders that 'she has no Latin name'.[13] If the name of the goddess defies translation, images of her nevertheless appear to be copied through the form of statues, simulacra, frescoes, engravings and paintings.

The method pursued here thus needs to be attentive to the ambivalent naming or the many valences of a given attribute. Dio Chrysostom has underlined the 'many names and many ways' of this constellation of deities: Fortune (*Tychè*) has been given many names among men. Her impartiality (*to ison*) has been named Retributive Justice (*Nemesis*); her obscurity (*to adèlon*), Hope (*Elpis*); her inevitability, Fate (*Moira*); her righteousness, Law (*Themis*).[14] In lines 3–13 of Mesomedes' *Hymn to*

Nemesis, the poet depicts a sophisticated tableau of her attributes and characteristics:

> You who restrain the empty snortings of mortals with an adamantine bit, and, hating the destructive hubris of men, you drive out dark envy. Beneath your wheel, ceaseless, trackless, the fierce fortune of mortals is ground down, and, escaping notice, you follow at men's heels, you force down the proud neck. You continually measure out life beneath your arm, you are forever nodding your eyes to your breast, mastering your 'zygon' with your hand.[15]

The word 'zygon', an attribute of the goddess, has been interpreted both as the balance of Justice and as the yoke of her chariot. Both interpretations are in fact right, as the poet develops several wordplays where one attribute can hide another. He rightly underlines how ancient iconographic representations, because of their ekphrastic nature, were always performed differently by orators seeking to enliven their portrait.[16] Instead of sticking to a clear-cut scheme with fixed attributes, each orator would craft his own refiguration of a popular narrative about a famous goddess. The most recognisable iconographic attributes of a given deity change over time. Allegorical creation needs some sort of consensus. A newly given attribute which stands on its own has no chance of surviving; it will fade quickly because it has not been shared widely as a recognisable feature of the initial matrix. Each allegorical performance may carry a strong cohort of elements rooted in a firmly established tradition, but at the same time it also needs to be garbed in the fashion of the day. Allegorical games play with lines of division and also with the controlled subversion of expectations.

Images in movement

More importantly, the two last lines of Mesomedes' *Hymn*, by insisting on her individual body parts (the reference to her forearm and the way she lowers her eyes to her bosom), depict with great acuity a body in action. In her role of moral corrector, Nemesis is swift and tense in her gestures: even her eyes, which appear to be static, are described as dynamic, as she looks downward to examine the scales. Weighing men's

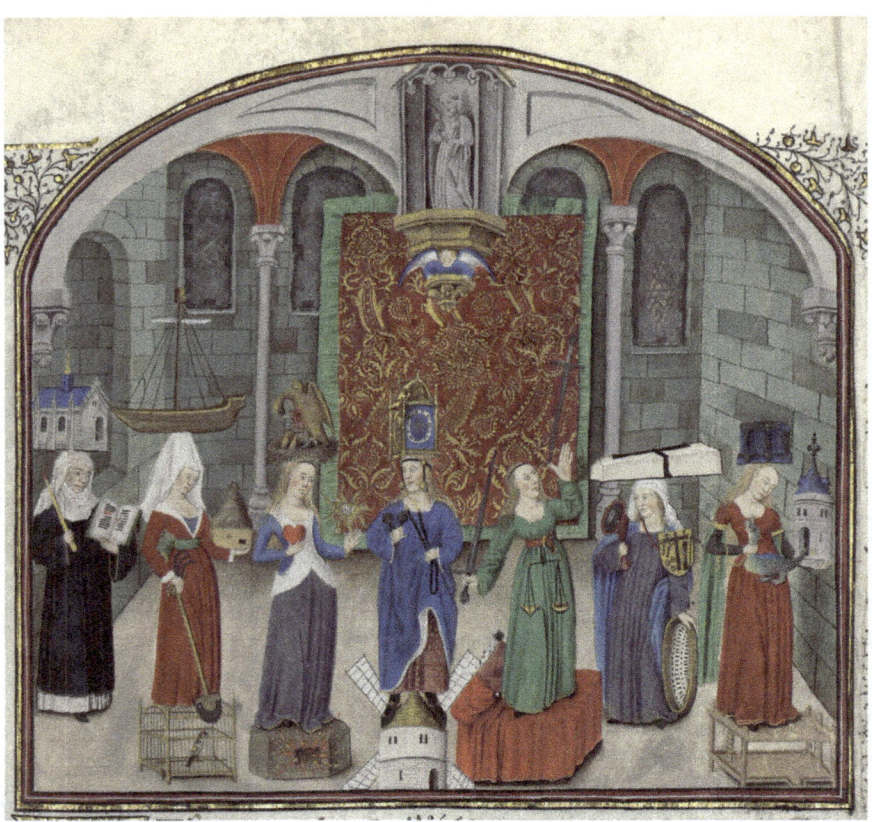

Figure I.1: Aristotle, *Ethics*, 1453–4, Ms. 297, fol. 17v. By permission of the Bibliothèque municipale de Rouen

lives, curbing destructive hubris and grinding down mortal wrong-doing, Nemesis performs a distinctive choreography. Instead of sitting at the goddess's foot, the attributes are held as instruments to be handled and used. In most of her emblematic appearances, Nemesis is depicted carrying a ruler as well as a bridle. One of Nemesis' often forgotten attributes is her forearm: in classical times, this portion of the anatomy was meant to equate to the length of a cubit. David M. Greene has observed that 'her limb is sometimes shown bared to the elbow' or 'crooked at a right angle, like a carpenter's square'.[17]

The manifestation of a well-established allegory hence combines commonplace appearances, where highly recognisable attributes are easily identified, with innovative patterns, where more recondite influences are put forward, in such a way that a common theme is reworked. Some of these inventions died out rather quickly, but it would be wrong to analyse these patterns of change in too fixed a mode. Our method aims at recovering the simple fact that these allegories were personifications, using the body's anatomical structure as a grammar of gestures. The most important attributes (the bridle for Nemesis, the scales and sword for Justice) are more than inert objects used in a one-way semiological process. Instead of simply accompanying the virtue, the most interesting occurrences of attributes are met when they are used as tools, as extensions of the user's anatomy. In a manuscript of Aristotle's kept in the Rouen Library (Ms. 297), Temperance *wears* the bridle instead of carrying it (Figure I.1). By doing so, she shifts perspective to pursue a slightly different end: the attribute is held as a mask to be worn; its power rests in its agency.

This observation leads us to identify at least two types of attributes: first, those which remain outside the virtue's body and second, objects that are manipulated, worn or used as a tool – such as the blindfold, the bridle or the sword. These attributes have a higher valence as their nature as tactile tools indicates that they are imbued with a prosthetic power. A phenomenological approach will show how a blindfold, a bridle or a sword are visible instruments that involve their users in various guises. Instead of simply being set aside as a distant object, the attribute is worn against a body. The allegorical body is a sensing surface, wearing and being worn, being at the same time both an agent and a patient. Moreover, the allegorical body superimposes two processes when seen through others' eyes: the body is being looked at wearing the bridle, but viewers at the same time sense imaginatively that they too may wear the bridle. The allegorical body hints at forms of worldly inter-relations. It is a medium able to unite viewers into an interpretative community. From the static attribute to the device, the operative aspects of these objects turn an abstract ideal into an experiential grammar of practical gestures, an orthopraxis which better marks the viewers' memory.

Justicia and vengeance

Through the trope of a highly ambivalent personification, the female figure of *Justicia* enters the threshold of the courtroom apparatus as a nexus of conflicting polarities. The American philologist James M.

Redfield opposes two passions: Aidos (pudor, reserve, feeling of shame in front of the community) and its opposed passion, Nemesis, which is an invading passion urging intervention in the business of others.[18] Aidos and Nemesis are a couple where Nemesis is the principle which urges us to act. Nemesis acts as Wrath above wrath, offering a perspective that sublimates the anger provoked by a personal conflict. Nemesis aims at tackling archaic violence by discharging it from its initial destructive powers. Is Justice's face always dispassionate? What are the iconographical conventions of depicting even-handedness, neutralising passions such as anger or wrath?

Lady Justice trampling on the emperor, the Pope, the sultan or the king questions the monopoly on legitimate violence: who will stand as warrant of retribution, exchange and arbitration between all these contestants of earthly justice? With her primary focus on ethics and the morality of behaviour, Lady Justice redraws the whole public theatre. Since judicial authority throughout the early modern period is a constant struggle between competing jurisdictions, Lady Justice presents herself as a vigilant virgin, keeping a true and ultimate watch over all of them. Yet her own agency in this endeavour is rendered in the shape of an ambiguous lady, dancing on dangerous thresholds. The immoderation and excesses of earthly governors are echoed in her ambivalent role as whimsical courtesan and arbitrary executioner.

The allegorical statue triumphs over these fractious authorities and tends to treat them all as the objectified counter-values of the group, but in doing so she takes on an opacity, the impersonal objectivity of a blindfolded figure, a numinous theophany which expresses a highly paradoxical embodiment of insoluble issues. Dismantling traditional visible orders, publicly exhibiting the hazardous spiral of judicial mechanics, Lady Justice reactivates a satirical theatre of violence, with its unbalanced play of forces and its puzzling apparatus. The allegorical image permits the easy internalisation of a subtle pattern of moral behaviour; it casts polite aspersions on the state monopoly of legitimate violence, as well as allusions to the executioner's masking of an archaic violence. Far from simply dispensing lessons of justice or instruction in good morals, the allegorical games of Lady Justice provide the imaginary crucible in which a new sense of civic urban space develops. The allegorical fountains of Justice in Swiss city-states unite collective appeals for staging new forms of fair judging processes. They institute new ways of seeing and experiencing the intertwinements of godly and human tribunals. Allegorical meaning sprouts from a fertile ground of multiplicity.

Before the law

Images of Justice are not to be identified as straightforward embodiments of a given concept: their value is as a power *before* the law, before the rationalisation of justice as a moral concept. A well-known maxim of Roman and canon laws explains that the prince (or the Pope) has all the laws in the shrine of his breast (*suo pectoris*). This metaphor, a juristic fiction, has been the object of many glosses, including those by Ernst Kantorowicz, Pierre Legendre and others. Kantorowicz reports one reading of this maxim by Cynus of Pistoia (1270–1336): the medieval jurist commented on the 'shrine of his breasts', noting that the doctors of law assembled into judicial courts so that the prince could speak 'through those mouths'. Kantorowicz adds:

> In other words the council of experts and crown jurists, are the 'shrine of the king's breast' because they really have all the relevant laws present to their mind which appears here as the 'mouth of the Prince', who speaks through his councilors.[19]

The highly creative use of juristic metaphors by Roman law glossators and their interpretative community lays a strong emphasis on metaphors of embodiment. Law is *viva vox*, it needs to be performed through polyphonic utterances, the fiction of the Emperor speaking through the mouths of his councillors, a mute figure articulating a higher voice through a sort of inverted ventriloquism.

More importantly, Kantorowicz reflects on the creative power of analogy. Allegories of Lady Justice perform the agonistic nature of the process, the symbolic roots of an abyss, a mystery tacitly enclosed within the mute eloquence of her acts. This volume aims at addressing the multiple challenges of a highly problematic collage: Lady Justice always remains an ambivalent image. Her power lies in the art of distraction. Her beautiful body and puzzling gestures shift the viewer's focus from the normative order of the trial scene to the hope of salvation in divine justice. Before the eyes of the condemned, as they make their way to the place of execution, she carries an ambiguous weapon, all the more sadistic as she entices with her décolletage. Doubt and scepticism arise frequently as to how to depict this fundamental ambivalence. Is Lady Justice simply an aesthetic distraction aiming to cover up the symbolic and actual violence of the law?

Sources

Humanities scholars have only recently started to accumulate various collections of objects digitised online. The open-source Rijksmuseum online database allows its users to collect high-resolution images of an ever-growing online image collection. Although these new sources add a constantly enriched archive of primary sources, retrieving images depends on the discursive limits of lexical indexes. Early modern images of Justice vary hugely in medium, size, location, setting, materials and condition. Allegorical images are frequently accompanied by mottos or aphorisms in Latin, Greek or vernacular languages, and sometimes these are to be read along with a meaningful caption (*subscriptio*). Images are too rarely indexed in any detail. The very act of indexing an image poses several problems and limitations, as it is the essence of an image to escape discourse. Generating indexes in order to fit narrowly defined themes relies on the tacit assumption that images may be reduced to keywords. Indexing is often so imprecise as to preclude any informed identification of what images actually depict. The original context, whether iconographic, cultural or material, is always distorted by the ways in which the medium is made available. Nevertheless, digital humanities platforms have shown the benefits to be derived from hypertextual public access to quantitatively important and still largely unknown corpuses. Breaking down the structures that contain images may help to gain access to them, seemingly abolishing logics of nation-states or institutions. However, image-mining is now more decontextualised than ever. So, this book also serves to assess the discrepancies between a world before digital search, where scholarship was rooted in a traditional method of accessing images, and today's scholarly practices, where developing a large-scale survey out of open-access collections as well as proprietary databases is both promising and challenging.

A close reading of why certain images attract viewers' attention is certainly needed. The ways in which images of Lady Justice act on their viewers differ notably. For example, inside the courtroom space, each actor will build their own reading of images according to a variety of factors. The controversial notion of 'visual literacy' is frequently used as a catch-all term that deliberately simplifies a complex process. Visual structuring processes such as iterative appearances, similar gestural patterns and codification of colours are to be scrutinised carefully. One important feature of judicial allegorical cycles is that their narratives were built on similar patterns, such as father–son diptychs where paternal relationships are meant to mitigate awe-inspiring retributive scenes. In the early modern Netherlands, the tradition of decorating aldermen's halls with *exempla justitiæ* panels was firmly established and widely disseminated. These impressive cycles – such as the *Legend of Trajan and Herkinbald* by Rogier van der Weyden for Brussels town hall (1439–50), the *Justice of Emperor Otto III* by Dirk Bouts for Louvain town hall, and the *Judgement of Cambyses* (1498) painted by Gerard David for Bruges town hall – offered judges visual depictions of notorious dilemmas about controversial judgments in the very space where legal cases were heard. These exemplary visual narratives have much in common, including an insistence on the fallibility of the judge, the ways in which the judge symbolically pays with his flesh for the faults of his own kin, and a penchant for the exemplary power of gruesome or atrocious violence justified by its supposed exemplarity.

These images of earthly judgments are very often counterposed with depictions of the Last Judgement inside the temporal courtroom. How did these two frames collide and what did this mean? How were visual experiences of the beholders modelled by the fearful presence of *exempla justitiæ*, or by scenes of the Last Judgement showing explicitly the decisions of a wrathful God? The conflation of the actual space of litigation with the imagined spaces of ancient types of exemplary judgments needs to be carefully gauged. Far from being pure ornaments, their insertion into the heart of litigation procedure directed the viewer's gaze and served to emphasise the importance of rituals, the ceremonial delivery of law's decorum. Are visual renditions of law's potential mechanisms of change structural elements of the verdict or only ancillary to law's design? What is the role played by *Justitia* in this context?

The two faces of Justice

Since the beginning, then, visual depictions of the image of *Justitia* were the object of competing linguistic renditions. Any humanist eager to go back to the origin of the symbolic tradition would have discussed at length the concepts of Dike, the tradition of *ekphrasis*, and the equipollence of the image of *Justitia* and the model of the righteous judge. Since antiquity, the birth of the personification of Justice as a goddess has been associated with the concept of the good judge.

Lady Justice becomes an object of aspiration and a support for identification: each judge may internalise the abstract concept of Justice in the form of an ideal ego, an aspiration of the self in the form of an attractive female body. This process of identification, however, remains ambivalent. The allegorical quality of Lady Justice is both sustained and undermined by the manifestation of a dynamic psychomachy. There is a fundamental ambivalence at the heart of her expression, which is rendered by a formal and stylistic asymmetry. On the one hand, she shows affection to good men, but, at the same time, she inflicts awe and terror without any compassion when she strikes evil wrongdoers. The judicial *imago* may thus be a benefactor and a protector of the sacred bonds of society, but she may well deploy lethal weapons to impose an authoritative and rigorous punishment. This depiction also authorises a psychoanalytic reading, where the concept of Justice is structured by the conjunction of the psychic agency of the superego and the existence of an inner voice, or 'voice of conscience', epitomising the sense of moral law. The allegory of Justice is to be understood as an object of fantasy, an ambivalent structure which is used as a moral compass, the bearer of love, desire and affection but also cruel injunctions and rigorous imperatives.

The allegorical language of personification, first devised by the ancient Greeks, gave a visual form to abstract ideas. In her study of images of Dike on coins, Helen North has argued that *Dikaiosynê/Justicia* was the only personification of the time that possessed a recognisable 'type'.[20] Aulus Gellius is frequently cited as he circulated widely the only information about how Justice was represented in classical antiquity, reporting a treatise left in a fragmentary state by the Greek Stoic philosopher Chrysippus. Conceived as the alter ego of the judge (as Chrysippus understands the role of the effigy of Lady Justice), she is assumed to act as a model of fair judgment, but the ways of seeing she triggers are often quite different from the noble ideal she aims at representing. Chrysippus' hypotyposis caters to an audience of artists (sculptors, painters) as well as an audience of orators. Justice is described as an asymmetrical figure, known to inspire fear in the wicked and courage in the just; to the latter, she presents a friendly gaze, while to the former, she is said to show a stern face. The entire text reads as follows:

> That Chrysippus skillfully and vividly represented the likeness of Justice in melodious and picturesque language. Most worthily, by Heaven! and most elegantly did Chrysippus, in the first book of his work entitled *On Beauty and Pleasure*, depict the face and eyes (*os et oculos*) of Justice, and her aspect, with austere and noble word-painting. For he represents the figure of Justice (*imaginem Justitiæ*) and says that it was usually represented by the painters and orators of old in about the following manner: 'Of maidenly form (*forma virginali*) and bearing, with a stern and fearsome countenance, a keen glance of the eye (*luminibus oculorum acribus*), and a dignity and solemnity which was neither mean nor cruel (*neque humilis neque atrocis*), but awe-inspiring.' From the spirit of this representation, he wished it to be understood that the judge, who is the priest of Justice (*antistes Justitiæ*), ought to be dignified, holy, austere, incorruptible, not susceptible to flattery, pitiless and inexorable towards the wicked and guilty, vigorous, lofty, and powerful, terrible by reason of the force and majesty of equity and truth (*vi et maiestate æquitatis veritatisque terrificum*). Chrysippus' own words about Justice are as follows: 'She has the title of virgin as a symbol of her purity and an indication that she has never given way to evil-doers, that she has never yielded to soothing words, to prayers and entreaties, to flattery, not to anything of that kind. Therefore, she is properly represented too as stern and dignified, with a serious expression and a keen, steadfast glance, in order that she may inspire fear in the wicked and courage in the good; to the latter, as her friends, she

presents a friendly aspect, to the former, a stern face.' I thought it the more necessary to quote these words of Chrysippus, in order that they might be before us for consideration and judgment, since, on hearing me read them, some philosophers who are more sentimental in their views called that a representation of Cruelty (*Sævitiæ imaginem*) rather than of Justice.[21]

The words of Chrysippus are quoted verbatim and in the original Greek. In this way, a constitutive ambivalence hints at two virtual pathways. Lady Justice's depiction likewise implies a constitutive tension between an all-powerful protectress and a punishing moral conscience. Indeed, she may well represent Cruelty rather than Justice. The secret rules governing her asymmetrical body highlight the body parts governing emotions: eyes, mouth, breasts, face. Hinting at diverse reactions, Lady Justice articulates the unwritten law of paradoxical gestures: stern but friendly, awe-inspiring and soothing, inexorable but empathetic or even desirable. The animating force of the moral law appears as the imaginary Other of the judge.

The moral allegory of Justice might seem to be a unique figure, locked in the hieratic countenance of a goddess, but on the cusp of Cruelty (Chrysippus' version). The fundamental question then becomes: how does this image appear to its viewers? How does the human being accept the claim for an allegorical rendition of Justice which seems both just and unjust? As we will see, Lady Justice is on the throne of judgment, but her multiple avatars never completely evacuate an element of injustice. Her body is often haunted by a sadistic polarity which blurs the distinction between divine justice and human institutions and highlights the necessity of bringing together both polarities: cruelty, punishment and lethal power are associated with desirability. Today, Themis is often viewed as the dispassionate version of a moral principle. Throughout the early modern period and before the waning of allegory, Lady Justice's iconographic formulae were often challenged by this paradox. If the painting of Justice is such a challenging venture, how can artists maintain an articulation of the inner psychomachy of the goddess without accentuating too vividly her cruel aspect?

Allegory as a medium for judicial reform

Allegorical depictions of Justice play a decisive role in courtroom symbolism. Lawyers are especially well equipped to comment on the significance of Justice's portraiture. Michel de l'Hospital, in his *De la Réformation de la Justice*, gives a detailed portrait of *Justitia* in the vernacular.[22] Chrysippus' canonical *ekphrasis* is the main *auctoritas*, but the French chancellor adds a full genealogy of this visual rendition by grounding it in an even more ancient tradition, that of the poets Orpheus and Hesiod. He summarises his own interpretation of the theme in the following words:

> I say that Justice is aptly figured by Orpheus, by Hesiod and other ancient poets, in the form of a chaste virgin coming from heaven, the daughter of Jupiter, in order to let us understand that Justice is a gift from God in imme-diate motion out of his goodness, and that she is kept as a precious and sacred thing between the hands of earthly powers in order to communicate herself to mortal men and let them live under her moral conduct and discipline.[23]

If his commentary underlines the duality of Lady Justice (her true motto, according to him, is *Parcere subjectis, et debellare superbos* [To spare the vanquished and subdue the proud], Virgil, *Aeneid* 6.853), he deliberately remains silent about her virtual tendency to cruelty. Instead of follow-ing Chrysippus' wit, he adds a final complacent depiction of Injustice, where she is depicted not as Justice's false sister but as her radical contrary: 'Injustice, on the contrary, speaks like a courtesan, approach-ing you with insistence and standing on ceremony, with a laughing face, a double-sided heart, a feigned discourse, deceptive and untrue.'[24] Michel de l'Hospital chooses to ignore the two-sidedness of Lady Justice, yet his take is understandable if we consider that images of Justice are themselves part of an institutionalisation process.

Michel de l'Hospital's account is an example of the many rewritings of Chrysippus' effigy of *Justitia* in a judicial context. The judicial image is used by prosecutors as ostensive and sensible proof to be produced inside the *hic et nunc* of courtroom space. The image is made more potent by its ability to revive the criminal process in its instantaneity: its ontological status (a memorable sign which is not grounded in a specific time frame) makes it easily mobilisable by popular affects. The intertwining of the prosecutor's speech, the action and the visual proof exhibited (the cloth tainted with blood) shows that images are referred to by orators in the course of their speech delivered in the courtroom. This interactive space promotes cooperative acumen and the ability to arouse emotions as the most immediate means of achieving persuasive effects.

Interpretative plurality

The method pursued here is Warburgian. After having collected and charted 987 allegories from 1450 to 1850, some schemas have been studied in depth, keeping in mind the need to identify meaningful gestures, beyond the apparently stable grammar of attributes. Marcel Proust's insights into the allegories of Giotto at the Arena Chapel in Padua reveal the difficulties in the reception of allegorical conceits. The narrator of *Remembrance of Things Past* admits that he had at first experienced no particular pleasure when he glanced at reproductions of Giotto's allegories which had been pinned down by Swann in the study room of Combray. Charity without charity, Envy without envy, Justice without justice:

> a Justice whose greyish and meanly regular features were identical with those which identified the faces of certain pious desiccated ladies of Combray whom I used to see at mass and many of whom had long been enrolled in the reserve forces of Injustice.[25]

Seen through the lens of a reproduction, Giotto's *Justitia* cannot touch the heart of the narrator; it only underlines his distrust and accentuates its most apparent features (exterior piety without charity, arbitrariness of social conventions during mass). Before experiencing them *in situ*, the narrator is only left with the vague and greyish impression that all three virtues, Justice, Charity and Envy, are nothing but caricatures of their noble ideals. He continues:

But in later years I understood that the arresting strangeness, the special beauty of these frescoes lay in the great part played in each of them by its symbols, while the fact that these were depicted, not as symbols (for the thought symbolized was nowhere expressed), but as real things, actually felt or materially handled, added something more precise and more literal to their meaning, something more concrete and more striking to the lesson they imparted.[26]

Instead of focusing on the allegorical conceits of Justice as semiotic objects immune to affective impulses, this remark leads us to question the ways of seeing and experiencing judicial symbols *in situ*. Allegories of Justice act as symbolic experiences incapable of being reduced to one exclusive way of seeing. The necessity of an *ambulatio*, a physical and experiential approach to symbols is in itself a necessary path to deconstructing the perilous notion of 'visual literacy'. The examining magistrate seeking to make a prisoner confess will use the power of symbols to 'more or less' unravel their mysterious gestures. On the contrary, the condemned, on the *via dolorosa* of his execution, might well look away, trying to evade the inquisitive order of judges or the vengeful enthusiasm of the crowd. Allegories of Justice, because of their paradoxical nature, challenge the very existence of a moral sense. They do not always act as deontological images, as many critics treat *exempla justitiæ*. Allegorical figures of Justice may also serve as exemplars of distrust, when an examining magistrate or a Christian priest uses them to obtain submission or publicly expose a vanquished opponent. In this extreme case, sadistic representations of Lady Justice may help the judge to accomplish his ritual execution without having to suffer in his own flesh from the anguish of the condemned man.

Thus interpretation is grounded in the process of decoding; it starts with the identification of a sign taken to be meaningful and derives meaning from it. Given that Law is generally understood as script, two other meaningful signs (gesture, speech) have generally been discarded, though they are equally able to convey meaning to wider audiences. Lady Justice, as an image of the Law, will always exceed the mere functionality of words. Lady Justice can express affects; as a body, she may appeal to emotional or artistic delight and thus call forth the phatic function of language, which is the essence and the foundation of the binding forces of legal norms. The emblematic representations of Lady Justice flourished with particular force throughout the early modern period. These images were part of a wider context. The Renaissance portrayal of ethical virtues as female figures added 'to the metaphorical dignity of woman, as baroque artists themselves point out'.[27] Indeed, one of the most significant advances in the sphere of female representation happens in the visual arts. These images of female virtues reflect a new aesthetic judgement of female beauty.[28]

Allegories of Lady Justice have been chosen because of their profound ambivalence. Women's fate in general is, at this time, closely related to the inescapable institution of marriage. Her subordination to her husband is grounded in Roman law, and her *deterior conditio*, supported by medical discourses, underlies her moral and judicial inferiority. Yet the allegory of Dame Justice often depicts an ambivalent virgin queen, a type of untouchable goddess who may also be turned into a raped woman, a courtesan, a bloodthirsty virago, or a hieratic and mute idol. What are the main differences in the notion of Lady Justice's embodiments? Has Lady Justice helped to improve the notional status of ethical virtues embodied by women vis-à-vis men? Is there something peculiar about this one allegory which would explain why she is still visible today?

One possible explanation is that Lady Justice is not concerned with the institution of matrimony. Her role is to foster and preserve a set of ethical virtues through a call to action. According to Plutarch (*De virtute morali* 440d), ethical virtues are opposed to contemplative virtues precisely in their use of passion (*pathos*) as topic and reason (*logos*) as form or figure. Ethical virtues are grounded in praxis, as virtues only become virtues in action. Lady Justice is depicted as a body in action, a binary posture, an ambivalent ethical standpoint. For a synthesis to be affective, the analysis of allegories of Justice must embrace the whole sphere of ethics: virtues also account for vices, their vicious counterparts. Andrea Alciato's emblems are inconceivable without these binary oppositions. By their profoundly ambivalent nature, vices and virtues are meant to achieve some sort of truth by bringing about contradictory stances. The European concept of Justice is a polyvalent notion, inherited from classical and patristic texts as well as from the foundational principles of Roman law. The figurative capacity of this concept may not only be represented by a thing, a person, an allegorical body or a narrative scene; it may also point towards mythology, mysticism, theology and ethics in its widest sense.

The polymorphous nature of images of Justice is part of a larger economy of cultural circulation: myths, ethics, theology, history and philosophy, as well as mysticism or esotericism, are fonts of their compositional context. A comprehensive modern cultural history of judicial gestures in Renaissance Europe has yet to be written. The present study aspires to a more modest endeavour: it aims at examining the sphere of Lady Justice's gestural ethics by concentrating on the dispositive spaces where her allegorical body has been inserted. It seeks to answer neither issues of connoisseurship nor questions about style, taste or attribution. It is intended as an attempt to show that the word and the notion of allegory is not an inflexible conceptual structure but rather a process, involving a wide range of meanings and interpretative paths. Instead of focusing exclusively on the making of these allegories, their genesis and genealogy, we will look at the frames of perception they offer. Are figures of Lady Justice able to manifest collective emotions? If the symbolic violence of the Law is grounded in the assumption that legal symbols are a powerful binding force for society, how do these symbols act in Renaissance Europe? According to Émile Durkheim, the only way that seemingly dispassionate punishment might be legitimised is by the manifestation of collective emotions.[29] The non-rational foundation of the process of imposing punishment opens up a radical standpoint addressing the ways emotions can reach some sort of collective meaning, by means of mimicry or contagion. Lady Justice embodies a highly ambivalent polarity; she is by essence oxymoronic. Her images play a role that perhaps Demosthenes and other orators might categorise in terms of the affective role of *hypokrisis*, both good and bad. Lady Justice is first and foremost staged as a sensible fragment inserted into a meaningful optical space of disposition. The disjunction between the two most represented attributes (measuring scales and punitive sword) is constitutive of the symbolic montage, but this scheme is only a tiny part of the overall picture available in early modern times.

'Precellence' of women?

The writings of Heinrich Cornelius Agrippa on the nobility and 'precellence' or pre-eminence of the female sex, along with works such as Symphorien Champier's *Nef des dames vertueuses*, borrow from Platonic and Neoplatonic sources, as well as mysticism, in order to provide insight into how to circumvent the excessive power of male tyranny, which prevails against divine justice and the laws of nature.[30] Agrippa declares the nobility of the female sex to be a sign of her mission and a token of her virtues. The praise of women is a central theme of his works; it is worth noting that after having looked for a position as a jurisconsult in Metz, Geneva, Fribourg and Lyon, after having served as a doctor, sometimes as an astrologist, Agrippa ended his *peregrinatio* by coming back to Mechelen, in order to accomplish the vows pronounced in 1509 towards Marguerite of Burgundy. His praise for the nobility and excellence of the female sex corresponds to the award of an imperial office in 1530. Marguerite died the same year. These feminist praises are often considered as part of a rhetorical exercise in oratorical declamation. In works such as Christine de Pisan's *Cité des dames* (1405–7), followed by many epigones, the litany of illustrious women belongs to a well-established tradition of praising the heroic fates of Ceres, Minerva, Nicostrata or Carmentis, who founded the Laws on the Palatine Hill and created the Latin alphabet.

As it is difficult to assess how conservative forces have maintained the tyrannical order of the male sex over women, one approach is to focus on practical expressions of female *fortitudo* such as the one granted to Lady Justice. While the legal order recognises various legal entitlements by means of which real women are to be classified – *puer* (*puella*), *virgo viripotens, marita, mater, gravida, lactans, vidua* are taxonomic descriptions requiring special dispensation in law – Lady Justice escapes this rigid taxonomical order in the realm of visual expression. She is often described as a *regina virtutum*, a noble lady, a *virgo*/maiden of exceptional beauty, an untouchable goddess situated beyond the institution of marriage. The topical question *an sit nubendum?* is nonsensical if we think of Lady Justice. She also escapes the physiological paradigm (*virgo/uxor/mater/vidua*) as her embodiment frequently uses ambivalence and various polarities to epitomise her distinctiveness. *Virgo viripotens*, in a legal context, means a nubile maiden, but in the case of Lady Justice, the pun on *virgo/virago* and her potential *virtus* comes to light with a specific relevance. Lady Justice brandishes the attributes of soldiers; she does not mirror natural hierarchies. The very embodiment of this curious allegorical montage challenges a frequently quoted commonplace of Roman law: 'Women are excluded from all civil and public offices; and thus, they may neither be judges nor magistrates, nor advocates; nor may they intervene on another's behalf in law, nor act as agents.'[31]

Roman law, as is well known, excludes women from public and civil offices. Women are debarred from jurisdiction, judgment, adoption, tutelage, guardianship and from acting on another's behalf. The *deterior conditio* of women is grounded in a set of dubious arguments perfectly expounded by Ian Maclean.[32] Conservative forces such as theology and law prevent major advances, but belief in the dignity of illustrious women or the allegorical representation of ethical virtues may add another understanding of why visual arts have blatantly expressed ideals of female *virtus*. If the legal interdiction is performed well, courtroom spaces may be adorned with female personifications of Justice. The question posed by Lady Justice entering the judicial process is the vexed issue of mimesis. To what extent is the embodiment of Justice in the female allegory of *Justitia* desirable in a criminal courtroom, where justice is being performed, rendered and heard? In order to prevent judges' emotional contagion triggered by mimicry, the author of the iconographical programme in Amsterdam town hall reserved a special treatment to female allegories of Justice. Lady Justice is depicted either as Divine Justice, holding an eyed sceptre, or as a mute Angerona, bound to the secrecy of instruction.

An ethics of affects?

Aristotle's definition of *Justitia* stresses its *affective* nature, the disposition of character towards Justice (*Nicomachean Ethics* 5.1). Cicero recalls that she is an *animi habitus*, while for Anselm (*Dialogo de veritate* 13), Justice is a *rectitudo voluntatis*. In this last sense, the *nomen justitiæ* may be understood as Charity. Saint Augustine elaborates this interpretation in his *Concerning Nature and Grace* 1.83–4: 'Charitas inchoata, inchoata justitia est; charitas magna, magna justitia est; charitas perfecta, perfecta justitia est' (Inchoate charity is inchoate justice, great charity is great justice, and charity accomplished is justice that has reached the point of perfection).

In this spirit, Justice will be primarily studied here as an iconic rendition of a specific affect. Before any judgment is pronounced or uttered, negotiated or inflicted, allegories are part of a spatial disposition that is installed to be viewed. Lady Justice is a peculiar allegory, a monstrous composite of contrary gestures. Her divine appearance and allegorical deployment are meant to overcome the monstrosity of human judgment: Lady Justice brings together two binary polarities, two sources of iconic agency, in the hope that both sides will be seen, during the judicial trial.

Walter Benjamin has shown persuasively how the emblems of the sixteenth and seventeenth centuries were fragmentary, dispersive, antagonistic and by nature piecemeal figurative embodiments of various knowledges.[33] Yet I argue in this book that symbolic acts are first and foremost experiences, not discourses, and as such they deserve a meticulous evaluation of what was intended, what was to be seen, and how their audiences would have responded. Our method is thus meant to obtain a suitable vantage point by leaving aside discursive reductions of images of Justice, in order to take a closer look at the analysis of what happens when a symbol appears inside the courtroom. Symbolic acts are performed within a spatial construct, and what follows is an attempt to get an idea of the 'otherness' of images of Justice when they are perceived (and not primarily read or commented upon) by all sorts of audiences.

Of the various factors on which we might focus in an analysis of images of Justice, I will dwell on the antagonism between the judge and his value-bearer. Lady Justice is born in Greece as a daimon of the good judge: the first depiction of her anatomy is of a paragon and as such is a depiction of the virtues of the *bonus judex*. Eyes, forehead, look, hands, gesture and her perfect proportions (according to the Greek canon) are chosen as a beautiful allegory to embody the ethics of the fair judge. The allegory of *Justitia* stands as a piecemeal figurative embodiment of ethical knowledge and know-how. Her anatomical composition is not primarily meant to exist as a discourse. It is part of a conversation, Chrysippus' dialogue 'of the beautiful and the pleasurable', an *ekphrasis* used to rejuvenate the ethics of judges, and the ambivalence of binary polarities: inflicting punishment and rendering to each their due, showing mercy towards the good-hearted and keeping an austere and stern watch over evil souls. The depiction of *Justitia* may be seen as a collection of professional gestures. She constitutes fragments of ethical wisdom, to be shared by all judges and to be transmitted inside the courtroom as shared judicial values.

In the truncated state in which images of Justice have come down to us, one major blind spot is rarely discussed: how did images of Justice enter the civic space of litigation? A viewer-reception theory is needed, if we want to ward off over-interpretation and misunderstandings due to several factors such as temperament, affects, intellectual categorisation of things, and cultural and educational backgrounds. The way in which an image is seen depends on the material conditions of its appearance (size, accessibility, tactility) but is also constrained by the metaphysical beliefs of the beholder. Is this image of Justice adequate in transmitting the sense of inflicting institutional punishment? Is the beholder able to make something out of it?

It is the very lack of cohesiveness and departure from dogmatic definitions that leads us to an understanding of emblematic representations of Justice as a form of portraiture. Lady Justice is a portrait, an effigy, a three-dimensional figure, and as such she always interprets the experience of the world as a fragment. According to each viewer of her multi-purpose bodily form, Lady Justice may embody a personal relationship to the ideal of divine justice, an overtly erotic enticement to the manifestation of Law's cruelty, or a pagan invitation to enjoy the mysteries of the flesh. As a visual portrait, she is *res picta* or *res ficta* and as such she is endowed with the power of referring beyond herself, *res significans*. Most scholars usually argue that as a picture, her visual nature does not allow her to possess speech. As a mute object, she supposedly needs a literary supplement to represent a linguistic conceit. The humanistic topos of *ut pictura poesis*, understood as the digestion of the power of images by verbal commentaries, is often used to privilege modes of commentary over ways of seeing, enacting a monopoly of learned interpretative skills over the affective nature of experiential forms of viewing Justice.

The intention of this book is to reverse this perspective. Lady Justice is not only a portrait of Justice; her figurative nature always escapes the interpretative skills developed by symbolic discourses. An image should not be reduced to a narrative in the first place. As a periegetic symbolic act, Lady Justice is part of a mental iteration of suggestive paths. She stands at the crossroads of multiple interpretative questions. The purpose of this reversed perspective is twofold. The first objective is to deny the view that symbols are mainly objects of discursive interpretative skills. The *symbolon* is an object cut into two pieces, and its paradoxical nature bears a fundamental ambivalence between object and subject. If Lady Justice's gestural eloquence is mute, it nevertheless conveys traces, engrams – patterns of behavioural practices which attempt to transform the ways viewers see them. The polysemic power of emblematic gestures, both in their specific compositional context and in the affective responses they trigger in various contexts and times, may disrupt the cohesion of all Lady Justice's attributes into a single didactic message.

Secondly, this book aims at developing a new approach to the study of allegoresis. The particular form of Lady Justice's portrait allows a fragmented perception of her body parts, and this is the reason why the modular approach towards allegories of Justice seems more appropriate than the choice of a single taxonomy. Representation is thus not to be viewed for its end product but for its process. The activity of representation is the dwelling place of truth, the only 'place' where truth is truly present. The method itself is not a privileged path to truth but something approaching a ritual form: it is continually making new beginnings in contemplating its object, thus resembling the multilayered method of allegorical interpretation. The appeal of allegory remains experiential – a sudden change of referentiality – and therefore ethical.

Notes

1. Unless otherwise referenced, all Latin quotations and their translations are from the Loeb Classical Library, <https://www.loebclassics.com/>.
2. Hans Belting, *Likeness and Presence: A History of the Image before the Era of Art*, trans. Edmund Jephcott (Chicago: University of Chicago Press, 1994).
3. See David Freedberg, *The Power of Images: Studies in the History and Theory of Response* (Chicago: University of Chicago Press, 1991); Wolfgang Brückner, *Bildnis und Brauch. Studien zur Bildfunktion der Effigies* (Berlin: Schmidt Erich Verlag, 1986).
4. The will is published in Carlo d'Arco, *Delle arti e degli artefici di Mantova*, 2 vols (Mantua: Giovanni Agazzi, 1857), vol. 2, p. 50, no. 63, where Battista Fiera is mentioned as 'Spectabile artium et medicinæ doctore Mag. Baptista fil. quem Pauli de la Fiera cive et habitante Mantuæ' (Admirable Doctor of Medicine and the Arts, Magnificent Baptista, son of Paulus de la Fiera, citizen and inhabitant of Mantua).
5. Battista Fiera, *De Justicia Pingenda Fieræ Mantuani Dialogus. Interloquutores Mantynias Momus*, in *Hymni Divini. Sylve Melanisius* (Mantua: Francesco Bruschi, 1515). The copy consulted is that of the Biblioteca Communale, Mantua.
6. Bianca De Divitiis, 'Castel Nuovo and Castel Capuano in Naples: The Transformation of Two Medieval Castles into "all'antica" Residence for the Aragonese Royals', *Zeitschrift für Kunstgeschichte* 76, no. 4 (2013), pp. 441–74.
7. See Michael Baxandall, *Giotto and the Orators: Humanist Observers of Painting in Italy and the Discovery of Pictorial Composition 1350–1450* (Oxford: Clarendon, 1971), pp. 112–14 (pp. 112–13), quoting Lorenzo Valla, 'In Bartolemaeum Facium Ligurem invectivæ seu recriminationes', vol. 4 of *Opera* (Basel, 1540), pp. 597–9. Here are the verses written by Antonio Becadelli, followed by my translation. Each of the verses is to be placed under the relevant allegorical figure: 'Iustitia/Te bone rex sequitur victas Astræa per urbes' (Justice. To you good king, who walks towards justice once the cities are conquered). 'Charitas. Te pietas et amor reddunt per secula notum' (Charity. May Piety and Love make you famous throughout the centuries). 'Prudentia. Agnoscit sociatque suum prudentia gnatum' (Learn to cultivate Prudence, if you want it to survive you). 'Fortitudo. Te dignum cœlo virtus invicta fatetur' (Fortitude. May this unconquerable virtue make you worthy to ascend to heaven). Valla continues, 'These flatteries seem to me simply banal, to say no more; and the verse he gives to any one figure could just as well be given to any of the others. As for mine, they are certainly not what Antonio said, "a nothing", beside his. I put them in the natural order I mentioned, with Prudence first: "Prudentia. Prima ergo virtutum, peragunt mea iussa sorores"' (Prudence. I'm therefore the first virtue, my sisters take their orders from me). 'Iustitia. Per me stat regis thronus et concordia plebis' (Justice. Through me, the King's throne is maintained as well as concord with the people). 'Charitas, or

Largitas. Celsius est dare nostra, suum quam reddere cuique' (Charity, or 'Largesse'. According to Celsius, to give my laws is to give to each one his due). 'Temperantia. Corporis illecebras plus est, quam vincere bella' (Temperance. I prefer to give myself over to the pleasures of the body than to win at war). 'Fortitudo. In gemmis Adamas, in moribus ipsa triumpho' (Fortitude. I triumph over diamond gems as I do over mores (moral rules, but also customs).

8. Ibid.

9. Timothy B. Husband and Michael Hoyle, '"Ick Sorgheloose . . ." A Silver-Stained Roundel in the Cloisters', *Metropolitan Museum Journal* 24 (1989), pp. 173–88; Timothy B. Husband, Madeline H. Caviness and Marilyn Beaven, 'Monograph Series I: Stained Glass before 1700 in American Collections: Silver-Stained Roundels and Unipartite Panels (Corpus Vitrearum Checklist IV), *Studies in the History of Art* 39 (1991), pp. 3–277.

10. The main centres for the dissemination of roundels are situated in the Lowlands: Amsterdam, Antwerp, Bruges, Brussels, Ghent, Haarlem, Leiden, Maastricht and Leuven. They also spread in German cities such as Nuremberg, Augsburg and Cologne.

11. See Émile Benveniste, *Noms d'agent et noms d'action en Indo-Européen* (Paris: Adrien-Maisonneuve, 1948), pp. 79–80; Emmanuel Laroche, *Histoire de la racine NEM- en Grec ancien (nemō, nemesis, nomos, nomizō)* (Paris: Klincksieck, 1949).

12. *The Greek Anthology, With an English Translation*, trans. W. R. Paton, Loeb Classical Library edition, vol. 4 (London: W. Heinemann; New York, G. P. Putnam's Sons, 1916), book 12, p. 193.

13. Pliny, *Natural History, Volume I: Books 1–2*, trans. H. Rackham (Cambridge, MA: Harvard University Press, 1938).

14. *Orations* 64.8.1–2, in *Dio Chrysostom, Vol. V: Discourses lxi–lxxx*, trans. H. Lamar Crosby (Cambridge, MA: Harvard University Press, 1951), p. 51.

15. Ernst Heitsch, *Die griechischen Dichterfragmente der römischen Kaiserzeit*, Mesomedes 3, qtd and trans. in Thomas R. Keith, 'The Fine Art of Horsing Around: A Note on Wordplay in Mesomedes' *Hymn to Nemesis', The Classical Quarterly* 64, no. 1 (2014), pp. 428–31.

16. See *LIMC*, vol. 6, s.v. 'Nemesis', 41, qtd in Keith, 'Fine Art of Horsing Around', p. 430 n. 13.

17. David M. Greene, 'The Identity of the Emblematic Nemesis', *Studies in the Renaissance* 10 (1963), pp. 25–43 (p. 29).

18. James M. Redfield, *Nature and Culture in the* Iliad: *The Tragedy of Hector* (Chicago: University of Chicago Press, 1975).

19. Ernst Hartwig Kantorowicz, *The King's Two Bodies: A Study in Mediaeval Political Theology* (Princeton, NJ: Princeton University Press, 1957), pp. 153–4.

20. Helen F. North, *From Myth to Icon: Reflections on Greek Ethical Doctrine in Literature and Art* (Ithaca, NY: Cornell University Press, 1979), p. 178 n. 3.

21. Aulus Gellius, *Attic Nights*, trans. John Carew Rolfe (Cambridge, MA: Harvard University Press; London, William Heinemann, 1927), 14.4.

22. Pierre Joseph Spyridion Dufey, *Œuvres inédites de Michel l'Hospital, Chancelier de France*, vol. 1 (Paris: Boulland, 1825), pp. 69–70.

23. Ibid., p. 70: 'Je dis que la justice est figurée fort proprement par Orphée, par Hésiode et aultres poëtes anciens, en forme d'une vierge chaste et pudique veneue du ciel, et fille de Jupiter, pour nous donner à entendre que la justice est ung don de Dieu mouvant immédiatement de sa bonté, et mis en dépost comme chose précieuse et sacrée entre les mains des puissances terriennes pour la communiquer aux hommes mortels, les faire vivre soubs la conduicte et discipline d'icelle.'

24. Ibid., p. 70: 'L'injustice, au contraire, parle comme une courtisane, vous aborde avec force et cérémonies, ung visaige riant, ung cœur double, ung parler affecté, pipeux et mensonger.'

25. Marcel Proust, *Remembrance of Things Past: Swann's Way*, trans. C. K. Scott Moncrieff (1913; London: Chatto & Windus, 1920), Part 1, 'Combray', p. 81.

26. Ibid., Part 1, p. 88.

27. Ian Maclean, *The Renaissance Notion of Woman: A Study in the Fortunes of Scholasticism and Medical Science in European Intellectual Life* (Cambridge: Cambridge University Press, 1980), p. 90.

28. As Peter Goodrich notes and elaborates, there is hubris in the positivistic excision and legalistic truncation of 'judgment' (written with fifth letter removed). Here, I follow the convention of spelling legal judgment without the first 'e' and moral and aesthetic judgement with the 'e'. See Peter Goodrich, 'Weird Judgment, Agon, Omniscience and the Absence of an "E"', *Ordine internazionale e diritti humani/International Order and Legal Rights* (2021), pp. 130–9.

29. Émile Durkheim, *The Division of Labor in Society* (1893; New York: The Free Press, 1997).

30. Heinrich Cornelius Agrippa von Nettesheim, *Declamatio de nobilitate et præcellentia fæminæ sexus* (On the Nobility and Excellence of the Feminine Sex), trans. Edward Fleetwood (London: Robert Ibbitson, 1652).

31. *Digest* 50.17.2 (*De regulis juris antiqui*): 'Fœminæ ab omnibus officiis civilibus, vel publicis remotæ sunt: et ideo nec judices esse possunt, nec magistratum gerere, nec postulare, nec pro alio intervenire, nec procuratores existere.' 'Judices' are defined as 'those who decided on the facts of a civil or criminal case, people on the *album judicium*'. See Maclean, *Renaissance Notion of Woman*, p. 112 n. 40.

32. Ibid.

33. Walter Benjamin, 'The Origin of German Tragic Drama' (1925), in *Schriften*, ed. Theodor Adorno and Gretel Adorno, 2 vols (Frankfurt: Suhrkamp, 1955), vol. 1, p. 182.

Chapter 1

Images of Justice

Images of Justice encompass a wide variety of pictorial expressions, and one of the goals of this book is to elaborate working definitions of the various relationships that images institute with the objects they represent. Traditional scientific disciplines that deal with figurative arts and images have almost always focused on art history, which primarily addresses artists, their biographies, styles, studios, the dating of artworks and attributions of their aesthetic value. Methodologically speaking, a legally conscious history of images needs a broader survey,[1] as it aims to deal with all images, not just the most aesthetic ones, which cater primarily for an elite circle of art experts.[2]

Many if not most of the secondary sources fail to make clear what defines or characterises an image of Justice. An icon, an emblem, as symbol or effigy does not have the same relationship to its archetype or prototype. An ontological approach to what is meant by the word *image* needs further critical elaboration. According to Georges Didi-Huberman, in Pliny's view (*Natural History* 35.1–17), 'imago' references a juridical genre where portraits were exhibited in a juridical space at the boundary of public and private law.[3] It is according to this line of division that images may be *just or unjust, legal or illegal*. Pictorial expressions do not originally refer to flat, planar objects. The word 'effigies' derives from the verb *effingere*, which was initially used to designate sculptural painting, especially artworks in clay. If the word was used to designate pictures and images, it also had a legal meaning. In the funerary cults from antiquity to modern times, the word 'effigy' stood for a plastic image of a deceased person, usually made of perishable materials such as wax, leather, clay or similar. At least until the nineteenth century, the practice of executing a sentence *in effigie*, that is, in or on the picture, was still prevalent in law. In an execution *in effigie*, a painting of the absent fugitive could be burned or a sculptural representation hanged instead of them.

The definition of the term 'simulacrum' is also instructive. Derived from the verb *simulare*, it initially meant 'to make similar', but the word is frequently associated with the verb *simulo* so as to suggest deception and delusion. Although it could generally be used to refer to an image, likeness or portrait, in antiquity it was mainly understood to designate the cultic worship of an image of a god. In addition, 'simulacrum' was also used to refer to images in dreams, as well as fantasies, shadows or spectres of the dead, opening up the path of inquiry into the imaginal. The Platonic distinction between 'imago' and 'simulacrum' has been influential up to modern times: 'imago' is permanent, stable and a-temporal while 'simulacrum' is changeable, material and temporal. 'Simulacrum' may have the connotation of a false image, but it may also indicate an attempt to emphasise the imaginary nature of the image in the mind (*eidolon*). The fear of idols regularly challenged legal doctrine. The exploration of the lines of division of an ontology of images of Justice is the ultimate task of a legal iconology.

This chapter pays special attention to the plasticity of images, to their iconic quality and material presentation as well as to the avenues of their dissemination, beyond the normative and linguistic order of the *ratio legis*. It uses as a case study a striking sixteenth-century effigy of Lady Justice to draw out the peculiar context in which early modern female embodiments of *Justitia* occurred. Here I give an analytical account of an allegorical image used by a German lawyer in a specific context, in order to make possible in due course a comparison with the allegorical conceits employed by lawyers of later periods.

Ekphrasis: Gregor Bersman

Gregor Bersman's image of Justice provides a beautiful and complex depiction of Lady Justice's anatomy as well as a conceptual glossary for the study that follows (Figure 1.1).[4] It is rooted in a Christian and Neoplatonic context. The depiction is of *Justitia* in an oval frame, similar to the shape of a printer's mark,[5] and it appears in an unusual layout.

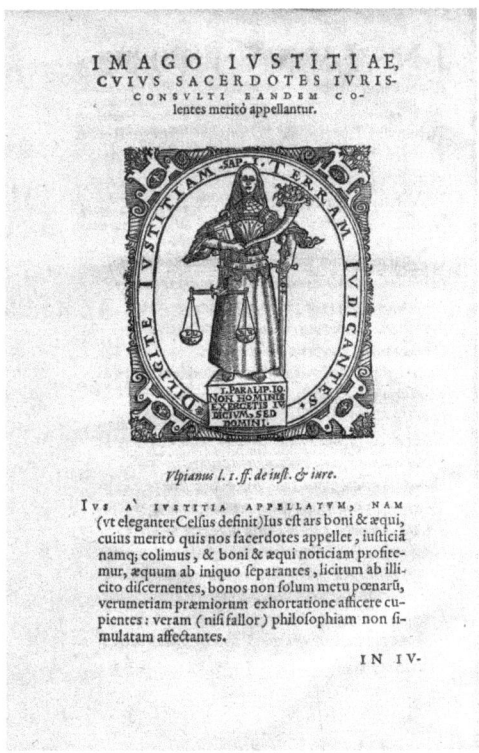

Figure 1.1: *Imago Justitiæ*, in Hartmann Pistoris, *Quæstionum iuris tam Romani quam Saxonici, liber primus*, 1579. Bayerische Stäatsbibliothek

The title above the illustration reads 'Imago Iustitiæ, cujus sacerdotes jurisconsulti eandem colentes merito appellantur'. The reference is to the *Digest* (1.1.1) where Ulpian claims that law being the creature of Justice, the jurisconsults are rightly called priests, for Justice is the goddess whom they worship and to whose service they are devoted. As Peter Goodrich has argued persuasively, the feminine genealogies of common law are rooted in a paradoxical 'gynætopia'. Although women are regularly said to have suffered from a *deterior conditio*, Justice is nevertheless allegorised in the shape of a female body.[6] Aulus Gellius (*Attic Nights* 14.4) famously reports that the allegorical figure of Justice is a paradigm of the just judge, as 'judicem Iustitiæ antistes est' (the judge is the priest of Justice). The word *antistes* refers to a superintendent, an overseer of a temple, or a high priest. In his *Oration on the Death of Alciati* (1550), Pietro Varondello used the honorific expression 'Justitiæ antistes' to characterise the Milanese jurist.[7] In his *Parerga*

(1539), Andrea Alciato goes beyond the laudatory use of the word to pay particular attention to the characteristics of legal expressions.[8] He hypothesises that the word *antistes* is etymologically related to the legal verb *antestor* 'to call as a witness', arguing logically that *antestor* probably derives from a contraction of *ante-testor, whilst *antistes* is derived from the prefix *ante-* and the verb *sto* 'to stand'.[9] Thus, *antistes* would primarily mean 'the leader of the persons called to testify'. This etymological suggestion reminds us that the expression *antistes Iustitiæ* may refer to the consultants of the goddess *Justitia*, who stand near an altar under the sky.

Here, the priestly power of *Justitia* is conveyed by an image, a visible signpost standing at the crossroads of law and theology. Lady Justice is standing as a hieratic full-length figure. The visive powers of *Justitia* are given close scrutiny. Legal iconology stands here as the ultimate justification of the ideal of a rule above men. Expressed through emblematic language, the *Imago Justitiæ* suggests that the rule of law needs to be introduced through the epiphany of the goddess. Gregor Bersman thus takes sides with Hotman, Cujas and many other sixteenth-century jurists, who firmly believed that Justice was a goddess. Commenting upon the fragment in the *Digest*, they regularly asked whether Justice was a *virtus* or a *dea*. Ernst Kantorowicz notes that they concluded that she must be a goddess, 'because the jurisprudents were called *sacerdotes* and there were no *sacerdotes virtutum humanarum*; hence Justinian must have defined *Justitiam deam, Iovis filiam*'. Cujas even goes as far as asserting that we do in fact worship Justice as if she is the most sacred goddess ('Justitiam namque colimus, quasi Deam sanctissimam').[10]

Kantorowicz has shown the centrality of the personification of the *Templum Iustitiæ* where Justice was placed in an intermediate position where 'she alone had a share in both Natural Law above and Positive Law below' though equivalent to neither. 'Iustitia herself was not Law. She was an Idea, a goddess who had the function of mediator, an *Iustitia mediatrix*, between divine and human laws.'[11] The excerpt from the *Digest* symbolises human laws, whilst the effigy of Lady Justice, showing the real presence of the goddess, embodies the eternally effective presence of divine law. The allegorical figure stands at the threshold of the legal text, its *fons et origo*.

Ekphrastic epigrams of Justice

To understand the complex work that Bersman's *Imago Justitiæ* is doing, it is necessary to have some sense of the tradition in which he was operating. The learned humanists had a special interest in *ekphrasis*, and their visualisation had already revitalised the most prominent examples of this tradition (the Calumny of Apelles, the Gallic Hercules and the statue of Occasio are probably the most well-known cases). The allegory of Justice had been the subject of several ekphrastic epigrams, frequently shaped into dialogues.[12] One of them, the *Dialogus de Justicia* (also appearing under the title *Iusticiae signo subscriptum*) is inserted into volume 1 of the *Carmina illustrium poetarum Italorum*, edited by Ioannes Matthaeus Toscanus, under the title *De vera Iusticia*.[13] The following epigram is attributed to a certain Ignatius Albanus, who is mentioned by Filippo Argelati as a protégé of Cardinal Federico Borromeo (1564–1631).[14] It is used as a prototype of the epigram in dialogue form in the *Institutio poetica* of the German Jesuit father Jacobus Pontanus (1542–1626).[15] The epigram reappears constantly in many early modern accounts of Lady Justice's symbolism, sometimes readapted to different contexts. A translation of the version given by Bernardino Dardano (1472–1535) is thus welcome:[16]

> What kind of goddess are you?
> Justice is my name.
> Why the fierce gaze?
> I cannot be bent in any way, and no interest touches me.
> From what country?
> From heaven?
> And who are your parents?
> Moderation is my kind father,
> And sincere Faith once carried me in its belly.
> What do you pretend to show with an open ear, while the other is not?
> To the righteous my help is offered: I am deaf to the wicked.
> Why is there a sword in your right hand? What is the role of the balance in your left hand?
> This one shows me busy punishing; this one is very accurate in weighing all rights.

Do you find any delight in walking alone like this? And would you be bored
   when you are accompanied?
It's because, Fabricius, there are few honest people these days.
Are you not without help in this poor appearance?
A righteous man who counts all the riches of the world for nothing,
will never consider it as its supreme good.[17]

This epigram frequently served as a rhetorical exercise for students training in forensic eloquence. In the edition of the *Carmina illustrium* already referenced, it is immediately followed by its counterpart *De falsa iusticia*, which is a formal inversion of it. Another poem, written by the German poet Euricius Cordus (1486–1535), entitled *In Iustitiam pictam*, is incorporated by Leodegarius a Quercu in his poetic miscellany.[18] Its incipit is very similar: 'Quod nomen tibi? Iustitiæ. Quid vult sibi libra?' The *Delitiæ poetarum Germanorum huius superiorisque ævi*, a popular anthology of neo-Latin poems edited by Janus Gruterus, also contains two compositions about the allegorical representation of Justice.[19] The first, entitled *Statua Iusticia*, is by Georgius Tilenus (first half of sixteenth century), and can be found on p. 865 of volume 2. The other, entitled *Iustitia Imago*, is by Joannes Lauterbach (1531–93), and can be found on p. 929 of volume 3.

The circulation of these Latin verses is a common practice among humanists. But vernacular versions also exist. One of them is of particular interest for us as it modifies the prototypical epigram quoted above to suit the illustration of a blindfolded Lady Justice. A print by Willem Jacobsz Delff, published around 1650 by Robert de Baudous, shows Lady Justice, blindfolded and holding her sword upward in her right hand, on a pedestal, staged on a *tableau vivant* between two judicial scenes in the background (the judgment of Zaleucus on her right-hand side and the judgment of Cambyses on her left-hand side) (Figure 1.2). The two trials taking place behind *Justitia*'s back (she is turned away) are performed on stages, with the audience in the pit. It is also noteworthy that the blindfold does not seem to entirely obscure her downward gaze, the band appearing to be slightly open at the bottom.[20] We will come to the particularities of Lady Justice's blindfold in Chapter 2. The vernacular epigram appears in French and Dutch in two columns, in the lower part of the print, between Piety and Peace. An English translation of the epigram shows how the original Latin poem has been adapted to print: *ekphrasis* is a combination of imitation and selection.[21] These ekphrastic dialogues are not set in stone, since the various guises of *ekphrases* show that they are never an exhaustive enumeration of a set of relevant signs. Rather, allegorical features demonstrate the problem of plurivalency in signs.[22]

Delff's poem revives the interrogative ethos of antique *ekphrasis*, in typical Lucian fashion: a beautiful sculpture, bearing enigmatic attributes, is expounded upon in a dialogue between the interpreter and the viewers of the statue. Novel features have been introduced to match the context of the Netherlandish audience of the print. Each attribute is carefully explicated in French and Dutch to cater for a wider public. The peripatetic interpreter is a figure of friendship ('l'Amy') who sympathises with the listener's/beholder's affects, as he is invited to see how much Justice is devalued in the earthly world. The role of the 'friend' is to draw attention to Lady Justice's attributes, of course, but by doing so he also draws attention to his own interpretative skills and his own set of values. The shared values are to the credit of an interpretative community: all viewers are invited to raise questions, to signal awareness of problems rather than offering any single viewpoint. The viewer is prompted to speculate for himself on the meanings of the attributes. In this way, images of Justice are presented in their didactic function.

Bersman therefore uses the traditional *ekphrasis* of Justice as the basis of a new pictorial realisation, developing an independent iconography, designed for learned lawyers and their interpretative communities. Instead of using the rhetorical resources of ekphrastic epigrams, written for a wider audience and not necessarily for a public of learned jurists, Bersman develops an unusually long and sophisticated poem, some appreciation of which is important to highlight the originality of its symbolism. For this reason, a translation of the first fifty-eight verses is available as an appendix to this chapter. It aims at describing a work of art, bringing before one's eye what is to be shown. It animates the mute statue by inserting it into a precise frame of reference. More than a simple window into a visible phenomenon, the *ekphrasis* must communicate the judgements and emotions of the describer. The setting of the woodcut between the title and a brief prose commentary at the bottom of the page highlights the interpretive role of the *ekphrasis*. This *Imago Justitiæ*

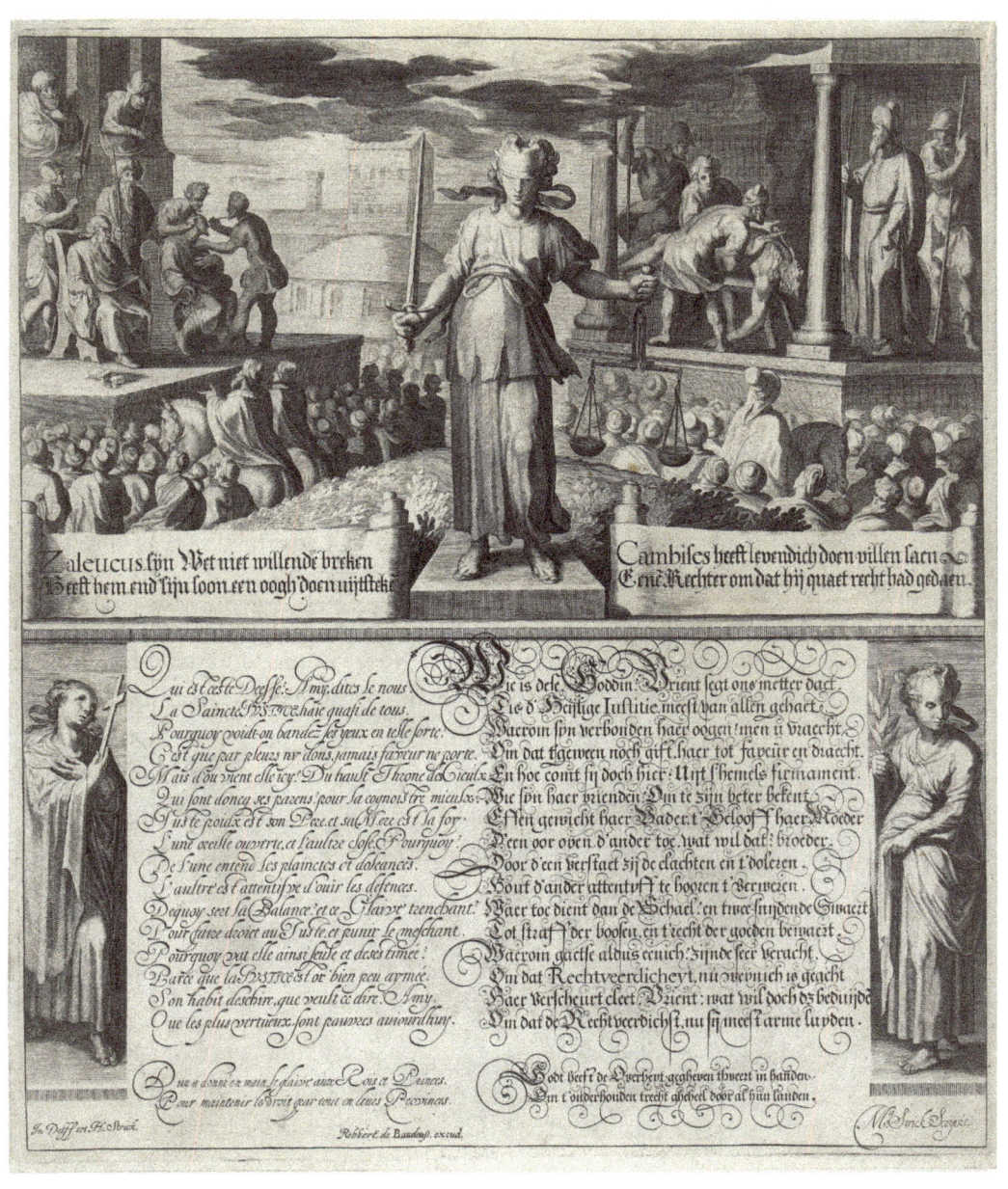

Figure 1.2: Willem Jacobsz Delff (print maker), Maria Strick-Bercq, *Lady Justice, between the Judgment of Zaleucus and the Judgment of Cambyses*, engraved print, 48.5 cm × 42.3 cm, published by Robert de Baudous, c. 1650. Courtesy of the Rijksmuseum, Amsterdam

does not stand alone as a mute icon, it is coined by the *sacerdotes juris-consulti* (priestly jurisconsults) as an image to worship. The surrounding *subscriptio* attributed to the definition of justice by Ulpian is carved out of the text of the *Digest* as a *sententia* capable of summarising a guide to moral conduct: separating right from wrong, licit from illicit.

Goddess *Justitia* and the paradoxes of *icones symbolicæ*

The verb *colere* 'to worship' used on the title page implies that the image of Lady Justice is understood as little more than a mere representation of an abstract idea. In order to define the type of divine quality which is involved in the figuration of Justice, the nature of the allegorical language in its relationship to the divine needs to be elucidated. During the early modern era, figures of allegorical Justice were interpreted in ways which the rational analysis of contemporary critics might ignore. Lady Justice was often depicted as an authentic goddess, rivalling the Virgin Mary. In his seminal article '*Icones Symbolicæ*: The Visual Image in Neoplatonic Thought', E. H. Gombrich investigated in depth how the Neoplatonic understanding of allegorical language and the art of devising symbolic images implied a genuine belief in their cognitive effect. The contemplation of symbolic images would then teach early modern men how to ascend high. The confusion between 'the sign and the thing signified, the name and its bearers, the literal and the metaphorical, the image and its prototype' was then essential to the functions of these images.[23] When he analyses why symbolic images were at the centre of lengthy philosophical speculations, Gombrich takes the example of Justice:

> Thus the painter who had to represent Justice in a city hall was not without a certain philosophical sanction if he first wanted to know what Justice 'looked like' in her supra-celestial dwellings. His humanist adviser would even know how to find out: If we only burrow deep enough into ancient and recondite lore we may find there an allusion to one of the images in which the ancient sages of the East hid their deep insight into the essence of Justice. It was Plutarch, for instance, who reported in *De Iside et Osiride* that the mythical Priest of Egypt represented Justice blind. To paint her blindfolded was thus to reveal a true attribute of the idea of Justice. The true Neo-Platonist may even

encourage one to go a step further and to assume that those whose eyes rest on the figure really do behold Justice, and that therefore their behavior may or must be affected by what they see [. . .] Justice welcoming the King at the city gate during a 'Glorious Entry' was perhaps conceived as more than just a pretty girl wearing a strange costume. In and through her, Justice herself had come down to earth to greet the ruler and to act as a spell and an augury.[24]

The divine nature of Justice

Bersman's depiction of an image of Justice *ad oculos* uses a symbolic *ekphrasis* to let the reader ascend to the divine nature of Justice. The whole poem is meant to be mysterious as it serves as a starting point for contemplation. One example of a similar blurring between representation and symbolisation can be seen in Marc-Antoine Muret's depiction of Astræa in Christophe de Thou's funeral poem (*Christophori Thuani Tumulus*) dated 1583. Is Astræa nothing but the metaphor of divine justice, that is to say a mere abstraction, or is she depicted as something existing by herself in a higher sphere? Ludwig Walther has noted that Marc-Antoine Muret was afraid of the French Inquisition, because he had called Astræa a goddess.[25] He felt deeply that this poetic licence might have sounded disrespectful and idolatrous. In his defence, he advocates that his use of the name Astræa is understood as nothing other than divine justice ('Ego tamen profiteor, Astræae nomina nihil aliud a me quam divinam justitiam intelligi').[26] Here, we may clearly witness that the divinity of Justice was highly suspect during the Counter-Reformation. Muret's position is over-cautious, a result of having been accused twice of heresy by the French Inquisition in 1553, accusations from which he had fled by escaping to Italy.

The goddess Astræa, quoted from the Iron Age of Ovid's *Metamorphoses*, appears as a central focus of the poem. Muret describes the social ascent of de Thou, who had been the first president of the Parisian parliament, which was also the Supreme Court, since 1562. The passage (verses 106–124) reads:

Here [i.e. in Paris] Astræa had long since built herself a dwelling place, here the ancient kings [of France] built her a marble temple with coffered ceilings at enormous expense, where two hundred fathers, the most exquisite heads, meet every day to honour the goddess in an orderly manner with venerable sacred acts and make final decisions about right and wrong and, inspired by the goddess, give information and through her advice steer the reins of the kingdom. Among these, the great Goddess herself puts de Thou in the first place and says 'You shall be the President of our Order'. High up on the ivory armchair, he represents the goddess' rule and gives punishments and rewards to the people. And immediately the deceits flee, the unfair favours flee far away and so do the bribes that corrupt the greedy spirits. Nothing more can hate; nothing can cause more anger. There is no longer any difference between the nobleman and the man of the people, between the poor and the man of great wealth, between the one who comes alone and the one who is accompanied on all sides by powerful friends. Everyone receives his right. The scales are the same for everyone.[27]

According to Ovid, Astræa, who represents the personification of justice following Aratus (*Phainomena* 96–136), is the last to leave the earth in the Iron Age (*Metamorphoses* 1.130–1). In Muret's poem, by contrast, Astræa has come back and now resides in Paris, while the personifications of injustice flee the city in reverse. The venerable goddess of Justice *inspires* the two hundred lawyers led by de Thou. They honour her with sacred rites and contemplation of her image, as she sits in the sacred Temple of Jurisprudence, endowing wise men with a superior knowledge of the Law.

In addition to the fairly common attributes of the sword and the scales, Bersman's printed figure also holds a book and a cornucopia, rather untypical attributes for *Justitia* and suggestive of an effectively syncretic fusion with the figures of *Lex* and Public Good. In turn, in the poem, she incarnates Astræa, Themis and Dike, and her avatars make her a versatile goddess. The emblematic nature of the portrait of Lady Justice, the aura of her image, and the mysteries of her attributes are all intended to depict a representation of the unrepresentable, an image-symbol demanding contemplation, enticing us to decipher it. In the 1579 Leipzig edition of the poem, the image is included in a particularly meaningful layout. The emblematic portrait of Lady Justice stands on one page, above the famous excerpt from the *Digest* where Ulpian gives his definition of Justice as derived from *Jus* – 'Jus a Justitia appellatum' (*Digest* 1.1.1). This configuration puts the image and the Justinian text on the same level of dignity. The effigy of Lady Justice announces through her sacred presence the transformation of the legal text into some sort of oracular word. In Goethe's analysis of the allegorical conceit, he states that its 'symbolism transmutes the phenomenon into an idea, the idea into an image, so that in the image the idea remains forever effective and intangible and, though expressed in all languages, inexpressible.'[28] The striking setting of the image and the legal text, a genuine emblematic montage, short-circuits the order of speech, the legal text and its *ratio legis*. Only an *imago legis* can perform the office of tracing the origin of *jus* to *Justitia*.

A judicial *ekphrasis*

Bersman's verses thus act here as a sort of prayer where the goddess is indeed offered as animate and present before our eyes. Svetlana Alpers noted that 'ekphrasis originated in late antiquity as a rhetorical mode of praising and describing people, places, buildings and works of art.'[29] Verity Platt adds that *ekphrasis* may itself become a 'form of worship' as 'the ekphrasis suggests that when experienced within the context of ritual – when the song can actually be heard – text and image can generate a "real" experience of the divine.'[30] If the *ekphraseis* of Callistratus were intended in antiquity as rhetorical exercises dealing with works of art and used as models to teach students the art of declamation, the *ekphrasis* of Justice composed by Gregor Bersman is reframed in a judicial context, as the vivid description of an image of Justice adapted to the readers of Hartmann Pistoris's *Quæstionum iuris*. Lady Justice's *ekphrasis* opens up a set of performative gestures aimed at serving as a model for the good judge. The forensic frame in which her visualisation is staged provides new ways to analyse ekphrastic agency. Beyond the traditional theoretical framework used to explain *ekphrasis* (the rivalry between literature and visual arts), this case enables us to expand the traditional viewpoint along with a new spectrum of its uses inside the legal sphere. Bersman's *ekphrasis* is unusually rich, offering the reader a veritable cornucopia through which, in a short time span, they may behold, witness and imprint in their mind the rules of moral and civic justice. Knowledge of Justice transmitted through a vision of its embodiment is higher knowledge. The vision of Lady Justice profoundly affects us, more than any rational argument.

Bersman's emblemology: the Leipzig context

Considering the poem's appeal primarily to jurists or judges, we need to pay close attention to the response it elicits from this particular audience. Gregor Bersman was a German humanist who has earned a name in literary history as a Latin poet.[31] His work includes hymnal poetry and the major forms of humanist classicism: elegies, epigrams, eclogues. In addition, he dealt with ancient authors and edited academic declamations and textbooks in the tradition of Philipp Melanchthon. The poem's dedicatee, Hartmann Pistoris, was an influential jurisconsult from Leipzig,[32] who took care of a number of the most important affairs of the Saxon Electorate under three governments for about eighteen years. People seeking justice would very often come to his estate, either to ask for his opinion or to consult his *Observationes Juris* (a collection of remarkable legal cases and disputes edited by him), which the author kept in manuscript form in Seußlitz at the time. In the dedicatory epistle (dated from October 1578, Dresden) of his *Quæstionum*, Pistoris claims that the administration of justice stands high above teaching, which is why he also chose it as his life's profession, and cites the words of Baldus in support of his view: genuine legal science is *digestive*: 'in scholis leges deglutiuntur, in palatiis vero-digeruntur!' (if one swallows laws in schools, one can only digest them in the courthouse). Considering them in their true function, the application to cases is the only way to join theory and practice.

The target audience for Pistoris's work are therefore those who are steeped in the concrete realities of courts. To better appreciate the significance of this reception, let me elaborate a list of some of the original features of Bersman's image. I will use the translated verses provided in the Appendix along with other emblematic signs appearing later in the poem. Since the poem contains no fewer than 136 verses, I will focus on only its most ingenious inventions.

Justitia quadrata

The goddess stands as *Justitia quadrata* (on a square or cubic stylobate).[33] Arnold Ehrhardt explains how the square shape was associated with the Greek word 'dikaiosyne', the first of the four cardinal virtues, closely connected to the number four, generating the link between the divine realm and the human microcosm.[34] The description of Justice as *quadrata iustitia* is frequently combined with the idea of the square universe and its harmony. 'Dikaiosyne' is the connecting bond between man (microcosm) and universe (macrocosm). The good man, says Simonides of Cos, is four-square: his spiritual appearance is similar to the harmony of the cosmos. The square stylobate depicted in the image helps to identify the nature of Justice here described. The engraving shows the divine Dike,[35] revered as an allegorisation of divine justice, unifying Christian and Pagan understandings of the four-square ground plan of the universe. Significantly, the square pedestal on which Lady Justice is standing, barefoot, is protruding, as if the cubic shape had come out of the oval frame. This protrusion of the frame makes the goddess even more present, giving her a supplemental aura.

Justice as *Puritas*

The anatomy of Lady Justice's body parts allows us to see beyond the straightforward denotations of her attributes. The focus on her face tends to soften the harshness of her attributes, infusing *rigor juris* with a sense of compassion. Lady Justice is not brandishing the lictor's *fasces* or reins here; her hair, 'pouring on her neck' in equal parts, as well as her ears 'covering both her temples', indicate, by their symmetry, that she is even-handed. Her mouth, eyes and chaste appearance signify that she is 'morally pure', 'without any fault or crime'. This is an important feature of her sacredness, which appears clearly in a print by Virgil Solis in which *Justitia* preserves herself from the impurity of directly holding an executioner's sword (Figure 1.3). She grasps the sword with a piece of cloth. The same pattern appears in a copy after Peter Flötner of a standing Justice, who is handling the deadly tool using a draped cloth, thus not directly touching the weapon (Figure 1.4). The cloth motif is a

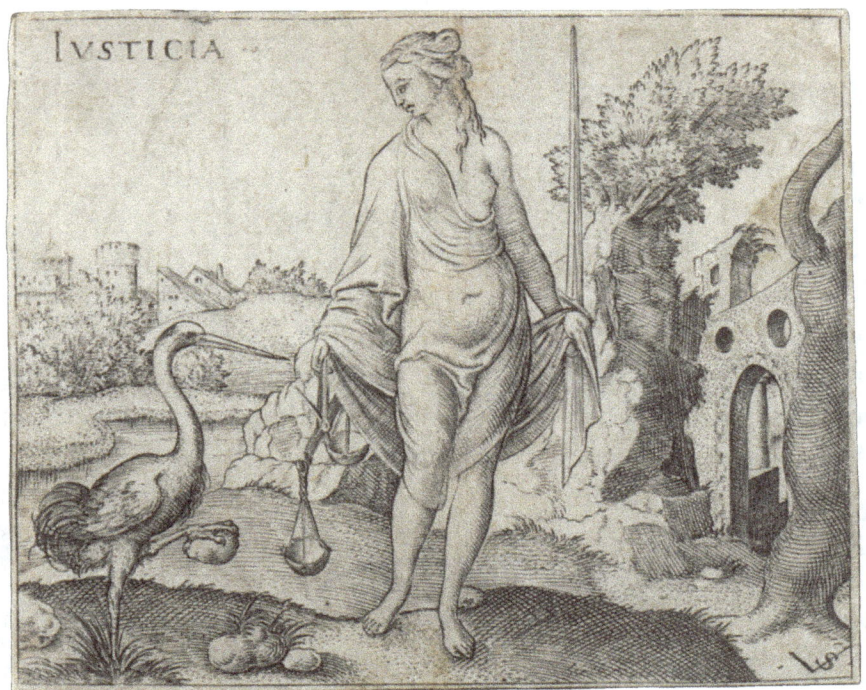

Figure 1.3: Virgil Solis, *Iusticia*, series of the seven virtues, print maker Virgilius Solis, c. 1524–62, 6.8 cm × 8.5 cm. Courtesy of the Rijksmuseum, Amsterdam

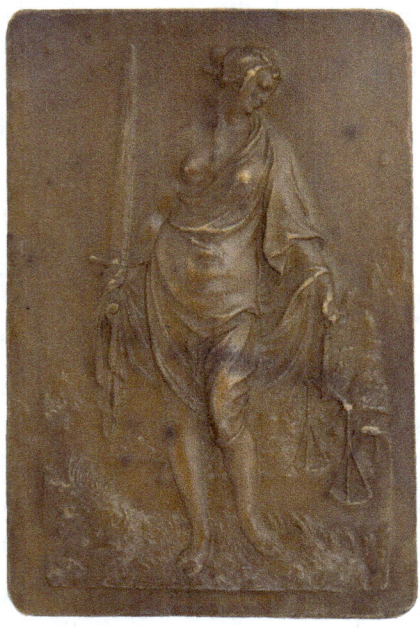

Figure 1.4: Copy after Peter Flötner (Thurgau, Switzerland, c. 1485–1546 Nuremberg, Germany), *Justice*, from the series *The Seven Virtues (Standing)*, plaque on electrotyped metal, 8.1 cm × 5.5 cm, early twentieth century (original from c. 1540). Courtesy of the Harvard Museum collections, Busch-Reisinger Museum

pictorial parallel to her blindfold, understood as a self-protective device against the atrocities of inflicting judgment. *Justitia*'s punishment needs to be presented as a ritual obligation, and not as a savage, human act of killing in which forbearance has no part to play.

A 'dress without pleat or knot' and the absence of artifice or 'false appearance' are in total correspondence with her face, posture and expression (she is neither frowning nor 'wrinkling her eyebrows' and her face is 'without ungrateful severity for others'). This moral purity is further enshrined in her armour, the *lorica justitiæ*.

The *lorica iustitiæ*

The breastplate (or hauberk) of Lady Justice is the visualisation of a well-known biblical metaphor, the *lorica iustitiæ* (Ephesians 6:14) and Isaiah 59:17: *indutus est iustitia ut lorica*, a potent and multifaceted emblem long associated with spiritual warfare. Early Christian exegetes have elaborated on the symbolism of the 'breastplate of righteousness' as a spiritual protection for its bearer. This rich symbolism had been taken up by several humanist authors. For instance, Erasmus' *Enchiridion militis Christiani* (Handbook – and Hand dagger – of the Christian Soldier), written in 1501 and first published in Antwerp in 1503, was a new iteration of the idea of the *miles christianus*, armed with the spiritual weapons of warfare (2 Corinthians 10:3) – the 'armour of God', the 'breastplate of righteousness', the 'shield of faith' and the 'helmet of salvation'.[36]

The iconographical depiction of the *lorica justitiæ* gained a certain popularity in the Renaissance period with the revival at the end of the sixteenth century of armour *all' antica*. The *lorica anatomica* depicts the detailed articulation of the torso's musculature, showing nipples and navel, as is the case with the figure of Lady Justice above the Santa Trinita Column carved in 1583 by Francesco Ferrucci del Tadda and Guglielmo della Porta (Figure 1.5). The tactile and erotic details reproduced on the porphyry sculpture exposes Lady Justice's vulnerability as if her cuirass was nothing but prosthetic skin. Her *lorica* bears the *gorgoneion* (a face-forward presentation of Medusa looking directly at the viewer) on the chest, *pteryges* (small mobile leather straps), a *cinctorium* (belt) with round buckle, and a flowing *paludamentum* (officer's cloak) in bronze, draped over her left shoulder. Her armour reproduces the cuirass of equestrian officers, the figurative expression of their military status.[37] This type of Nemesis is symbolic of Roman imperial power, and some third- and fourth-century examples have Nemesis dressed in full military cuirass and cloak, the very image of the victorious general.[38]

Bersman's composition adopts the rhetorical pattern of the *miles christianus* for Dame Justice, turning a virile model for Christian faith into a female allegory. Armour, like weaponry in general, was male gendered in early modern societies. Bersman's verse refers explicitly to a male hero, Aeneas, whose cuirass is described as *loricam ex aere rigentem* (Virgil, *Aeneid* 8.621–2). 'Rigentis' describes a stiff, bronze type of

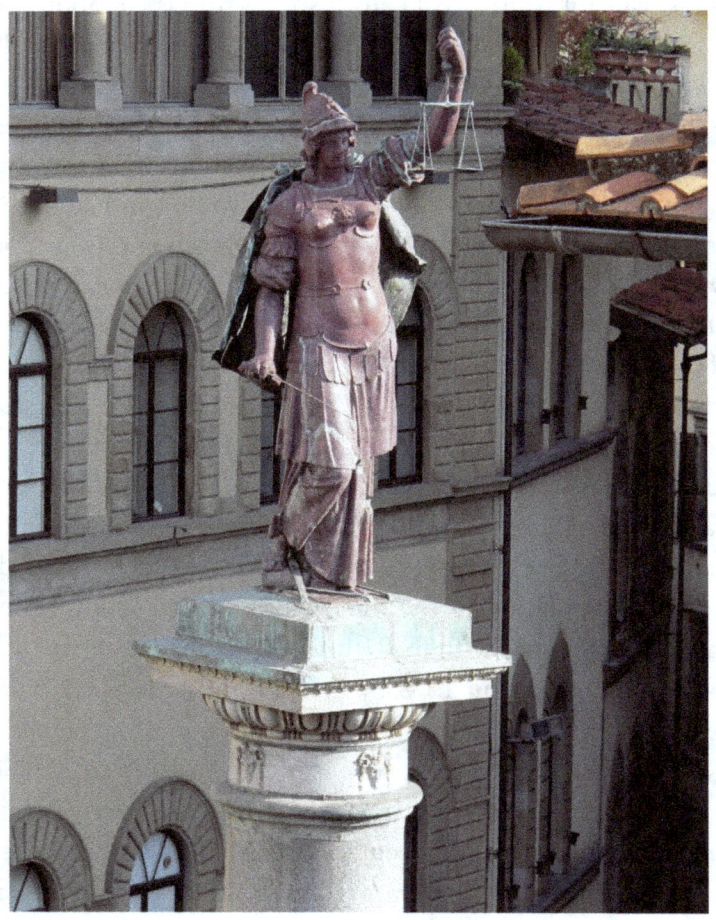

Figure 1.5: Francesco Ferrucci del Tadda, *Lady Justice Standing above the Santa Trinita Column*, 1583, Piazza Santa Trinita, Florence. Wikimedia Commons

cuirass, able to stand upright, a solidly constructed shape, moulding muscles sharply. In Roman times, this type of anatomical cuirass was usually associated with a high-ranking Roman officer, or indeed the emperor himself. Here the breastplate clothes *Justitia* from collar to waist. Decorated with fluted surfaces in the German fashion, it is adorned with flaring ridges that radiate from the waist.

Nevertheless, Bersman primarily interprets the *lorica* as a protective device. Her armour, says Bersman, is 'not intended to inflame one with wrath.' 'Justice', the poem argues, 'defeats crime with gentleness, without ever scarily grinding its teeth at anyone, without demanding anything by shouting or through blows.'

Book, scales and cornucopia

Bersman revives here a lost emblem of Aequitas when he adds to the panoply of *Justitia* a cornucopia. In Roman coins, the goddess *Dikaiosynê/Aequitas* is commonly depicted with a balance in the right hand and an ear of grain in the left. A similar pattern shows that the goddess holds in her left hand a whole cornucopia. These coins all date from the imperial period, from Augustus onwards.[39] The horn of plenty is also given a judicial meaning as, says Bersman, it 'teaches how to safeguard the accused, the wealth of licit acts'.

The 'book in her elbow' is a more original facet of the emblem, and relates to the iconography of Nemesis. According to Bersman, the book, held in the right hand, symbolises the equivalence of laws and rights ('leges' et 'jura'[40]) transmitted by legal codes. The poet insists on the body part where the book is placed: 'Why is she willing to bear as ornaments books in her elbow?' The word *cubitus* stands for a body part (forearm or elbow) *and* for a type of measure (cubit). Since the salient characteristic of her hair and ears is symmetry, a token of even-handedness, the *cubitus* is also invested with special significance. The Vitruvian proportions of Lady Justice's body strike many chords at the same time. In the traditional representations of the ancient goddess Nemesis, the attribute of the cubit-rule is often exhibited by a movement of the forearm.[41] It is first intended to draw the spectator's attention to the symbol of measure, but it also echoes the direct relationship between the measure of the cubit and that of the human forearm. The *cubitus* appears as an attribute of Alciato's Nemesis in his emblem 'Nec verbo, nec facto, quenquam lædendum' (Injure no one, either by word or deed).[42] Alciato was inspired by an anonymous epigram of the *Planudean Anthology* (16.223) 'On a statue of Nemesis', which reads: 'Nemesis warns us by her cubit-rule (πῆχυς[43]) and bridle neither to do anything without measure nor to be unbridled in our speech.'[44] The engraver of the Wechel edition exploits the detail, showing her left elbow clutched in the right hand holding the bridle (Figure 1.6).

David M. Greene sees the iconic insistence on the representation of the *cubitus* by a clutched elbow as 'a rather desperate attempt to suit the picture to text on a misapprehension of *cubitus*', adding, 'The Alciatian commentators tied themselves into knots pontificating over the apparent ambiguity; the huge edition of Joannes Thuilius (Padua 1621) devotes an eighth of its four-page, double-columned gloss on this emblem to this one point.'[45] We think on the contrary that this anatomical detail is not an error. It has a genuine symbolic significance and testifies to the interest of the emblematists in the body of

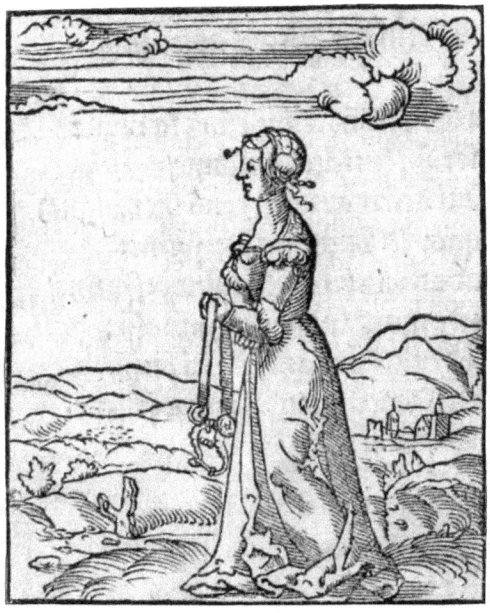

Figure 1.6: Andrea Alciato, *Livret des emblemes* (Paris: Chrestien Wechel, 1536), C2v, emblem 'Nec verbo, nec facto, quenquam lædendum'. By permission of the University of Glasgow Archives & Special Collections, Stirling Maxwell collection

Nemesis. The 1621 edition commentary by Thuilius is instructive. Thuilius claims that

> the word *cubitus* is used ingeniously, not in its primary meaning, as a limb but as a unit of length, based on the distance from the elbow to the end of the middle finger, the cubit of twenty-four fingers or six palms. This cubit rod is similar in shape to the elbow that bends the arm at a right angle. It was called a ruler in Latin and a *gnomon* in Greek. Painters hold the cubit for a measure of a quarter of the body.[46]

Far from engraving a whimsical invention, the cubit-rule is understood as a type of measuring rod, which finds its symbolic root in the proportions of the body. In Mesomedes' *Hymn to Nemesis*, which contains a full list of the goddess's attributes, she is called 'Winged Nemesis, balance of life' who 'continually measures life under (her) cubit-rule'.[47] The root meaning of the expression in Greek ('beneath her forearm') is also present in the poet's mind.[48] It is not insignificant to recall that on the diorite stele of the Babylonian Code of Hammurabi, the king on his throne also holds a measuring rod.

It is a Greek idea to indicate standard measures not under the abstract form of a scale, a unit or a rule, but by figuring those parts of the body from which the measures were initially derived. The body of Dame Justice, in this respect, is far more than a purely aesthetic envelope. Articulating the multiple meanings of *cubitus* (forearm, cubit-rule and cubit), she stands in the agora as the *Justitia agoranomos*; she holds the symbolical office of the magistrate guaranteeing the exactness of measures. She arouses trust and harmony through her practical wisdom (*phronesis*) and virtue (*aretē*), conveyed by *gestus* and *motus corporis* and not necessarily by logical demonstrations.

The insistence on the correct use of the scales is an important feature of her gestural ethics, as Chapter 3 will further elaborate. For now, we will simply point out that four verses, inspired by Ausonius (*Eclogues* 96.11–12), indicate Bersman's particular attention to the correct handling of the scales.[49] The just judge must examine fairly, weighing everything 'on the platform of a fair scale'; the angle must form equal lines and the 'fingers hitting the scale' must announce that the device is 'neutral'. Bersman probably worked closely with the engraver because the drawing of the scales contains two groups of letters which he alludes to in his poem and in the marginal note to the verses: the letters LL (for *Leges*) are written above the R (for *rigor*), and the characters §§ (for *Jura*) are visible above Æ (for *aequitas*). Equity mitigates the rigours of strict law, tempering the harsh effects of written laws. In Bersman's view, the notion of *aequitas* is equated with the moral concept of *bonitas* (verse 71). Bersman here follows Guillaume Budé, who had noted that *aequum et bonum* were a pair synonymous with Aristotle's *epieikeia*, thus equating *aequitas* to *bonitas*.[50] Bersman's idea of equity follows Melanchton's theory,[51] which was focused on checking the compatibility of the law with rules of higher justice (verse 69: 'legum scita sacrarum'), illustrating a peculiarly Lutheran approach to the concept of equity.

The sword: *alienum opus facio*

In the course of the poem, Bersman uses three near-synonyms for 'sword': 'gladium', 'ensis' and 'mucro' (a *sword*, a poetic synonym[52] and a *blade*).[53] Since precise vocabulary is one of the trademarks of a lawyer's art, a note on the use of these terms is not superfluous. These were popular examples of synonyms in late antiquity as grammarians almost always mention the same group. The fifteenth-century grammarian Martianus Capella used this trio as an example for the concept of *plurivocum*: 'A *plurivocum* is when one thing is called by many names, as gladius; for both *ensis* and *mucro* signify the same.'[54] Boethius further elaborates on this triad to make a philosophical distinction between formal and numerical unity, a pivotal argument in his *De Trinitate*. The same object, he says, can be referred to by many different names – *gladius*, *mucro*, *ensis* – without being three different objects.[55] These three words regularly appear as canonical examples of synonyms, frequently taken up in chorus by most grammarians. In his *De Copia Verborum ac Rerum*, Erasmus quotes the words *ensis* and *gladius* as examples of 'synonyms of grammar' that enrich the store of words.[56] But a certain Pseudo-Sergius (c. 500), praising the mastery of *copia verborum* – a linguistic cornucopia – attempted to distinguish between them: 'One says *ensis* when it is a question of combat, *gladius* in general, *mucro* when it is a worked object.'[57] Bersman certainly uses these parasynonymous terms to demonstrate a like mastery. The sword depicted in the image is not particularly ornamented, it has a globular pommel, a broad blade, straight quillons, and the hilt seems undecorated. The bare sword, though, seems to underline the warlike posture of the ruler as the bearer of the *jus gladii*, but it is carried downward and not brandished. Moreover, since God's Word is frequently compared to a sharp sword which brings punishment, the biblical mottos inscribed around the frame and below the pedestal of *Justitia* gain special significance.

Lady Justice wears a ring on her wrist which allows her to hold in one hand three different objects: the book in her elbow, the scales on her wrist and the horn of plenty. Her left hand neither grasps nor brandishes the sword. She slightly supports its guard with her left thumb, while the point of the downward sword rests on one of the edges of her pedestal. She holds four attributes in balance (twice as many as usual) without appearing overloaded. This paradoxical equilibrium reveals a challenging symbolism as well. Lady Justice's sword bears three enigmatic letters, 'A.O.F.' As explained in a marginal note, 'Alienum op(us) facio Esaiae 28' refers to Isaiah 28:21 and introduces us to the paradoxes of God's 'strange work', that is, God's death-dealing work.[58] Just as God's wrath is strange to him because it is alien to his nature, Lady Justice's use of wrath is 'strange' as it assumes a foreign character to her. Wrath is not an attribute of God. God's Justice being the 'measuring line' (Isaiah 28:17), following 'the plumb-line of righteousness', it is meant to be perfectly fair. God's 'strange work' opens up to the paradoxical nature of his work of judgment. One of the greatest challenges to Christian faith is when God seems to be actively malevolent, sending affliction to his people.

Martin Luther likewise speaks of God's *opus alienum*, his alien work.[59] Through his exposition of two kinds of works of God, Luther explains that the first one (*Opus Alienum Dei*) involves killing and taking away hope, whilst the second one (*Opus Proprium Dei*) speaks of forgiveness, love and encouragement. The idea is that the God who kills and who enriches life is to be understood in his wrath and in his grace. Because of sin, God must judge, kill and destroy. To make men righteous, his 'alien' work must precede and accompany his 'proper' work. Humbling, bruising and beating down serve as an entrance into grace.

While the impenitent may receive only the severity of the wrath of God, the penitent recognise the merciful intention which lies beneath it, and thus receive the grace of God. But Bersman's vision of Justice differs from Luther's. Putting the motto 'Alienum opus facio' on *Justitia*'s sword, Bersman seems to suggest that Justice is the mediator of the wrath of God when she brandishes her lethal weapon. Bersman seeks to find points of consonance between Lutheran theology and the humanistic conception of *Justitia*.

Bodily synecdoches

Bersman's head-to-toe description of Lady Justice brings the arrangement of her body parts into a powerful symbolism. What is of particular interest is the order in which the items are placed, and which body parts are included. This poem serves as a key entry point for this book as the allegorical figure of Lady Justice is depicted as a body with multiple histories. Many of the marginal notes focus on bodily synecdoches, as if the poem was meant to draft a blazon of Dame Justice. It is not a typical blazon poem though, as the author's intention is not to write a catalogue of the desirable corporeal features of his beloved. His attention deliberately avoids any indecorous detail or sexually charged body part. Eyes, mouth, hair, neck, chest, hands, elbow and feet are not used for their erotic valence. Thighs, breasts, belly, buttocks and genitalia are left aside, covered up by armour. These bodily synecdoches charge *Justitia* with a higher symbolic power, while (perhaps) eliding some of the troublesome physicality of her female body.

The record of the meaningful signs of the body proceeds from head to heels, *a capite ad calcem*, following the structure of divinatory tradition. Her body is carefully constructed through text and image as a series of semiotic signs to be decoded and read. The head-to-toe anatomising principle provides a treasure trove for Bersman, who aims at rewriting Aulus Gellius' portrait of Justice. The marginal note to verse 19, 'oculi acres et recti', refers explicitly to the quotation of Chrysippus recorded in Aulus Gellius (*Attic Nights* 14.4.4), in which the eyes of Justice are described as *acres, recti et immoti* (penetrating, direct and unmoving).[60] In his adage *Iustitiæ oculus. A paragon of Justice*, Erasmus explains Chrysippus' wording as follows: 'It is important that one who is to judge rightly should not allow his gaze to be diverted this way or that from what is honest.'[61]

On the whole, it should be noted that the etching depicts an image of irenic Justice. Even if she is clothed with armour, *Justitia* does not wield the sword with any degree of military vigour. Her body is in sharp contrast with nude portraits of Justice as she is conspicuously covered so that only her forearms, face and feet are left exposed. This masking of Lady Justice's body is surprising. Instead of showing usual standards of bodily display such as 'heroic nudity', the engraver has opted instead to concentrate upon a body shrouded with clothes. Her power to rule is especially signified through the use of a tight-fitting, all-concealing ceremonial garment. Her court robe, covered by an armour worked with exquisite designs, is thought to be a talisman, protecting and demarcating her semi-divine body. But the insistence on the carefully delineated garments also has a mnemonic function. As the unknown author of the *Rhetorica ad Herennium* explains:

> We ought to set up images (*imagines agentes*) of a kind that can adhere longest in memory. And we shall do so if [. . .] we dress some of them with crowns or purple cloaks, for example, so that the likeness may be more distinct to us; [. . .] The things we easily remember when they are real, we likewise remember without difficulty when they are figments, if they have been carefully delineated.[62]

Conclusion

Bersman's verses are therefore remarkable. They include a rare blend of surprising attributes associated with the anatomy of Dame Justice. Recovering many of the lost emblems of Justice, he masterfully creates a syncretic image, combining antique sources and biblical mottos with Justinian's foundational texts. Transcending different historical contexts, his *Imago Justitiæ* subsumes various salient features to animate Lady Justice's body in a polysemous and imaginative way. Lady Justice's *ekphrasis* enables the audience to become witnesses to a novel emblematic process: it aims at persuading judges to live up to their model, as they discover right before their eyes an embodied, sensual and affective portrait. The ethical power of *ekphrasis* transforms a mere portrait into a deontological device. Bersman's image of *Justitia* constructs an alternative project for the administration of justice, attempting to activate an image in order to show the ideals of justice in their most desirable form. She stands as the allegorical shadow of every judge, constructed as the parallel model for the jurist's ethics. Bersman's image shows how the agency of *ekphrasis* attempts to convey the legal truth residing in art.

The implications of this judicial *eidolopoiesis* need to be clarified. The trope of *eidolopoeia* was considered by rhetoricians to be an ideal vehicle for ethics. *Eidolopoeia* (or *simulachri effictio*) was a special kind of *prosopopoeia*, which had the rhetorical power to bring gods down from heaven with great persuasive force. This rhetorical technique, whereby characters are brought back from the dead, would attempt to fashion a spirit in order to make a contemporary point.[63] In a more general sense, the word is used to describe a figure in which a speech is attributed to the deceased, a ghost, an idol or – most particularly in this context – an image. The word also hints at the *eidolopoiike techne*, a technique for producing images, whereby images are created and enlivened.[64] The taste for the Greek terminology of *eidolopoeia* also brings into prominence the forensic notion of *enargeia* (translated in Latin as *evidentia*).

The vividness of the pictorial expression of this *Imago Justitiæ* goes beyond the pure representational necessity of depicting an object which is probable or simply plausible. In order to offer his image to fictitious eyewitnesses, *evidentia* demands more than the creation of an imaginary image with which to see what Bersman is speaking about. Image production, *eidolopoiesis*, means more than presenting to the eye what is described by words. Through the imaginal, where the 'real' and the 'imaginary' are allowed to intertwine, contaminating each other,[65] the *eidolopoeia* of Lady Justice restructures speech into a perceptual space which changes the mere representation in the vision into a pre-essential haptic experience, where the beholder is being penetrated by the image. Embedded in a layout combining a quote from the *Digest* and a full-length portrait of Lady Justice, the *ekphrasis* serves as a signpost of legal *auctoritas*, an attention-arresting device which also functions as a deontological allegorical image. The living portrait of Astræa/Themis/Dike provokes emotional intensity as it appears as an apparent epiphany of the goddess to the onlookers. In painting an exemplary image of Justice, Bersman allows Pistoris's readers to visualise a paragon deserving of imitation. Aulus Gellius' quotation from Chrysippus had set the initial pattern: his effigy of *Justitia* was meant to serve as a model of the *juris antistes*. Bersman proposes a model of moral conduct towards which readers should aspire, but he also adds a sophisticated image, bearing at least four types of inscriptions: title, motto, hieroglyphic letters and legal quotation.

Bersman's *ekphrasis* is strongly bound to tradition: his depiction of Justice as implacable and merciful at the same time develops an antique *topos*, the artful combination of two or more contradictory emotions in one figure. Many epigrams in the *Greek Anthology* depict images of Medea at the time of slaying her children and being at the same time full of rage and moved by pity.[66] Chrysippus' account of the figure of Justice

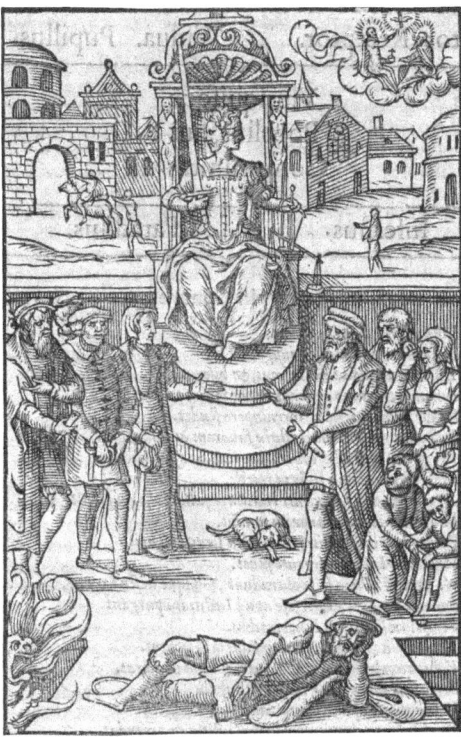

Figure 1.7: Joos de Damhouder, *Mundanæ Justitiæ Effigies*, in *Praxis rerum criminalium* (Antwerp: Jean Beller, 1562). By permission of Numistral, Bibliothèque de l'Université de Strasbourg. Licence ouverte/Open licence

shows a similar articulation, as she was said to 'inspire fear in the wicked and courage in the good; to the latter, as her friends, she presents a friendly aspect, to the former, a stern face' (Aulus Gellius, *Attic Nights* 14.4.1–2). Henry Maguire noted that this characterisation was applied by Byzantine historians to imperial persons. It was also

> used by Mesarites, around the year 1200, to describe the mosaic of Christ Pantocrator in the Holy Apostle. We are told that 'His eyes, to those who have achieved a clean understanding, are gentle and friendly and instill the joy of contrition in the souls of the pure in heart [. . .] To those, however, condemned by their own judgement they are scornful and hostile and boding of ill; the face is wrathful, terrifying, stern and filled with hardness.[67]

So too, the mixed passions of Dame Justice will give rise to a wide number of iconic solutions, one of them being the *facies duplex* (half clear-sighted/half masked) of the face of the goddess in her portrait featured in the *Praxis rerum criminalium* by Joos de Damhouder (Figure 1.7). Since *Justitia* is in essence a binary image, an efficient portrait of Justice seems to lie somehow between *proposon poiein* (to confer a mask or a face) and *eidolon poiein* (to craft, make, reproduce or imitate a fictitious image). Using mimesis through its cognitive, moral and aesthetic aspects, the judicial use of visual entities aims at creating 'mimethical' images (*eikones êthôn, eikonismoi*).

Appendix: translation of Gregor Bersman, *Imago Justitiæ*, in Hartmann Pistoris, *Quæstionum iuris tam Romani quam Saxonici, liber primus*, 1579, verses 1–58

Whoever you are, you will find that the face and hands
reproduced in this painting are like a miniature representation of Astræa,
She used to hold her eyes like this, her hands as well and mouth
When worship had not yet been scorned, she used to
Show herself in mortal assembly
And she would visit in person the homes of the chaste. (Catullus 64.384–6)
Come near, ô Clio, you who keep the memory of these happy deeds treasured
   up in your mind, teach Me the signs of this virgin and meditate with me
   on the secrets of this picture:
Since the earth was stained with unspeakable crime (Catullus 64.397)
No one was allowed to see the living face of the Goddess.
You too, Hartmann, remarkable ornament of the *gens Pistoriadis*,
Of whom the imperial court is also proud, if you are unoccupied, allow me a
   bit of your time,
Once I have reflected on your verses, I will report what the muses have
   dictated.
Am I deluded? Or are those who render justice represented
By lictor's *fasces* and reins held by governing rulers?
Before anything else, look at the mouth of this chaste Virgin,
Look at the two beaming orbs of her eyes, their direct light,
See her hair, pouring on her neck, by the law of 'an eye for an eye' (Propertius
   4.4.58),
Indicating that she is morally pure, without any fault or crime,
Her hair is not dyed with iron-rust, it lacks artifice:
The sharpness of her mind, which lies, hidden in secret retreats,
Guides us towards truth and care for order.
And here, you can see her ears, covering both her temples,
Which the impartial judge applies to both parties,
And soften up her long robe (*stola*) with a stick, as it is lamenting when reach-
   ing her feet.
A dress without pleat nor knot, really not like the long syrma-robe with a long
   train, trailing on the ground, like dotted tail feathers.

Indeed, as the one who knows both parties pronounces only one sentence,

No one can be esteemed as an even-handed judge unless he declares unbiased sentences:

Thus, *gravitas* furnishes it, and not wrinkling its brows,

Her face without ungrateful severity for others,

And her speech without any false appearance or sweet ornament,

Hiding poison in her cruel breast, framing pitfalls and breaking down legal barriers.

But why then is my breast protected with an armoured shield,

And why do I see a stiffened bronze cuirass made of strips of mild steel plate?

Obviously, this cuirass sustains the mind like a vigorous oak,

And it indicates a brave soul that lacks the fear of death (Juvenal 10.10.357).

These pieces of armour are not intended to inflame one with wrath,

Nor to model themselves on criminals,

Neither by entreaty nor by bribery, they continue on the righteous path of the just.

But Justice defeats crime with gentleness, without ever scarily grinding its teeth at anyone, without demanding anything by shouting or through blows.

Moreover, why is she willing to bear as ornaments books in her elbow,

Why is she supporting the two pans of her scales in her right hand?

What about the cornucopia, filled with fruits and flowers?

This teaches how to safeguard the accused, the wealth of licit acts and how her devotion becomes a habit: the rule of justice is the directress of life, the sacred knowledge of laws.

Naturally, in the city, a cult was established for her, along with Faith and Peace,

Embracing sisters who were born twins: their pedestal is enriched with fertile lands and a cluster of Abundant goods, gold altar furniture

Onto which the Muses with their brother have placed their penates.[68]

Notes

1. Costas Douzinas, 'The Legality of the Image', *The Modern Law Review* 63, no. 6 (2000), pp. 813–30.
2. W. J. T. Mitchell, *Iconology, Image, Text, Ideology* (Chicago: Chicago University Press, 1986).
3. Georges Didi-Huberman, 'The Molding Image: Genealogy and the Truth of Resemblance in Pliny's *Natural History*, Book 35, 1–17', in Costas Douzinas and Lynda Nead (eds), *Law and the Image: The Authority of Art and the Aesthetics of Law* (Chicago: University of Chicago Press, 1992), pp. 71–88.
4. Gregor Bersman was born 10 March 1538 in Annaberg and died 5 October 1611 in Zerbst.
5. The German printer Andreas Gutterwitz used an ornamental framework with an image of *Justitia* in his 1548 edition of Melanchton's *Grammatica*, and it has survived in just one copy, that of the National Library in Stockholm. His use of *Justitia* is unique and it is uncertain whether the *Justitia* image should be regarded as his printer's mark, according to Kristina Lundblad, 'The Printer's Mark in Early Modern Sweden', in Anja Wolkenhauer and Bernhard F. Scholz (eds), *Typographorum Emblemata: The Printer's Mark in the Context of Early Modern Culture* (Berlin: De Gruyter, 2018), pp. 227–56 (p. 238, fig. 7).
6. Peter Goodrich, 'Gynætopia: Feminine Genealogies of Common Law', *Journal of Law and Society* 20, no. 3 (1993), pp. 276–308 (p. 283): 'Justice is a temporal yet internal image (*ymaginem*) which triggers recollection of who we are by virtue of reminding whence we came.'
7. Henry Green reproduces a written copy of this rare work, Pietro Varondel's *Oration on the Death of Alciati*, in *Andrea Alciati and His Books of Emblems: A Biographical and Bibliographical Study* (London: Tröner, 1872), p. 286.
8. Andrea Alciato, *Parergon iuris libri tres* (Lyon: Simon Vincent & Jean Barbou, 1538), book 2, ch. 20, p. 100: 'veteres latius testis significationem accepisse: siquidem qui nunc testis est, olim superstes, et antistes est dictus. Quisquis igitur rogatus alicui adesset, superstes dicebatur, quia super ea re, qua de agebatur, stabat. [. . .] Eadem ratione dictus est antistes, et antestatus, et antestor verbum, et antistitor pro testificatore. [. . .] uidetur ergo testis quasi antestis, per aphæresin dictus, sicut et institor, quasi antistitor.'
9. Alciato notes that the frequent orthography *antestis* for *antistes* had to do with an influence from *superstes*. Isidore of Seville (*Etymologies* 7.12.16) claims that 'Antistes sacerdos dictus ab eo quod ante stat'. On 'testis', see also Venantius Fortunatus, *Carmina* 4.4.5: '[Leo] testis et antestis.'
10. Ernst H. Kantorowicz, *The King's Two Bodies: A Study in Mediaeval Political Theology* (Princeton, NJ: Princeton University Press, 1970), esp. pp. 110–11 (p. 111 n. 70), quoting Hotman, commenting on *Institutes* 1.1 (Venice, 1569) and Cujas, commenting on *Digest* 1.1.1, *Opera*, vol. 7 (Prato, 1839), col. 12.
11. Kantorowicz, *King's Two Bodies*, pp. 110–11.

12. Godelieve Tournoy-Thoen has listed them in 'Le manuscrit 1010 de la "Biblioteca de Cataluna" et l'humanisme italien à la Cour de France vers 1500 (III)', *Humanistica Lovaniensia* 27 (1978), pp. 52–85 (pp. 63–5).

13. Ioannes Matthaeus Toscanus (ed.), *Carmina illustrium poetarum Italorum*, vol. 1 (Paris: Gorbinus, 1576), p. 48.

14. Filippo Argelati and Giuseppe Antonio Sassi, *Bibliotheca scriptorum mediolanensium . . .*, vol. 1 (Milan: in aedibus Palatinus, 1745), book 2, col. 14.

15. Johann Buchler, *Institutio poetica ex R. P. Jacobi Pontani e S. J. libris concinnata* (n.p.: n.d.), p. 84.

16. On Bernardino Dardano, see Carlo Vecce, 'Bernardino Dardano. Un poeta italiano alla corte di Luigi XII', in Gabriella Almanza Ciotti, Sandro Baldoncini and Giulia Mastrangelo Latini (eds), *Studi in memoria di Antonio Carlo Possenti* (Macerata: Istituti editoriali e poligrafici internazionali, 1998), pp. 559–73.

17. 'Quæ dea? Iusticia. Ecquid torvo lumine? Flecti / Nescia sum, lachrimis nec moveor precio. / Unde genus? Cælo. Qui te genuere parentes? / Mi Modus est genitor, clara Fides genitrix. / Cur gladium tua dextra gerit, cur leva bilancem? / Ponderat hec causas, percutit illa reos. / Cur sola incedis? Quod copia rara bonorum est, / Hecque ferunt paucos secula Fabricios. / Aurium aperta tibi cur altera, et altera clausa est? Una patet iustis, altera clausa malis. / Paupere cur semper cultu? Iustissimis esse / Qui cupit, ingentes nemo paravit opes.'

18. Leodegarius a Quercu (Léger Duchesne, from Rouen), *Farrago poematum ex optimis quibusque et antiquioribus et ætatis nostræ poetis selecta*, vol. 2 (Paris: Aegidium Gorbinum, 1560), fol. 260r.

19. Janus Gruterus (ed.), *Delitiæ poetarum Germanorum huius superiorisque ævi*, 6 vols (Frankfurt: Nicolaus Hoffmannus, 1612).

20. I owe both remarks to Peter Goodrich.

21. (My translation):

> Who is this goddess? Friend tell us.
> Holy JUSTICE hated by almost everyone.
> Why do we see her blindfolded?
> It's because, no favours are ever granted neither under the effect of cries
> nor under the effect of crying.
> But where does she come from?
> From the high Throne of Heaven.
> Who then are her parents? To know her better:
> Just Weight is her Father and her Mother is Faith.
> One ear is open and the other is closed. Why is that?
> From one she hears complaints and grievances.
> The other is attentive to hear the defences.
> What is the use of her balance? and what about this sharp Sword?
> To uphold the righteous and punish the wicked.
> Why does she go so alone and misjudged?
> Because today JUSTICE is much unloved.
> Her torn garment, what does it mean? Friend,
> That the most virtuous are poor today.

God has given the sword in hand to Kings and Princes.
To maintain the law by all in their Provinces.

22. In Figure 1.2, the text in French and Dutch in script was translated by Maria Strick.

> Qui est ceste Deesse? Amy dites-le nous.
> La Saincte JUSTICE haïe quasi de tous.
> Pourquoy voidt-on bandez ses yeux en telle sorte?
> C'est que par pleurs ny dons jamais faveur ne porte.
> Mais d'où vient elle icy? Du hault Throne des Cieulx.
> Qui sont doncq ses parens? pour la cognoistre mieulx:
> Juste poids est son Pere et sa Mere est la foy.
> L'une oreille ouverte, et l'aultre close. Pourquoy?
> De l'une entend les plainctes et doleances.
> L'aultre est attentive d'ouïr les defences.
> Dequoy sert sa Balance? et ce Glaive trenchant?
> Pour faire droict au Juste et punir le meschant.
> Pourquoi vat elle ainsi seule et desestimée?
> Parce que la JUSTICE est or bien peu aymée.
> Son habit deschire, que veult ce dire? Amy
> Que les plus vertueux sont pauvres auiourd'huy.
> Dieu a donné en main le glaive aux Rois et Princes.
> Pour maintenir le droit par tout en leurs Provinces.

23. E. H. Gombrich, 'Icones Symbolicæ', in *Gombrich on the Renaissance, Volume 2: Symbolic Images* (London: Phaidon Press, 1985), p. 125.
24. E. H. Gombrich, 'Icones Symbolicæ: The Visual Image in Neo-Platonic Thought', *Journal of the Warburg and Courtauld Institutes* 11 (1948), pp. 178–9.
25. Ludwig Walther, 'Die Monodia des Marcus Antonius Muretus zum Tod des Pariser Parlamentspräsidenten Christophe de Thou (1583) – Idealbilder von Humanismus und Gerechtigkeit', in Ivo Volt and Janika Päll (eds), *Quattuor Lustra: Papers Celebrating the 20th Anniversary of the Re-establishment of Classical Studies at the University of Tartu* (Tartu: Tartu University Press, 2012), pp. 273–303.
26. Ibid., p. 275.
27. Ibid., p. 275: 'Hic sibi iam pridem sedes Astræa locavit: / Marmoreum hic illi templum, laqueataque tecta / Sumptibus immensis reges statuere vetusti: / Quo bis centeni, lectissima pectora, patres / Conveniunt, quot eunt soles, mactantque verendis / Rite deam sacris, et certo fasque nefasque / Fine regunt, ipsaque afflante oracula reddunt, / Consilioque suo regni moderantur habenas. / Hos inter primo ipsa loco Dea magna Tuanum / Collocat: et Nostri princeps, ait, ordinis esto. / Ille Deæ imperium, solio sublimis eburno, / Exsequitur, pœnasque viris et præmia ponit. / Nec mora: diffugiunt fraudes, fugit improba longe / Gratia, quaeque avidas pervertunt munera mentes, / Nil

odium, nil ira potest; discrimine nullo, / Nobilis an plebeius, inops an divite censu, / Solus, an hinc illinc magnis stipatus amicis, / Consequitur ius quisque suum: trutina omnibus æqua est.'

28. W. Goethe, *Maximen und Reflexionem. Nach den Handschriften des Goethe- und Schiller-Archivs* (Weimar: Verlag der Goethe Gesellschaft, 1907), nos 1112 and 1113: 'Die Symbolik verwandelt die Erscheinung in Idee, die Idee in ein Bild, und so, dass die Idee im Bild immer unendlich wirksam und unerre- ichbar bleibt und, selbst in allen Sprechen ausgesprochen, doch unasprechlich bliebe.'

29. Svetlana Alpers, '*Ekphrasis* and Aesthetic Attitudes in Vasari's *Lives*', *Journal of the Warburg and the Courtauld Institutes* 23, no. 3/4 (1960), pp. 190–215.

30. Verity Platt, *Facing the Gods: Epiphany and Representation in Graeco-Roman Art, Literature and Religion* (Cambridge: Cambridge University Press, 2011), p. 4.

31. See Friedrich August Eckstein, 'Bersman, Gregor', in *Allgemeine Deutsche Biographie*, vol. 2 (Leipzig: Duncker & Humblot, 1875), pp. 507–8. In 1549, Bersman attended the Meissen princely school St Afra, where he was eagerly encouraged in Latin poetry under the rector, Georg Fabricius. In 1555, he enrolled at the University of Leipzig to devote himself to philological and medical studies. There, he met Joachim Camerarius the Elder, who gave him the opportunity to publish his poetic works and give samples of his Latin eloquence. After obtaining his master's degree in 1561, he went on study trips to Strasbourg, France and Italy, where he used the lessons of the most impor- tant humanists of the time and gained insight into the working methods of the Paduan physicians. In the late autumn of 1564, he went to Wittenberg, from where he was appointed to a teaching position at Schulpforta in 1565. As early as 1568, he returned to Wittenberg, where his lectures on Melanchthon's *Libelli de anima* provoked the first attacks of the orthodox Lutherans. In 1571, he accepted a call to Leipzig as professor of poetics and in 1575, succeeded Camerarius as professor of ancient languages and ethics. In the same year, he married Magdalene Helbdorn. He joined the circle of those who refused to sign the Formula of Concord in 1580. Consequently, he was deprived of his office in the dispute over Calvinism and expelled from his home and city. In 1581, he received an offer as rector of the Gymnasium Franciscum in Zerbst. On 30 January 1582, he took up the post and kept it until his death. Bersman is described as an irritable and vehement spirit, who also had to cope with many difficulties in his private life (such as early deafness). He worked mainly with the Latin poets (Virgil, Ovid, Lucan, Horace) but also edited the Greek poem of Manuel Philes (c. 1275–c. 1345), Περὶ ζῴων ἰδιότητος in 1596 and translated it into Latin verse. For didactic purposes, he wrote the *Erotemata rhetorices* and *Dialectices* (1593), edited after Melanchthon. His Latin poems are light and fluent, and he wrote on all kinds of occasions such as *Carmina, Epithala- mia, Encomiastica, Epicedia, Tumuli, Elegiæ, Lusus*, first collected in 1576 and then increased to two volumes in 1592. He also signed a poetic paraphrase of the Psalms, of which sixty-two first appeared in 1594, followed in 1598 by the whole Psalterium. Several Latin festive speeches were printed separately.

32. We learned this from Christian Gottlieb Haubold, *Legis judiciariæ utriusque Saxonia regia utitur origines* (Leipzig: ex Officina Walmonia, 1809). Hartmann Pistoris von Seußlitz und Hirschstein (born 22 January 1543 in Leipzig; died 1 March 1603) was a German jurist and Privy Counsellor to the Saxon Electors. Like his father Simon Pistoris the Younger, Hartmann began his law studies at the University of Leipzig under the guidance of his father and his elder half-brother, Modestinus Pistoris von Seußlitz, before completing some years of study at Italian universities. After his return from Italy, he was relatively quickly appointed assessor of the High Court and in 1574, assessor of the Schöffen-stuhl. In 1576, he was called by the Elector August of Saxony to be appointed a member of the College of Court Counsellors and promoted to Privy Counsellor. He held this office until the death of the Elector. He then retired to his country estate, Seußlitz Castle, to acquire further lands and properties. He advised the Electoral Saxon governments in office at the time, repeatedly performed his function in the Court of Appeal, and drew up numerous expert opinions for local and foreign princes. See Roderich von Stintzing, *Geschichte der deutschen Rechtswissenschaften*, vol. 1 (1880; Leipzig: Wentworth Press, 2018), pp. 258–89.

33. Filippo Picinelli, *Mundus symbolicus, in emblematum universitates formatus, explicatus*, vol. 2 (Cologne: Thomas and Heinrich Theodor, 1715), book 21, col. 1, p. 188: 'Est ergo justitia quadrata, inquit apud Joannem Cartagenam S. Clemens Alexandrinus, omni ex parte aqualis, et similis in verbo, in abstinentia a malis, in beneficentia, in perfectione cognitionis, nusquam alio modo claudicans' (Justice is therefore square. It is therefore a complete whole of which all the parts, similar to themselves, correspond exactly to each other: words, actions, abstinence from evil, good works, perfect knowledge, nothing lame in it).

34. Arnold Ehrhardt, 'Vir Bonus Quadrato Lapidi Comparatur', *The Harvard Theological Review* 38, no. 3 (1945), pp. 177–93.

35. After Clement of Alexandria, *Stromata* 7.102.2ff. See *Clement of Alexandria, Miscellanies Book VII*, ed. Fenton John Anthony Hort and Joseph Bickersteth Mayor (Cambridge: Cambridge University Press, 2010).

36. Erasmus, *Collected Works of Erasmus*, vol. 66, *Spiritualia: The Handbook of the Christian Soldier*, trans. and annot. Charles Fantazzi (Toronto: University of Toronto Press, 1988), pp. 1–127.

37. Hubert Devijver and Frank Van Wonterghem, 'The Funerary Monuments of Equestrian Officers of the Late Republic and Early Empire in Italy (50 B.C.–100 A.D.)', *Ancient Society* 21 (1990), pp. 59–98.

38. M. B. Hornum, *Nemesis, the Roman States, and the Games* (Leiden: Brill, 1993), pp. 32–8; see especially pl. X, a relief from Egyptian Thebes, Cairo Museum (*LIMC*, Nemesis, no. 165), mentioned by Emma J. Stafford, 'Nemesis, Hybris and Violence', in Jean-Marie Bertrand (ed.), *La violence dans les mondes grec et romain* (Paris: Sorbonne, 2005), p. 207.

39. *LIMC*, vol. 3, s.v. *Dikaiosune*, pp. 386ff.

40. Bersman *Imago Justitiæ*, verse 77: 'Quam leges et iura valent, tot prodita libris.'

41. Monica Mărgineanu Cârstoiu, 'Némésis et la coudée. Un édicule votif de Tomis', *Caiete ARA* 2 (2011), pp. 53–68.

42. Andrea Alciato, *Emblematum liber* (Augsburg: Steyner, 1531), emblem 104, 'Assequitur, Nemesisque virum vestigia servat, / Continet & cubitum, duraque fræna manu' (Nemesis follows on and marks the tracks of men. In her hand, she holds a cubit-rule and harsh bridles). See David M. Greene, 'The Identity of the Emblematic Nemesis', *Studies in the Renaissance* 10 (1963), pp. 25–43 (esp. pp. 29–30).

43. The Greek word πῆχυς means 'forearm', 'cubit'. However, when used as an epithet of Nemesis, it means 'cubit-rule'. See Henry George Liddell and Robert Scott, *A Greek–English Lexicon* (Oxford: Clarendon, 1940).

44. *The Greek Anthology*, trans. W. R. Paton, Loeb Classical Library edition, vol. 5 (Cambridge, MA: Harvard University Press, 1918), book 16, nos 223 and 224, p. 293.

45. Greene, 'Identity of the Emblematic Nemesis', p. 29 n. 54.

46. Andrea Alciato, *Emblemata cum commentariis* (Padua: Tozzi, 1621), p. 159, cols 1–2: 'cubitum hic ingeniose accipi non in significatione primaria, pro cubito manus; sed pro ulna, sex palmorum mensura [. . .] a similitudine cubiti, cum ad rectos angulos brachium flectitur, accipi pro instrumento Architectorum quod ex regulis duabus ad angulum rectum coagmentatis conficitur, gnomona Græci nominant, ut Latini normam. [. . .] Cæterum qui cubitum duobus constare palmis dicunt, digitos omnino quatuor & viginti commemorant: dicunt enim cubiti spatium id esse, quod ab extremis unguibus in medium brachii angulum por sensum est, illus quidem sesquipedale. Pictores cubitum quartam corporis humani partem volunt esse. Didici etiam ab Architectis, tegium cubitum (is mensuræ nomen) maiorem communi tribus digitis.'

47. Ernst Heitsch, *Die griechischen Dichterfragmente der römischen Kaiserzeit*, vol. 1 (Göttingen: Vandenhoeck & Ruprecht, 1963). The hymn is preserved with musical notation. See J. G. Landels, *Music in Ancient Greece and Rome* (London: Routledge, 1999), pp. 258–60.

48. Thomas R. Keith, 'The Fine Art of Horsing Around: A Note on Wordplay in Mesomedes' *Hymn to Nemesis*', *The Classical Quarterly* 64, no. 1 (2014), pp. 428–31.

49. Bersman, *Imago Justitiæ*, verses 67–8 and 73–4: 'Sic judex iusto libellæ examine causas / Pensat et æquata ius lance cuique rependit' and 'Hoc libræ sibi nempe volunt elementa bilancis, / Quæ neutro inclinans digitis pellentibus exit.'

50. Guillaume Budé, *Annotationes in Pandectas* (Lyon: Gryphe, 1551), pp. 9–10. Budé had influentially noted that Accursius, the author of the *glossa ordinaria*, was wrong when he distinguished *æquum* from *bonum*. See Accursius *ad* 'Bono publico', D.41.3.1.

51. See Lorenzo Maniscalco, *Equity in Early Modern Scholarship* (Nijhoff: Brill, 2020).

52. According to Quintilian, *Institutio Oratoria* 10.1.11–14.

53. The assemblage of *gladius*, *ensis* and *mucro* is a classic example of synonymy (a number of words can signify the same thing), which refers to the covering of the same reality with different garments. See John of Garland, *Liber synonymorum* (1496; Antwerp: T. Martinus, 1507, v. 12): 'Various synonymous words contain one idea, as one thing is called *mucro*, *gladius*, *ensis*: by these three

nouns the same thing is signified.' Millicent Inglis Thomas, *Cassell's Compact Latin Dictionary* (London: Cassell, 1961) suggests that the word may be derived from *clades*, which in turn is derived from the Greek verb κλαΔάΣαI 'to brandish'.

54. Martianus Capella, *De Nuptiis Philologiae et Mercurii*, 4.357 (Leipzig: Adolfus Dick, 1925), p. 164.

55. Boethius, *De Trinitate*, in *Theological Tractates and the Consolation of Philosophy*, trans. H. F. Stewart, E. K. Rand and S. J. Tester (Cambridge, MA: Harvard University Press, 1918), § 3, 172.141, p. 28.

56. Erasmus, *De Copia Verborum ac Rerum*, 1534 edn, in *Collected Works of Erasmus*, vol. 24, *Literary and Educational Writings; 2*, ed. Craig R. Thompson (Toronto: University of Toronto Press, 1978), p. 8.

57. Pseudo-Sergius, *Explanationes in artes Donati, Grammatici Latini, ex recensione Henrici Keilii GL*, vol. 4 (Leipzig, 1855–80), p. 538 1. 2: 'ensis enim in proelio, gladius generaliter dicitur, mucro in opere'.

58. Isaiah 28:21: 'For the Lord will stand, just as at the mountain of divisions. He will be angry, just as in the valley which is in Gibeon, so that he may accomplish his work, his strange work (*alienum opus eius*), so that he may complete his work, his work which is foreign even to him.'

59. Martin Luther, *Werke* (Weimar: Böhlau, 1883–1993), WA 1, 357, 6–10; *Luther's Works* (Philadelphia: Fortress; St Louis: Concordia, 1986), LW 31, 44. See Jos E. Vercruysse, 'Gesetz und Liebe: Die Struktur der "Heidelberger Disputation" Luthers (1518)', *Lutherjahrbuch* 48 (1981), pp. 7–43 (p. 13).

60. Chrysippus, 'Περὶ τοῦ καλοῦ' (About what is beautiful-honourable), fragment 1, in *Stoicorum veterum fragmenta*, vol. 1, ed. Hans Friedrich August von Arnim (Stuttgart: Teubner, 1964), 3.197–8.

61. Erasmus, *Collected Works of Erasmus*, vol. 35, *Adages III iv 1 to IV ii 100*, trans. and annot. D. L. Drysdall, ed. John N. Grant (Toronto: University of Toronto Press, 2005), p. 448, IV i 11, 'Justitiæ oculus'.

62. *Rhetorica ad Herennium*, trans. Harry Caplan (Cambridge, MA: Loeb Classical Library, 1954), 3.22.37. Written in the 90s BCE, the work was originally attributed to Cicero, but the author is unknown.

63. See Nicolas Reusner, 'Idolopoeia', in *Elementorum Artis Rhetoricæ libri duo* (Lavingen: Emanuele Salcero, 1571), ch. 29: 'Quid est Idolopœia? Idolopoeia est, cum persona nota veluti excitatur ab inferis, et producitur cum oratione'.

64. See Plato, *Sophist* 235b–236c. Plato had divided the image-making art (*eidolopoiike techne*) into the 'likeness-making art' (*eikastike techne*) and the 'fantastic art' (*phantastike techne*). Artists creating *phantasmata* abandon the truth.

65. Chiara Bottici, *Imaginal Politics: Images Beyond Imagination and the Imaginary* (New York: Columbia University Press, 2069).

66. *Palatine Anthology*, 16.135, 136, 138, 139, 140, 143.

67. Henry Maguire, 'Truth and Convention in Byzantine Descriptions of Works of Art', *Dumbarton Oaks Papers* 28 (1974), pp. 111–40 (p. 133 n. 117), quoting Nikolaos Mesarites, *Description of the Church of the Holy Apostles at Constantinople*, ed. and trans. Glanville Downey (Philadelphia, PA: American Philosophical Society, 1957), p. 870.

68. I express my thanks to Dr William M. Barton, for his helpful comments on a first draft of this translation.

Quisquis in hac pictos tabula vultusque manusque
Conspicis, Astrææ simulacrum in imagine parva:
Sic oculos, sic (crede) manus, sic ora ferebat,
Cum, non dum spreta terris pietate, solebat
Mortali sese terris ostendere cœtu,
Sæpius atque domos præsens invisere castas.
Hûc ades, ô Clio, quæ temporis acta beati
Condita mente geris memori, me virginis hujus
Signa doce, et mecum picturæ arcana revolve:
Quandoquidem scelere imbuta tellure nefando
Haud ulli nunc viva Deæ datur ora tueri.
Tu quoque, si vacat, exigui mihi temporis usum
Indulge, decus ô gentis Pistoridos ingens,
HARTMANE, Augustam cuius non pænitet aulam:
Dum, meditata tibi, refero dictante Camœna.
Fallor, an hæc speciem reddentis iura figurant,
Et populi fasces, regnique tenentis habenas?
Iam primum, castæ quæ Virginis aspicis ora,
Atque oculorum orbes, radiantes lumine recto,
Collaque plaudentes alterna lege capilli,
Candorem, moresque notant sine crimine culpæ,
Nec fuco seclique sui ferrugine tinctos:
Ordinis et curam, nec lævum mentis acumen,
Quod jacet abstrusum latebris educere verum.
Hinc auresque vides, velantes tempora, binas,
Quas parti judex accommodet æquus utrique,
Atque stolam molli plangentem verbere talos,
Quæ sulcis spiraque carens, haud syrmate longo
Verrit humum, qualis stellatæ cauda volucris.
Nam veluti partes, qui, quam cognoverit ambas,
Jus uni dicit, censeri iudicis æqui
Nullus honore potest, quamvis pronunciet æquum:
Sic illum gravitas ornat, non horrida rugis,
Et nullo vultus aliis ingrata rigore,
Nec specie fucata levi, nec melle politi
Sermonis, diro celans in pectore virus,
Insidiasque struens, iurisque repagula frangens.
Sed quid ego clypei munitum tegmine pectus,
Atque orbes video loricæ ex ære rigentis?
Scilicet hæc valido suffultam robore mentem
Indicat, atque animum mortis terrore carentem.
Quique, nec irasci velit, aut inflectere sonti,
Nec prece, nec precio, recti iustique tenorem.

Sed placidus delicta domet, nec dentibus umquam
Horrendum infrendat, fremitu nec verbera poscat.
Quid sibi vult porro libri, libræque bilancis
Gestamen, cubitus quæ dexter sustinet ambo:
Inque manu cornu, pomis et flore refertum?
Discitur, ut tutela reis sit, copia fandi,
Et studia in mores abeunt: vitæque magistra,
Normaque iustitiæ est, sacrata scientia legum.
Scilicet hanc, cum pace fides, complexa sororum
Unigenas coetus, colit et sibi destinat urbem:
Fertilis hanc uberque soli, et fecunda bonorum
Congeries ditant, aerisque aurique supellex,
Qua posuere suo Musae cum fratre penates.

Chapter 2

The paradoxes of
Lady Justice's blindfold

One of the most disputed questions about representing Lady Justice is that of her blindfold.[1] Since its invention in the second half of the fifteenth century, it has generated a constantly growing body of glosses and interpretations, and considerable scholarly debate.[2] Sightlessness is problematic: is it a sign of disability or a token of impartiality? One way of contributing to this debate is to show how the blindfold is polysemic: as a word and as a representation it remains ambivalent. An investigation into several interpretations of Lady Justice's attributes by lawyers, orators and legal humanists demonstrates its different uses, meanings and functions. The noun itself, *velum* (a veil, a curtain, but also the curtain covering a theatre) is less frequently used than the verbs associated with the process of blindfolding: *oculis velatis*, *oculis tectis* and *oculis obductis*. If the gesture of blindfolding Justice cannot be reduced to a stable nomination, the veiling of her body is also unstable. To translate the idea that Justice is essentially a mediator between divine and human law, her composite body is at the heart of various blindfolding processes. The blindfold is first and foremost the strange indicator that Lady Justice has experienced a conversion. *Justitia* can exist without head or without ears; her head can be covered by bandages, impairing her sight but also shifting her perception of the world around her. Ancient authors associate the myth of Astræa with the gesture of turning her back on mankind during the ages of her decline. Her volitional departure, triggered by the desire to avoid the sins of humanity, is an extraction process that is similar to that of blindfolding. Many other Latin words translate the Renaissance French vernacular *bandeau* and, as we will observe, the idea of blindfolding is conveyed (by texts and images alike) in a great variety of ways.

The allegory as a composite body

The blindfolding of Lady Justice is a skilful symbol traversing the epochs. Lady Justice's blindfold can be seen as a *velum* covering her eyes, but it can also relate to what Ovid (*Metamorphoses* 5.110) calls a *velatus tempora vitta*, 'a head covered with bandages', which may be a verbal translation of what Gaspard Heuvick painted in 1589 (Figure 2.1).

The Flemish painter invents an allegory of Justice to adorn the court-room in Audenarde town hall. Justice is blindfolded and seated on a throne. Behind her head we can read 'præmium et poena' (reward and

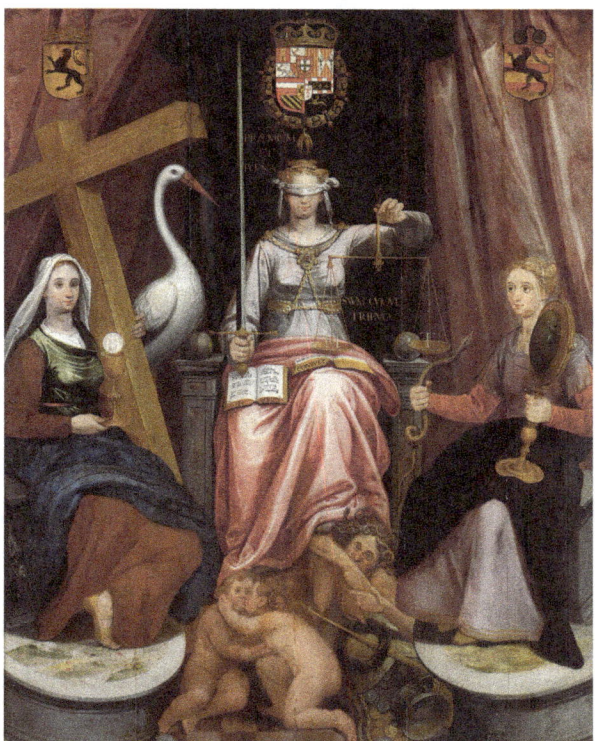

Figure 2.1: Gaspard Heuvick (or Gaspar Hovic), *Justitia*, 1589, oil painting on panel, 150 cm × 125 cm. Oudenaarde, Museum Oudernaarde en de Vlaamse Ardennen. Photograph by Dominique Provost

punishment). Visually, Heuvick's invention contains letters inscribed into the surface of the space represented, and the written golden letters between the two pans of the scales attract the attention of the viewer. One side bears the initial capital M for 'meum' (mine) and the other bears the initial capital T for 'tuum' (thine). The will (*voluntas*) of Lady Justice is represented as a double gesture, perfectly firm and balanced: the sword (incumbent *poena*) is brandished vertically, whereas the tips of the scales are somehow magically balanced by a force that exceeds human vision. Specialists in historical metrology – that is, the science of measurement – argue that the magical aura surrounding scales might be due to the fact that the physical principle on which these instruments function remained mysterious for a long time, at least until the discovery of 'mass' in modern physics.[3] The allegorical body of Lady Justice sits on a throne under a shroud or curtain (one of the senses of the Latin *velum*) high up before humanity. Lady Justice's body is designed so as to remain composite and multivalent. Aby Warburg's bushman might wonder how a 'natural' human body can hold an evenly balanced scale along with an upright sword in a perfect and steady gesture, if the eyes are covered by some kind of cloth band. The answer is that the body of *Justitia* stands as a composite structure capable of mediating between two orders of reality: ideal justice and human deeds. The figures of the letters (M and T) celebrate, as Leon Battista Alberti would put it, the pictographic language of hieroglyphs as an esoteric language of eternity.[4] Allegories only gesture towards meaning. By doing so, they trigger diverse lines of interpretative response to the image. The absurdity of Justice's gesture indicates immediately to the beholder that a literal exegesis is inappropriate.

Ancient grammarians explain that the word 'allegory' implies *alla* 'other' and *agoreuein* 'say': the trope which says one thing but signifies something else. As a rhetorical trope and as a method of commentary, the process is crucial to any understanding of the articulation between textual interpretation applied to a reference text and the interpretative plurality triggered by images. Renaissance humanists often stress the importance of Heraclitus (sometimes called 'the Allegorist'), who lived perhaps towards the end of the first or the beginning of the second century CE.[5] He introduced the term *sêmainein*, in reference to the interpretation of the oracles who neither speak openly nor conceal their meaning but rather 'indicate' it. When allegorised, the oracles of divine law may thus be interpreted by means which have little to do with deciphering codes. The earliest purpose of allegorical criticism might have been to interpret the oracles of divine laws in Homer and Hesiod. But before any gloss, the allegorical impulse is an appeal: it first drives the viewer to astonishment, indicating that the seat of intelligence might be located in the heart. The oddity of the gesture is a way to signal that something is hidden beyond Nature.

Today, scholars frequently treat allegory, as opposed to metaphor, as the systematic application of transferred or hidden senses of terms in an extended passage or argument. Allegorical images of Justice tell quite a different story. Allegorical readings of Heuvick's painting may be focused on particulars, but in order to come to a coherent interpretation, the interlocking network of references must be reconstructed. Lady Justice serves here as a paradigm for virtuous behaviour. As a heroine of exceptional integrity, she becomes an exemplar of wisdom and endurance in service to divine law. Visually speaking, Heuvick substitutes writing for representation, spelled out in the centrally focused fragment 'suum cuique tribuere.' The beholder may then accede to the intended meaning of the allegory by means of a reading, from the enigmatic letter of the Law to its enshrouding within the open books of the Codes and the *jura propria* of Customs. The reading of the letter of the Law may then serve as the frame of reference for understanding the whole composition. Pictorial composition is interpreted through the cardinal texts of the *Digest*, but as an icon it hints towards premodern classical rhetoric.

Heuvick's Justice encapsulates a fourfold method of *compositio*: the letter (M & T), the adage (ancient wisdom here conveyed by an elliptical motto), the attributes (visual conventions are perfectly respected) and lastly, the personification (Lady Justice as the embodiment of a figurative body). Only once the *compositio* is understood as an overall structure does allegorical interpretation become possible. But this does not imply that the eyes of the beholder will stick to the 'authorised' interpretation of the allegorical content displayed in the picture. Anyone who is prepared to delve more deeply into the routes indicated by *Justitia* will recognise that allegorical reading is an initiation charged with wisdom. The allegorical body of *Justitia* is plausible rather than true, its *raison d'être* is to give an ethical interpretation of the inevitable conflict between human and divine laws.

On her right side, an allegory of Piety – with a stork, and holding a chalice and an enormous wooden cross – would be salient to a viewer who wished to articulate a lenient interpretation of the principle of Equity. On her left side, Prudence, with her traditional attributes – a snake, recalling the biblical 'estote prudentes sicut serpentes' (be wise like serpents, Matthew 10:16) and a convex mirror with a handle – might resonate differently to the spectator who notices the shadowy bodies reflected in the convex surface of the mirror facing *Prudentia*. Beneath her feet, Envy is crawling, trying to grasp the fallen heavenly riches (sceptre, golden coins). The appearance of the blindfold itself is unusual. Normally, tying a double knot at the back of one's head is enough to keep the blindfold from slipping. Here Heuvick has designed a peculiar blindfold with two different prominent knots on either side of *Justitia*'s face. The blindfold itself seems more prominent than in other representations, the band longer than usual and its two edges reaching her shoulders. The blindfold is firmly placed over the ears; its two knots add a symmetrical dimension that echoes the even-tipped pans of the scales.

A phenomenological approach to allegory

The ubiquitous nature of allegorical imagery in the physical spaces of early modern Europe should not obscure the fact that these images, when located in courts, serve as visual memoranda of judicial duties. The focus of this chapter is multilayered: it aims to offer new modes of defining the power of the visual allegory of Justice. Far from seeing the allegory as a singular vehicle for abstract and transcendent meaning, underpinning stable conventions designed to articulate fully formed ideas, this research aspires to approach the uses and functions of an incarnate form within the legal sphere from a phenomenological per-spective. Lady Justice is a sensual and spiritual body. In methodological terms, allegory is subjected to an analysis that balances a semiotic trend, articulated in early modern times by iconological coding, with a more phenomenological depiction,[6] focused on cognition and frames of perception, pertaining to individuals as part of a *civitas*. The examples analysed here aim to reveal the essential dynamic function of a civic allegory – its invention and composition, derived from iconological treatises and emblematic sources, its role in the dissemination of meanings and the ways in which the image is perceived by different audiences – in order to question more generally the extent to which this device fulfilled didactic, persuasive, mnemonic, evidential and deontological functions.

Allegory as a word receives an appropriate focus because, much in the same way that the visual allegory is always in tension, the word *allegoria* itself pertains to different configurations and rhetorical traditions. Any attempt at a definition of the visual allegory of Justice shows that this device is always a struggle between figure and conceit, image and Idea, or compositional coherence and perceived multivalence. I will argue here that the visual allegory of Justice, as a civic theophany or divine apparition, excludes all sorts of contact between the figure (the embodiment) and the Idea (divine justice). The blindfold is more than a semi-latent attribute: it is the *index animi* (sign indicative of the inward gaze, i.e. the soul). It indicates that Lady Justice's body is meant to be perceived as a theophany, situated *beyond* the standard regime of visibilities. Walter Benjamin remarks of Baudelaire's reflection upon this notion, that allegory is a relic re-enacted by memory. The cardinal force of the virtue of Justice (in both senses of *virtus*: an impulse or an ethical stand) is to be found in her struggle with the ambivalent essence of the blindfold.[7]

Why is the allegory of Justice still easily identified today? How can we explain the constant revival of her paradoxical gaze? One approach to answering these questions is to look at the ways in which the allegory of Lady Justice has been used as a vehicle or medium inside the legal sphere. The allegorical process institutes a different time and space than the one which is experienced during a court session or recorded in the writing of *consilia*. Courthouse designs, civic spaces as well as mental spaces must be scrutinised if we want to observe wherein the power of images of Justice lies.[8] Images are able more vividly to express an order or a normative message because they act as substitutes for real people (judges). The notion of performativity applied to images is sometimes overemphasised. The anthropology of images may serve to question whether representations of Justice are in any sense performative *imagines agentes*: if no direct line of causality exists between the image and subsequent actions, an image often contributes as a strong feature for performativity within symbolic acts. Moreover, if the people represented can affect us through their images, the reverse is also true. We produce images to honour or dishonour people. Wolfgang Brückner and David Freedberg have underlined the distinct role of effigies in legal practice and mob violence.[9]

The very notion of representation is a two-sided coin. On one side, a representation is a mental thing. On the other side, something is represented inside it. Too often, this Janus-faced nature of representation is quickly rephrased by the following: a representation possesses a content. Thus, we are naturally tempted to think that the *res* signified is expressed by a signifying 'form'. But we need to be aware that the very essence of a representation is dynamic. The way we experience symbolic forms is different from the mental process we project onto them. As Jean-Pierre Changeux and other neuroscientists have shown, the human brain proceeds exactly in the opposite manner to the entry/exit functioning mode which has been long postulated by cybernetics.[10] The human brain projects, on a permanent basis, onto the world, in a spontaneous endogenous manner. 'Mental representations' are attempts to impose upon an exterior reality which is intrinsically meaningless. This projective activity, generating mental forms, constitutes an essential predisposition of the human brain towards creation.

Early modern allegories of Justice can be apprehended through the bi-modality of seeing. Maurice Merleau-Ponty's phenomenology of art has taught us the ways in which the eye always implicates the body. Ways of seeing a symbolic picture are and remain an inchoate process. When we see pictures, we are physically feeling what we are seeing. This aspect is made even more crucial when we deal with images of Justice. A wound in the flesh, a scene of martyrdom, a gouge on the side is always registered in the body of the viewer more vividly than we tend to admit.

Early modern lawyers and their interpretation of the blindfold

The enigma of *Justitia*'s blindfold is probably one of the best examples of an emblematic process:[11]

> the emblematic processing of traditional materials would seem to involve two distinct sequential procedures consisting, at least by implication, of the fragmentation of well-known allegorical works or traditional sign systems and the subsequent recombination of fragmented elements into new and striking signifying units.[12]

The blindfold is borrowed from traditional allegories (Cupid, the Synagogue) so as to be recombined in a striking new configuration. As an official token of impartiality, it aims to disseminate the idea that Justice is no respecter of persons. Nevertheless, as is well known, it started out as a negative attribute in a satirical woodcut in the lawyer Sebastian Brandt's *Das Narrenschiff* (The Ship of Fools, 1494). But the image is inherently paradoxical. Is Lady Justice blindfolded by painters, by the king, by God or is it a self-imposed hindrance to viewing? Does the blindfold deprive of sight, enhance an inward gaze, or render Justice's sight more acute? Is the blindfold a way of indicating that Justice cannot see or cannot be seen? It is not simply an enigma; it is the depiction of the blindfold itself that remains paradoxical.

In an attempt to reconstruct the power of allegory within the legal sphere and the legal profession, judicial *actio* will be examined first. Many orators use the theme of the blindfolding of the goddess to unfold a concept of mute eloquence. Traditional uses of visual allegories may well interact with functions that are more familiar to legal practice, such as its evidential and deontological characters. The image of Lady Justice often appears to freeze social categories into a totalising scheme, yet the very selectivity and seriality of these images undermines any attempt at a unitary reading. The plurality of viewers (legal scholars, lawyers, judges, litigants, citizens, the condemned) suggests that these images resonate differently and lead potentially to contrasting perceptions. In comparison with an erudite jurist who proposes an iconological reading harnessing meaning to a particular, telling detail – Morelli's 'clue'[13] – a litigant might experience allegory in its more provisional and fugitive affects. Judicial allegories are to be analysed on the premise that several specific inter- pretative communities react differently to allegorical imagery, and that the issue goes well beyond the notion of visual literacy.

Clarity and ecstasy

The blindfolding process is often referred to as an error, a crime com- mitted against ancient wisdom and ancient texts. According to the Renaissance thinker Cælius Rhodiginus, the symbol of Justice is the eye, *Justitia* must see, she is *oculatissima*. Her eye is 'justitiæ servator', Jus- tice's servant. Chrysippus, in his treatise on the nature of beauty and pleasure (Aulus Gellius, *Attic Nights* 14.4), likewise insisted upon her sight and the keen glance of her eyes.

A striking example of a paradoxically blindfolded *Justitia* appears in a roundel engraved by Jacob de Gheyn II, c. 1593 (Figure 2.2).

The band covers only half of her revolving eyes, and along with her half-open mouth and hardened nipples, it makes her look as if she were in deep ecstasy. Crowned with laurels, her ecstatic mind expands her interior sight and spiritual awareness: she stands as the exact opposite of strict justice, the kind that seeks to effect adequate compensation. This *furor justitiæ* goes beyond the mere norms of human justice. Her excess shows the enthusiasm of pure love as she embodies the superior sight of divine justice. Lady Justice represented in the convex and circular shape of a shield acts as the visual depiction of the Latin legal proverb *In gremio legis* 'In the bosom of the law', which translates the idea of being 'under the protection of the Law'. But here, the depiction of an erotic body stages a free-standing act of stat- uary, contrasting with the six other virtues of the series, which are depicted in more traditional poses. Instead of painting, like Heuvick, a more or less inscrutable hieroglyph, the engraver celebrates Justice as Ecstasy, more than a century before Gian Lorenzo Bernini would use the same ambiguous articulation to carve his famous Saint Teresa of Avila in quite a different context. The ecstatic lady has a dual appeal to the learned and the unlearned. Without any accompanying text

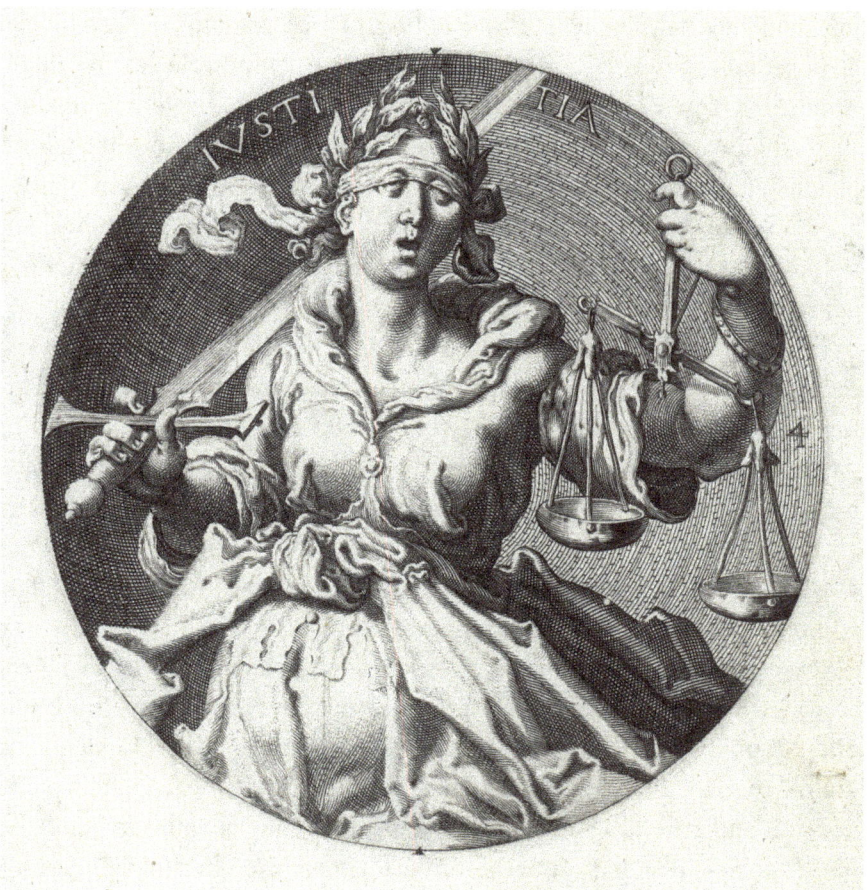

Figure 2.2: Workshop of Jacob de Gheyn II, *Justitia*, c. 1591–5, engraving, diameter 14.5 cm, JUSTI/TIA series of seven virtues. Courtesy of the Rijksmuseum, Amsterdam

except for the fragmented wording IUSTI/TIA, she carries her sword very negligently, as would a warrior, and the gesture of her fingers covering the invisible tip of the well-balanced scales makes the beholder fear that they might fall.

Is the blindfold an attribute?

When the unruly meanings of the blindfold are framed as an attribute, the sign still remains ambiguous: the official language tends to interpret it in a positive way, whereas many contemporary viewers still see it as proof of her helplessness. Blindfolding Justice remains a paradoxical gesture: its polysemy suggests the possibility of multiple textual interpretations, transforming the figure into a different emblem according to the will of the viewer. The paradoxical nature of the blindfold is productive: is it a sign of blindness? A token of impartiality? A necessary avoidance of lucidity? A momentaneous oblivion to the evidence put before the eyes? A mark of ecstasy? A shameful stigmata? A trick? A game? A mark of derision?

Indeed, the blindfold's effect may exceed the intention of its creators; that is why conflicts about what are considered to be the correct attributes of Justice never end. Judges will not necessarily argue for a sign of virtuous celebration as they are well aware that it is a potentially derisive mark. The question arises again as to when a representation of Justice as an institution needs to be displayed publicly. The same is true for the citizen: depending on their view of Justice as an institution, they will or will not opt for an irreverent disfiguration of *Justitia*.

It is because the blindfold is in essence ambivalent that it has generated a wide array of glosses or alleged misinterpretations: the blunt opposition between a clear-sighted Justice and a blindfolded one is unable to seize the complexity of this articulation. Justice's sight is paradoxical, and it is too simplistic to state that sight is valorised and the failure to see, derided. In early modern times, the blindfold remains a powerful *symbolon*; it bears multiple valences, the conflation of which is essential to the process. As a token of mutual identification, the *symbolon* is imbued with tension. The blindfold may serve as a *punctum* of indifference, a point of intersection between Law and Violence, a threshold where the suspension of the boundary between the inside and the outside enables a dialectics of transformation.[14] Justice wears an enigmatic blindfold, as an index of mystery and not as a straightforward signifier. The only method which seems relevant to apprehending the variegated nature of Lady Justice's blindfolds is to look at the frames of reference that her images institute.

Renaissance lawyers were very much aware of the paradoxical nature of this symbol: Justice's blindfold revives the paradoxical games of legal aphorisms: *audi* (or *audite*) *et alteram partem*. 'Hear – singular or plural – the other side' is built on a dialogic principle: Justice must be dynamic and enigmatic; it needs a powerful symbolism to articulate the fact that legal words both complement and contradict one another. Judicial discourse is itself constituted by a vast network of interlocking texts. The very essence of adjudication may only be honoured by a paradoxical emblem. To consolidate this stance, a collection of accounts of how these blindfolds were viewed and translated into texts will help to sharpen the focus of this study.

Clear-sighted Justice in Greek and Roman antiquity

According to classical authors, the goddess of Justice was clear-sighted. Athenaeus (*The Deipnosophists* 12.65) recalls that several ancient peoples made effigies of Justice with a golden face and golden eyes. This was meant to signify that Justice had to be similar for all citizens. Plato says that Justice 'looks abroad' (*foras spectat*) and that she is the 'trustworthy observer' (*fida speculatrix*) of others (Apuleius, *De Platone* 2.7.229). According to Cælius Rhodiginus (*Lectiones Antiquarum* 29), the symbol of Justice is an eye, and her gaze is penetrating. Aulus Gellius, the second-century jurist and rhetor, has reproduced in his *Attic Nights* (14.4), from Stoic sources in Greek, an *ekphrasis* of *Justitia*, taken from Chrysippus, who is 'an awe-inspiring virgin with penetrating eyes' (*luminibus oculorum acribus*) and 'with some venerable grief in her dignity'. The object of this appearance was that she might 'inspire fear in the wicked and courage in the good; to the latter, as her friends, she presents a friendly aspect, to the former, a stern face'. A further purpose was to set an example for the good judge, who 'ought to be dignified, holy, austere, incorruptible, not susceptible to flattery, pitiless and inexorable towards the wicked and guilty, vigorous, lofty, and powerful, terrible by reason of the force and majesty of equity and truth'. This famous passage is regularly quoted by humanist lawyers and orators alike.

Another source is less frequently quoted: Diodorus Siculus mentions a statue of Justice in Egypt which stands before the doors of Truth without a head. In his *Hieroglyphica* (1556), dedicated to Cælio Curione and devoted to the theme of Justice, the poet and humanist Pierio Valeriano gives an interpretation of acephalous Justice (Figure 2.3):[15] it signifies that her head needs to be inside the clouds, as a sign of divinity, that

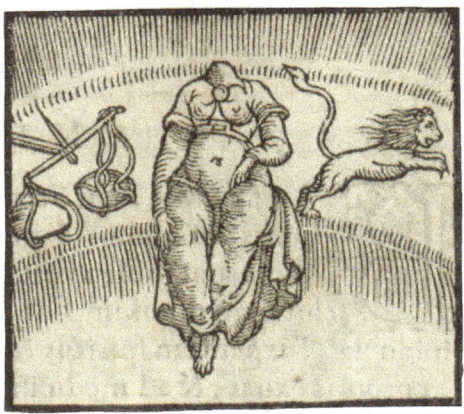

Figure 2.3: Pierio Valeriano, *Astræa/Justitia*, figure of an acephalous *Justitia*, wooden engraving in *Hieroglyphica, seu De Sacris Ægyptiorum aliarumque gentium literis commentarii* (Basel: Isengrin, 1556; Lyons: Thomas Soubron, 1595), reproduced from the 1595 edition, p. 579. E-Rara, Zentralbibliothek Zürich, Rc 129, <https://doi.org/10.3931/e-rara-24697>, Public Domain Mark

Justice has no head. He adds that when sitting on the Aeropagus, Athenians had their head covered by a veil, so as not to arouse the gaze of spectators.

Sebastian Brandt and the fool blindfolding Justice

Except in this last case, *Justitia* was known in antiquity for her clear-sightedness. The idea of placing a blindfold over her eyes emerged around 1494, as is well known, in Germany. In the first edition of *The Ship of Fools* by the humanist lawyer Sebastian Brandt, a woodcut showed a jester covering the eyes of Justice with a blindfold (Figure 2.4). The blindfold was intended to imply an absence of judgement and was originally meant to mock Justice and criticise the ignorance and dishonesty of the courts. In this derisive context, the blindfold was not considered an attribute like the sword or the scales: instead, it was temporary; an obstacle created by human folly. Brandt expects his readers to remove Lady Justice's blindfold and restore her penetrating gaze.

In *The Ship of Fools* Lady Justice is shown blindfolded by Dame Folly. Dame Folly, *Moria*, will later become even more famous for having blindfolded the major authorities of the time in Erasmus' *Praise of*

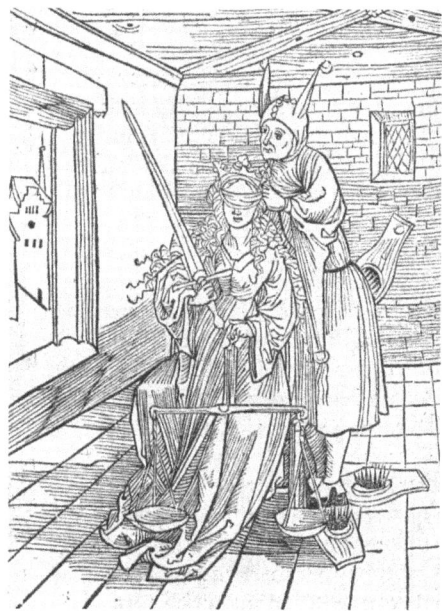

Figure 2.4: Sebastian Brant, *Stultifera navis: narragonice perfectionis nunquam satis laudata navis*. [Basel]: [Johann Bergmann von Olpe], [1. März 1497]. Universitätsbibliothek Basel, UBH DA III 2, https://doi.org/10.3931/e-rara-4622/ Public Domain Mark

Folly.[16] Lady Justice appears then as one of the many victims of a wave of paradoxical eulogies. She is the object of an 'energetic inversion',[17] her dignity compromised by an irreverent gesture. She is staged in a carnival play where Folly ironically advises her listeners not to be too impressed by the exterior marks of her supposed wisdom. Jean-Claude Margolin has noted that *fascia* (headbands) decorated the *pilleus* (Phrygian cap) of Doctors of Theology at the University of Paris.[18] Lady Justice enters the realm of allegorical games with a severe handicap: the *signum* of academic *dignitas* has been turned into a mark of their foolishness. This irreverent gesture will lead to a growing number of controversial interpretations. But as an image, it is a gesture and not a discourse. The target, for Sebastian Brandt, is not divine justice. It is human justice, embodied by earthly judges.

The 'official' explanation of the blindfold is that Lady Justice without eyes or hands cannot be corrupted. Blindfolds make it harder for her to solicit or receive bribes. Her eyes are covered so that the rich and the poor appear the same. This we read in an inscription written in the antechamber of the old Tübingen town hall, where Justice is painted blindfolded on a mural. In Cesare Ripa's *Iconologia*, one of the eight models for the depiction of Justice is blindfolded. The device acts as a filter, aimed at eradicating passions and clarifying knowledge: 'Justice's eyes are bandaged and thus she cannot see anything that might cause her to judge in a manner that is against reason.'[19]

An astute interpretation by Pierre Ayrault

In 1576, Angevin criminal lawyer Pierre Ayrault published an influential treatise on judicial procedure called *L'ordre, formalité et instruction judiciaire*. In it, he argued that every suspect must receive a formal judicial proceeding with cross-examination of witnesses in order for the justice system to work properly:

> We say that even if Justice is blindfolded, she is not blind. As when she's seeking truth (which is the task of the investigation procedure) she rightfully opens her eyes. It is only when truth has been obtained that she blindfolds her eyes in order to judge.[20]

Jacques de Cater's emblematic verses

In a later engraving by Jacques de Cater dated 1645, the blindfold has become a powerful attribute of impartiality (Figure 2.5). The upright sword and the even scales reinforce the clarity of what was at first a disconcerting attribute.

Justice is seated on her throne, and the Latin text in the cartouche below the image underlines her incorruptibility by dwelling on the significance of the blindfold:

> True Justice is blind and deaf, but this blindness is not due to the fact that the object of her desires is gold, and her deafness is not due either to the fact that she is often exposed to rich promises. She sees too much, if she sees gold; she hears too much, if she listens to flattery. And nonetheless she's able to see, but at the same time she is blind. And she's able to listen and nonetheless she is deaf. She uses her faculty of sight to investigate

the motives of the crimes she punishes and to evaluate the merits that she greets with rewards; however, she is blind, so as to be no respecter of persons.[21]

The emblematic text indicates that conflict about whether the blindfold ought to be valorised had already generated a number of possible misinterpretations. Whether this explanation of the even-handedness of Justice convinced his readers is not known, but the message is conveyed through a dialogic poem, not by means of a doctrinal discourse. It does not attempt to flatten the enigma of the blindfold.

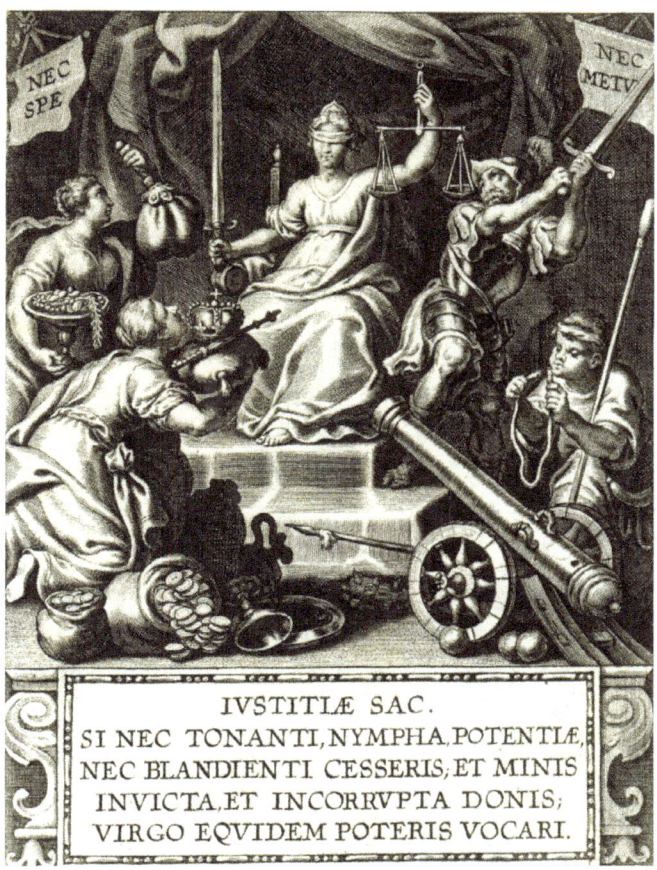

Figure 2.5: Jacques de Cater, 1593–1657, *Virtutes Cardinales Ethico Emblemata Expressae* (Antwerp: ex officina Plantiniana, 1645), produced by Balthazar Moretus II, p. 11. Courtesy of the Hathi Trust; original source: University of Illinois at Urbana Champaign

(Extra-)sensory perception

One rationale often argues that the blindfold, by removing direct sight from the judges, urges them to focus on their hearing of the cause instead. Many painters, says Olav Worm, have put a blindfold on Lady Justice's face, so as to prevent her from looking at litigants, in order to focus on an auditory perception of the trial and give to everyone their due.[22] In Roman law, the testimony of eyewitnesses is not trustworthy because ocular testimony alone is not sufficient to prove that someone is guilty. Where possible, lawyers sought to convert hearsay or single-witness testimony into a record established by multiple eyewitnesses. The blindfold here has an evidential function: it is meant to avoid the limited perception of an ocular testimony in order to focus instead on the legal principle of *audi alteram partem*. Just as an osteopath blindfolds his apprentices in order to teach them how to concentrate only on their tactile abilities, putting on a blindfold may enhance other senses.

Taken together, sculptural virtuosity and Latin mottos almost never signal in the same direction. In the words of D. H. Lawrence:

> The artist usually sets out – or used to – to point out a moral and adorn a tale. The tale, however, points the other way, as a rule. Two blankly opposing morals, the artist's and the tale's. Never trust the artist. Trust the tale. The proper function of a critic is to save the tale from the artist who created it.[23]

Instead of being caught up in the moralisation of the allegory, a viewer might first applaud the pleasure of the senses. Conversely, it could be argued that aesthetic pleasure channels the imagination to a contemplative intellection of Justice as an ideal. In the judicial sphere of legal *actio*, the allegorical body of Lady Justice might distract jurists from their focus on case law.

The diaphanous blindfold

When the blindfold is diaphanous, clearly showing eyes wide open, it becomes a sign that the bandage's function is not that of removing sight. It acts more like a filter; it indicates that *Justitia* is a gifted seer. Sometimes the blindfold is nothing but a piece of transparent gauze; it lets us see her meditative gaze. Several artists craft a type of thin gauze blindfold, through which *Justitia* can be seen to look. In an anonymous print showing Oliver Cromwell as Lord Protector in 1653, *Justitia*'s melancholy eyes are also perfectly apparent through her blindfold (Figure 2.6).

Lastly, the allegorical portrait of Ferdinand III, 'defensor Justitiæ', engraved by Michel Natalis in 1645 shows, through another transparent

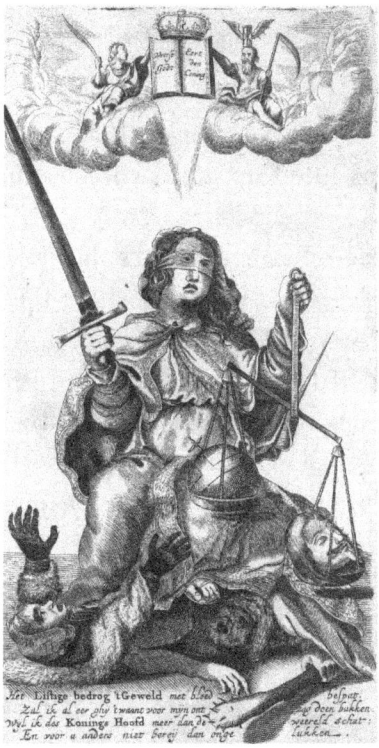

Figure 2.6: Workshop of Claes Janz Visscher (II), *Satirical etching of Oliver Cromwell after the dissolution of Parliament and his appointment as Lord Protector on 16 December 1653. Justitia* weighs the severed head of Charles I in scales against the world. Courtesy of the Rijksmuseum, Amsterdam

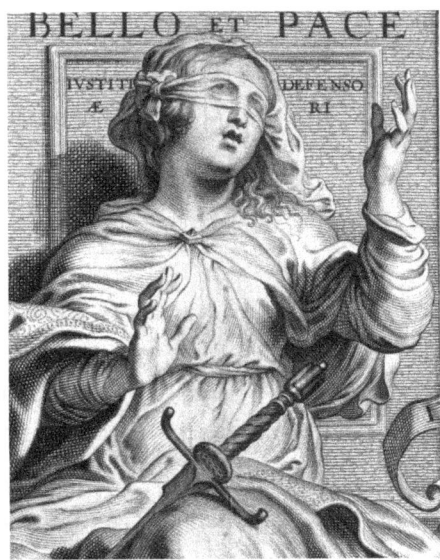

Figure 2.7: Michael Natalis (print maker) after a drawing by Abraham van Diepenbeeck, Antwerp, 1645. Engraved portrait of German Emperor Ferdinand III as 'defensor Justitiæ' with an allegory of War and Peace. Blindfolded *Justitia* sits below the Emperor's statue. Courtesy of the Rijksmuseum, Amsterdam

blindfold, the expressive gaze of *Justitia* looking up towards the sovereign, her hands lifted up, her sword balanced on her left knee (Figure 2.7).

Through her wide-open eyes, charitable Justice is modulated by mercy, affording a degree of leniency where the rigour of Law would be expected and deserved. Charitable Justice allows her compassionate eyes to pop out from the blindfold; she reshapes what is 'just' in light of what she sees, between the imperatives of war and peace. These examples of translucent blindfolds show the variable polysemy of the bandage: the blindfold is a visual index for an ambivalence about *Justitia*'s sight.

In praise of blindness

Other contemporary testimonials show that Justice's blindfold is a constant object of paradoxical interpretations. An early seventeenth-century French humanist lawyer, Jacques Gouthière, wrote a paradoxical eulogy of blindness, in which he comments expansively on *Justitia*'s

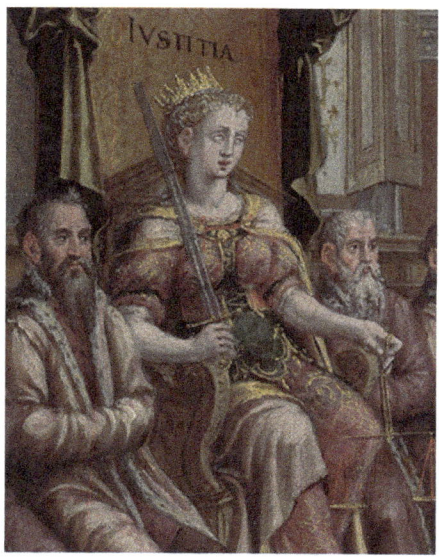

Figure 2.8: Hans Vredeman de Vries, *Justitia and Injustitia*, 1594–5, from a seven-part cycle of paintings for the Council's Grand Chamber of the Main City Town Hall in Gdansk. Oil on canvas, 140 cm × 200 cm. Gdansk, Historical Museum, MHMG/S/R/1

blindfold. His piece is entitled *Tiresias, or in praise of blindness* (*Tiresias, seu cæcitatis encomium*):

> At first, Lady Justice was clear-sighted, as we know from Aulus Gellius quoting Chrysippus and from other ancient testimonies [. . .] So why do we put a blindfold on *Justitia*? Does it signify that Dame Justice serves the blind circumstances of the time? Or is it because she seems to find in an iniquitous situation an example on which to meditate? A thing she wouldn't be able to do if she didn't show some blindness of the mind. Or does she wear a blindfold because her piercing eyes dazzle with the lightning she throws, while her eyes look up at the ultimate summit of Law, the extreme right (*summus jus*), which often produces extreme wrong (*summa injuria*)? Or does she wear a blindfold to signify that Justice defines herself as a constant and perpetual will to grant every person his or her due? It is this last hypothesis that seems the most relevant to me because Justice's blindfold will serve Reason. Her will is similar to a blind person who is driven by Reason only.[24]

This explanation is close to the one we find in Ripa's *Iconologia*, the 1611 Paduan edition of which mentions, as noted before, that the blindfold aims to clarify knowledge. The blindfold prevents false judgment and keeps her reason free of bad influences: it indicates that Justice is a matter of inner conscience. Wearing the blindfold enables her to see the true dimensions of equity and reason. As a sign of metaphorical blindness, the blindfold may also be a sign for an inward-directed gaze. This volitional blindfolding is not a hindrance, rather, it is a sign that she draws upon an inner source of wisdom, to allow for an equitable judgment.

Hans Vredeman de Vries likewise depicts Lady Justice as a blind woman whose corneas have a cloudy appearance (Figure 2.8). The eye, as a small detail in the face of the figure represented, is usually hardly visible.[25] De Vries artfully shapes her opaque orbs as a pictorial means to make blindness manifest. This is an appropriate formula by which to visualise blindness: both closure of the eyes and the blindfold are avoided. It links her visually to the positive representation of blind seers such as Homer or Tiresias. In de Vries's highly skilled hands, blindness becomes a marker of divine election.

Continuing objections to the portrait of a blindfolded Justice

The lawyer Nicolas Reusner makes a strong criticism of the use of the blindfold as a proper attribute of Justice. In one of three speeches he devotes to the theme of the Theban judges, written in 1581, he warns against its use:

> The allegory of Justice is of a virgin goddess, eyes closed or blindfolded so that men's faces will not disturb or move her when she pronounces her judgment. Indeed, instead of using her eyes, she should focus on her hearing when pronouncing her judgment. From this point, she must evaluate and reach the truth of the trial. But these two things, as far as I can judge, seem ridiculous to me. Because of this attribute, the allegory may also signify the following: either it means that the magistrate might sometimes turn a blind eye to vices and crimes or it might also signify that the knowledge and perception of all that occurs are not always relevant to the investigation of cases, because, as is often the case, the magistrate ignores or dissimulates

what has happened, if he wants the others to continue to rule in peace and serenity. [. . .] As far as I'm concerned, I'm fully against this opinion as I am highly convinced that the good prince, or the magistrate, not only should not be blind, but also should never turn a blind eye to the case.[26]

Reusner underlines here that the application of the bandage can be understood as trying to limit, rather than focus, Justice's knowledge of a given case. As a well-trained lawyer, Reusner gives a cynical explanation of the blindfold, as undermining judicial integrity.

Another sceptical opinion is voiced by Georges de Scudéry, in 1647:

I wonder whether those who have represented Justice with a blindfold have done a judicious painting of her, as for me I think on the contrary that she should have a clear-sighted vision. If I were to depict her, I would give her instead the multiple eyes of Argus, rather than the blindness of Oedipus or Tiresias. It is my opinion that the Lynx shouldn't have a clearer sight than Kings, because Kings hold the sword of Justice in their hands. To hit without being able to see, to weigh without seeing are things that hardly satisfy me and I find these gestures without great reason. I know that what the ancients meant by this blindfold was that Justice is no respecter of persons, but I think it would have been far more appropriate to represent her as an imperturbable goddess.[27]

More than a century later, the inappropriateness of the blindfold would be carried further. In 1782, the Royal Censor Jean-Baptiste Robinet links blindfolding to the fallibility of torture:

Justice is painted blindfolded, so as to signify that she is no respecter of persons. Couldn't this emblem also mean that she gropes along, blindly seeking the motive of crimes, in a similar way as in those games where a child, blindfolded with a handkerchief, pursues the others and is obliged to name the one he captures? Tortures, invented to extort confessions from defendants' mouths, are they really appropriate for discovering the truth we are looking for?[28]

Robinet echoes here the rising opinion of encyclopedists about torture, promoting the reforms of Beccaria before the Revolution.

Sculpting Justice: the coexistence of a clear-sighted and blindfolded Justice

As sculpture is a three-dimensional art, the blindfold invites explora-tion primarily through the sense of touch.[29] In the old Amsterdam town hall (now the Royal Palace), the Antwerp sculptor Artus Quellinus the Younger in 1665 produced not one but two allegories of Justice, provid-ing an institutional or purposive solution to the tension we have observed between a clear-sighted and blindfolded Justice.[30]

The first, located inside the courtroom (*Vierschaar*), is blindfolded. Following Ayrault's and André de Nesmond's models, Lady Justice, when seated in the courtroom, needs to be blindfolded as she is about to pronounce her judgment. She is paired with Prudence to underline her crucial role in delivering criminal sentences, including death penal-ties. The second, displayed in the entrance hall, is clear-sighted. The statue here represents the goddess in her search for truth and equity, holding a sceptre bearing a radiant eye.

These allegorical choices are derived from what E. H. Gombrich termed the 'principle of decorum' (or fitness to the subject).[31] In each case, the artist's choice reflects a sensitivity to the different purpose of each room. In the engraved account of the building published by the artist's brother Hubertus Quellinus, the principle of decorum is detailed thoroughly: the pairing of Prudence with a blindfolded Justice is appro-priate to the function of the Justice Chamber, where criminals are to hear their sentence before its execution. The figures represented are meant to inspire awe.[32] Clear-sighted Justice, on the other hand, is placed in a public location that concerns everyone; the instructive emblem is the radiant eye, as a symbol of Justice's protection of and vigilance towards all her citizens.

The polysemy of the blindfold

Let us now turn towards a sophisticated pamphlet addressed anony-mously to Henri IV. In *La Justice en son throsne. A tres chrestien Henri IIII Roy de France*, printed in Rouen by Jean Petit in 1609, an anonymous orator dwells copiously on the various significations which can be attached to Justice's blindfold or 'bandeau', a translation of the Latin *fascia*.[33] The text is a *prosopopoeia* and it is thus Justice herself who speaks, addressing her respectful remonstrances to the king with a rich diet of metaphors. The speech is metaphorically overlarded. Justice first explains that her blindfold is a device aimed at keeping her indifferent when hearing trials, but she immediately adds that 'her eyes are never closed', that 'her blindfold is intended not to blind her vision, but to allow her to see better'. She further elaborates the paradoxical essence of the blindfold through two oxymoronic images: 'the sun, which is only visible when seen through a cloud' and 'a diamond, which shines even better in the dark'. This plethora of significations gains its coherence from the reference to the king's authority. The blindfolding process may act as a way to control the potential disobedience of citizens. It is interpreted as a royal diadem surrounding the king's head with glory. The blindfolding power exerts a fascination (and *fascinatio*, as Pierre Legendre has noted, is a way of tying someone with bandages).[34]

It is, at the same time, a sign of obedience to the king, a token of chastity, and a device to uncover men's imperfections. Its circular shape reminds us that Justice is always active. The most original explanation is probably the following: 'the blindfold says that men blindfold me with their passions'. It reverses the agency of the blindfolding process: Lady Justice's sight grows dim and the blindfold indicates Lady Justice's disability in facing the troubled waters of passions. In this discourse composed by Justice herself, the cornucopia of meanings adds considerable wealth to the process of interpreting the enigmatic device. Is Lady Justice blindfolded by God, by a painter, or by the king? Is it an act of self-limitation? The numerous combinations suggested in this poetical praise introduce a strong bond between the king, *fons justitiæ*, and Lady Justice's agency. Justice belongs to the monarch. This is a metaphor especially well adapted to France, where blindfolded figures of Justice are scarce, often being replaced by the representation of the king as the only source of justice.

André de Nesmond's remonstrance

The theme of the diadem that sparkles best in the night is further developed in a final example worthy of an in-depth analysis. It is a remonstrance entitled *Le bandeau ou le diadème de Justice* delivered by the magistrate André de Nesmond at the opening session of the Parliament of Bordeaux, on Saint Martin's Day, 1613.[35] The text is forty-two pages long, so the following account will stress only the main points of the argument. The discourse is remarkable for the wealth of its erudition and the complexity of its symbolic thinking. His first concern is to state that antique painters should be blamed for having forgotten to put a blindfold on Lady Justice.[36] The magistrate criticises what he understands as a *læsa maiestatis*. He wishes to rectify the fault by honouring Dame Justice with a blindfold or a diadem. His goal is settled from the very beginning: the new attribute is intended to make Justice more venerable. The author gathers all the positive valences of the blindfold he can find or invent. All his interpretations are supported by long and thorough quotes in the Latin or Greek of ancient authorities.

The first reason given is that Astræa, when abandoning the earth during the Iron Age, fleeing from the new wickedness of humanity, blindfolded herself and became the constellation Virgo. In her quality of goddess, Astræa wears a blindfold.[37] The magistrate then underlines that Justice, as a most sacred institution, is rightly covered with a blindfold.[38] The next argument praises Lady Justice's virginity. As a symbol of modesty and chastity, the principal rationale for blindfolding Justice is to protect her integrity. As a sign of secrecy, veils are used by priests and magistrates alike. Codinus is cited in reference to courtrooms in early Constantinople where curtains were displayed to protect the secrecy of tribunals.[39] Furthermore, the blindfold is properly a sign of mourning: Lady Justice regrets and mourns her sad functions, especially when she has to ordain criminal judgments. This meaning is associated with the ancient rite of covering the eyes of the statues adorning Roman amphitheatres, to prevent them from seeing the blood spilled by gladiators.[40]

The blindfold is also understood as a *flammeum*, that is to say a bridal veil.[41] As the Roman bride wore the *flammeum* as a good omen for a lasting marriage, a symbol of constancy and lifelong fidelity, Lady

Justice's blindfold demonstrates her respectability. De Nesmond insists on the specific pattern of this veil: Lady Justice wears a blindfold not to prevent herself from seeing but to avoid being seen. The double nature of the blindfold is evident here: it can be used as a filter but also as a protective device.

De Nesmond then comes to his core argument: the significance of the 'emblem' and the 'declaration of the symbol' is, unsurprisingly, that Justice is no respecter of persons and that she should not favour anyone in terms of quality or rank.[42] He adds that the eye has the hieroglyphic meaning of 'favour'. In an echo of Ayrault, de Nesmond points out that Lady Justice does not need to become blind; she ought to remain clear-sighted when she investigates the case but she must put back her blindfold when it is time to pronounce judgment.

The last part of the remonstrance is the most adventurous. De Nesmond refers to the *splenium* (a bandage) used by Roman lawyers to cover up their eyes, such as Pliny the Younger says about Regulus (*Epistles* 6.2). De Nesmond interprets the *splenium* as a sort of mask (*persona*) or blindfold signifying that lawyers should not consider persons but only equity and the generality of the case.[43] The last part of the speech is devoted to transforming the blindfold into a diadem.[44] It might relate again to a pun on *fascia* (a headband or blindfold) and *fasces* (a bundle of rods, symbol of coercion). The blindfold here becomes a sign of the power and authority of Justice: it is a royal bandage or diadem, suitable for a queen. The orator invents a peculiar diadem which is to cover her eyes, adorned with precious gems symbolising each of Justice's virtues.[45] De Nesmond transforms a potentially derisive mark into a glittering sign of honour.

The eye of the law

Indeed, the diadem has proved a highly productive counterpoint to the blindfold. In some cases, Lady Justice is blindfolded but also wears a diadem adorned with a third radiant eye, the eye of the law.[46] Romeyn de Hooghe proposes this inventive formula in an allegorical print celebrating the princes' marriages concluded in 1680 (Charles II of Spain and his wife, and Charles XI of Sweden and his wife, both married the same year) (Figure 2.9).

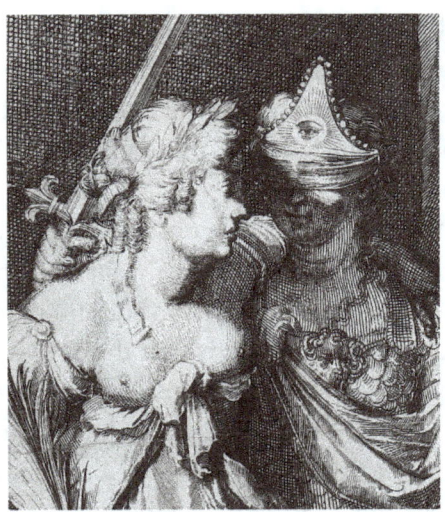

Figure 2.9: Romeyn de Hooghe (print maker), allegorical print on the princes' marriages of 1680/1681 (Willem III and Hendrik Casimir II) below the dedication to and arms of four Amsterdam mayors. *Justitia* and *Pax* kissing. Courtesy of the Rijksmuseum, Amsterdam

Justitia wears a blindfold but, at the same time, a pyramidal diadem hosts the eye of judgment. The presence of this overarching third eye exerts a dual role, invoking both surveillance and protection. The third eye may seem redundant but, worn on armour, or as a diadem or a jewel to show its supranatural essence and its separation from normal vision, it indicates a higher vision. The Genoese painter Giovanni Andrea de Ferrari gives another subtle variation (Figure 2.10).

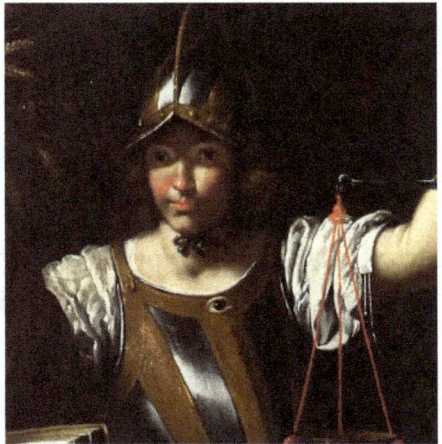

Figure 2.10: Giovanni Andrea de Ferrari, *Justitia*, painting, c. 1620. Musei di Strada Nuova, Genoa. Google Arts Project

Lady Justice is not blindfolded, but the shadow projected by her helmet onto her vision obscures her sight. A third eye on the upper edge of her armour indicates her superior vision. The conjunction of the shadow and the omnivoyant eye adorning the armour is a more natural way of depicting the paradoxical sight of the goddess than the odd accumulation proposed by de Hooghe. This solution also predates the ingenious painting produced later by Sir Joshua Reynolds, in which the shadow projected by her hand covering her gaze is reminiscent of her blindfold (Figure 2.11).

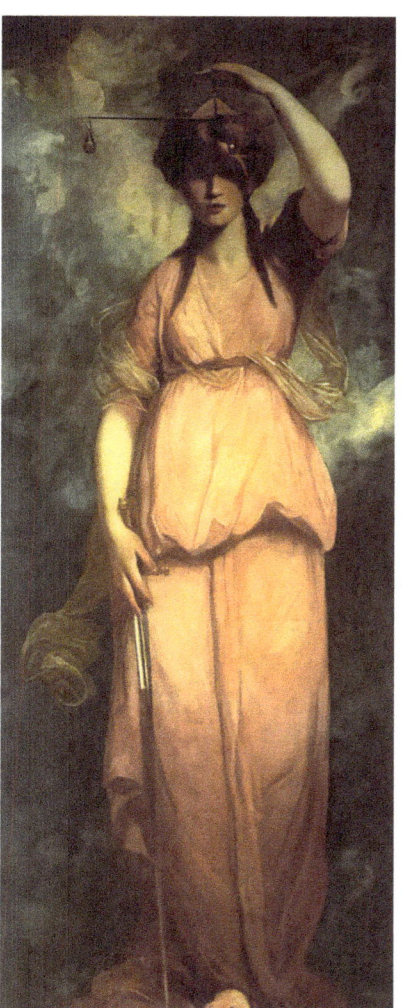

Figure 2.11: Sir Joshua Reynolds, *Justice*, west window of the gothic chapel of New College, Oxford, 1779. Wikioo.org

Conclusion

This chapter has tried to introduce new findings into a well-worn debate. The accounts of the blindfold given by humanist lawyers and orators indicate the acute and vivid character of its ambiguities. The allegorical impulse involves many shifts in frames of perception: far from portraying the body of Lady Justice as a hieratic matron, her postures show that she stands at the edge of several thresholds.

The process of blindfolding is ambiguous at several levels; it solicits a true art of interpretation. Thanks to its reversible agency, the blindfold indicates a process which cannot be reduced to the simple idea of impartiality. When Justice is seen as a royal prerogative, it cannot be associated with an ambiguous attribute such as the blindfold. At the same time, lawyers admit that the depiction of a blindfolded Justice is appropriate to limited moments in the process of judgment. Lady Justice may be blindfolded by jesters or painters, by the king or by God. She might use the device as self-imposed hindrance, so as to deprive herself of sight, to enhance an inward-looking gaze, or to render her sight more acute. The device of the blindfold is reversible: it may indicate that Justice cannot see or that she cannot be seen. Its ambivalence lies in the potential reversal of its agency. The blindfold can either attenuate or separate Lady Justice's vision from the human world: it can obscure, absorb, disperse or interfere with human justice. Acting as a refracting lens, it may contain positive or negative valences.

The blindfold is not simply an enigma; it is the depiction of the blindfold itself that remains paradoxical. In his *Theory of Justice*, John Rawls famously built on this positive meaning to define the essence of Justice as its 'veil of ignorance'.[47] Despite the assumption that allegory is dead, Justice's blindfold is still a source of widely shared fascination.

Notes

1. A first version of this chapter appeared in Stefan Huygebaert, Georges Martyn, Vanessa Paumen, Eric Bousmar and Xavier Rousseaux (eds), *The Art of Law: Artistic Representations and Iconography of Law and Justice in Context, from the Middle Ages to the First World War* (Cham: Springer, 2018), pp. 201–21.
2. Ernst Von Moeller, 'Die Augenbinde der Justitia', *Zeitschrift für christliche Kunst* 17 (1905), pp. 107–22, 141–52; Lodovico Zdekauer, *L'idea della giustizia e la sua imagine nelle arti figurative* (Macerata: Bianchini, 1909); Chaim Perelman, *Études de logique juridique* (Brussels: Bruylant, 1966); Erwin Panofsky, *Studies in Iconology: Humanistic Themes in the Art of the Renaissance* (New York: Harper Torchbook, 1967); John Rawls, *A Theory of Justice* (Cambridge, MA: Harvard University Press, 1971); Otto Rudolf Kissel, *Die Justitia. Reflexionen über ein Symbol und seine Darstellung in der bildenden Kunst* (Munich: Beck, 1984) Robert Jacob, *Images de la justice. Essai sur l'iconographie judiciaire du Moyen Âge à l'âge classique* (Paris: Le Léopard d'Or, 1996); Paulo Ferreira da Cunha, *Arqueologias Jurídicas. Ensaios Jurídico-Humanísticos e Jurídico-Políticos* (Porto: Lello, 1996); Christian-Nils Robert, *Une allégorie parfaite. La Justice: vertu, courtisane et bourreau* (Geneva: Georg Éditeur, 1993); Christian-Nils Robert, 'Naissance d'une image: la balance de l'équité', *Histoire de la Justice* 11 (1998), pp. 85–97; Werner Schild, *Bilder von Recht und Gerechtigkeit* (Cologne: DuMont, 1995); Mario Sbriccoli, 'La triade, le bandeau, le genou. Droit et procès pénal dans les allégories de la Justice du Moyen-âge à l'âge moderne', *Crime, Histoire et Sociétés* 9, no. 1 (2005), pp. 33–78; Michael Stolleis, *The Eye of Law: Two Essays on Legal History*, trans. Thomas Dunlap (Abingdon: Birkbeck Law Press, 2008); Judith Resnik and Dennis Curtis, *Representing Justice: Invention, Controversy, and Rights in City-States and Democratic Courtrooms* (New Haven, CT: Yale University Press, 2011); Peter Goodrich, *Legal Emblems and the Art of Law:* Obiter Depicta *as the Vision of Governance* (Cambridge: Cambridge University Press, 2014); Adriano Prosperi, *Justice Blindfolded: The Historical Course of an Image* (Leiden: Brill, 2018; first published as *Giustizia bendata. Percorsi storici di un' imagine*, Turin: Einaudi, 2008); José M. González García, *The Eyes of Justice: Blindfolds and Farsightedness, Vision and Blindness in the Aesthetics of the Law* (Frankfurt: Vittorio Klostermann, 2017).
3. Massimo Leone, 'The Frowning Balance: Semiotic Insinuations on the Visual Rhetoric of Justice', *Semiotica* 216 (2017), pp. 41–62.
4. See Renée Watkins, 'L.B. Alberti's Emblem, the Winged Eye, and His Name, Leo', *Mittellungen des Kunsthistorischen Institutes in Florenz* 9, nos 3 and 4 (November 1960), pp. 256–8.
5. *Heraclitus: Homeric Problems*, eds and trans. Donald A. Russell and David Konstan (Atlanta, GA: Society of Biblical Literature, 2005).
6. Cristelle L. Baskins and Lisa Rosenthal (eds), *Early Modern Visual Allegory: Embodying Meaning* (Aldershot: Ashgate, 2008).

7. Bainard Cowan, 'Walter Benjamin's Theory of Allegory', *New German Critique*, special issue on Modernism, 22 (Winter 1981), pp. 109–22.

8. David Freedberg, *The Power of Images. Studies in the History and Theory of Response* (Chicago: University of Chicago Press, 1991).

9. Wolfgang Brückner, *Bildnis und Brauch. Studien zur Bildfunktion der Effigies* (Berlin: Schmidt Erich Verlag, 1986); Freedberg, *Power of Images*.

10. Jean-Pierre Changeux, *La beauté dans le cerveau* (Paris: Odile Jacob, 2016).

11. Daniel Russell, *Emblematic Structures in Renaissance French Culture* (Toronto: University of Toronto Press, 1995).

12. Daniel Russell, *The Emblem and Device in France* (Lexington, KY: French Forum, 1985), p. 164.

13. For an analysis of the Morellian method, see Carlo Ginzburg, 'Morelli, Freud, and Sherlock Holmes: Clues and Scientific Method', in Umberto Eco and Thomas Sebeck (eds), *The Sign of Three: Dupin, Holmes, Peirce* (Bloomington, IN: Indiana University Press, 1984), pp. 81–118.

14. Giorgio Agamben, *Homo Sacer: Sovereign Power and Bare Life*, trans. Daniel Heller-Roazen (Stanford, CT: Stanford University Press, 1998).

15. Pierio Valeriano, *Hieroglyphica sive De Sacris ægyptiorum aliarumque gentium literis commentarii* (Basel: Isengrin, 1556; Siena, 1616), p. 797.

16. In Erasmus, *Praise of Folly* (*Encomium Moriæ*) (Basel: Johann Froben, 1515), p. 109, Folly mocks theologians: 'Do not be surprised to see them (theologians), on days of public controversy, with their heads so tightly bound in their blindfolds (*fasciis*), otherwise they would burst'. 'Tot fasciis' is glossed in a marginal note: 'Id potissimum videmus in doctoribus apud Parisios, quorum capita tot fasciis sint obvolute, ut vix possint evolvere sese. Dissilit autem, quod ruptum in varias partes, minutim solvitur' (We see it especially in the Parisian doctors whose heads are surrounded by so many blindfolds that they have difficulty unrolling them themselves. It explodes because it bursts into many pieces and is reduced to rubble; my translation, because English translations choose the word 'caps' instead of 'blindfolds' for *fasciis*).

17. Aby Warburg introduces the concept of 'energetische inversion' (energetic inversion) in his *Mnemosyne Bilderatlas*. See Sigrid Weigel, 'Epistemology of Wandering, Tree and Taxonomy. The System Figuré in Warburg's *Mnemosyne* Project within the History of Cartographic and Encyclopaedic Knowledge', *Images Re-vues*, special issue, 'Survivance d'Aby Warburg', 4 (2013), art. 15.

18. Jean-Claude Margolin, 'Parodie et paradoxe dans l'"Éloge de la Folie" d'Érasme', *Nouvelles de la République des Lettres* 2 (1983), pp. 27–58.

19. Cesare Ripa, *Iconologia* (Padua: Tozzi, 1611), p. 203.

20. Pierre Ayrault, *L'ordre, formalité et instruction judiciaire, dont les anciens Grecs et Romains ont usé ès accusations publiques, conféré au style et usage de notre France* (1576; Paris: Laurent Sonnius, 1615), p. 547: 'Qu'on peint à cette occasion la justice bandée, et ne luy laisse l'on que l'ouye libre. Nous disons que la justice, pour estre bandée, n'est pas aveugle, que pendant qu'elle cherche la vérité (ce qui se faict en instruisant), elle ouvre à bon escient les yeux. Est-elle trouvée? Elle les bande pour juger.'

21. My translation.

22. Olav Worm, *Danicorum Monumentum libri sex* (Copenhagen: Joachim Molt-ken, 1643), book 5, p. 425: 'Justitiam mihi adumbrare videtur. Caput grande oculis destitutum, inter bestias duas locatum, Justitiæ, vel Judicis justi emblema est. Pingitur a multis justitia velata facie, it non tam personas litigantes aspiciat, quam causas auribus percipiat.'

23. D. H. Lawrence, 'The Spirit of Place', in *Selected Literary Criticism*, ed. Anthony Beal (New York: Viking Press, 1966), p. 297. I owe this quotation to Desmond Manderson.

24. My translation. Jacques Gouthière, *Tiresias, seu de Cæcitatis & Sapientiæ cognatione* (Paris: Heirs of Nicolas Buon, 1618), pp. 25–6: 'Quid vero causæ fuerit, ut Justitiæ oculis velum opponeretur? An quod illa cæcis temporum difficultatibus quandoque serviat, vel in magnis exemplis aliquid habere videa-tur ex iniquo, quod sine quadam mentis cæcitate esse non potest? Vel quod acutiores illius oculi suo fulgore hebetentur, cum ad summum jus illud respici-unt, ex quo summa sæpe injuria nascitur? Aut quia Justitia constans & perpetua voluntas definitur? Quod probabilius puto: voluntas enim rationi ancillatur, atque ut cæca a ratione sola ducitur in iis, quæ constanter prudenterque fieri solent. Et cæca voluntas ab intellectu lumen accipit & movetur. Ab hac Cæci-tate Justitia merito laudatur, ut hoc tritum vetustate proverbium, Quicum in tenebris? Quod in una re dictum latissime patet, ait Tullius, ut in omnibus factis re non teste moveamur.'

25. See Moshe Barasch, *Blindness: The History of a Mental Image in Western Thought* (New York: Routledge, 2001), esp. pp. 38–40.

26. Nicolas Reusner, *De officiis Magistratus et Subditorum in Republica tam civili quam literaria oratio* (Lavingen: Leonard Reinmichel, 1581): 'De Statuis prin-cipum et judicum Thebanorum Orationes Tres', oratio prima, B5v: 'Quo modo etiam nonnullos justitiæ imaginem effinxisse video: quæ DEA sit, & virgo, oculis clausis, aut velo obductis: ne hominum vultu (si Dijs placet) eam flec-tatur, aut pertubetur: quippe quæ non tam oculorum, quam aurium judicio uti: & ex eo veritatem, bonitatemque, causæ metiri debeat. Ridicule sane hoc utrumque: quantum ego judicare possum: quum illud potius ex eo significetur: aut in hominum sceleribus, & flagitiis magistratum aliquando connivere debere: aut non omnium eorum, quæ accidunt, perspicientiam, cognitionem-que ad eum pertinere: quum satius sit, multa saepe, quæ fiunt, magistratum ignorare aut certe dissimulare: si & tranquille sibi & alijs jucunde imperare velit. [. . .] Ego vero contra sentio, Auditores: & omnino ita mihi persuasum habeo: bonum principem, aut magistratum non modo non cæcutire, sed nec ullo modo connivere opportere.'

27. Georges de Scudéry, *Discours politiques des Rois, dédiez à Monseigneur le Cardinal Mazarin* (Paris: Augustin Courbé, 1647), pp. 192–3: 'Je ne sçay si ceux qui ont représenté la Justice avec un bandeau, ont fait une Peinture judic-ieuse, car pour moy je trouve au contraire qu'elle ne sçauroit voir trop clair. Je lui donnerois plustot les yeux d'Argus, que l'aveuglement d'Edipe ou de Tiresie, si j'avois à la dépeindre: & selon mon sens, le Linx mesme ne doit pas mieux voir que les Rois, qui tiennent seuls l'Espée de cette Justice en leur main. Fraper sans voir, & peser sans voir, sont des choses qui ne satisfont gueres, & où je

trouve peu de raison: je sçay bien que l'Antiquité a voulu dire par ce bandeau que la Justice doit estre *sans acceptation des personnes*: Mais il valoit bien mieux la representer comme une Deesse, que rien n'est capable d'esbranler, que de nous dire tacitement, qu'elle a besoin de ne voir pas, pour s'empescher de commettre des injustices. Il est donc très-necessaire, que les Rois ne se laissent pas aveugler par leurs passions; qu'ils pèsent avec jugement les choses qu'ils déterminent, & qu'ils se servent de l'Espée [. . .] discrettement.'

28. Jean-Baptiste Robinet, *Dictionnaire universel des sciences morale, économique, politique et diplomatique ou Bibliothèque de l'homme d'état et du citoyen*, vol. 27 (London: Libraires associés, 1777), p. 458, art. 'Question. De l'usage de la Question (torture)': 'On peint la justice avec un bandeau sur les yeux, pour marquer qu'elle ne fait acception de personne. Cet emblème ne pourroit-il pas signifier aussi qu'elle marche à tâtons dans la recherche des crimes, à peu près comme ces jeux où un enfant, les yeux bandés d'un mouchoir, poursuit les autres, & est obligé de nommer celui qu'il prend? Les tortures inventées pour extorquer, de la bouche des accusés, sont-elles bien propres à découvrir la vérité qu'on cherche?'

29. See Inge Kroppenberg, 'Blind Bodies of Justice. Æsthetics and Law in Johann Gottfried Herder's Sculpture', in Werner Gephart and Jure Leko (eds), *Law and the Arts: Elective Affinities and Relationships of Tension* (Frankfurt: Vittorio Klostermann, 2017), pp. 251–70.

30. González García, *Eyes of Justice*, pp. 167–9.

31. E. H. Gombrich, 'The Use of Art for the Study of Symbols', *American Psychologist* 20, no. 1 (1965), pp. 34–50.

32. Hubertus Quellinus, *Architecture, peinture et sculpture de la maison de ville d'Amsterdam, représentée en 109 figures en taille-douce*, vol. 1 (Amsterdam: Gérard Valk, 1719), p. 4, fig. XVII: 'Cette Planche représente la Chambre de Justice [. . .] C'est en ce lieu qu'on lit la sentence aux Criminels avant leur exécution; c'est pourquoi on y a placé ces deux statues, la Justice et la Prudence [. . .] Tout ce qu'on y remarque n'est capable que d'inspirer de la terreur par le rapport qu'ont toutes les Figures à la punition des coupables' and 'Les Planches précédentes renferment des emblèmes propres aux lieux particuliers auxquels elles servent d'ornements: Celle-ci contient une instruction générale pour tous les hommes: Aussi est-elle placée dans un lieu ouvert à toutes sortes de gens.'

33. *La Justice en son throsne. A tres chrestien Henri IIII Roy de France* (Rouen: Jean Petit, 1609), pp. 38–9, copy of the Bibliothèque municipale de Lyon: 'Tousiours, oüy tousjours le bandeau devant les yeux, ce bandeau que ce paintre me donnoit, pour ne faire point exception de personne, pour n'avoir nul chois & nul respect de grandeurs: tout m'estant indifferant, oüy en tous mes iugements, oüy prononçant mes arrests, oüy en rendant mes oracles: & iamais pourtant les yeux fermés, pour voir ce que le droit ordonne. Mais tousiours le bandeau devant les yeux, ce bandeau Royal, qui entourne de gloire votre front, & le cerne de grandeur et de pompe. Tousiours cet objet, à fin qu'on ne me puisse obiecter aucune desobeissance; tousiours les yeux vers vous, qui estes les yeux mêmes, par lesquels j'y vois, la lumiere de laquelle j'esclaire, le Soleil, par lequel j'illumine le monde. Le bandeau devant les yeux; non pas pour n'y voir, mais

bien pour y voir mieux; le bandeau devant les yeux pour cacher l'esclat de ma splendeur & le pouvoir plus aisément communiquer aux hommes, non tant pour couvrir ma puissance, que pour descouvrir la faiblesse de ceux qui, à travers les nuages du monde, ne peuvent voir à clair. Qui cache ma vertu & tasche d'imperfections les hommes. Si le Soleil à travers une nuée se laisse voir à tous, sans qu'il soit affaibli, si le diamant jette bien mieux son feu dans les ténèbres qu'en plein jour. Bandeau pour dire que les hommes me voilent de leurs passions; Bandeau pour en mieux voir les hommes, & considérer leurs actions sans estre considerées; Bandeau comme dans les cieux, d'où Dieu contemple les humains; Bandeau comme l'écharpe du ciel, à l'entour de laquelle ces deux beaux luminaires roulent incessament pour esclairer le monde; Bandeau enfin r'attaché des deux bouts, pour dire que le commencement est la fin, & en la fin est mon commencement, tousiours en action, pour le repos de tous.'

34. Pierre Legendre, *Leçons VIII. Le crime du caporal Lortie. Traité sur le Père* (Paris: Fayard, 1989). I would like to thank Peter Goodrich for making this suggestion to me.

35. André de Nesmond, 'Neufiesme Remonstrance faicte en Parlement à l'ouverture de la Sainct Martin, l'an 1613: le bandeau ou le diadème de Justice', in *Remonstrances, ouvertures de palais et arrets prononcés en robe rouge* (Poitiers: Antoine Mesnier, 1617), pp. 360–402, <http://gallica.bnf.fr/ark:/12148/bpt6k94691k>.

36. Ibid.: 'Les peintres anciens, à ce qu'il nous semble, se sont fort oubliez de n'avoir donné à la Justice un Voile, ou bien un Bandeau pour luy seiller les yeux, ou pour luy couvrir tout à fait le visage. C'est pourquoy, s'il nous est permis de corriger la faute de l'antiquité, nous luy donnerons aujourd'huy un Bandeau, ou Diadème, qui luy sera aussi séant & convenable pour exprimer ses fonctions, & son principal office, que pourroient estre les faisseaux, l'épée, ou les balances, les espis ou les rameaux d'olivier, les ailes & le caducée, ou le pourfil de visage descrit par le Philosophe Chrysippus [. . .] au lieu de descouvrir et exposer la Justice pour représenter sa beauté à cette grave assemblée, nous luy couvrirons le visage d'un voyle pour la rendre plus vénérable [. . .].'

37. Ibid.: 'C'est le Voyle dont elle s'affeubla apres le siecle d'or escoulé [. . .] comme en ce siecle d'argent l'iniquité & la malice eurent fait leur entrée au monde, deslors la Justice ne se laissa plus voir.'

38. Ibid.: 'Or que ce voyle ou bandeau appartienne à la justice, il se void par tous les tiltres & raisons qui ont peu mouvoir les anciens de se servir de voyle ou les donner à d'autres en tiltre d'honneur: Le premier peut estre en qualité de Déesse, ou à raison de la divinité présumée.'

39. Ibid.: 'Voires mesmes la coustume de porter des voyles glissa peu à peu jusques aux Officiers de l'Estat, & aux Magistrats, car ils faisoient comme par honneur pendre des voyles és lieux où ils traictoient des affaires concernant leurs charges, lesquels voyles ou rideaux s'appeloient VELA SECRETORUM, d'autant que ces lieux, où ils manioient les affaires d'Estat, se nommaient SECRETA. [. . .] Les Origines de la ville de Constantinople par Codinus font mention de certains rideaux ou voiles posez & tendus [. . .] qui estoit le parquet des Juges.'

40. Ibid.: 'En quatriesme lieu, on pourroit dire, que la justice se doit couvrir le visage pour tesmoigner le deüil qu'elle porte lors qu'elle est contraincte d'oster

& d'arracher par force ce qui est injustement usurpé par d'aucuns, pour le donner aux autres affin d'introduire l'equalité, & sur tout lors qu'elle est contraincte de se ranger à la sévérité & à la punition, comme il faut faire nécessairement aux iugements criminels. [. . .] Disons qu'on donnoit pour ce sujet le voyle ou le Bandeau à la justice, pour ne voir le sang humain espandu, comme on donnoit iadis des voyles aux statues des Dieux, qui estoient eslevées dans le Cirque Romain, affin qu'elles n'eussent horreur du sang qui se respandoit par les Gladiateurs, ne pouvant à cause de leur immobilité destourner le visage. [. . .] Ce regret de la Justice en ses tristes fonctions, ne se pourroit mieux exprimer que par un visage voylé.'

41. Ibid.: 'Nous pourrions pour un cinquiesme tiltre donner le Bandeau à la Justice [. . .]. C'est le symbole d'une honneste & chaste matrone, qui ne veut ny voir ni sçavoir ce qui se fait hors l'enclos de sa maison, comme la Justice doit estre tellement attentive aux affaires du Palais, & à ce qui est du bon ordre de sa maison, que la curiosité ne la tente jamais de regarder autre part, c'est pour cette raison principallement qu'on donnoit jadis aux femmes le jour de leurs nopces, le flammeum [. . .]. Et c'est peut estre pour cette raison que nos Maieurs peuvent avoir donné le Flammeum ou le Bandeau à la Justice.'

42. Ibid.: 'Cette regle et position, à sçavoir que la justice ne fait par faveur ny plus ny moins, c'est la signification de l'Embleme, c'est la declaration du Symbole du voyle & Bandeau dont nous seillons les yeux à la justice, voulant dire, qu'elle ne doit pas regarder les personnes, qu'elle doit estre, comme disait Platon dans le Protagoras, *personae non acceptatrix*, qu'elle ne doit pas favorizer aucun par considération de la qualité & condition de la personne, car l'œil & le regard c'est le Hyeroglyphique de la faveur [. . .]. Et la consideration des personnes faict mal aux yeux de la justice: C'est donc pour cette consideration qu'on luy bande les yeux.'

43. Ibid.: 'Cette regle position, à sçavoir que la justice ne fait par faveur ny plus ny moins, c'est la signification de l'Embleme, c'est la declaration du Symbole du voyle & Bandeau dont nous seillons les yeux à la justice, voulant dire, qu'elle ne doit pas regarder les personnes, qu'elle doit estre, comme disait Platon dans le Protagoras, personae non acceptatrix, qu'elle ne doit pas favorizer aucun par considération de la qualité & condition de la personne, car l'œil & le regard c'est le Hyeroglyphique de la faveur [. . .]. Et la consideration des personnes faict mal aux yeux de la justice: C'est donc pour cette consideration qu'on luy bande les yeux.'

44. Ibid.: 'Ce que la besace était pour Antisthène et le bâton pour Diogène, c'étaient ce que la cotte d'armes est pour le général, la tiare pour le Pontife, le bâton recourbé pour l'Augure; ainsi ce qui est propre à Justice, c'est son VOILE: Ce voyle sera vrayement son Bandeau royal ou Diademe, car il est très certain que le Diademe iadis n'était autre chose qu'un bandeau fait de quelque matière lente et ployable [. . .]. Or la iustice, au dire d'Orphée, est une grande Royne, & une Déesse fort puissante, de façon que nous pouvons lui donner le Diademe, lequel aussi d'ailleurs est une espèce d'ornement des femmes, selon Prudence [. . .] de façon qu'il vous peut, ô Saincte iustice, convenir en tant que Royne, [. . .] en tant que Déesse, puis que vous estes potissima Dia, entant

que Vierge, puis que vous estes *iustissima Virgo semper amans homines*. [. . .] à la justice nous luy ferons descendre son Bandeau royal sur les yeux. [. . .] Nous voulons bien retenir cette simple matiere de fin lin, pour façonner un Bandeau à la justice, & quitter l'or et la sculpture à part: Mais les pierreries, nous les voulons retenir pour en estoffer son Bandeau, car aussi sçavons nous que le masque ou splenium des Advocats estoit ainsi figuré et greslé de perles. [. . .] Nous graverons donques sur le Bandeau ou *splenium* de Justice, les plus belles perles des vertus, sœurs germaines et compagnes de la justice.'

45. Ibid.: 'Car les vertus sont dénotées par le Bandeau & par les perles; Quant au Voyle ou Bandeau, qu'il soit la figure des vertus, il ne se void pas si souvent que le contraire, d'autant que par le voyle ordinairement les vices & mauvaises inclinations sont entendues. [. . .] Pour les pierres precieuses elles sont aussi marques des vertus [. . .] Or la justice selon Theognis & Aristote comprend toutes les vertus, c'est l'amas, le receuil, la fin & la confection de toutes les vertus assemblées en une: Et principallement disons nous que la justice est comme l'abrégé de toutes les vertus Cardinales [. . .] la justice est *unum ex quatuor*, car elle contient la Force, la Prudence et la Tempérance.'

46. See Stolleis, *Eye of the Law*.

47. John Rawls, *A Theory of Justice* (Cambridge, MA: Harvard University Press, 1971).

Chapter 3

Lady Justice's fingers: gesture and meaning

The ways in which *Justitia* holds her attributes is always an object of careful depiction. What are the gestures appropriate to the *dignitas* of Lady Justice? How are these gestures codified in this domain? In the dialogue *De Justicia Pingenda*, Momus questions the challenging task of capturing the right gestural depiction of *Justitia*.[1] Because *Justitia*'s bodily gestures tend to run riot, Momus delivers a surreptitious sabotage of her supposed dignity. While showing the discrepancy between symbol and meaning, Momus' carping critique points out one major problem: how can several gestural systems coexist in the one body? Lady Justice is probably one of the few allegories depicted as ambidextrous, using both hands equally well. This chapter analyses Lady Justice's fingers, showing that the scales of Justice must be presented as true measure: the positioning of the fingers is used in a variety of ways to indicate the principles of honest weighing. This chapter aims to look at the 'immense care and learning' which was spent on the depiction of Lady Justice's gestures.[2] Is it possible to capture the essence of Justice in the form of a gesture? Are Lady Justice's distinctive gestures a prefiguration of what could be called an allegorical characterology?

Lady Justice's gestural system is complex and varied: it involves bodily and facial gestures; variants are oriented to the left or to the right, and their symbolic perception is always influenced by orientation. The diversity of cognitive and experiential modes suggested by Lady Justice's gestures might explain the reasons why this allegory has persisted over centuries. *Justitia* repeatedly challenges viewers to experience different levels of engagement: her keen eyes trigger intuitive and emotional reactions, while the careful weighing – the ponderation – of the scales induces a ratiocinative and intellectual movement. Her body is frequently treated as a nexus of multimodality where archetypical gestures are reduced to a minimum. The calculative spectrum of possible responses to her gestures may be revealed through closer inspection. Clearly, Lady Justice is opposed to static being. Her allegorical stance is not rigid: it is a play, a performance, a pageant in action. A serious exploration of the advantages of allegory over other cognitive methods lies in understanding gesture as the depiction of symbolic action in the world.

The ancients used specific designations for each finger: *pollex, index, medius, annularis, minimus.* Bruno Roy underlines that these designations are inspired by their form (*pollex, minimus*), their situation (*medius*), or their function (*annularis, index*).[3] If we want to assess the chironomic force of *Justitia*'s hand gestures, we need to address cultural variations in the meaning of particular gestures, from ancient forms to early modern reiterations.

Selecting salient features is crucial to gestural recognition, since hand gestures are very rich in shape variation, motion and expressiveness. A viewer-based approach has been preferred, identifying the major tendencies used to represent the fingers and static hand postures of Lady Justice. But even this method is not always reliable. It freezes motion and it is not applicable to the dynamism of a three-dimensional sculpture. In trying to build a taxonomy of Lady Justice's hand postures, the first distinction to be made is to oppose 'autonomous gestures', which occur independently of speech, from 'gesticulation' accompanying speech. Another appropriate classification is to distinguish mimetic from deictic gestures. Based on the data I have collected from approximately one thousand images, the following findings will evidence the main features employed by artists throughout the period under consideration (from 1450 to 1850). In the sphere of allegorical representation, the most discriminating gestures are also the most expressive ones. This is the reason why computer-assisted hand posture recognition cannot detect the salience of the specific gestural composition of allegories. Allegorical images need to be rooted in their anthropological context: a quantitative approach is needed, but the main difficulty is to detect what has changed drastically in our understanding of non-verbal communication. During early modern times, the hand was variously used as an instrument for counting, a mnemonic tool or even an apotropaic sign.

This study aims to classify the characteristic patterns or 'signatures' of gesture, as meaningful signs in the representation of Justice. The overall goal is a semantics of the hand's postures. One of the main issues is to cope with the variable shapes that the same gesture may exhibit. We also need to question the rarity of some representations. The framework adopted here is that of classifying iterative patterns. Template matching has been used to confront several prototypes of Lady Justice's hand gestures. Once the prototype has been sufficiently documented (namely by visual and textual sources), it may be evidenced as an archetype, thus creating a historical gradient. The number of images surveyed is high, in order to catch even the most minute differences in posture. A small vocabulary of gestures offers a convenient way to grasp the iterative nature of allegorical postures. Some gestures (e.g. the use of a pointing finger) appear to be of cross-cultural or universal significance, whereas others are less commonly utilised. In the sphere of judicial *actio*, hand gestures that accompany speech in conversations are of particular interest as they complement verbal communication.

Gestural expressivity

In a Netherlandish engraving entitled *Amanda est Justitia* (Lady Justice must be loved) (Figure 3.1), her body is restricted to the depiction of her bust as in a secular close-up portrait. The elaborate design of her gestures sets up a contrapuntal relation between the two visible attributes: the sword's upward handle is set at the same height as the axis of the scales. The strategy is to give to both gestures equal impact so as to suggest that Justice should be moderated by Temperance. The Augustinian motto reads 'excessive Justice tends to sin, whereas a moderate Justice renders men perfect'.[4] The gestural system combining her two most common attributes, sword and scales, is not to be understood as a mere accumulation of static objects. Lady Justice holds a light and versatile sword together with manageable scales:[5] the manner in which the sword is gripped is to be compared with the dexterous handling of her scales.

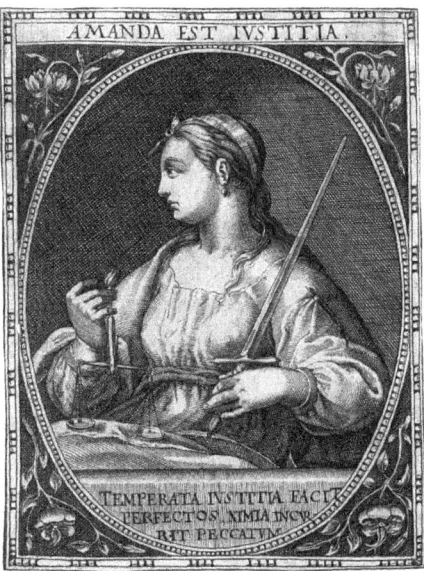

Figure 3.1: *Amanda est Ivstitia*, dated c. 1576–1625, Graph. C: 570.6. Herzog August Biblio-thek, Virtuelles Kupferstichkabinett

Instead of focusing on the impersonal agency of the scales, the allegorical posture of Lady Justice insists on the subjective agency of its user. As Massimo Leone has insightfully noted, parts of the human body were used in Ancient Egypt to bind the weighing process to an embodiment of adjudication.[6] In one of the Coffin Texts – a collection of ancient Egyptian funerary spells written on coffins beginning in the First Intermediate Period (c. 2181–2055 BCE) – weighing is personified in demonic form. The dead address the sun god Re with a prayer for help: 'Save me from this God with occult shape, whose eyebrows are the beams of the scales [. . .]'. This curious image stresses the subjectivity of a weighing procedure generated by the emotional reaction of the judge as seen expressed on his face. In other visual representations of the weighing of the soul, the penis of Thoth seems to be a part of the indicative system of the scales.[7]

In most allegorical representations, the essential feature of the scales is equilibrium; but the representation of *Justitia*'s iconic attribute is sometimes distorted by perspective, and the equipollence of the pans is often disturbed by the agency of its user. In *Justitia*'s gestural system, both attributes complement each other and the allegorical conceit rests on a gestural *compositio*. Lady Justice is a personification, and the way she embodies the weighing mechanism is subjected to various body postures and hand gestures. As we will examine in this chapter, her body articulates two symmetrical grips which reuse a well-established visual genealogy. Throughout the early modern period, the mechanical agency of the balance is conceived as an extension of her body.

André Chastel indicates the richness of the approach: gestures are specific thresholds where signifiers convey signified entities.[8] The expressive gesture stands as a key feature in the enhancing of the affective power of the composition. Visual symbols allow us to see a rather complex concept all at once, whereas discursive speech is linear and its successive words can only impart the same meaning at greater length. As a representation of the unrepresentable, the symbolic body of Lady Justice offers one complete image of a complexity which is more accessible to intellectual intuition. Lady Justice is not a mere sign which stands for an abstract concept; she is at the same time a physiological body, an ambiguous form (*forma anceps*) and sign of institution.

The extended middle finger as part of a mnemonic technique

Further intriguing patterns need investigation. Hand gestures carry a strong symbolic component as they are constitutive of all human activities (prehensile movements, visual judgement and experimental measurement). In an unusual engraving by Hendrick Goltzius (1558–1617) dating between 1585 and 1589, also executed by Jacob Matham, the movement of Lady Justice's middle finger deserves close analysis (Figure 3.2). It may allude to a symbolic correspondence with the mystical interpretation of Christ's fingers, as elaborated in the *Life of Christ* by Johann Eberard Scheifler:

His hand has five symbolic fingers. [. . .] 1. The first one, the smaller one, the little finger signifies obedience [. . .] 2. The second finger, called 'ring finger' was in relation with the piety of our Saviour, and it is with this finger that he touched the heart of the sinners [. . .] 3. The third finger, stronger and more vigorous than the ring finger alludes to the astonishing sacrifices of Christ throughout his life [. . .] This finger indeed has three articulations: one stands for his ability to do good works. Another one stands for his aptitude for distinguishing iniquity from equity and vice versa. The third articulation signifies works of mercy. 4. The fourth finger is the one used for preaching, and that is

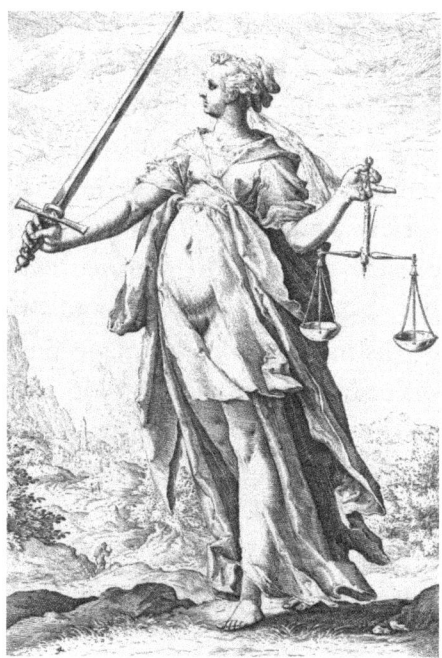

Figure 3.2: Jacob Matham (engraver) after design by Hendrick Goltzius, *Allegory of Lady Justice*, c. 1585–9, middle finger extended. Courtesy of the Rijksmuseum, Amsterdam

why it is rightly called 'index' [. . .]. The fifth finger of Christ is the Passion of Jesus our Lord. [. . .] The little finger of our hand stands for humble, favourable and joyful obedience. [. . .]. The third and middle finger, which is also longer, **stands for justice** with its triple articulation: restitution of extorted property, payment of debts, and punishment of crime. The fourth finger (index) stands for prudence, with its triple articulation: memory of the past, intelligence and penitence, and foreseeing of the future. The fifth finger of our hand is the thumb, which symbolises generous fortitude, with its two articulations: the audacious attack of arduous tasks and the courage that endures hardship.[9]

This rare level of specificity reveals a wider symbolic nexus. Each finger of the hand is paired with a virtue. This detail refers to practices of the Late Middle Ages in which the hand, frequently used as an instrument for counting, served as a mnemonic device for the contemplation of the Passion.[10] Those at prayer would count off the stations of the Passion on their fingers, and each one of them was assigned to a segment of a finger. This arithmetical piety enjoined the persons praying to train in the virtues in a very practical way. Note here that this sophisticated interpretation is a Christian rewriting of ancient gestural practices, seeking to avoid any obscene, insulting or scatological connotations. Here, the middle finger serves to articulate an economy of salvation in addition to being symbolic tool for remembering that justice is a distributive principle as well as a punitive act. But the *medius* (middle finger) also bears earlier valences under the *digitus impudicus* paradigm. When the middle finger is singled out, it serves first and foremost as a beckoning signal. A clear distinction is to be made between an extended middle finger used as a fixed mooring point for counting and a *medius* in motion, used to express greetings (*index salutaris*), or conversely used to express an act of shaming (*digitus infamis*).

Goltzius shows that he is well aware of these mnemonic uses of the hand: training in the virtues is a key aspect of understanding how symbolic practices influenced daily life. The elucidation of the symbolic meaning of *Justitia*'s middle finger contains a threefold definition of Justice: the three joints of Christ's middle finger are depicted carefully in the engraving; one of them is, according to Scheifler, a symbol of Christ's 'aptitude for distinguishing iniquity from equity and vice versa'. The triple joint may also refer to three examples of earthly justice: the precision of the legal vocabulary ('restitution of extorted property, payment of debts, and punishment of crime') describes the concrete implications of earthly law. Dame Justice's middle finger becomes a point of articulation between divine and human law.

Goltzius's engraving also suggests how the hand – instrument of instruments, according to Aristotle – may serve as a transmitter of ethics and as an ethical guide. Goltzius often alluded to the distinctive physiognomy of his own hand in his print work: his right hand had been severely burned when he was a year old, leaving him crippled for life. The artist's hand became something like his signature; he did a number of drawings of it, and even used it, while travelling, to establish his legal identity. With the example of the outstretched middle finger of *Justitia*, Goltzius shows how the hand becomes the locus of virtues where each finger joint may serve as a metonym for a very concrete mnemonic and practical art.

Transitory hieroglyphics

The *modi significandi* of hand gestures are figuratively treated as though they constitute mute relations to things, in either the mode of hieroglyphs or common emblems. Mimetic language has no predefined ability to signify, as gestures are always means without ends, fragments of a wider nexus. Andrea de Jorio's definition of the nature of mimetic language (*linguaggio mimico*) excludes the possibility of achieving a genuine alphabetic language, comparable to other alphabetic systems that can be described through syntax and grammar. Instead, the nature of gestural meaning pertains to the class of 'lingue emblematiche, le quali esprimonsi per via di geroglifici.'[11] This emblematic language of gestures cannot be reduced to any lexicon. He refers to Francis Bacon's judgment, according to which gestures are 'transitory hieroglyphics' – a term adopted by several other authors, including Wundt, Efron and Tyler: 'Gestures are transitory hieroglyphics and are to hieroglyphics as words spoken are to the written, in that they abide not; but they have evermore, as well as the other, an affinity with the things signified.'[12]

Gestures are not signs in the semiotic sense of the term. They do not have fixed meanings established by an arbitrary coding or a universal social convention. Instead, they serve as an illustration of cultural differences in perception, tied to a context-based paradigm which shifts over time and space. Ray Birdwhistell states that 'gestures' (conventionalised motor symbols) are socially learned and he adds that the process of learning these 'motor patterns' is largely unconscious.[13] These liminal remarks aim at putting Lady Justice's gestural action into perspective. Are ideographic gestures (non-mimetic) more appropriate to Lady Justice's dignity than mimetic ones, sometimes depicted as histrionic gesticulation?

Lady Justice seems to resist any purely descriptive taxonomy. It is more useful to understand her gaze, hand gestures and expressive gesticulations dialectically. One method is to follow Quintilian's account of the classification of gestures. The Roman orator's starting point is a restrictive classification of gestures in order to examine the pragmatic variation that hand gestures may bring to speech acts. This method gives a solid ground to the analysis of the gestural paradigms of Lady Justice throughout the early modern period. Our hypothesis is that

Quintilian's revival during the early modern period may also explain how allegorical sculptures in civic spaces (marketplaces, courthouses, tribunals) are shaped according to newly reappraised rhetorical arts.[14]

The horn gesture as apotropaic

Although quite rare, another example of *Justitia*'s finger posture deserves a detailed analysis. In *Allegory of Justice* (1537), a painter from the circle of Lucas Cranach the Elder (c. 1472–1553) painted *Justitia*'s left hand in an unusual but telling position: she holds the balance in a typical apotropaic gesture, intended to ward off bad luck (Figure 3.3). A belief in *malocchio* or *iettatura*, the evil eye capable of inflicting harm or misfortune, is commonly associated with protective measures. One of these is the 'horn' gesture: index and little fingers are extended while the other fingers are bent down towards the palm of the hand. Charms depicting a hand imitating the horn gesture were also common. Here, the horn gesture is a defensive weapon. Ancient and

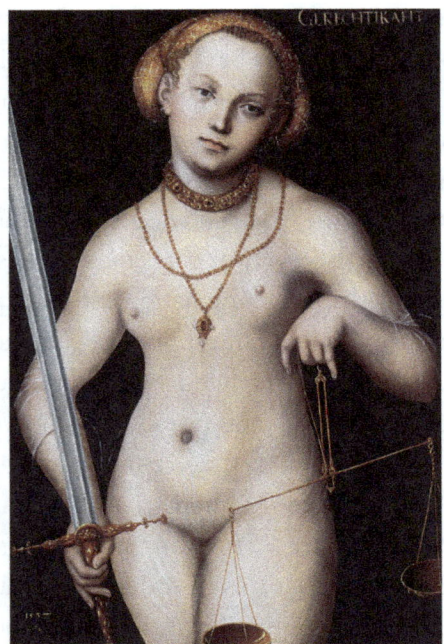

Figure 3.3: Lucas Cranach the Elder circle, *Allegory of Justice*, 1537. Private collection. By permission of Michael Hofbauer

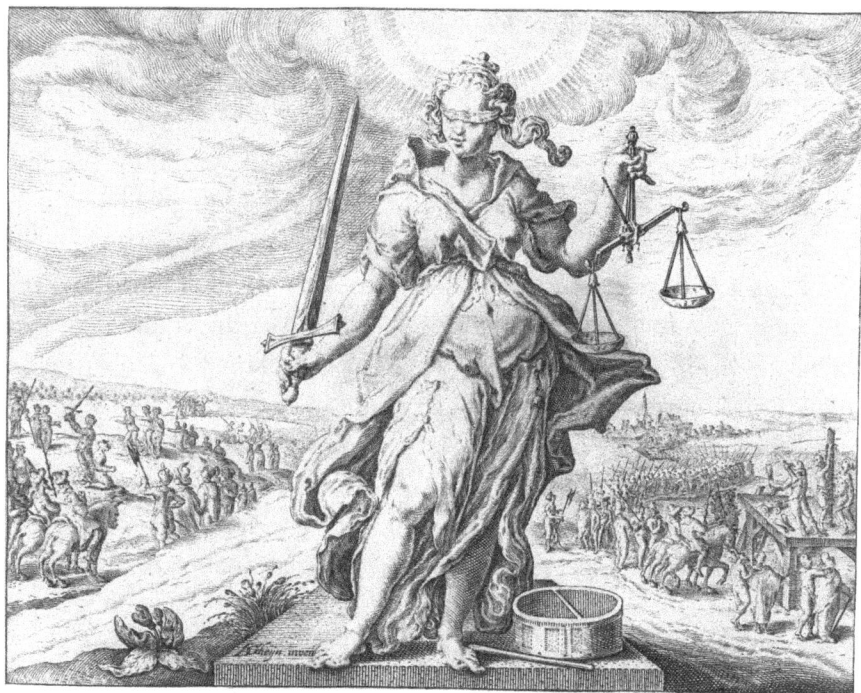

Figure 3.4: Jacob de Gheyn II, *Allegory of Justice*, 1598. Horn gesture. Courtesy of the Rijksmuseum, Amsterdam

modern ethnographic literature gives ample evidence of this pattern. The same gesture appears in Fra Filippo Lippi's *Portrait of a Woman with a Man at a Casement* (c. 1440) to protect the soon-to-be married young woman's fertility.[15] Lady Justice holds the scales using a *mano cornuta* aimed downward like a suspended amulet. The gesture may suggest that the instrument itself is in danger of bewitchment. *Justitia* needs to protect the balancing power of the scales from the evil eye. Her hand does not only hold a conventional attribute, but instead her fingers indicate a supplementary meaning: the scales need to be cautiously instrumental; they are used as an extension of her body.

In a later engraving by Jacob de Gheyn II dating from 1598 (Figure 3.4), the same horn gesture is present, but this time, it is explicitly directed towards a gruesome theatre of punishment, situated in the background of the scene. Such apotropaic gestures are part of Lady Justice's legal ritual: symbols not merely as signs representing things already known but felt to possess an efficacy and agency all their own.

Deictic index and judicial *actio*

The index finger – also known as the pointer – may be used simultaneously to call attention, to point towards the all-seeing eye of God, and to mediate between two orders of reality (divine justice and human codification). This gesture is particularly well represented by Bernardo Strozzi's *Madonna of Justice*, a large altarpiece commissioned by the city of Genoa and destined for the Hall of the Great Council in the Palazzo Ducale in around 1620–5 (Figure 3.5).[16] The pointing index finger of the Madonna is directed towards the open book of the Bible, bearing the injunction 'Suprema lex esto' (May this be the supreme law), while an angel placed in front of the Virgin indicates the attributes of Justice (lictor's *fasces* and a measuring plumbline). This is, in fact, one of the most common and codified gestures, but the conflation of Lady Justice with the Virgin produces an impressive compositional pattern.

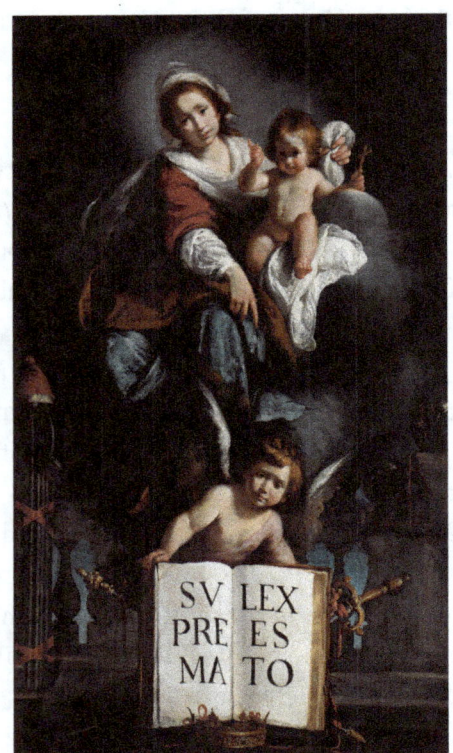

Figure 3.5: Bernardo Strozzi, *Madonna of Justice*, c. 1620–5, from the Hall of the Great Council in the Palazzo Ducale of Genoa. Louvre Museum, Department of Paintings

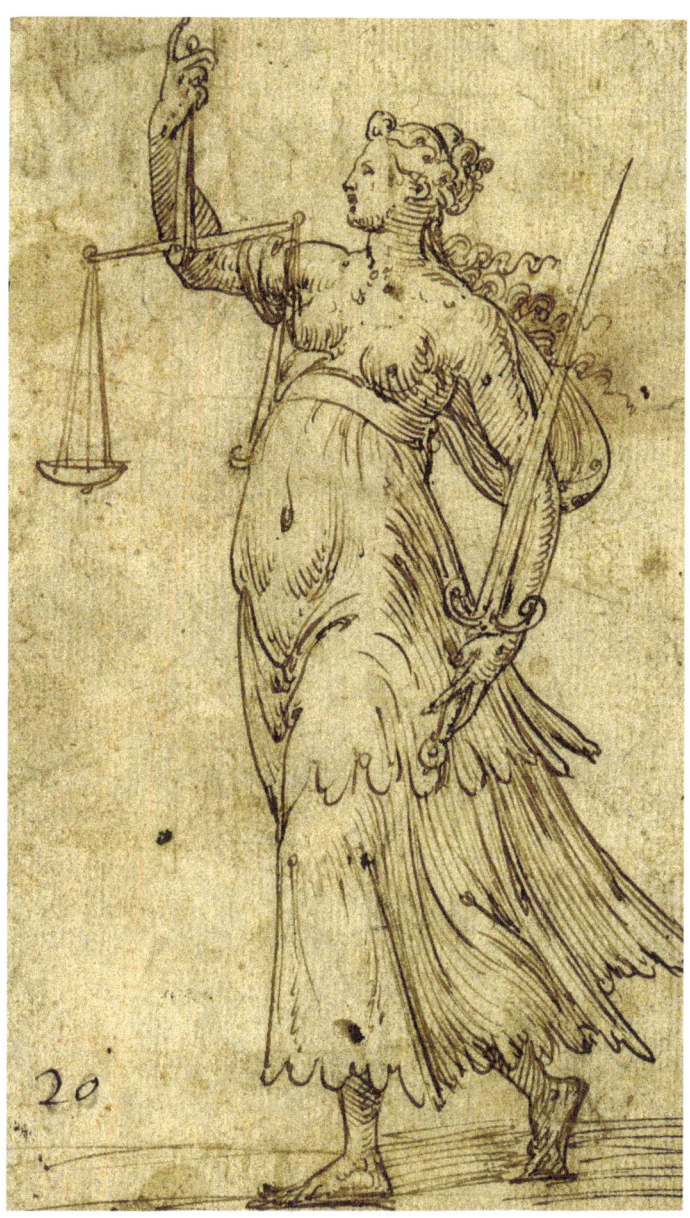

Figure 3.6: Anonymous drawing attributed to Lambert Lombard, sixteenth century, inv. AN 1175. © The Trustees of the British Museum

An anonymous late sixteenth-century drawing of Justice attributed to Lambert Lombard shows Lady Justice lifting her scales in her right hand, with an index finger emphatically pointing towards the heavens in a particularly strong deictic gesture (Figure 3.6). The index finger points to the frame of reference where the mute but eloquent body acts and reinforces the persuasive rhetoric of the allegory by offering to ground abstract ideas in concrete actions. This emphatic gesture embodies the binding force of Law. Its expressiveness is key to understanding allegorical conceits. A pointed index finger alludes immediately to the silent rhetoric of the orator. The hand gesture appeals particularly to lawyers and orators, who, since ancient times, have been trained in the use of specific gestural methods.

In his *Chirologia, or The Natural Language of the Hand*, John Bulwer suggests that the index finger, pointed upward with great vehemence, is a threatening gesture, brandished in the mode of terror.[17] This sign (*terrorem incutio*) may stand here for the punitive force of Justice, brandishing her attributes in a particularly vehement stance. Such a strong deictic gesture, especially when it is expressed in allegorical language, conveys a meaningful emphasis on the expressive force of judicial *actio*. Allegory becomes a model for animated eloquence.

The same gesture appears in a narrative judicial scene depicted on an enamelled leather box by an anonymous artist (Figure 3.7). The pointing index finger holds a balance, its beam pointed upward towards the

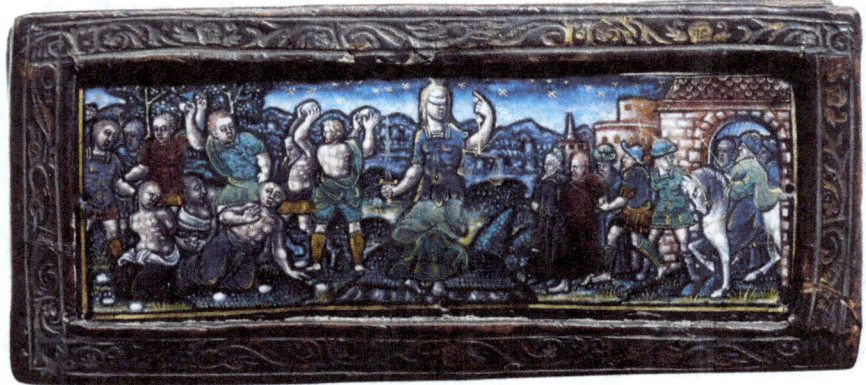

Figure 3.7: A stamped leather coffer with a polychrome enamel plaque depicting an allegorical scene of Justice, Limoges, late sixteenth century. Christie's database of auction sales

emperor seated on his horse (bottom right) and his court. On the left-hand side (*ad sinistram*, a bad omen) of the scene, three slaves are savagely stoned. Lady Justice, blindfolded, points her index finger up to heaven, and this may indicate that her judgment derives from God's will.

In a later representation of Lady Justice, the Dresden court painter Christian Schiebling depicts fourteen life-size virtues in the shape of baroque female figures, actively engaging the viewer.[18] *Justitia*, placed on the south wall, points an index finger towards the spectator, involving the viewers in contemplation of heroic virtues (Figure 3.8). Her deictic gesture shows that Justice has a strong communicative nature. Her allegorical stance serves as a fictive medium to lead the audience into the dance of virtues.

A final example will show the enduring expressivity of this gestural language of deixis. Given that allegorical compositions are often reduced to conventional patterns, strong deictic gestures are the preferred bearers of the affective component of the composition. In an early nineteenth-century anonymous allegorical painting, Lady Justice's left index finger

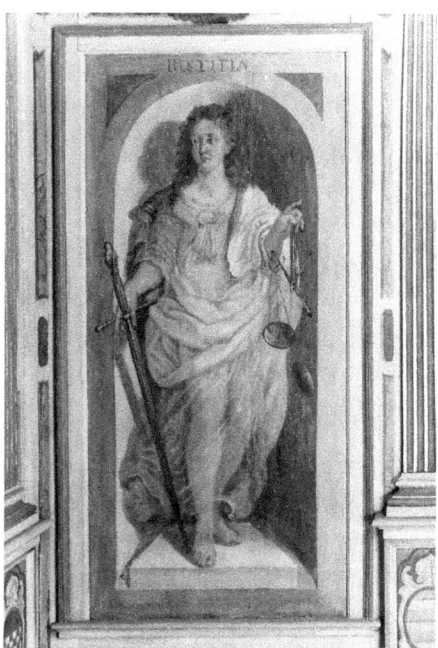

Figure 3.8: Christian Schiebling, *Justitia*, c. 1634, south wall of the manor house salon, Hoflößnitz, Radebeul, Kreis Meissen, Germany. SLUB Dresden, Deutsche fotothek. Photograph by Henrik Ahlers

is pointed towards the Eye of the Law and at the same time holds the balanced scales, while her right index finger shows an upward sword used as a heavy bookmark in the open books of the newly drafted *Code Civil* (1804). At her feet lies a thinner volume of the *Lois Civiles*. In this straightforward composition, Lady Justice's body acts as an animated indicator of three orders of Law: divine law, suggested by the hieroglyph of the overarching eye, watches over the institution of the Napoleonic Code, directly inspired by God, with which earthly human civil laws are in harmony. This allegory of Law offers a visual representation of the proclamation of the 1804 'Loi sur la réunion des Lois civiles en un seul corps sous le titre de Code Civil des français', as drafted by the four legislators of the French Civil Code: Félix Julien Jean Bigot de Préameneu, Jacques de Maléville, François Denis Tronchet and Jean-Étienne-Marie Portalis.[19] As a modern code of law which made a clean break with the past, the new act of legislation is embodied in the strong deictic gestures of a female body. Lady Justice indicates a paradigm shift, and her eloquent gestures invent a new way of *legem instituere*.

Gripping and handling

Hidden or discarded scales

The scales are generally held with a cautious gesture, striving for balance. But sometimes they are depicted less obviously and in other configurations. Andrea del Sarto executed a rather unconventional allegory of Justice for a series of frescoes on the life of Saint John the Baptist for the San Giovanni Battista Scalzo Cloister in Florence. The grisaille of Justice (from a series of four virtues flanking the doors) was finished between 1515 and 1523 (Figure 3.9). The confraternity's oratory enclosed highly esteemed works of art: Sarto's frescoes attracted artists who wanted to execute drawings after his models. Lady Justice, a full-length female figure, is shown in frontal view, standing in a niche, holding a monumental executioner's sword downward in her right hand. Her left hand hides a large portion of the right pan of the balance under a bulky piece of drapery: only one side of the bending scales remains visible. Below is inscribed 'Diligite Iustitiam qui judicatis terram'. This pattern is quite

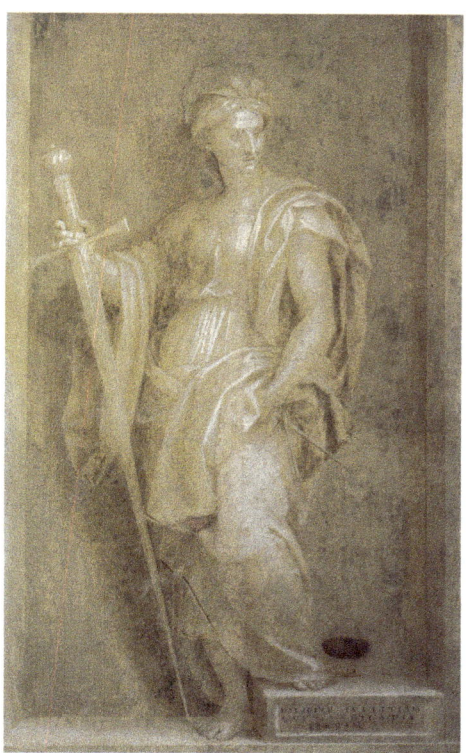

Figure 3.9: Andrea del Sarto, *Allegory of Justice*, cycle of the life of Saint John the Baptist, San Giovanni Battista Scalzo Cloister, Florence, grisaille, c. 1515–23. Kunsthistorisches Institut in Florenz Phototek. Photograph: Kunsthistorisches Institut in Florenz – Max-Planck-Institut. Photographer: [Rabatti – Domingie]

rare; it outwits the viewer, who is trained to identify the allegory by recognising its two major attributes. Deliberately hiding the mechanical agency of the balance illustrates the virtue of Justice in a religious cycle. While the judicial rhetoric of law aims at figuring a visible equipollence of the pans of the scales, Andrea del Sarto has chosen a radically different stance. The size of the executioner's sword compared with the invisibility of the scales offers a way to meditate on punitive justice and the economy of salvation. While contemplating the tribulations of the life of a saint, his pious and sinful deeds, the spiritual assessment cannot be reduced to a merely quantitative measurement.

A study of three figures of Justice and two figures of Temperance by Antonio Palma (c. 1510–c. 1575) shows three patterns for Lady Justice holding her attributes (Figure 3.10). The first posture depicts her with her face leaning towards the scales, sword held in a relaxed gesture and

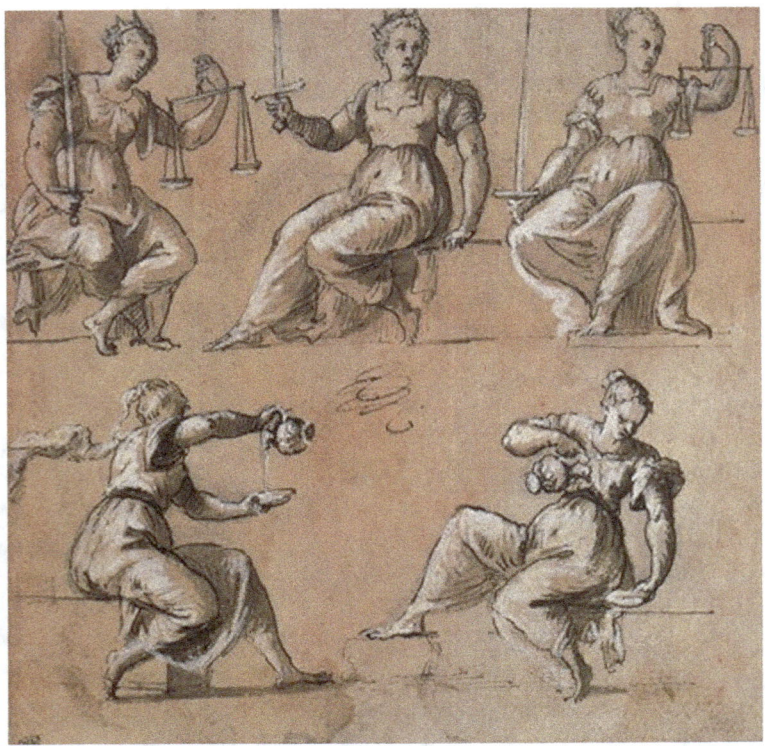

Figure 3.10: Antonio Palma, *Study of Three Figures of Justice*, inv. 5727 recto. Louvre Museum, Department of Graphic Arts

legs crossed (Clement Justice). The second shows her right arm extended with an upward sword, while the scales are barely noticeable (Punitive Justice). The third depicts her in an intermediary position, as she equitably uses both attributes: the sword is lifted upward, while the scales are held steady (Equitable Justice). The three poses are not redundant; they indicate with minute variations a nexus of gestural options.

Power grip and precision handling

The study of the prehensile movements of Lady Justice's allegorical body demonstrates how the intended activity, doing justice, influences the pattern of the grip represented. As the paleoanthropologist John Russell Napier suggests, the main distinction to be discerned in the analysis of the movement and posture of the human hand is between the power grip and precision handling: 'These patterns provide the anatomical basis for all prehensile activities, whether skilled or unskilled.'[20]

The artificial body of Lady Justice combines both. Her right hand wields the sword in a power grip whereas her left hand holds the scales in a precision-handling gesture. The combination of two archetypal anatomical gestures may explain why this allegory is still alive today. Images of Justice give expression to the *coincidentia oppositorum*, a mode of being which manifests itself in contradictory ways and therefore cannot be reduced to rigid concepts. Lady Justice is a multivalent image with a wide pattern of meaningful stances and gestures. To reduce an image to an abstract terminology by restricting it to a single frame of reference is to destroy its power as an instrument of cognition. Beyond any analytical description, images always convey more than words.

Among the transient attributes she has been given over time, some have faded away. She is no longer depicted with an ostrich or a sieve. These iconological conceits have died out quickly. Nevertheless, she remains a powerful binary symbol, all the more striking in its polarity. The sword is an example of a stable grasp: the object becomes a tool, understood as an extension of the hand. Equally important for the daily work of the hands, a dynamic grasp, which involves measurement, including repositioning the fulcrum in the hand, is represented in how she holds the scales.

In the power-grip pattern, the dynamics of gripping produce a particular mode of holding as the fingers have to clench around the object to hold it firmly. In the precision-handling pattern, the object is held between the tips of the thumb and the index finger in order to render it immobile. While holding the scales, Lady Justice seizes both pans within the compass of the hand. She is able to manipulate them by pushing or lifting the hand as a whole or by means of the individual digits. The combination of the two hand gestures is particularly significant, as the power grip emphasises security and stability whereas the precision handling underlines dexterity and sensitivity. Allegorical gestures are all the more salient for their symbolic meaning. These sculptures are made for groups, not for individuals. They hint at a universal grammar for prehensile postures. In this case, the allegorical body shows that grasping displays an exemplary form of embodied knowledge. These observations are predicated on the contiguity of reality and representation.

Hendrick Goltzius, followed later by his stepson Jacob Matham, has treated her hand gestures in a particularly prominent *maniera*. The comparison of the two versions of the drawing of Lady Justice discussed below offers a contrasting grammar. In the first version (Figure 3.11), Lady Justice's left arm is raised and outstretched, showing the tips of the middle finger and thumb pressed together in an unusual precision-handling pattern. This is an image of measuring and balancing: the image values the tactile experience of mensural effort. One tip of the scale is purposely extended through the rectangular frame, probably in order to suggest, in a typical mannerist strategy, a framing effect evoking the set of scales as an everyday object.

Instead of depicting the allegory of Justice as a figure constrained mechanically to hold to her conventional attributes, Goltzius used the sharp contrast between the power grip and precision handling to depict a body that operates in the world. The illusion is carefully staged: the allegorical figure is seated on a staircase, in front of a balustrade over which she extends her hands and arms. The second version (Figure

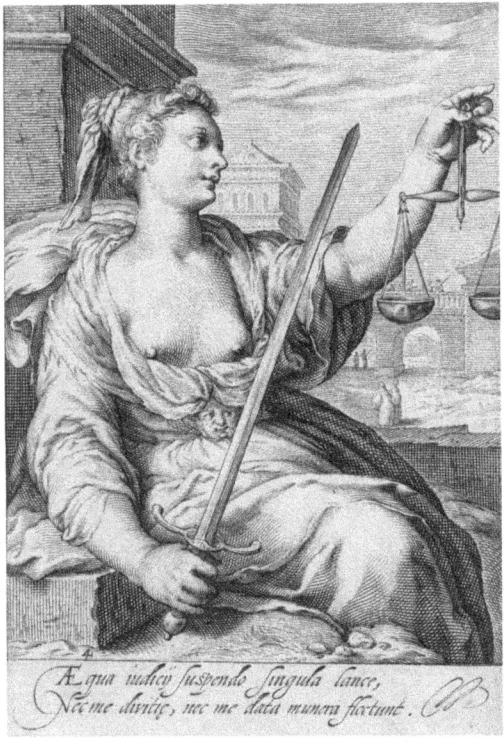

Figure 3.11: Jacob Matham (engraver) after Hendrick Goltzius (inventor), *Allegory of Lady Justice*, 1597, 'Aequa judicii suspendo singula lance / Nec me divitie, nec me data munera flectunt'. Courtesy of the Rijksmuseum, Amsterdam

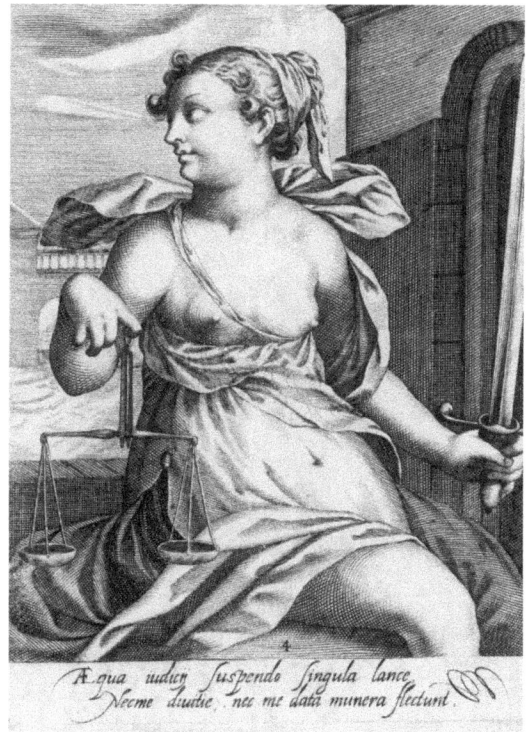

Figure 3.12: Dietrich Krüger (engraver) after Gabriel Weyer (inventor), Balthasar Calmox (printer), *Allegory of Lady Justice*, 1614, 'Aequa judicii suspendo singula lance / Nec me divitie, nec me data munera flectunt.' Herzog Anton Ulrich Museum, Dkrüger WB 3.20

3.12) signals another configuration: Lady Justice now holds the scales in her right hand and the sword is upright in her left hand. She uses her index finger as a digital grappling hook to raise the scales and keep them in equilibrium. The index finger arching forward and inward serves to direct a downward hook, and her arm is bent to compensate for the fact that only one finger is in use.

The power-grip pattern as a visual rhetoric for a firm metrological order

As has been noticed before, Lady Justice almost always uses precision handling to hold the scales. The depiction of an honest weighing relies on a strong pattern, which emphasises the role played by the thumb and index fingertips as a meaningful signature visually signalling an invisible property: weight. But occasionally the hand holding the scales uses a power grip, giving Lady Justice a posture more appropriate to *Fortitudo*.

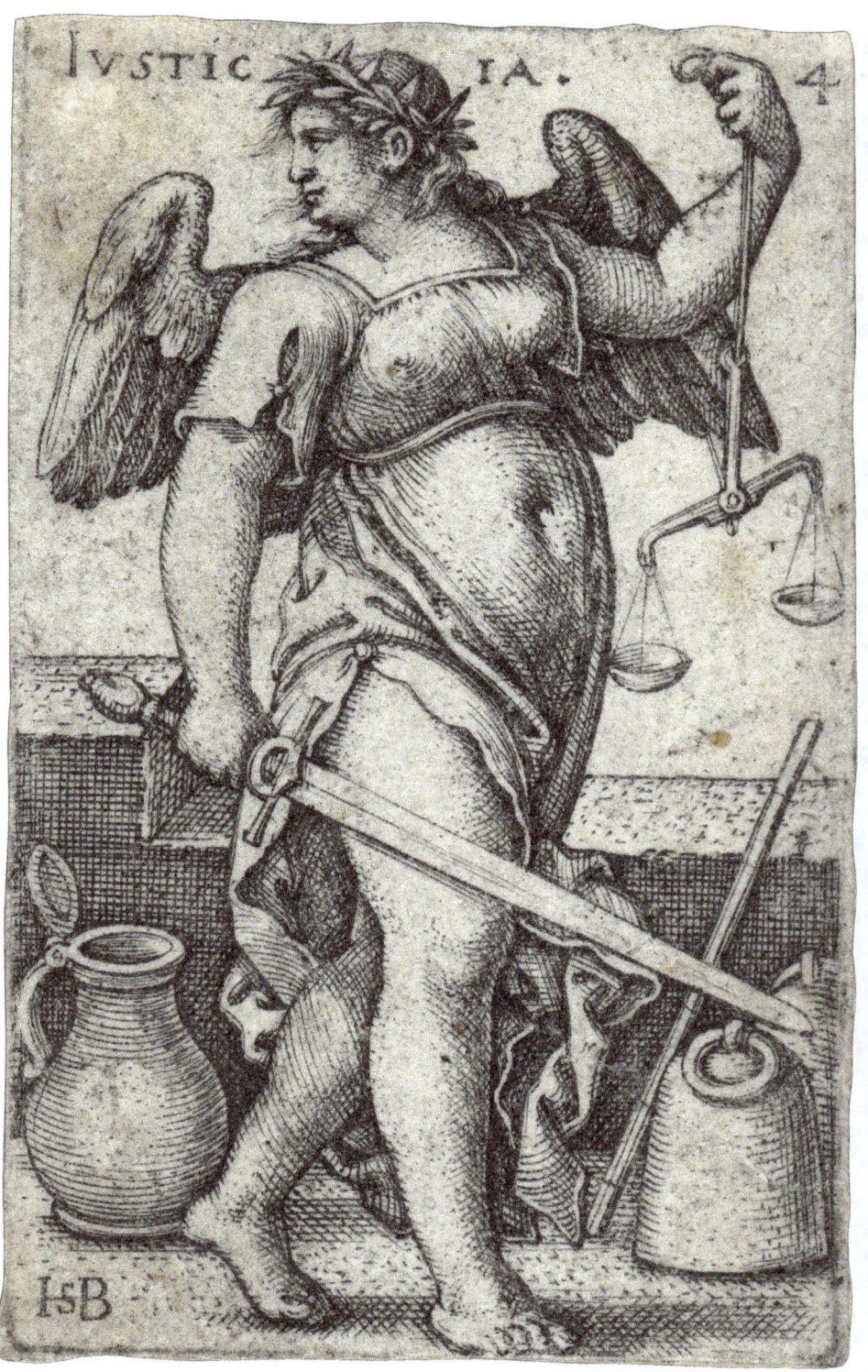

Figure 3.13: Hans Sebald Beham, *Justicia*, 1539. Courtesy of the Rijksmuseum, Amsterdam

In 1539, Hans Sebald Beham depicts a winged Justice holding the scales firmly by the *summitas lini* (the end of the cord) and folding all fingers onto it, looking in the opposite direction (Figure 3.13). At her feet, three objects allude to ancient metrology, which is to say, the science of measurement – a *muid*, a weight and a meter. Errors, frauds and disputes in the act of weighing were a common feature of early modern times, as measurement was dependent on a variety of parameters: 'the origin of merchandise, the place and role of economic agents depending on whether they were selling or buying, the nature of customers and their role on the international market, depending on whether they were exposed to foreign currency.'[21]

Lady Justice's power grip over the scales serves to indicate who controls metrological power. Her binding role, to avoid disputes and frauds, is to signal that her weighing ability is located above any earthly system of measure. Her wings suggest that her power is divine, magical, located above any human intervention. She does not allow a better grasp of the various measures of the world; her grip is rather a visual rhetoric aiming at imposing a superior order, wherein political influences condition the economical rules of trade. Beham evidences the visual distortion of both physical and juridical weighing, indicating that the hand gesture of a winged *Justitia* will firmly put an end to indefinite quarrels. Lady Justice, depicted here as Fortitude, appears as the mediator of collateral agencies. She stands as the indispensable virtue of fair trade and honest merchants, vouching for the correct measure of the objects at her feet. Her hand gesture reigns over everyday adjudication used by merchants in current transactions.

Holding the scales: an archetype of honest weighing

As an archetype of honest weighing, Lady Justice's scales serve to evidence the proper method of weighing to avoid fraud. In a strikingly detailed piece of legislation in the *Theodosian Code*, Constantine singles out those who are fraudulent in measuring, slyly giving a turn to the scale with their fingers in order to press down the pans:

> When gold is paid, it shall be received with level pans (*æqua lance*) and equal weights (*libramentis paribus*) in such a fashion, that the end of the

cord (*summitas lini*) is held with two fingers, the remaining three being free and extended towards the tax-receiver (*susceptor*) so as not to depress the weights (*pondera*) by restraining either of the pans suspended from the tongue (*examen*) of the balance, but so as to permit the level and equal movement of the balance (*stater*).[22]

This remarkably precise text provides the essential rules on how to depict an honest use of the scales. The insistence on weighing honestly echoes Leviticus 19:35–6: 'Do not use dishonest standards when measuring length, weight or quantity. Use honest scales and honest weights.' The correct finger position already appears in the iconography of the goddess Aequitas/Dikaiosynê in Alexandrine tetradrachms at the end of the Aurelian period.[23] The goddess is depicted with her right hand

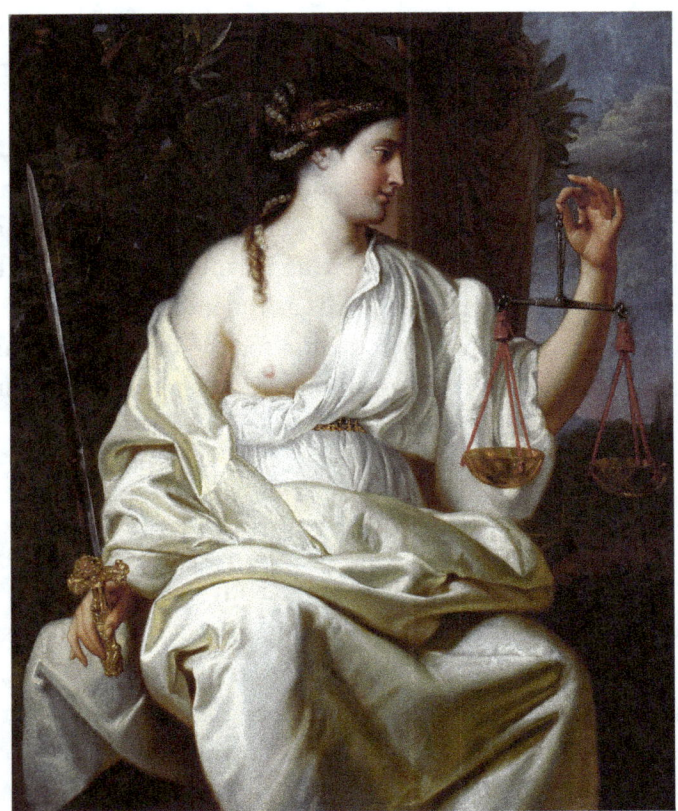

Figure 3.14: *Allegory of Lady Justice*, Flemish School, end of seventeenth century. By permission of the Ashmolean Museum, Oxford.

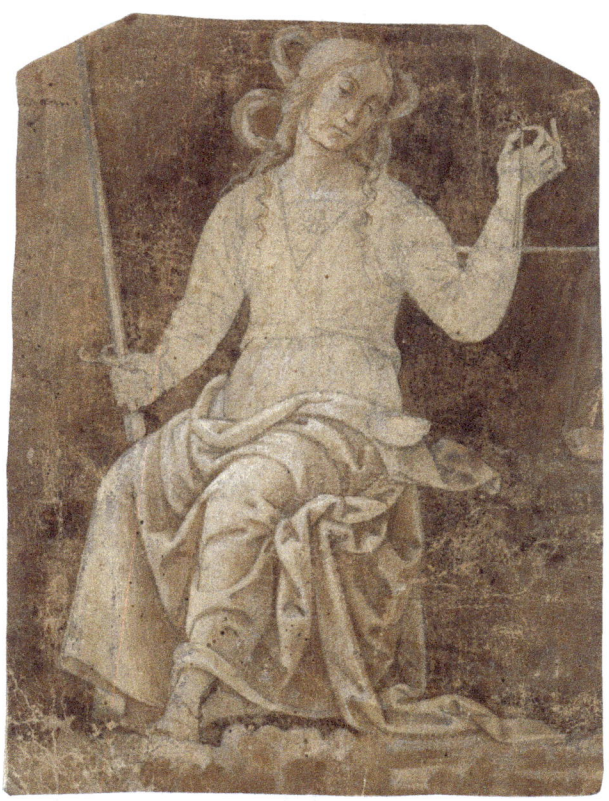

Figure 3.15: *Allegory of Lady Justice*, Perugino circle, c. 1510–23. By permission of the Pierpont Morgan Library, New York

showing three fingers only: the first two fingers hold the two pans of the scales, while the other three are shown in extension, intentionally standing away from the weighing instrument. It is important, according to the legal text, that the free fingers be visible to the official controller of weighing procedures (the *zygostatai*) to establish the justness of the process.

The correct posture of the fingers is carefully depicted by several early modern artists (Figure 3.14). An artist from the circle of Perugino adopts this pattern as early as 1510–23 (Figure 3.15). So does Marten de Vos in an engraving executed by Crispin de Passe the Elder, a full-length portrait of Dame Justice (1580–8) (Figure 3.16). The scales are held in her left hand and suspended by a cord (*summitas lini*) to avoid any depression of the pan (*lanx*). The first two digits (thumb and index finger) hold the top of the instrument, whereas the three other fingers

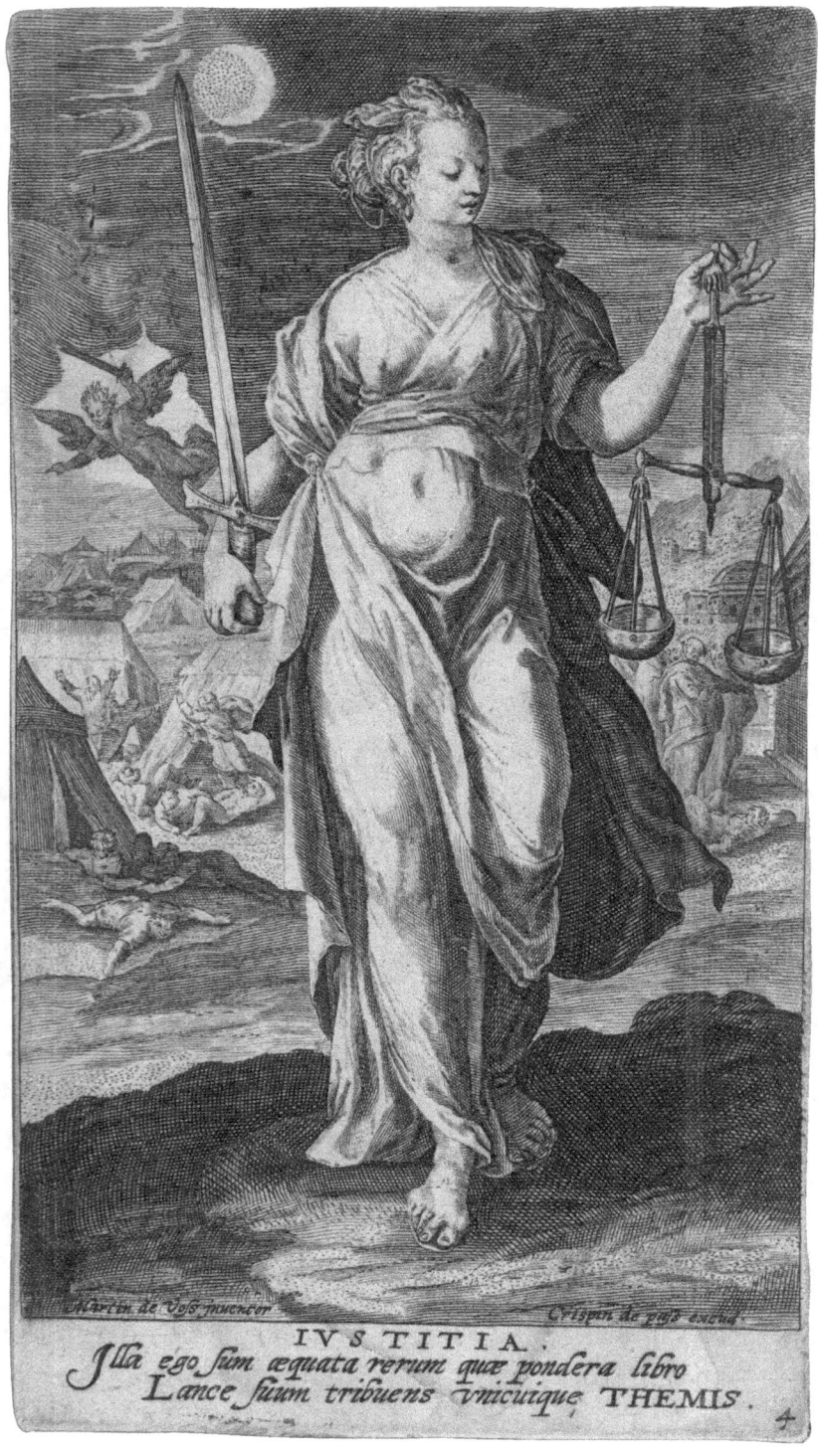

IVS TITIA.
Illa ego sum æquata rerum quæ pondera libro
Lance suum tribuens vnicuique THEMIS.

4

Figure 3.16: Martin de Vos in an engraving executed by Crispin de Passe the Elder, a full-length portrait of Dame Justice, 1580–8. Courtesy of the Rijksmuseum, Amsterdam

are shown outstretched and separated. The Latin motto added below insists on the obligation of just weighing: 'Illa ego sum aequata rerum quæ pondera libro lance suum tribuens unicuique Themis' (I, Themis, am the one who puts in balance equal things by their weight and I am the one who renders to each his due by using the levelled pans of the scales). The very essence of Justice (render to each his due) is compared to the subjective agency of Themis. Her watchful eye checks the equipollence of the pans in front of a reward scene whereas behind her right hand holding an upward sword, a scene of punishment is depicted.

A slight variation is introduced in a version of Dame Justice engraved after Hendrick Goltzius by his stepson Jacob Matham, in 1597 (Figure 3.11). Instead of using the first two digits, *Justitia* holds the axis of the balance with her thumb and middle finger, leaving her index finger free to point. The Latin motto inscribed below also hints at the importance of just weighing: 'Aequa judicii suspendo singula lance / Nec me divitie, nec me data munera flectunt' (I suspend my judgments only to the force of a level scales / Neither wealth nor gifts will bend me). The hand posture combines here a deictic gesture (pointing index finger) with a mimetic one (the weighing of a balance such as everyday merchants use). In this context, Josse de Damhouder's Janus-faced Justice, who appears to be giving a turn to the scale with her left little finger, adds an intriguing pattern to the depiction of mundane Justice (Figure 1.7). Damhouder probably indicates here the antithetical power of legal performance in delivering the law.[24]

The watchful eye combined with precision handling

One particularly skilful rendition of honest weighing is Raphael's allegory of Justice, from the Room of Constantine in the Vatican Palace (Figure 3.17). Commissioned in 1509, it has usually attracted scholars because of the presence of a naturalistically painted ostrich as an arcane hieroglyph for justice.[25] But the way *Justitia* holds her scales, at the height of her acute vision, also needs elaboration. The unusual finger posture (index and middle finger outstretched and simultaneously holding the scales in equilibrium) is related to the agency of her watchful eyes. The precision handling of the fingers converges with the axis of her vision so as to convey the idea that she herself acts as the ancient

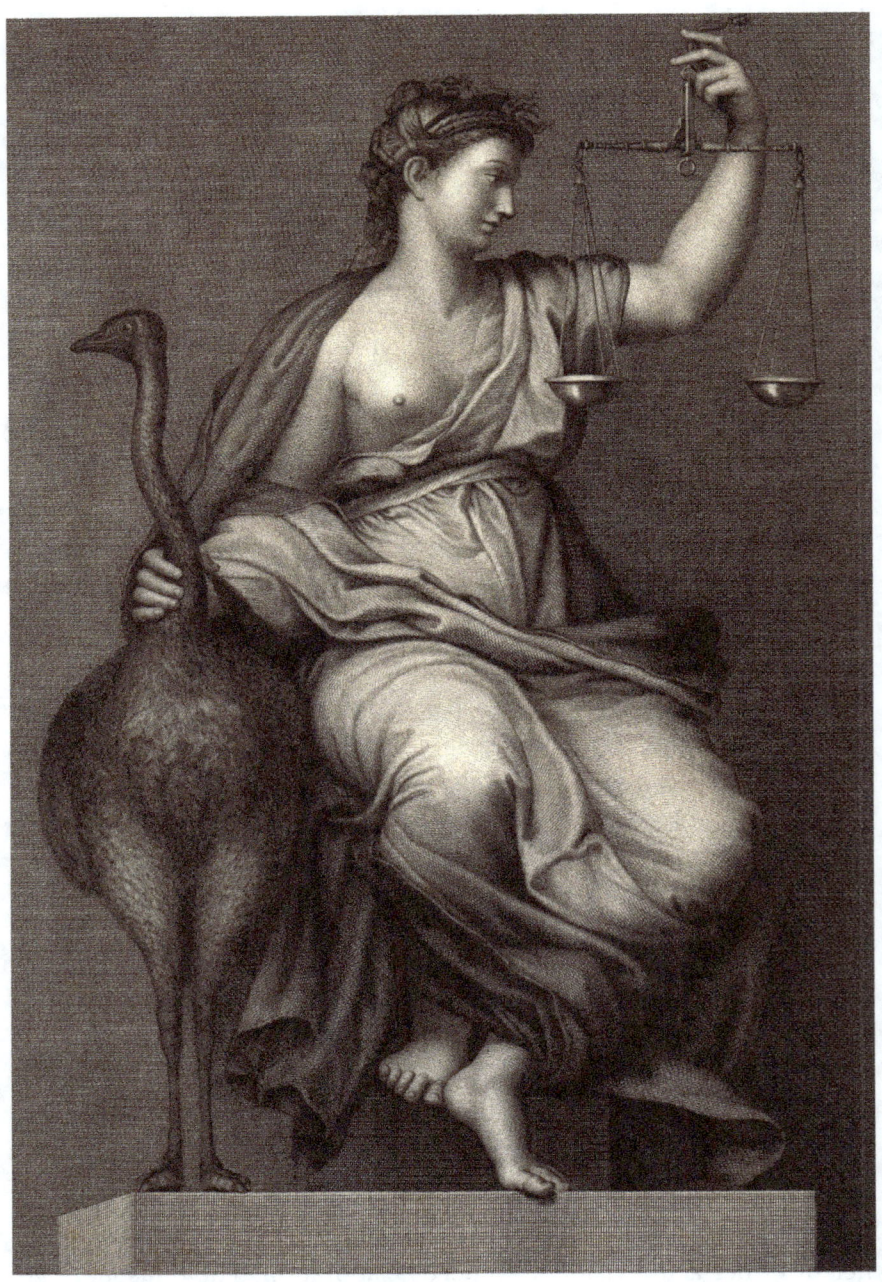

Figure 3.17: Copy of Raphael's *Justitia*, Room of Constantine, Vatican Palace. *Figure of Justice*, Harvard Art Museums/Fogg Museum, Gift of Regina Slatkin. Photograph © President and Fellows of Harvard College, 1979.344 Harvard Museum

zygostatai (the official controllers of the weighing procedures). Eye gesture and hand gesture converge in a strikingly efficient composition. Raphael indicates that a watchful eye over the weighing process best conveys the idea of an equitable Justice.

The motion of the eye is also a gesture; it adds a supplementary binding force to the depiction of weighing. In one of the earliest treatises devoted exclusively to the art of gestures, *L'arte de' cenni* (1616), the lawyer Giovanni Bonifacio (1547–1645) describes and elucidates a vast and comprehensive range of bodily actions.[26] His goal is to deal with the mute expressiveness of body language in order to show how all liberal and mechanical arts make use of this knowledge. One of these meaningful gestures is especially assigned to Justice: 'Voler veder il tutto' (Wishing to see everything). In his account of bodily gesture, vision is pinpointed as her most active gesture: her eyes are living manifestations of her symbolic agency. While a gesture may be defined as a physical movement of the hands, arms, face or body with the intent to convey meaning or information, Lady Justice's active eyesight is granted a penetrating agency of its own:

> The gesture of *Justitia* is to aim at seeing each thing with piercing eyesight, just as it is expected from the judge. Plato says that *Justitia* sees everything and it is for this reason that Ancient priests called her 'seer of all things'. Apuleius swears by the eye of the Sun and the eye of Justice: Ancient theologians stated that *Justitia* came from the middle of the throne of the Sun to signify that, just as the Sun does, she watches, moderates and maintains all things. [. . .] Just as ears are the principal instruments for the knowledge of things, eyes are better testimonies as they are more trustworthy.[27]

Conclusion

As anthropologists know well, the gestural grammar sketched here cannot be reduced to a firm chronology. Depictions of gesture change over the course of the *longue durée*, by slow reiterations or invisible twists. The principle of decorum is often more telling than the evolutionary gradient. Instead of seeing the scales as an objective instrument of measurement, and thus an appropriate symbol of fairness, we found that the body of Lady Justice assigns her subjective agency to weighing justly. Ideally, mutual confidence should characterise honest weighing. *Justitia's* holding of the scales should reflect both a correct handling of the fulcrum and a careful balance of the pans. The advent of a new mechanical and experimental know-how (weighing precisely with chemists' scales or manipulating a weaponised sword) is entrusted to a female allegory who is supposed to prevent metrological disorders. Law is depicted as a conjectural science as citizens should not be deceived into believing in the power of righteous metrics. Lady Justice's avatars, however, often reflect attacks on her *gravitas* and *dignitas*. She is frequently depicted as a perverse figure, playing shrewd games to circumvent the laws of good measurement. The image of Lady Justice is thus either highly admired or cynically dethroned. She finds herself caught in an inescapable trap: Justice is bound to a divine impulse, imposed on her from above, but she also exercises her discipline on earth, engaging with intricacies, false weights and metrological variations. Lady Justice cannot escape the paradoxes of her body, as a closer inspection of her posture in the next chapter will show.

Notes

1. Battista Fiera, *De Justicia Pingenda Fiera Mantuani Dialogus. Interloquutores Mantynias Momus*, in *Hymni Divini. Sylve Melanisius* (Mantua: Francesco Bruschi, 1515; reprinted as *De iusticia pingenda: On the Painting of Justice: A Dialogue between Mantegna and Momus*, trans., intro. and notes James Wardrop, London: Lion and Unicorn Press, 1957; and in Italian translation as 'De Iusticia pingenda Baptistæ Fiæræ Mantuani Dialogus', trans. Rodolfo Signorini, in Luca Chiavoni, Gianfranco Ferlisi and Maria Vittoria Grassi (eds), *Leon Battista Alberti e Il Quattrocento: Studi in Onore di Cecil Grayson e Ernst H. Gombrich*, Atti del Convegno Internazionale (Mantua, 29–31 October 1998) (Florence: Leo S. Olschki, 2001), pp. 381–434. A Portuguese translation is now available online, ed. Marcilio Franca Filho, Bruno Amaro Lacerda and France Murachco, <http://www4.uninove.br/ojs/index.php/prisma/article/viewFile/3206/2140>.
2. E. H. Gombrich, '*Icones Symbolicæ*: The Visual Image in Neo-Platonic Thought', *Journal of the Warburg and Courtauld Institutes* 11 (1948), pp. 178–9.
3. Bruno Roy, 'À propos d'un geste antisémite décrit par Huguccio de Pise', in *Le geste et les gestes au Moyen Âge* (Aix-en-Provence: Presses Universitaires de Provence, 1998), pp. 557–70.

4. Saint Augustine, *Corpus scriptorum ecclesiasticorum Latinorum*, vol. 50, *Quæstiones Veteris et Novi Testamenti* (Vindobonae: F. Tempsky, 1908), p. 41, quæstio XV. Temperantia justitia facit perfectos, nimia incurrit peccatum.

5. The most widely used scales (*libra, lanx, statera, trutina*) at this time included a central pivot and two pans. *Trutina* was a large scale with two trays, and *statera* and *moneta* are names for the smaller scales of similar structure. The reliability of its equilibrium is ensured by the equidistance of the pivot from the scales as well as by the uniformity of the standard weights employed in weighing.

6. Massimo Leone, 'The Frowning Balance: Semiotic Insinuations on the Visual Rhetoric of Justice', *Semiotica* 216 (2017), pp. 41–62.

7. Christine Seeber, *Untersuchungen zur Darstellung des Totengerichts im alten Ägypten* (Munich: Deutscher Kunstverlag, 1976).

8. André Chastel, *Le geste dans l'art* (Paris: Liana Lévi, 2001).

9. Johann Eberhard Scheifler, *Vita Christi Concionatoria tribus libris comprehensa, primus liber* (Dillingen: Heirs of Joannis Caspari Bencard, 1697), pp. 302–3; my emphasis: 'Habet manus ista quinque symbolicos digitos. [. . .] 1. Primum minimus digitus Christi auricularis significat obedientiam [. . .] 2. Secundus digitus, qui vocatur medicus, erat ingens pietas Salvatoris, qua venam cordium peccatorum tetigit [. . .] 3. Tertius digitus annularis robustior, fortiorque cæteris erant miræ operationes Christi per vitam ejus [. . .] Hic etiam digitus trinos habet articulos; unus est potentiæ ejus in operando [. . .]. Alter erat justitia ejus in discernendo iniquo ab aequo, ac vicissim. Tertius articulus erat operæ misericordiæ. 4. Digitus quartus erat ejus prædicatio, unde merito vocatur index [. . .] Digitus Christi quintus fuit passio Domini Jesu.' The same author adds: 'Minor digitus in nostra manu sit humilis, facilis, hilarisque paritio, & obedientia. Secundus digitus medicus sit temperantia continens, modesta, ac abstinens. Tertius isque medius, ac longior digitus est justitia cum triplici articulo, restitutione ablatorum, debitorum persolutione, ac maleficiorum punitione. Digitus quartus & index est prudentia, cum articulo itidem trino, praeteritorum memoria, poenitentia intelligentia, ac fururorum providentia. Quintus digitus in manu nostra pollex est generosa fortitudo, habens geminos articulos, audacem agressionem arduorum, fortem perpessionem durorum.'

10. Thomas Lentes, 'Counting Piety in the Late Middle Ages', in Bernhard Jussen (ed.), *Ordering Medieval Society: Perspectives on Intellectual and Practical Modes of Shaping Social Relations*, trans. Pamela Selwyn (Philadelphia: University of Pennsylvania Press, 2001), pp. 55–91.

11. Andrea de Jorio, *La mimica degli antichi investigata nel gestire napoletano* (Naples: Dalla stamperia e cartiera del Fibreno, 1832), p. 2.

12. Francis Bacon, *The Advancement of Learning* (London: Henrie Tomes, 1605), book 2, 16.3.

13. Ray Birdwhistell, qtd in Tsuyoshi Kida, 'Appropriation du geste par les étrangers: le cas d'étudiants japonais apprenant le français', unpublished thesis, Université de Provence, 2005.

14. During the Late Middle Ages, the oratory part of Cicero's writings was largely ignored. In 1416, a complete manuscript of Quintilian's *Institutio Oratoria* was

discovered by Poggio Braccioloni in Saint Gall. See Jean-Claude Schmitt, *La raison des gestes dans l'Occident médiéval* (Paris: Gallimard, 1990), p. 370 n. 58. The impact of this discovery had a long-lasting influence throughout the fifteenth and sixteenth centuries.

15. J. Russell Sale, 'Protecting Fertility in Fra Filippo Lippi's *Portrait of a Woman with a Man at a Casement*', *Metropolitan Museum Journal* 51 (2016), pp. 64–83.

16. See M. C. Galassi, in *Bernardo Strozzi*, exhibition catalogue Rome, 1995, p. 43; C. Manzitti, *Bernardo Strozzi*, exhibition catalogue, Turin, 2012, pp. 159ff.

17. John Bulwer, *Chirologia, or The Natural Language of the Hand* (London: Thomas Harper, 1644), p. 166.

18. This figure is part of the allegorical programme of the salon of the manor house of the Saxon ruler of Hoflößnitz in Radebeul (c. 1634), executed by the Dresden court painters Christian Schiebling (1603–63) and Centurio Wiebel (1616–84).

19. *Code Civil des Français* (Paris: De l'imprimerie de la République, 1804), book 3, ch. 20, 'De la prescription'.

20. John Russell Napier, 'The Prehensile Movements of the Human Hand', *Journal of Bone and Joint Surgery* 38-B, no. 4 (1956), pp. 902–13; John Russell Napier, 'The Evolution of the Hand', *Scientific American* 207 (1962), pp. 56–62.

21. Leone, 'Frowning Balance', esp. p. 9.

22. *Theodosian Code* 12.7.1 *de Ponderatoribus*: 'Aurum quod infertur, æqua lance et libramentis paribus suscipiatur: scilicet, ut duobus digitis summitæ lini retineatur, tres reliqui liberi ad susceptorem emineant, nec pondera deprimant, nullo examinis libramento servato, nec aequis æ paribus suspenso statere momentis.' Michael F. Hendy, *Studies in the Byzantine Monetary Economy c. 300–1450* (Cambridge: Cambridge University Press, 1985), p. 329.

23. Filippo Carlà, *L'oro nella tarda antichità: aspetti economici e sociali* (Turin: Silvio Zamorani Editore, 2009), pp. 99–101.

24. Julie Stone Peters, *Law as Performance: Theatricality, Spectatorship, and the Making of Law in Ancient, Medieval, and Early Modern Europe* (Oxford: Oxford University Press, 2022).

25. Judith Resnik and Dennis E. Curtis, 'The Jayne Lecture: Representing Justice: From Renaissance Iconography to Twenty-First-Century Courthouses', *American Philosophical Society* 151, no. 2 (2007), pp. 139–83; Una Roman D'Elia, *Raphael's Ostrich* (University Park: Pennsylvania State University Press, 2015).

26. Born to a noble family in Rovigo, Bonifacio had practised as a lawyer and magistrate in Treviso, Venice and Vicenza. He also published several legal treatises and a history of Treviso. In his learned treatise, he acknowledges his debt to Andrea Alciato, Achille Bocchi or Pierio Valeriano. His interest in emblems, hieroglyphs and symbols is stated at the very beginning of his treatise.

27. The full quote is the following: Giovanni Bonifacio, *L'arte de' cenni: con la quale formandosi favela visibile, si tratta della muta eloquenza, che non e' altro che un facondo silentio* [. . .] (Vicenza: Francesco Grossi, 1616), p. 141, § 37: 'E Gesto di giustizia il voler veder ogni cosa con acutissima vista come al Giudice si richiede. Platone dice, che la Giustizia vede il tutto, e percio da gli antichi

Sacerdoti fù chiamata – veditrice di tutte le cose. Apuleio giura per l'occhio del Sole, e della Giustizia: Egli antichi Teologi dissero, che la giustizia usci di mezzo il trono del Sole per significare che, come il Sole, rimira, modera e mantiene tutte le cose. Da che non discorda quel detto: *Oculi Domini multo plus lucidiores sunt super Solem, & circumspicientes omnes vias hominis, & corda intuentes in absconditas partes.* [Eccl. 13] A. Gellio attribuisce alla Giustizia occhi acri, retti, & immobili, per esprimer che il Giudice non deve volgersi dall' honesto quà, e là rimirando, ma immobilmente sempre il giusto contemplare. Judex cuncta mirari debet, cio è per rimas inspicere, e come disse colui da picciolo pertugio cavare gran luce [. . .] Sicome gli orecchi sono principale instrumento d'apprender la cognitione delle cose, cosi à far fede sono più certi gli occhi; onde anco da i Leggisti è detto testis de visu quello che e buono, e sicuro. E Plauto chiama le mani d'una rossiana oculate, non orecchiute, perche solo credono quello che vedono, non quello che odono. Et Horatio dice che: *Segnius iritant animos demissa per aurem/Quam quæ sunt oculus subjecta fidelibus.* /Et Giustiniano chiama *oculatam fidem*, quando la cosa evidentemente è sottoposta a gli occhi & certissima, & è noto il proverbio che dice: *Pluris est oculatus testis unus quam auriti decem.* Cicerone cosi spiego questo cenno. *Ego autem cum omnia collustrarem oculis, animadverti colunt illam, etc.* Questo gesto di vedere il tutto s'attribuisce a Dio. [. . .].'

Chapter 4

Lady Justice's posture: sitting, standing or walking?

What looks stable and hieratic, through the figure of a sedentary Justice, may be no more than an artificial harmony. Far from naïve modalities inherently inferior to her attributes, the question of posture possesses a unique capacity to foster mindfulness, bodily empowerment or threshold awareness. Law lives in the multisensory performances of gestures. We tend to overlook some of the most obvious physical postures because we are not aware that they retain symbolic significance. Sitting or standing poses are carefully scrutinised, as they bring to light the more hidden connections between temperaments, passions and the signs they can produce, just as jurists must continuously examine the motion of the body, facial expressions and any gesture, if they are to judge well. Allegories of Justice also reveal the motion of the soul.

Manifestations of judicial impartiality have attracted scrutiny in legal scholarship for centuries. Yet, we lack studies of how judicial postures and gestures convey specific meanings and how they play a role in influencing and transmitting lay impressions of judicial values. The judge's sedentary posture is part of his gestural ethics and is said to reveal his judicial temperament. This chapter aims at restoring the symbolic meanings of these postures: Lady Justice is not always depicted sitting down; far from it. Standing, animated by a warrior *virtus* or a desire to flee, *Justitia* lends herself to surprising metamorphoses. After a discussion of Justice's temperament, this chapter considers images of Justice seated, then standing, then walking, before finally leaving the court for the public square and the quotidian life of the city.[1]

Judicial temperament

This study starts with an account of the medical language of the perfectly balanced body. Since Justice is said to be an affection of the soul, it is in our interest not to ignore the humoral basis of ancient physiology. The absence of passionate movements of the mind echoes a physiological ideal, the notion that there is a correct humoral balance for achieving health and equanimity. Medieval physicians believed that there was an original stability of the physiological constitution of men, a balance of qualities, a distribution of humours, then named *temperamentum ad iustitiam*.[2] Following Galen and Avicenna, they discussed the notion of *temperamentum* (constitution) in terms of *temperamentum ad pondus* and *temperamentum ad iustitiam*. The first involves a perfectly tempered constitution, lying at a middle point between two extremes. The second, the *temperamentum ad iustitiam*, always implies the notion of 'proportion', thus varying from case to case. Moreover, the physical constitution *temperamentum ad iustitiam* was called *realis*, since only a proportioned rather than an exact (*punctualis*) configuration of humours may be effectively applied to natural entities. In this medical context, the *temperamentum ad iustitiam* was considered the ultimate archetype for reaching health.

In his anatomical treatise, *Physiologia* (1567), the French physician Jean Fernel, explains how a complexion is moderated by *iustitia* or *pondus* and gives the following account of the *temperamentum ad justitiam*:

> We will grasp mentally a midpoint of the whole span that is encompassed; being separated from these limits by an equal interval, it will be called both eukraton (i.e., temperate) and symmetron (i.e., consistent and moderate): and not simply, but in its own kind and form. It is like justice, absolutely even-handed, because it has achieved that honorable and consistent fairness by which, freed (so to speak) of all details and parts, it conducts itself to good effect, in integrity and in conformity to its nature, and faultlessly carries out every function to which its nature directs it.[3]

Fernel's understanding of the humoral doctrine through the notion of justice is important for two reasons. On the one hand, he presents the prevailing assumptions about the nature of human temperaments which underlay the Renaissance system of medical theory, in order to give a *physical* definition of justice. Humoral theory posits an interdependency between the body and emotions. On the other hand, he gives to the medieval understanding of the *temperamentum ad justitiam* a causal explanation, in typical Aristotelian fashion.

This medical account opens up an investigation into the character of the judge and challenges the assumption according to which good judgment is properly characterised by emotional distance and disconnection of the mind. Indeed, as we shall see, the postures of Lady Justice both endorsed and challenged that belief. The supposed incompatibility of empathy and judicial 'objectivity' emerges as a crucial concern. The jurist Guillaume Maran (1549–1621), from Toulouse, admits that in a fiery trial, the judge may find it difficult to contain his strongest emotions:

> I freely confess that it is very difficult and almost impossible that in a thorny trial stings and bites should not be encountered and that where there is emotion and restraint there should not be heat and fire, which pushes and emanates words of ardour, and are contrary to our style, which God wanted us to mark by his own example (and by) the mark of the gentleness and cordial humility that Jesus Christ wanted to teach us by his word and deeds.[4]

This is why textbooks dealing with judicial ethics usually recommend a certain caution in behaviour. The judge must avoid anger at all costs. Maran alludes here to the deadly sin of wrath, frequently compared in the Old Testament to thorns and nettles. *Justitia* is the antithesis of *libido vindictae* (the wicked will to be avenged), one of the main features of wrath. In a print from a series of nine woodcuts depicting scenes of the life of Christ combined with depictions of the sibyls dating from 1521 to 1523, Jacob Cornelisz van Oostsanen and Lucas van Leyden draw a meaningful contrast between *Justicia* and *Ira* (Figure 4.1). The allegorical portrait of *Justicia*, holding an upright sword, stands between the mockery of Christ (top left) and the scourging of Christ (top right). Below, the allegory of *Ira* (a tyrant with a scimitar) stands between the Tiburian sibyl holding a maimed hand, in memory of the hand of the guard who inflicted a blow on Christ at his trial (bottom left), and the Agrippan sibyl, carrying

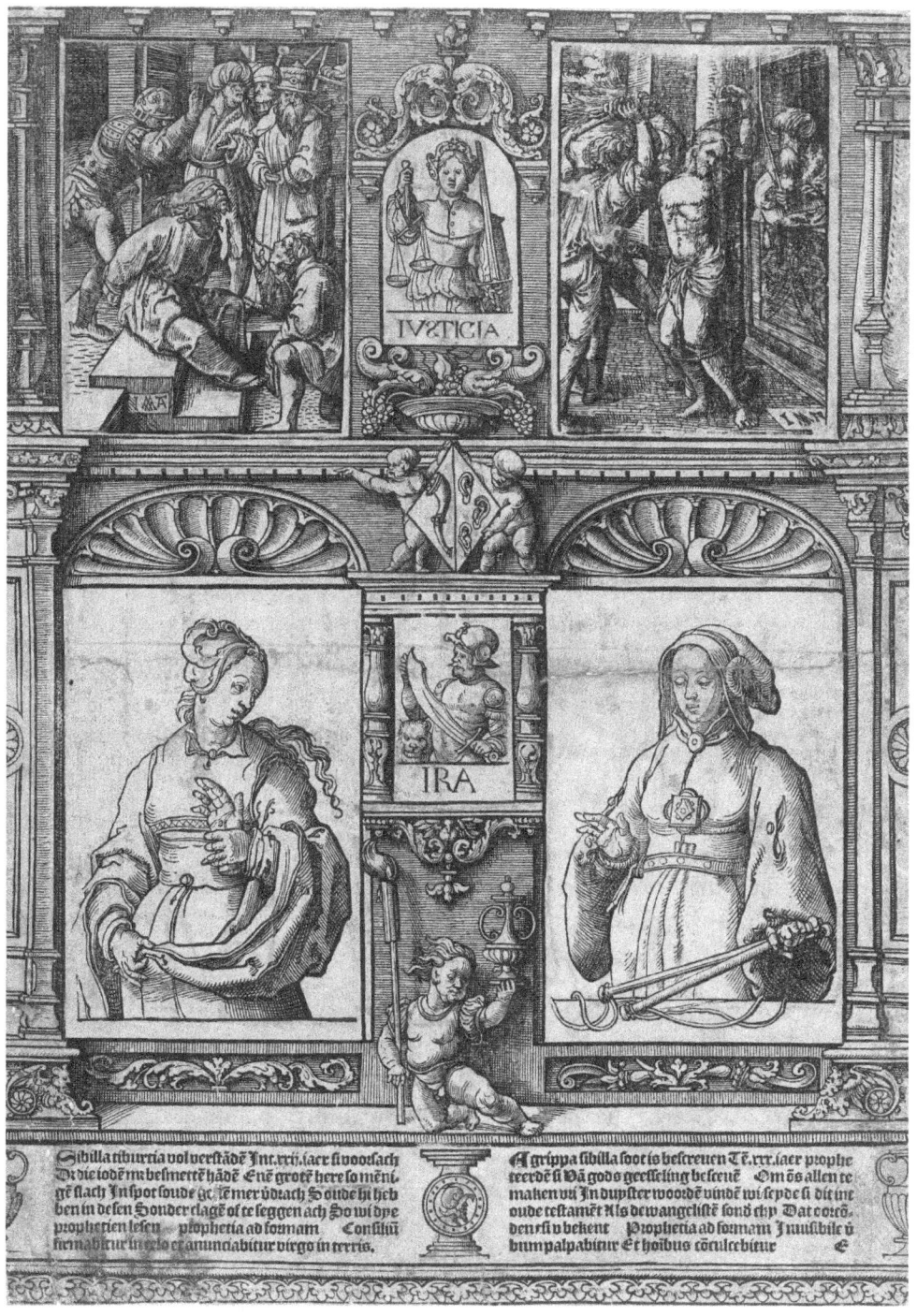

Figure 4.1: Jacob Cornelisz van Oostsanen and Lucas van Leyden, c. 1521–3, representations from the life of Christ with sibyls, virtues and vices. Top: *Justicia* between the mockery of Christ and the scourging of Christ; bottom: *Ira*, between the Tiburian Sibyl and the Agrippa sibyl. Courtesy of the Rijksmuseum, Amsterdam

a whip, as a reminder of the scourging of Christ. The print opposes Lady Justice's sword, an image of God's anger, a good kind of wrath, against Wrath's scimitar, held by a zealous tyrant, a vicious portrait of the effects of hatred on man. In the overall context of the iconographical programme, developed by explanatory notes in Dutch and Latin, the sibyls are considered as the ancient visionaries who prophesied the birth, suffering and resurrection of Christ. In his analysis of the print, Huigen Leeflang argues that the appearance of Justice between the mockery and the flogging of Christ can almost be called ironic.[5]

If he does not want to arouse contempt, the judge must find the right distance, which presupposes seriousness but also benevolence, authority without excessive familiarity. Jean de Coras, in his *Petit discours des parties et office d'un bon et entier juge*, claims:

> The judge must therefore make himself easy and accessible to the litigants with an honest seriousness, while not admitting them out of private familiarity, from which arises contempt, or even, as Theophrastus said, hatred and enmity. This is why Lacides Cyrenian, an officer of King Attalus, replied that one should look at the images, that is to say the Kings and Magistrates, only from a distance, especially as an extended familiarity diminishes the admiration of their authority.[6]

It should be noted here that the kings and magistrates themselves are referred to as 'images'. If 'image' is to be understood here in the sense of a 'representation that is the object of worship or veneration', the role of the image as 'model, paragon of virtue' must also be emphasised. De Coras defines a proper ethical distance, necessary for the office of the good judge; it relates to what the Romans called *dignitas*, a certain presence assured by the office, and which the individual must simply inhabit, occupy, but with which, as an individual, he is never confused.[7]

As a trope which aims at conferring *dignitas*, corporeal allegory may serve to articulate the concept of ethical distance. Law and order is more often conveyed as a physical static countenance; priority is given to postures where the ruling figure is seated on a throne. Nevertheless, figures of Lady Justice oscillate between sitting and standing postures, showing that the issue of judgment remains a source of tension between the judge's body and his innermost feelings.

Sitting judges

The majority of early modern and classical allegories of *Justitia* high-light her role as a sitting goddess: as an avatar of the sitting judge, her body is meant to represent a figure of authority empowered by its dignity and stability. In his treatise on *Mundane Justice*, Josse de Damhouder wrote that those who administer Justice need to be seated, in order to enunciate their judgment in a serene and free state of mind, because it is in the quiet posture of *recte sedendo* that the mind finds wisdom and prudence.[8] The injunction for judges to be seated when pronouncing their sentence is even explicitly quoted in the *Summa* (a manual of moral theology) of Antoninus, a Dominican friar and Arch-bishop of Florence from 1446 to 1459: 'Laws have ordained that the judge, while proffering his judgment, has to be seated in order to judge in a calm state of mind.'[9]

When the chiefs of the Greek army constituted themselves into a court to rule on the respective claims of Ajax and Ulysses to the inher-itance of the arms of Achilles, the debate opened as soon as the judges had taken their seats. The act of taking one's seat corresponds precisely to the opening of the trial, as Ovid records (*Metamorphoses* 13.1): 'Consedere duces, et vulgi stante corona' (The chiefs were seated, and the soldiers formed a circle round them). In this sense, sitting indicates that one has entered the judicial space, even though the meeting happens outside the courthouse precincts.

The effects of the sitting posture are intertwined with professional habitus. If this posture is designed to encourage calm mental states, it also serves as what Pierre Bourdieu calls a *habitus*, a mental disposition that structures the experience of a human agent by incorporating objec-tive social conditions in him or her in the form of custom, but without determining his or her nature.[10] Gestural *habitus* exists, alongside what manifests itself in symbolic capital such as skills, taste, clothes or emblems. Acquiring competence in these types of behavioural norms is what we mean by acting like a lawyer. This is why they are particularly well adapted to the ethics of emblematic literature coined by jurists. The motif of the sitting judges appears in Andrea Alciato's emblem 'In Senatum boni Principis' (In the Senate of a Good Prince) at verses 5–6:

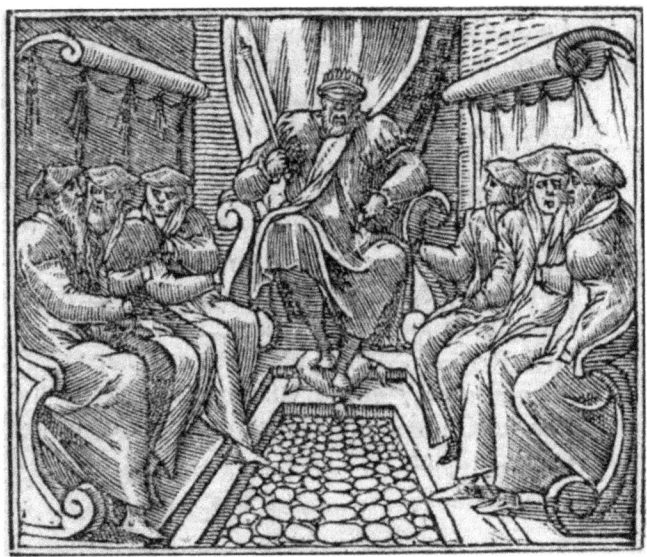

Figure 4.2: Andrea Alciato's *Emblèmes*, 'Sur le Senat d'ung bon Prince', illustration of the 1549 Lyons edition, Macé Bonhomme for Guillaume Rouillé, p. 176. By permission of the University of Glasgow Archives & Special Collections, Stirling Maxwell collection

'Cur resident? Quia mente graves decet esse quieta Iuridicos, animo nec variare levi' (Why do they sit? – Because lawgivers should be grave, of a calm mind, and not change with inconstant thoughts).[11] The illustration of the emblem in the 1549 Lyon edition by Macé Bonhomme (Figure 4.2) shows the presiding judge elevated on a throne, surrounded by the three essential attributes of royalty: the crown, the sceptre and the cushion under his feet.

In the 1621 Tozzi edition, the commentary by Joannes Thuilius ('Why do judges sit?') offers a lengthy response. The commentary starts with a dazzling array of legal sources, quoted in full, starting with Justinian's *Novels* (82.3): 'Ordinary judges shall sit continually, they shall hold court in the Royal Basilica and in the various halls where they at present preside.'[12] Another source from the *Novels* (71.1) is added, underlining that the sitting posture is considered a privilege: 'We decree this in order that they [i.e. persons of illustrious rank] may not be compelled to be seated with the magistrates, when the latter decide their cases, or to stand before them as litigants, which would be equally improper.'[13] To these quotes, Thuilius adds ancient authorities such as Aulus Gellius (*Attic Nights* 6.8), where Scipio, engaged in the siege of a town, once 'sat holding court in his camp'.[14]. He also refers to an epistle by Pliny the Younger (*Epistles* 6.33) where the judges sitting at the Centumviral Court contrast with the advocates, appearing on both sides.[15] The most interesting quotes, though, refer to Cicero's speeches. In *Pro Rabirio Postumo* (6.9.7–8) he distinguishes between the office of the juror and the duty of the *praetor* or judge: 'I have gone through all judicial offices, I have been the accuser in causes of extortion and rapine, I have likewise *sat* on a jury, and *presided* as praetor or judge in criminal causes'.[16]

Thuilius also borrows his argumentation from poetical sources, such as a verse taken from Propertius (4.18.37), 'Minos sits as the judge of the infernal abode'.[17] Thuilius concludes that 'Judges are seated because it is proper for them to be grave, still and of calm mind, and not easily moved.'[18] The concluding remarks are first drawn from the Bible (Exodus 18:13): 'Moses sat to decide disputes among the people.'[19] Christ is said to be sitting on his throne of glory 'in sede maiestatis suæ'. The sitting posture, says Thuilius, denotes a quiet body. One of the most telling examples refers again to Cicero (*Brutus* 24), who replies to his interlocutor: 'facilius sermo explicetur, sedentes agamus' (To make the interview easier, let's talk in a seated position!). In an elegant oxymoron, Cicero joins the verb *agere*, whose common sense expresses movement, and which here relates to speaking, to the present participle *sedentes* (while remaining seated), which expresses the opposite idea.[20] Thuilius adds that the sitting posture mirrors the judge's equanimity. The judge ought to project the institutional values of dignity, authority and stability.

In his description of *Mundane Justice*, Damhouder lists the sitting posture as the first 'proprietas' of Justice and he gives a similar account of this characterisation.[21] The judge needs to be calm and of independent mind, *ab humanis affectibus desfæcato* (from whom all human feeling has been expelled). To a panoply of biblical examples, he adds Aristotle's testimony: 'In quiescendo enim et sedendo anima sit sciens et prudens' (Sitting and resting, the soul becomes knowing and cautious). But the Latin translation of the quoted fragment (*Physics* 7.3.247b10) actually corrupts Aristotle's original text: 'For it is by the fact that the soul achieves calm by abandoning its natural turmoil that one becomes prudent and skilful.'[22] This corrupted Latin translation of Aristotle's fragment was widely circulated at the time. Damhouder introduces the idea of sitting, where Aristotle's text speaks only of 'appeasing the soul' (*tô gar kathistasthaï tên psukhên*).

In his *Tractatus de sententia e re iudicata*, Sigismondo Scaccia (1564–1634), judge, lawyer and auditor of the Inquisition in Malta, states:

> The reason for this disposition is that the soul, in the position of bodily rest, becomes more prudent; for the movement of the body corresponds to the movement of the soul, which therefore does not enjoy the firmness of reason. But when the body sits down, the soul works intelligently, and thus becomes more prudent; the intelligence is therefore not distracted by any other operation.[23]

Scaccia adds that in the seated position the judge enjoys majesty, hence the need to pay him greater respect, which is why the parties, unlike the judge passing sentence, must stand.[24]

The legal status of the sitting judge

Judicial posture was also subject to regulations, as the French jurisconsult Cardin le Bret attests:

> Judges must be seated while judging and giving their opinion. Chapter XII
>
> At all times and in all places, Judges have been accustomed to dispensing justice, not by standing or walking, but by sitting on seats or chairs ordered for this purpose in all courts where justice has been accustomed to be dispensed. [. . .]. That is why our Mercurials of 1581 prohibit the Councillors [. . .] from allowing the public prosecutors or the parties to plead before them on leaving the Palace, in the lower courts of that palace, or in the streets outside, but to go and hold their hearing in the large public prosecutors' room, sitting on one of the public prosecutors' benches, on pain of nullity [. . .].[25]

The behavioural strictures of judicial rituals drew many lawyers to break the rules. To pass a judgment standing, or at any rate not sitting, was one of the examples of *nullitas ratione modi*. The invalidity of judgments and decrees pronounced by the standing judge (*stans*) is ordinarily questioned by civilists and affirmed by canonists. In an amusing passage from Rabelais' *Tiers Livre* reporting the trial of Judge Bridlegoose, we are told that a judgment delivered standing, or anyhow not sitting, is void.[26] The judge needs to be *sedens*; if he is not, the judgment is subject to annulment on appeal. Rabelais pokes fun at the glossator's expense: 'quid si in culo doleret, quod sedere non posset. Item qui si in ipsa sede nec sederet, nec staret: sed jaceret?' (What happens if his arse hurts and he is not capable of sitting down? And what if he is not able to sit in that seat, if he can't stand in it either, but he has to lie in it?). And what if the judge was sitting on a horse? In a high tower? On a swing? Giovanni d'Andrea discussed the rule in detail, putting forward several exceptions in which a judgment pronounced by a standing judge remains valid; for example, 'in the case of fear, when the judge might proclaim (sitting) on a horse so as to flee immediately after proclaiming the sentence'.[27] In his *Arresta Amorum*, Benoît Le Court addresses the same *casus perplexus*.[28] But instead of giving a pragmatic explanation, he prefers to answer by quoting Plautus (*Mostellaria*, line 1103), when the slave Tranio answers, 'my mind is much sharper when I'm sitting down'.

The mocking of the magistrates' sedentary posture is a counterpart to their elevation. In his panegyric to Emperor Anastasius (491–518), written in Constantinople by the sixth-century author Priscian, the sitting judge is explicitly compared to a celestial image: 'Judicis, ipse sedens, cœlestis imago, / Per te respondes populis oracula sancta' (You yourself, image of the heavenly judge, want to sit in judgment, you yourself give your sacred answers to the people).[29]

Sedendo et dormiendo?

This identification between sitting, quietness and a certain form of wisdom can be found in several sermons of Master Eckhart. Commenting on Luke 2:46 (Jesus was sitting in the temple and preaching), he writes, 'That he was seated means resting. For he who sits is more ready to do clear things than he who moves or stands. Sitting means rest, standing means work, moving means instability'.[30]

In a short story entitled 'Sedendo et Quiescendo', Samuel Beckett revisits the Aristotelian topos.[31] Using the quotation 'Sedendo et quiescendo anima efficitur prudens' (By sitting and remaining quiet the soul gains wisdom), he deliberately undermines the convention of philosophical quietism, implying that it amounts to slothfulness. The seated

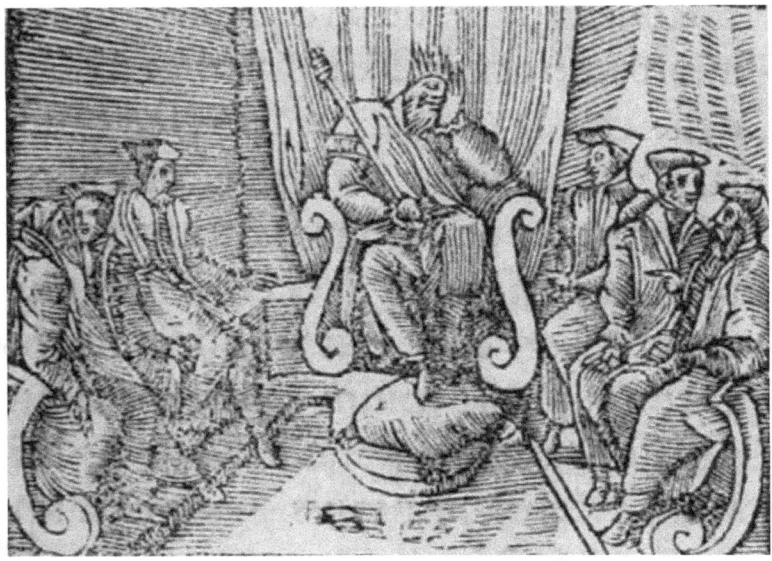

Figure 4.3: Pierre Coustau, *Pegma cum narrationibus philosophicis* (Lyon: Macé Bonhomme, 1555), p. 209. Illustration of the emblem 'In perfunctoriè iudicantes. Μήδὲ δίκην δικάσῃς πρὶν ἀμφοῖν μῦθον ἀκούσῃς' (Against judges who are indifferent to the causes they defend. Don't give judgment until you have heard both sides of the case). By permission of the University of Glasgow Archives & Special Collections, Stirling Maxwell collection

position of the judges may also lead them to sleep. An emblem by the French lawyer Pierre Coustau (1555) warns against this peril, indicating the presiding judge's sleeping posture by a typical melancholic gesture (Figure 4.3). Its French version, by Lanteaume de Romieu, bears the title 'Contre les Juges dormans au siege & puis se reveillans se tiennent au cleret' (Against Judges sleeping on their seats, and when waking up, abusing claret wine).[32] The epigram below adds:

> Against judges who are indifferent to the causes they defend.
> Until both sides have been heard, it is impossible to judge. While Philippe Aemathius was delivering his judgments to the people, an immense torpor invaded his exhausted members. As he was finally active, he threw his vows into the urn. Ignoring the details of the trial, he judged the accused guilty. While the lawyers are so exhausted that they become hoarse from debating an abstruse trial, sleep often overwhelms the bodies of the magistrates. How can you measure the pros and cons of an obscure case if your limbs go numb in the middle of the pleading?[33]

The weaknesses of the flesh also affect judges, who are here subjected to a fierce satire. The possibility of creating bridges between affectivity and rationality is not an easy task: what appears as an outer sense of deepened awareness, concentration and insight may hide the simple fact that the judge has fallen into numbness. The motif of the well-fed or drunk judge is particularly developed by Daumier's *Men of Justice* lithographs of 1845. To heighten the satiric content, the judge's reclining posture is easily trivialised by caricature: it is a fragile thing that can be shattered by very minor misconduct. Because the judge's throne is subjected to public scrutiny, a minimal postural shift will immediately mark a moral decline. Any representation of judges' seated postures is ethically invested. The implicit judge's transgression is to have brought forward the shocking collapse of the *otium/negotium* distinction. Judicial matters belong to the forum, the realm of serious business, and they are strictly opposed to *otium* where heavy consumption of wine, food, conviviality and sex are possible. Sir Edward Coke also warned against the dangers of law being a *sedentariam vitam* and a short life for that reason.[34]

In his penetrating study of judicial ritual, Antoine Garapon summarises the antagonism between the standing and the sitting postures:

> The accuser rises up, stands up, rebels, opposes; he accuses, points, creates a bodily and scenic rupture: it is the standing magistracy. The judge sits, listens, takes opinions, his gestures are less visible, less spectacular, he does not move, he deliberates, he turns his head to one side and to the other, he is thoughtful: this is the seated judiciary. The image of the man standing evokes a confrontation, and moreover the lawyer will in turn stand up to reply. That of the seated man evokes tranquillity, serenity and stability. We stand up to confront each other; we sit down to exchange.[35]

The essential difference between judges seated on their throne ('magistrats du siège') and standing lawyers ('l'avocat requiert debout') is a structuring feature of the judicial ritual. The accusatory posture is a body that stands up, denounces and opposes itself, index pointing towards the erring individual. On the contrary, the decision-making process as well as the act of rendering to each their due involves a sitting posture. The seat itself invokes the sacred order where Justice appears.

The judge as 'throne-sharer of Dike'

In an important study, Ernst Kantorowicz demonstrated the iconic tradition of the representation of rulers next to the personified virtue of *Justitia*.[36] The expression 'throne-sharer of Dike' appears in several inscriptions dedicated to governing officials and rulers of the third century CE. This feature was not entirely new, as Dike and Themis were the natural companions to rulers and kings. Yet Kantorowicz shows how the motif of the throne-sharing companions of the king, understood as *nomos empsychos* (living law) was also applied to judges and governors and more often in Hellenistic and late Roman than in medieval times. The qualification 'throne-sharer of Dike' was applied to a judge sitting on a tribunal from which righteous judgments were drawn. But there is also some evidence that the idea was conveyed symbolically, by means of artistic figures placed on the right and left sides of statues or images of judges. The pattern of 'allegorical synthronismoi', linking princes with civic virtues, survived throughout the Middle Ages. In his treatise *Questiones de juris subtilitatibus*, probably written in the middle of the twelfth century, Placentinus depicted *Justitia* enthroned in the centre of the sanctuary, with Reason above her head and with Equity in her arms.[37] The iconic pattern of *Justitia* as throne-sharer of civic virtues is fairly common, though with some variation. *Justitia* may be descending from above, indicating her divine status, or embracing the monarch or the judge in a more intimate gesture. The antique and medieval roots of this pattern are of interest here as Lady Justice sometimes emancipates herself from the ruler's *tutela*.

Lady Justice's throne

Lady Justice's throne often represents an image of the world revolving around her: her seat is as important as her sitting posture. In his 1658 textbook for children *Orbis Sensualium Pictus* (Visible World in Pictures), the Czech pedagogue John Amos Comenius insists that 'Lady Justice is painted sitting on a square stone as she ought to be immovable' ('Justitia pingitur, sedens ut lapide quadrato, nam debet esse immobilis') (Figure 4.4).[38] The phrasing recalls a sentence found in Barthélemy de Chasseneuz's *Catalogus Gloriæ Mundi*,[39] quoting Baldus (in his *consilium* 327, no. 4), that the 'prince ought to be motionless, as a cornerstone'

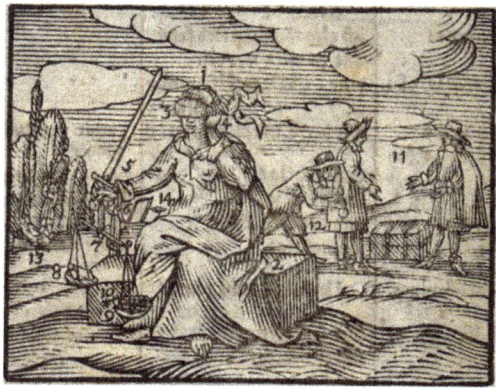

Figure 4.4: John Amos Comenius, *Orbis sensualium pictus* (Nuremberg: Michael Endter, 1658), p. 240. *Justitia.* Private collection

('princeps debet esse immobilis, sicut lapis angularis'). Lady Justice, like the prince, must not vary in her opinions and ought to remain a model of constancy, infallible in her decisions. The same idea features in the frontispiece to John Case's *Sphæra Civitatis*, where Queen Elizabeth is depicted embracing a series of concentric spheres representing the virtues of good government (*Ubertas Rerum, Facundia, Clementia,*

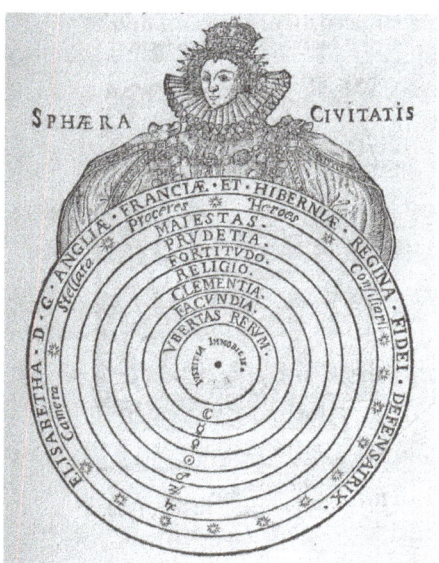

Figure 4.5: John Case, *Sphæra civitatis*, woodcut printer's device on title and diagram with portrait of Elizabeth I on verso, woodcut initials, modern brown morocco gilt, e.g. 4to (Oxford: Joseph Barnes, 1588). Courtesy of the Newberry Library

Religio, Fortitudo, Prudentia and *Maiestas*) (Figure 4.5).[40] The sphere is marked by the motto *Justitia immobilis*, as she reigns on the central axis, the earth. The metaphor of an immovable Justice also applies to the judge's ethics, as Guillaume Le Rouillé (1494–1555) asserts in his *De Justitia et injustitia* (1529), although he adopts a more straightforward metaphor, a column: 'Iudex immobilis debet esse ut columna' (The judge must remain immovable as a column).[41]

Standing Justices: the myth of Astræa

Astræa as an allegorical body in motion

If *Justitia* is predominantly depicted in a stable posture, seated on a throne, the identification of *Justitia* with Astræa, walking away from the evils of the world, suggests a completely different paradigm. This influential myth derives from a famous description in the first book of Ovid's *Metamorphoses* (1.149–50). After the Golden Age of Saturn, the Silver Age of Jove and the sterner Bronze Age, came the Iron Age, when evil was let loose. War came, Piety lay vanquished and the virgin Astræa, last of the immortals, abandoned the blood-soaked earth. Drawing from Greek sources, Ovid expanded the myth originally narrated by the astronomical poet Aratos in which, having left the world in disgust at humanity's wickedness, the virgin Justice took up her abode in the heavens as the constellation Virgo.[42] Astræa embodies disturbing emotions such as anger or despair, thus enabling the judge to see them from another perspective.

When Lady Justice stands for the goddess Astræa, she is depicted in movement. Her return was to signal the dawn of a new golden age. The aesthetic paradigm of Astræa's flight from the sinful earth and ascent to heaven adds dynamism to the usual posture of *Justitia sedens*. In his *Georgics* (2.458–74), Virgil links the destiny of Astræa to a Messianic prophecy, suggesting the ending of the old world and the coming of the kingdom of Saturn. Every time some new Augustus seemed to put an end to discord and bloodshed, the Virgilian myth of Astræa's return came back to collective memory, half magic incantation, half promise from above. A pagan promise, but one which Christians made their own very early on, retaining the Virgilian resonances of regeneration, fruitfulness and the return of civil peace. For England, victorious in the battle waged against her by Philip II, Queen Elizabeth had been this Astræa, which Edmund Spenser celebrated in *The Faerie Queene*:

Now when the world with sinne gan to abound,
  Astræa loathing lenger here to space
  Mongst wicked men, in whom no truth she found,
  Return'd to heaven, whence she deriv'd her race;
  Where she hath now an everlasting place,
  Mongst those twelve signes, which nightly we doe see
  The heavens bright-shining baudricke to enchace;
  And is the *Virgin*, sixt in her degree,
  And next her selfe her righteous ballance bee.[43]

The myth first flourished in the territories of the Venetian Republic, which had a long tradition of representing Venice under the guise of *Justitia*, claiming to be Justice herself (*Venecia-Justitia*), as David Rosand has shown.[44] In the Doge's Palace, the Scala dei Giganti attributed to Pietro Lombardo (1435–1515) is adorned by winged victories in the spandrels of the supporting arcade. One of them carries a scroll with the inscription 'Astrea duce' (Under Astræa's leadership), summoning the Venetian patriciate to follow the doge into a new golden age.[45] She is depicted as a dancing victory (*Nike*) with fluttering draperies, billowing garments and windblown ribbons. The entire decoration of the courtyard of the Doge's Palace celebrates the new *Aetas aurea* or golden age of the Venetian Republic, with Astræa as its chief virtue. Venice could also be described as the sister of Astræa.[46]

In England, the elegant figure of Astræa was also one of Elizabeth's favoured personæ. One hundred years later, Charles II again chose this subject to illustrate his return to power. In his bedchamber at Whitehall, *Astræa Returns to Earth*, painted by John Michael Wright (1617–94), the king is held aloft by three cherubim and hailed by Astræa herself, dressed in flowing robes and cloud-borne (Figure 4.6).

Astræa as *Justitia victrix*

In 1563 in Piazza Santa Trinita in Florence, a free-standing figure of *Justitia* was set atop a large column of ancient Egyptian granite taken from the baths of Caracalla in Rome, a gift from Pius IV to the duke

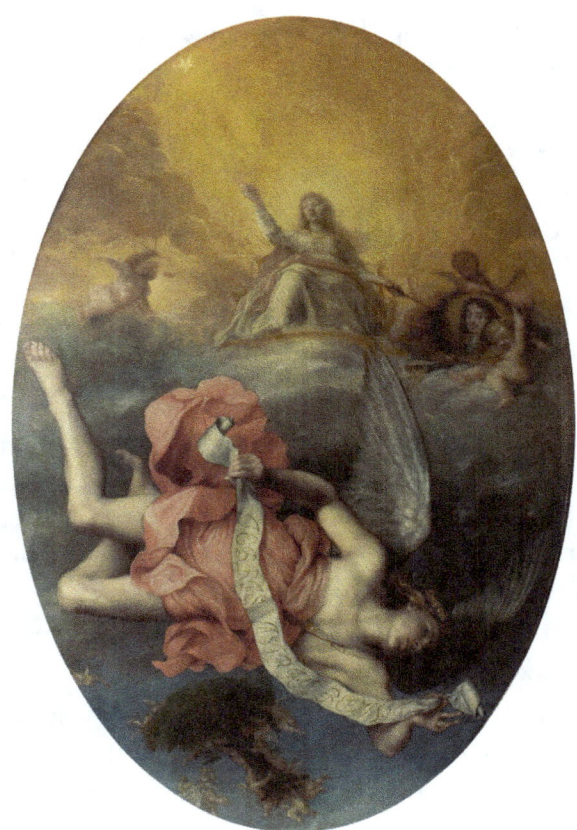

Figure 4.6: John Michael Wright, 1617–94, *Astræa Returns to Earth (The Apotheosis of Charles II)*. By permission of Nottingham City Museums and Galleries and Bridgeman Images

Cosimo I de' Medici. Originally designed in terracotta by Bartolomeo Ammannati, the statue was replaced in 1581 by a sculpture in ancient red porphyry carved by Francesco Ferrucci del Tadda (1497–1585) (Figure 4.7). Porphyry was valued for its hardness and durability and long associated with the Imperial East. It took Francesco Ferruci del Tadda, the first sculptor since classical antiquity to carve porphyry on a large scale, and his son, eleven years to complete the work. After its placement, presumably to balance the proportions, Ammannati covered its back with a cloak of copper.

Standing on top of a Roman column, such triumphal elevated statues frequently served to commemorate military victories. The granite shaft was considerably taller than any other column in the city. The statue, her right hand wielding an unsheathed sword and the left raising a pair

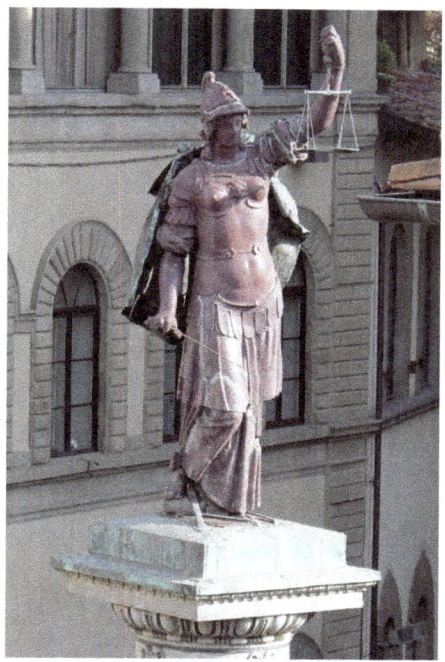

Figure 4.7: Francesco Ferrucci del Tadda, *Lady Justice Standing above the Santa Trinita Column*, Piazza Santa Trinita, Florence, 1583. Wikimedia Commons

of scales, represents *Justitia victrix*.[47] The stylistic fusion of Astræa and Victory, in a monumental setting, served to designate Cosimo as the warrant of Justice as well as signifying his military prowess. It was theatrically set into the urban space of Florence, where the Piazza Santa Trinita was used for festive triumphs and other ceremonies. Situated at a key nodal point between via de Tornabuoni, via delle Terme and Borgo Santi Apostoli, it dominates the square. Its gigantism echoes the return of the golden age under the duke's good governance.

The myth of Astræa was frequently reworked as imaginative, multi-temporal allegories of a contemporaneous reality. Their figural structure at the same time preserved the historical event and interpreted it as a new revelation. Moreover, recurrent iconographical themes built a common symbolic pictorial language, while imitation and emulation conferred on the resulting artwork a novel historical and ideological significance. Astræa thus became an archetype of victorious and messianic Justice, bridging the gap between the civic and non-civic spaces of the city.

The departure of Astræa from earth

A less frequent theme is the departure of Astræa from the blood-drenched earth, driven up to heaven by human wickedness. Her renunciation affords an opportunity to paint her in an unusual position, with her back to the viewer. Marcantonio Raimondi's *Justitia* (from a series of the seven virtues) stands in a recessed archway evocative of classical architecture, in a dynamic walking posture, showing her shoulders and seen almost entirely from behind (Figure 4.8).[48] Her transparent garment is subtly erotic and allows a precise delineation of the buttocks.

As images of Astræa became more familiar to people in early modern city cultures, her gestural vocabulary was more explicitly preserved, and changes or subversive re-enactments of the myth more easily detected.

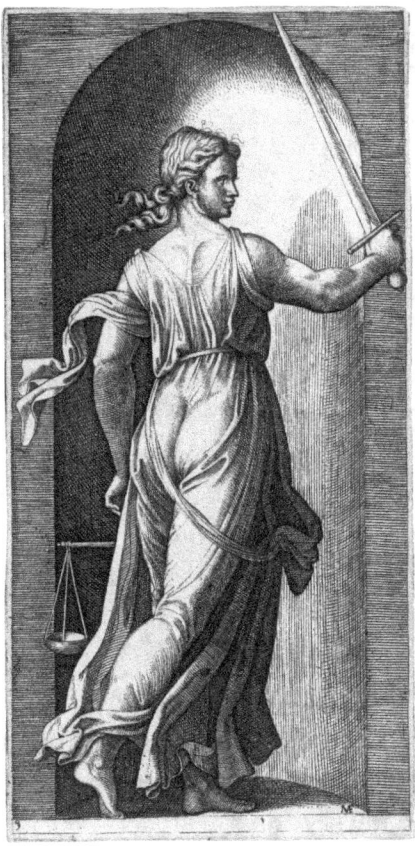

Figure 4.8: Marcantonio Raimondi, after Raphael, *Justitia*, plate 3 from series *The Seven Virtues*, c. 1516–18, engraving, 21.5 cm × 10.5 cm. Courtesy of the Rijksmuseum, Amsterdam

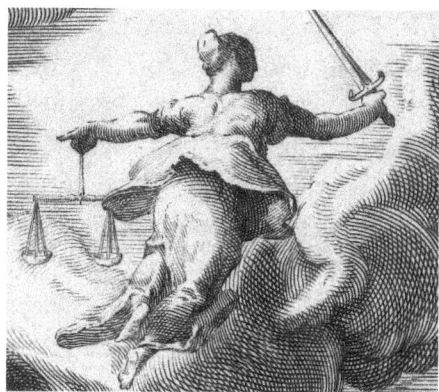

Figure 4.9: Hendrick Goltzius, Ovid's *Metamorphoses* (series title), *The Iron Age*, character-ised by Mars, War and Rapine, engraving on paper, RP-P-1882-A-6348, detail of Lady Justice, turned away. Courtesy of the Rijksmuseum, Amsterdam

Hendrick Goltzius (1558–1617) depicted the flight of Astræa in his plate representing *The Iron Age*, one of fifty-two plates illustrating the first book of Ovid's *Metamorphoses*, in a work published by Claes Jansz Viss-cher in 1589 (Figure 4.9). The God of War, Mars, stands at the centre, brandishing an oversize executioner's sword (gallows may be seen in the background, as well as scenes of atrocities or chaos), at his feet discarded armour, a drum and a cannon. Astræa is depicted as a tiny figure in the upper right corner, cloud-borne, spinning and twisting as she turns her back on the earth and flees. Her complex serpentine posture demon-strated Goltzius's paramount technical virtuosity. His departure from the traditional conventions of the myth is striking. Astræa is portrayed as small and powerless in comparison with giant Mars in the foreground. Goltzius's depiction of the Iron Age highlights the loneliness of Astræa, flying above an expansive vista of mischiefs. The effect is similar to Pieter Brueghel's treatment of Justice where the figure of Christ appears only as a tiny figure, off to the right, in the background. Brueghel completely shifted the aerial perspective; everything in his landscape turns away from the disaster, onlookers ignorant or indifferent.

Astræa, the *Diva Fugax*

The visual dynamism of Astræa escapes the suffocating formalism of the judge's gestural ethics. For these reasons, her twists and turns last longer in imagination and memory than static postures. In Nicolas de Nancel's

(1539–1610) account of the entry of Prince François d'Alençon, brother of the French King Henri III, into Tours, on 28 August 1576, Astræa is depicted as a winged goddess, with a blue garment strewn with stars ('Astræa alata et cærulea, stellisque conspicua').[49] She is the *Diva Fugax* par excellence: 'Where are you running so fast goddess? Why do you fly faster than the wind? Let us stop the movement of your wings' ('Quo tu diva fugax? Aura cur ocyor omni, / Sic revolas? En remigium tibi frangimus alae').[50] De Nancel's verses enhance Astræa's swiftness by characterising her with the Homeric epithet *fugax*. Astræa executes a wide range of movement motifs, from poised postures to spinning motions: her wings suggest flight. Her mobility attracts attention and facilitates remembrance by the simplicity and comprehensibility of her postures.

The countless returns of the goddess Astræa

The figure of Astræa is regularly used in triumphal entries during the early modern age. As noted earlier,[51] her appearance as a visible figure welcoming the king at a city gate was perhaps conceived as a genuine symbolic act, similar, says E. H. Gombrich, to a 'spell and an augury'.[52] Lady Justice's performances reached into the city, blurring the boundaries between the symbolic realm and physical urban space. Civic pageants often challenged these distinctions. Among numerous examples, Charles the Fifth's entry into Messina on 20 October 1536 was the occasion to set up a golden scaffold in front of the cathedral. The city hired numerous workers to construct the pageant. The scaffold read: 'Under his laws, peace reigns, and the goddess Astræa visits his lands.'[53]

In the *Triomphante Entrée de très illustre dame Mme Magdeleine de la Rochefoucauld [...] Faicte en la ville et université de Tournon le dimanche vingt-quatrième du mois d'Avril 1583*, Honoré d'Urfé stages for the spouse of Comte Juste-Henri de Tournon festivities to celebrate their marriage, under the auspices of the goddess Astræa.[54] While the noble lady is invited to pray with her husband in front of Saint Julien Church, a statue of Discord placed on scaffolding is burned down and replaced immediately by Concord, with a sceptre surrounded by two auspicious crows. Tournon is praised as a wise apostle of good governance: he combines all the virtues (Fortitude, Prudence, Faith, Justice, Loyalty and Courage) in one body: 'You know this, O Themis, / And you, common Father, almighty God, who has put / In it, the divine spirit of this lovable Tournon / Of your eternal goods, a marvelous treasure.'[55] Themis is the overarching principle of all the other princely virtues: she acts as a witness to warrant that the prince-governor possesses all the necessary virtues expected for good governance. 'La Deesse Themis, qu'il prise et caresse / Luy procure des autels' (The Goddess Themis, whom he honours and caresses / Provides him with altars). Honoré d'Urfé puns on Tournon's surname 'Juste' as a radical for Justice and later adds 'il aime Thémis dont il porte le nom' (He loves Themis, whose name he bears).[56] While the pun may seem trivial to us today, such games went hand in hand with the celebration of court ethics in early modern times. Figures are set as *tableaux vivants* on platforms or scaffolds, installed at street corners, sometimes hidden by curtains, unveiled at the right moment to the eyes of the passers-by. Civic pageants were powerful tools of legitimation.

The myth is invariably reorchestrated for kings and queens, Popes and emperors. The topos is also exploited by parliamentarians, in a judicial context. Astræa's return to parliament reminds them of their duties. In 1612, the French poet Vincent Voiture published his *Hymnus Virginis seu Astrææ*.[57] The poem, 120 verses long, describes the flight of Astræa caused by human wickedness during the Iron Age and her return under the favourable auspices of the first president of the Parliament of Paris, Nicolas de Verdun, a model for the good conduct of all judges of the tribunal: 'At nunc, cum vitium rigido sub judice desit, [. . .] Virgo redi' (But now, as vice has disappeared under the action of a strict judge, the virgin has come back, verses 14–16). Frequently adapted to the here and now of judicial discourse, Astræa's flight and return became a leitmotif in the speeches made by parliamentarians at the start of each new year.

Astræa before the peasants

According to Virgil (*Georgics* 2.458–74), peasants were the last to give *Justitia* a refuge before she departed the earth and flew into the sky. Petrarch reported this particular story: 'When Justice departed from the earth / She left her last footprints among them (the husbandmen).'[58] This infrequent episode gained special importance as it was the occasion of describing the simple life of peasants as a sign of their genuine justice. In his *Mythologiæ*, Natale Conti, commenting on this passage, describes their rustic life and emphasises their authentic relationship with Justice. He furthermore links the departure of Astræa from earth to the fact that human laws were put in writing, in the form of 'Astræa's wills':

> Poets have written that Justice fled the earth and flew into the sky. This natural equity that was rooted in the hearts of men left the place it had in their minds, as a great list of laws was gradually written down, in order to curb the malice of men. As long as men were simple, they had a better soul; since so many codes of laws were composed and promulgated in the city by jurists, this ancient simplicity gradually began to leave the townspeople, and those who did not understand Astræa's will well withdrew to the fields.[59]

The peasants become the ultimate guarantors of natural equity, the witnesses of a mythical Justice inscribed in souls and hearts, not yet corrupted by the labyrinth of writing. Walter S. Gibson has insightfully noted that in Joos de Damhouder's effigy of mundane Justice (Figure 4.10), first published in Antwerp in 1564, the 'woodcut shows the peasant figure as the very foundation on which Justice rests'.[60] In the accompanying text Damhouder stresses that,

> At the feet of Lady Justice, you can see a lying figure, a wretched peasant, a figure of the common people overwhelmed by misfortune, on which we have put the name of everyman (unusquisque). He, like the other wretched people painted above, is in heavenly paradise, because there, after all

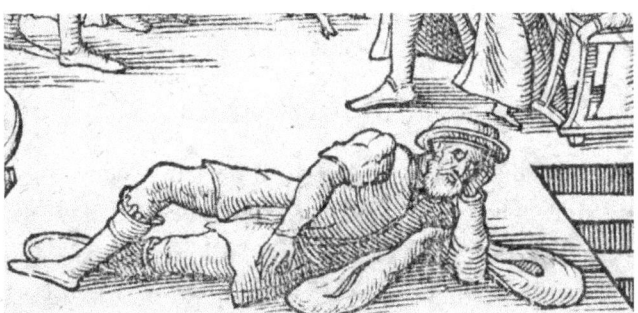

Figure 4.10: Joos de Damhouder, *Mundanæ Justitiæ Effigies* (Antwerp: Jean Beller, 1564). By permission of Numistral, Digital Library of the University of Strasbourg

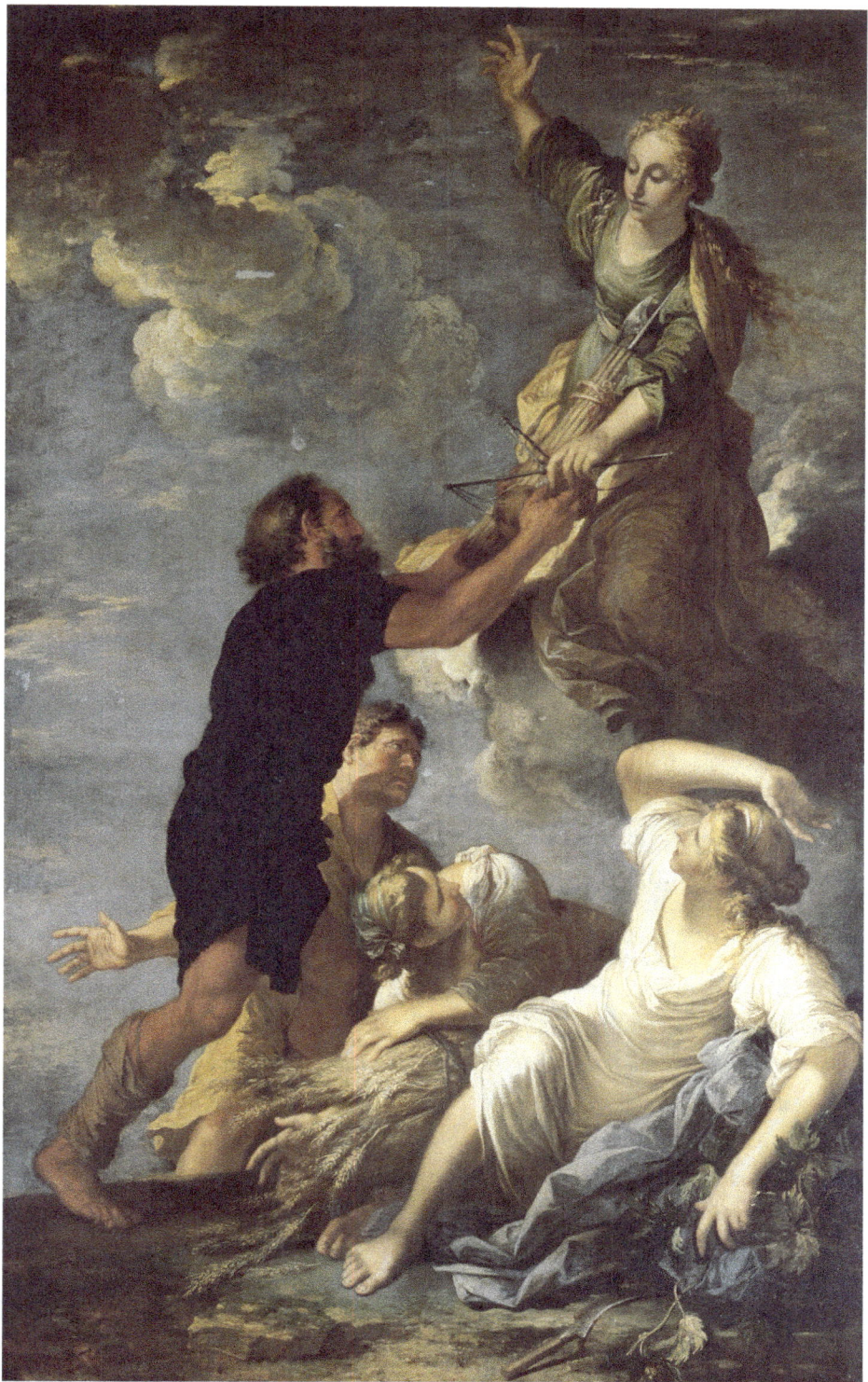

Figure 4.11: Salvator Rosa, *Justice Appearing to the Peasants*, c. 1640. Kunsthistoriches Museum, Vienna. By permission of Bridgeman Images

these trials, after so many injustices, it is true, severe, but endured to the end, with patience and good faith, imbued with the hope of a more equitable Justice, common people hope to participate in the true life that awaits them.[61]

The figure labelled 'unusquisque popellus aut communitas' (everyman, common people, rabble or community) at the bottom of the illustration is depicted lying, dreaming in the foreground. The peasant's point of view on Justice is privileged. Holder of natural equity, he represents Justice before the law, rights that precede writing.

In his painting *Justice Appearing to the Peasants* (c. 1640), Salvator Rosa depicts the same episode, focusing on the appearance of Justice to the peasants before leaving the earth (Figure 4.11). Here, peasants are conflated with shepherds and they are granted an exemplary status. Instead of following the tradition of depicting peasants as leading foolish or vicious lives, Salvator Rosa prefers to show their virtuous nature and their honourable estate. Idealised in a classicising fashion, they welcome Astræa to her last dwelling place, providing her a refuge. The peasants' passions are depicted with tragic dignity. The attributes of Lady Justice are entrusted not to representatives of imperial, papal or royal power, but to the peasants themselves.

Rosa, like Conti, celebrates the distant origins of law, in which the laws of equity were inscribed directly in the hearts of men. Richard W. Wallace notes that Rosa, in his enthusiasm for Stoicism and simple rustic life, has depicted the goddess surrendering her attributes (*fasces*, scales and sword) to the shepherds, before her final flight to the stars.[62] Her right arm is raised in a sign of proclamation, the classical gesture of *adlocutio* given by Roman orators. The peasants are struck by her divine appearance; the intensity of their emotions makes them collapse. In order to bridge the ever growing distance between magistrates and the people, the myth of Astræa was considerably reworked in the seventeenth century. The idea of a direct link between the peasants and the goddess is a conscious attempt to create a novel imagery. It is more attuned to a depiction of *Justitia* as patroness of the peasants, nourishing all the inhabitants of the earth at the same time. Later representations of Lady Justice's flight are indicative of another turn, this time announcing rebellion and sedition.

Seditious Lady Justice

A late example, dating from the eighteenth century is particularly telling. Entitled *Justitia relegata flecti nescia*, it commemorates the exile of the French parliament on 9/11 May 1753 (Figure 4.12). Lady Justice, stiffened by her stoic posture, suffers with dignity the exile inflicted upon her. This intaglio, distributed by French parliamentarians at a time when a major political conflict opposed them to the monarchy, belongs to a collection of twelve engraved plates published in 1755 to celebrate the rebellion of the magistrates against Louis XV, which culminated in the exile of parliament between 1753 and 1754. The print was sentenced to be burnt on 28 May 1753.[63]

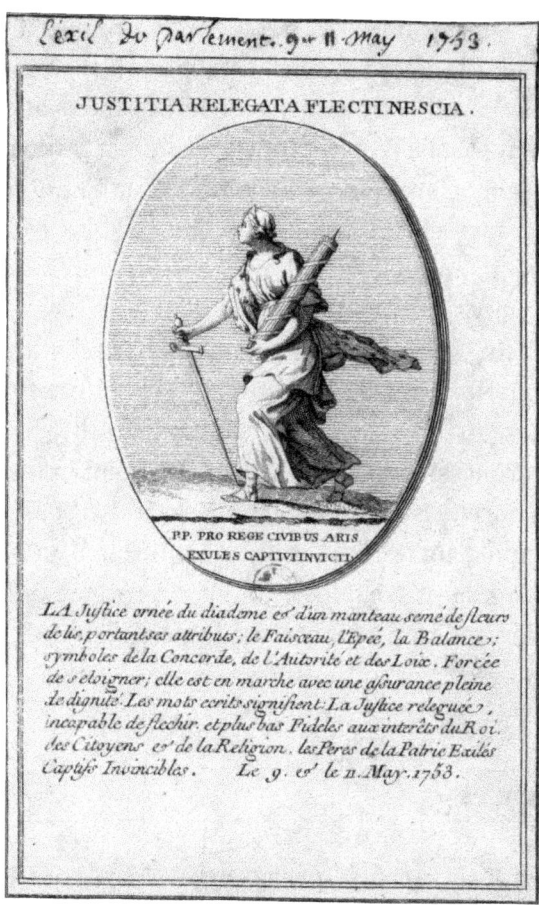

Figure 4.12: Anonymous, *Justitia relegata flecti nescia*, etching, BnF, Est., Qb1, M97111. By permission of the Bibliothèque nationale de France

This seditious print provides an unusual representation of Justice on the move, busy climbing a hill, in a voluntarist pose. Far from suffering her infamous relegation, she treads an arduous path. The motto and the text underneath the medal describe Justice as 'forced to walk away' ('forcée de s'éloigner'). But in reality this is not the case, for Justice is determined to exile herself, walking with a decided step and 'unable to falter' ('incapable de fléchir'). Marked by an 'assurance full of dignity' ('assurance pleine de dignité'), she radically reworks the usual hieratic gestures of the goddess sitting motionless on her throne. Instead, she leans on her sword as on a walking stick; the trays of her scales on her back are barely visible. In her left arm, she holds the lictor's *fasces* as if she were brandishing a torch to illuminate her path. A lapidary inscription at the bottom of the print claims her loyalty to the interests of the King, the Citizenry and Religion. It is signed with the insolent words, 'we, the fathers of the fatherland, exiled, captive but invincible'. This figure of a stubborn Justice, exiled but undefeated, is not primarily remarkable for its handling of her attributes; she *acts* as a body that has entered into resistance. It is above all a question of reviving a highly conventional allegorical code by animating it with a warlike *virtus*, a courageous pose, gestures tended by a lively emotion.

Lady Justice is one actualisation of the various female allegories which haunted city spaces and the ephemeral festivities of early modern cities. Before being the subject of a continuous and at times strenuous exegesis, which often enough dwelt only on the interpretation of her attributes, Lady Justice may be viewed with fresh eyes as a body in motion. Her various stances mark a climactic point in the early modern period, whose novelty is exemplified by the role that sculpture had come to play. A sculpted image, especially when located in a liminal space (threshold, staircase or corridor) can be interpreted as an impulse to question the demarcation between the enclosure of the courtroom and the day-to-day agenda of court officers.

Walking Justices

A standing Lady Justice gains a special appeal when she is figured, on foot, in a dynamic walking posture, such as in the allegorical figure executed in 1783 by the French sculptor and academician Étienne-Pierre-Adrien

Gois (1731–1823) (Figure 4.13). Lady Justice was a striking figure of 6.5 feet designed specially to adorn the staircase of the Cour des Aides in Paris. In his guide describing the monuments of Paris, Luc-Vincent Thiéry informs us of the exact location of the statue:

> On entering the Galerie Mercière, we find in its middle the entrance that leads up to the Cour des Aides: it is announced by two Ionic columns, crowned at the entablature of this gallery, and surmounted by the King's coat of arms. [. . .] The staircase lit from above produces a great effect [. . .] At the junction of the staircase, the Statue of Justice by M. Gois, one of the King's Sculptors, can be seen. It is placed in a niche crowned by a pediment.[64]

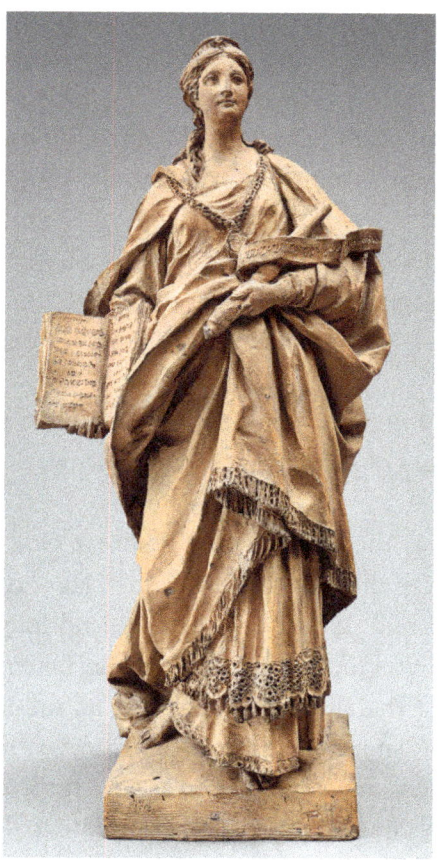

Figure 4.13: Étienne-Pierre-Adrien Gois, *Justice*, terracotta modello of the marble sculpture executed in 1783 to adorn the staircase of the Cour des Aides, Paris. RF 2653, 35 cm × width 15.6 cm × depth 15 cm. Louvre Museum, Department of Sculptures

The sculpture is set in a broad staircase, lit from above. Wielding a sceptre in her left hand, the figure holds the open book of laws in her right hand. A long gown decorated with precious fringes and embroideries gives a glimpse of the solemn and slow movement of her walk. The statue was presented at the Paris Salon of 1785 under the title 'The Royal Power holding the book of Laws' (*La Puissance Royale tenant le livre des Lois*). The book of Laws is inscribed with the legend, in black letters, 'In legibus salus' (Salvation is found in laws). In his choice of motto and attributes, Gois follows here the recommendations of Lacombe de Prezel's dictionary of iconology, published in 1779, where the allegory of Law is described as follows:

> LAW: She has been represented under the symbol of a majestic woman, sitting on a Tribunal with a diadem on her head, a sceptre in her hand and an open book at her feet, on which is written this sentence: *In Legibus Salus*.[65]

In another contemporary iconological source published in 1770, Jean-Raymond de Petity adds a further explanation:

> LAW. She has a radiant diadem to mark that her origin is holy. The sceptre she holds indicates her authority; and the open Book with the words, *In Legibus Salus*, signifies the reward she promises to those who obey her.[66]

But instead of sitting, Gois opts for the dynamism of Justice walking, under several drapery folds, activated by the viewer's perambulation on the staircase.

The sculptor was the son of Edme Philibert Gois, employed by the Office of the Clerk of the Judicial High Court. He was thus familiar with the judicial world and its rituals. The piece no longer exists, but the *modello* in terracotta (today preserved in the Louvre) shows how the walking posture of the allegory, along with its full-length motion and gestures, and ideally situated at the primary entryway to the central building of the courthouse, must have acted as a perfect *cicerone* for the busy magistrates as they climbed the majestic staircase to the Cour des Aides.

The figures of *Justitia* adorning judicial spaces are often distinct from those designed to be seen by a wider public. Gois sculpted an image for magistrates, capable of reflecting the image of *dignitas* they wished to

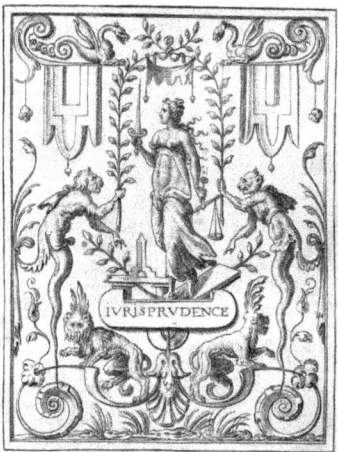

Figure 4.14: Étienne Delaune, *Juriprudentia*, c. 1570. Paris, Bibliothèque nationale de France

imprint on their profession. In a similar vein, the allegory of Jurisprudence – not to be confused with Dame Justice – gives an account of the difficulties of good judgment primarily addressed to magistrates. In an early drawing by French artist Étienne Delaune (1518/19–83), belonging to a series of drawings on the theme of the liberal arts,[67] Jurisprudence is depicted in profile as a woman standing, marching to the left. She walks onto an unstable wooden device, towards a mason rule, one of the pans of her scales masked (Figure 4.14). This paradoxical standing posture, between instability and stability, olive branches and mason rule, indicates the very nature of the path towards equity: Jurisprudence walks cautiously; her equilibrium results from a well thought-out compromise between the exercise of Justice and the knowledge of rules. She needs to be able to pivot quickly, if any unforeseen element comes up.

Fountains of Justice: spatial location and communal function

The examples analysed so far have offered novel insights into the variety of meanings of sitting and standing postures. Depending on the context, Lady Justice can appear as an adjudicating Justice when she is sitting or as a vindicative or militant Justice, defender of the weak or the oppressed, when she erects herself and brandishes her minacious sword. But she also acts as a liminal figure, a sort of divinity of the crossroads, performing a dynamic march aiming at shifting the perspective of the viewer. Freed from the primary obligation to signify, Lady Justice appears first as a way to organise space differently. We will now address the problem through the case of fountains of Justice. With these final examples, a new spatial configuration is achieved: erecting a standing Justice above a column in the middle of a marketplace is a deliberate strategy to enhance its communal function. Lady Justice is much more than a mere allegory in the narrow sense of the term: she becomes a pivotal focal point organising a visual dialogue with citizens. Of particular importance is the insertion of the figure of *Justitia* on the architectural structure of a public fountain, given pride of place in the agora and offered to the panoptic gaze of an entire urban community.

As vital sources of drinking water, the public fountains of the early modern period were proudly built as civic monuments, frequently located in front of the city council. Michael Baxandall remarks that 'the public fountain, ceremoniously delivering water to the community, is an emblem of local well-being and collective identity'.[68] Many statues and fountains of *Justitia* were placed in town squares in northern Europe next to newly erected buildings, testament to a nascent public sphere.[69]

Reformed cities: a new vision of Justice

In the major squares of Swiss and German reformed cities, a standing figure of Lady Justice, erected atop a column, often appears as a focal point, crowning a fountain located at a major axis of urban space. The first one, attributed to the sculptor Hans Gieng (Fribourg, 1525–62) was erected in Bern in 1543 (Figure 4.15). Probably of Swabian origin, Hans Gieng is recorded as having become a citizen of Fribourg and a member of the craftsmen's guild in 1527. After being repaired and repainted for the first time by Humbert Mareschet in 1584 and 1589,[70] the sculpture underwent a second restoration, mainly of the stonework, in 1668–9. Slightly under life-size, Gieng's polychrome Lady Justice stands above a polygonal basin atop a fluted column shaft of 5.2 metres (the total height of the complex is 6.25 metres). Blindfolded, an upward sword in her right hand and scales in her left, she stands in a pronounced *contrapposto*. Her costume is antique: her feet are laced in sandals, her gown, vividly pleated, is close-fitting and attached only at the middle of her body, with double-laced sleeves. Her

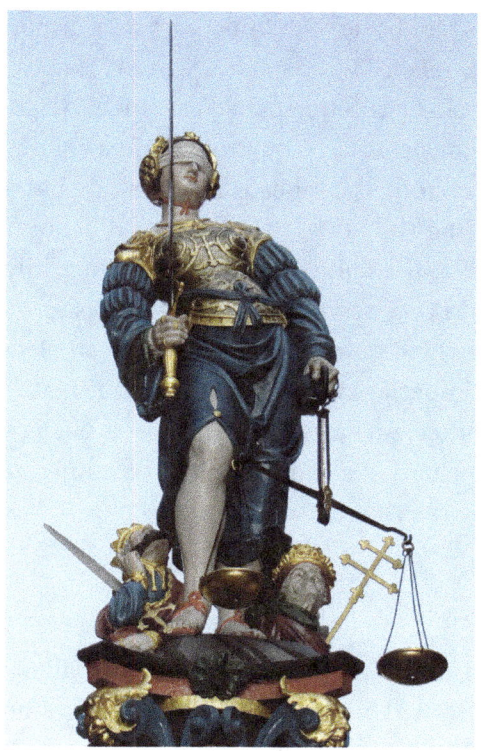

Figure 4.15: Hans Gieng, *Fountain of Justice*, 1543, Bern. Wikimedia Commons

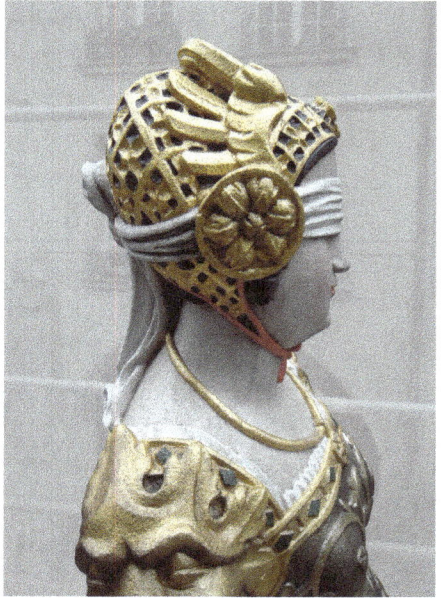

Figure 4.16: Hans Gieng, *Fountain of Justice*, Bern, 1543, detail of the head. Wikimedia Commons

right knee is uncovered. She wears an ornamental armour with arabesque decoration in low relief. The epaulets are in the shape of lion heads, and her blindfold is held by rosette-shaped ear shields (Figure 4.16).

The pedestal consists of a strong ring shaft, a volute wreath with four male masks with humped foreheads and hanging beards in the corners of the slab, figuring the Pope, the emperor, a Schultheiss (magistrate, head of the city) and a sultan, as symbols of worldly powers. At the feet of Justice, the Pope wears the tiara and the bishop's cross; the sultan, a turban-like entwined pointed hat and a Saracen blade; the emperor, a crown and the imperial sword; and the Schultheiss, a beret and his golden chain of office. All have their eyes closed. Gieng's statue, executed in 1543, can be regarded as an archetype of numerous Swiss fountain statues erected in the sixteenth century.

Divine justice and earthly rulers

The articulation of divine justice with world rulers was particularly pronounced in Bern. The Bernese fountain shows how divine justice stands above the potentates, just as a virtuous state triumphs over worldly powers. Divine justice was a prominent political theme in Protestant Bern, because justice, according to the word of God, counted for more than a prince's word.[71] In a 1558 stained-glass window by Hans Rudolf Manuel for a Bernese bailiff, Lady Justice's divine character is indicated even more clearly (Figure 4.17).[72] Winged, she stands on a cloud brandishing a threatening sword against four worldly rulers. The iconography of a stained glass by Anton Wyss dating from 1578 adopts a similar configuration (Figure 4.18).[73] In the centre, the blindfolded, blonde-curled Justice is enthroned on the globe. Concealing her naked body under a red cloak, she holds up a sword in her outstretched hands. The Pope and three crowned temporal rulers and a citizen with a fur cap are depicted beneath her throne in a wreath of clouds. The four basic figures of four earthly powers were seen as embodiments of the four types of rule: theocracy (Pope), monarchy (emperor), autocracy (sultan) and republic (Schultheiss). The cloud motif adds another reference to heavenly judgement, recalling Proverbs 8:15–16: 'Through me kings, sovereigns and governors make just laws. Through me princes act like princes, from me all rulers on earth

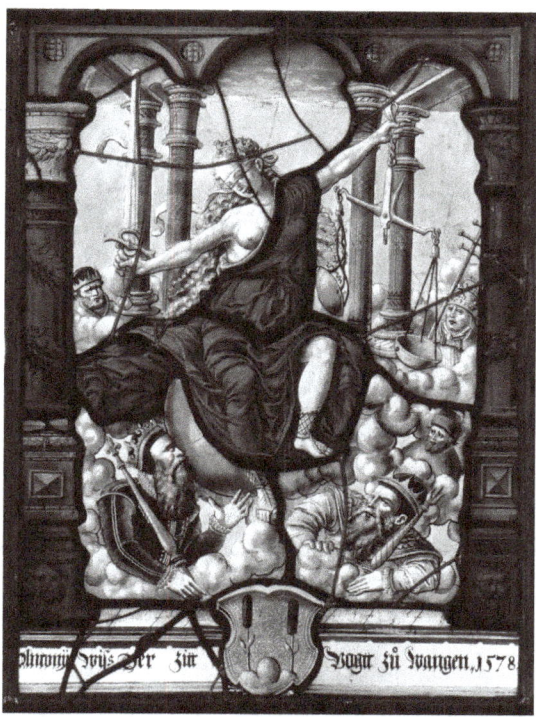

Figure 4.17: Hans Rudolf Manuel, stained-glass window for a Bernese bailiff, inv. 20036.595. Bern History Museum. Wikimedia Commons

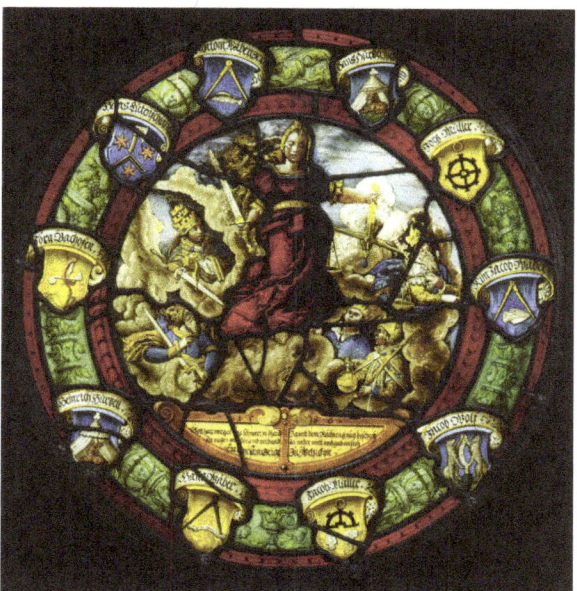

Figure 4.18: Stained glass, *Anton Wyss with the Justice over the World Rulers*, anonymous artist, 1578, 43.7 cm × 32.7 cm, Reformed Church of Aarwangen, sll, 1b, Inventory Berne *Corpus Vitrearum*

derive their nobility.' Divine justice stands above worldly dominion, transcends earthly rulers, and shows its independence of rank and name. This iconography was very influential. It communicated a Republican spirit cherished by Swiss free cities.[74]

In the late sixteenth century, the formula spread quickly and was known from numerous stained-glass objects and designs. The prototype of Gieng's statue was copied in Neuchâtel (by Laurent Perroud, in 1545–7), Solothurn (also by Laurent Perroud, in 1561, painted by Hans Shilt), in Lausanne (by Laurent and Jacques Perroud, in 1584–5), in Boudry (1610), in Cudrefin (by Benoît Magnin, in 1605), in Aarau (in 1643, by Heinz Henz, painted by Balthasar Fisch), in Bienne (by Johannes Hesch, in 1650, replaced by a new statue by Jean Boyer, in 1714) and in Burgdorf (by Joseph Füeg von Urs, in 1757). In Aarau, the fountain of Justice used to stand next to the pillory in Rathausgasse, where the Court was seated in the Middle Ages. Later, the fountain was moved to the church square. In Neuchâtel, Bienne and Lausanne, the statues were oriented towards the façade of the town hall, which was then the centre of judicial activities. In the German city of Worms, a

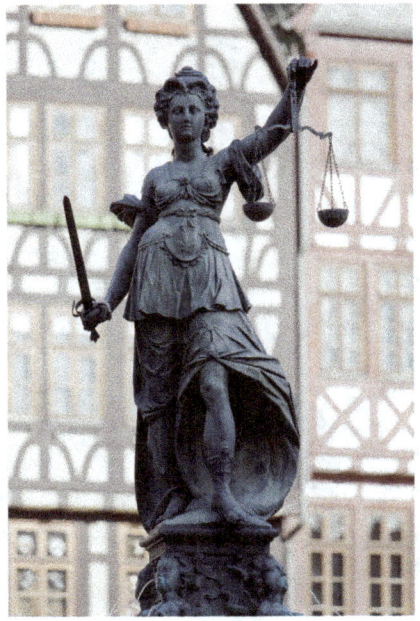

Figure 4.19: Frankfurt, *Gerechtigkeitsbrunnen* (Fountain of Justice), Römerberg Square. Photograph by the author

fountain of Justice was erected in front of the Late Medieval town hall, then used as a civic court.

In Swiss free cities, the model of the fountain of Justice endured for more than three centuries, profoundly shaping the landscape of the city: Lady Justice, engaged in favour of distributive and coercive justice, one of the weightiest issues of communal politics, also rules over the allocation of public water. Wells or ponds were an essential part of urban social life: as a source of water for households and as a place of work for washing clothes, fountains occupied the squares, and defined a district, a neighbourhood. They were, above all, meeting places. Lady Justice, a virgin, a ruler and a warrior, towers over the receptive basin of public waters. Many civic fountains at the time feature images of Justice. She stands as the monumentalised focal point of public space, overseeing the equitable distribution of the water of life.

Lady Justice on the forum

In Frankfurt, a *Gerechtigkeitsbrunnen* (Fountain of Justice) was erected in 1611 in the middle of the central square, Römerberg, where a fountain had existed since 1543 (Figure 4.19). The free-standing fountain figure faces the town hall; her gaze is directed towards the place where justice was meted out. The town hall was not only the seat of the city council but also the court of lay assessors and the criminal court. An octagonal trough made of red Main sandstone with a diameter of 6.5 metres forms the foundation. The statue of the goddess was set atop a stone column with siren statues and reliefs of virtues. The sculptor Johann Hocheisen (1595–1635) received 200 guilders for his work, and the painter Philipp Uffenbach (1566–1636) adorned it with colours, and was paid 37 guilders by the city council. The form of the fountain is well documented as it was already depicted in the coronation diary of Emperor Matthias in 1612. In a print commemorating the event, the trough was covered with an artificial rock group reaching to the top of the column. These ceremonies were witnessed by crowds held at bay by guards, adding an element of popular participation. In the days of the Holy Roman Empire, the fountain of Justice was turned into a wine fountain during the emperor's coronation ceremony (Figure 4.20). The primary purpose of the wine was to fulfil the archducal office, as he was

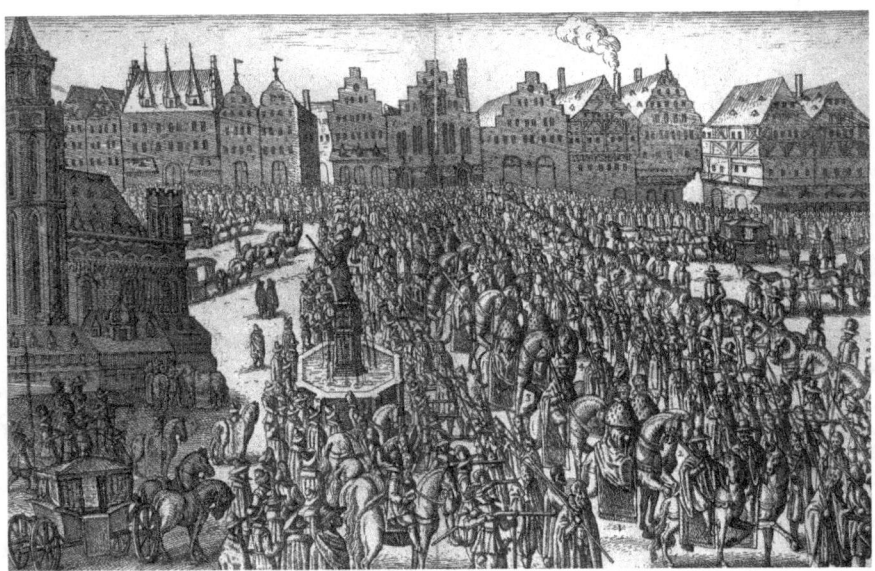

Figure 4.20: Fountain of Justice turned into a wine fountain. Entry of the electoral princes in 1612 in Frankfurt am Main, engraving by Athus Gotthard, *Electio et Coronatio Serenisss.*, Francfort am Main, Officina de Bry, 1612. Courtesy of the Herzog August Bibliothek, Wolfenbüttel

expected to offer a cup of wine to the new emperor during the ceremony. After that, the nobility usually left the wine fountain to the people. The fountain on display today is a copy by Friedrich Schierholz, dating from 1887 and financed by the Frankfurt wine merchant Gustav D. Manskopf.

In Regensburg, the *Justitiabrunnen* is located on Haidplatz, its most important and centrally located town square (Figure 4.21). A simple wooden fountain was erected in 1551; following a decision by the city council, a stone fountain was built from 1656 to 1659. It consists of an octagonal trough with a raised podium, a high, four-sided pedestal for the larger-than-life statue of Justice. The allegory is depicted with elaborate garments, showing her left breast bared. In her right hand, she holds the sword raised vertically, and with her left arm slightly bent, she holds the scales. On the right side of the figure, at ground level, a crane stands as a symbol of vigilance. The contract to build the fountain was awarded to the master stonemason Leoprand Hillmer in 1656. It is closely linked to the agreement between the ecclesiastical states and the Protestant magistrate of the imperial city, which was sealed by Emperor Ferdinand III in 1655 and settled a long-standing dispute over the immunity of ecclesiastical property. This formed an essential basis for the Regensburg religious peace, which was crucial until the end of the

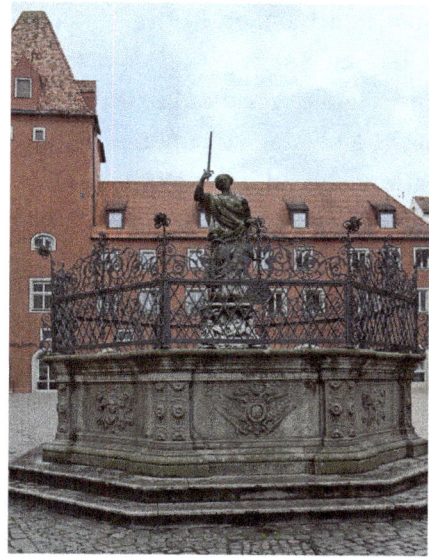

Figure 4.21: Regensburg, *Justitiabrunnen*, by Leoprand Hilmer. Photograph by the author

old Empire. The fountain of Justice on Haidplatz is therefore closely connected to the fountain of Peace, which stood in the large courtyard of the old town hall. Justice and Peace were thus visually linked.

Lady Justice seated primarily acts as an adjudicative figure, involved in procedural law, investiture or homage rituals. Erected figures of Justice are much more attuned to their witnessing communities. Often standing on square pedestals, larger than life, they are looked up to by the people. Displayed in public spaces, their accessibility to the wider public is key. Lady Justice erected on a square stone becomes the nation's virtue for it is the virtue of each citizen. More fundamentally, the erection of standing Justices above monumental fountains is a context-specific trend, closely related to the affirmation of Swiss free cities under the Reformation.

Conclusion: in the orbit of Dame Justice

Allegories pervaded the civic spaces of early modern cities. They were perceived as concrete effigies, active three-dimensional bodies opened up to various frames of perception. In the cases examined here, the postures of Lady Justice are linked to the spatial frames in which she performs. Instead of being solely viewed as a beautiful courtesan, belonging to an unreachable world of luxurious decorum, Lady Justice sometimes becomes the pivotal axis upon which plaintiffs, defendants or judges are repositioned to fulfil their judicial roles. This operation, by which Lady Justice shifts the usual *habitus* of frame and perception, serves as an enduring way of reminding us that affective justice emanates directly from the allegorical impulse and not from legal definitions.

Dame Justice stands as a mysterious daimon, behind or before the judge's purview. The frames she institutes as a silent image need to be carefully scrutinised. Is not her silent presence meant to question the office of the jurist himself? The sacred judge, as a mouth producing the oracles of the Law, sits next to a mysterious Lady. Her trials and paths are not straightforward; they belong to a *methodos*, they always hint at a salutary *periegesis*. In his Salon in 1767, Diderot reflected on the form that a judicial allegory should take when it comes to making it a cathartic instrument. His sharp criticism of the *Triumph of Justice*, painted by Louis-Jean Jacques Durameau, did not imply a pure and simple rejection of the allegory:

> I admit, however, that if painting has ever been allowed to use allegory, it is in the *Triumph of Justice* [. . .] But I claim that whoever throws himself into allegory imposes on himself the need to find strong [. . .], new [. . .], striking [. . .] sublime ideas.[75]

As we take leave of Lady Justice's majestic entries, one last and late example will illustrate the necessity of rendering a powerful symbolisation of Justice's body in action.[76] Pierre-Paul Prud'hon's impressive *Justice and Vengeance Pursuing Crime*, intended for the great courtroom of Paris's Palais de Justice, widely disseminated in French courthouses through numerous copies, is probably one of the most compelling images of Justice produced for a judicial setting. However, Proudhon initially proposed an allegorical composition (Figure 4.22) quite different from the panel presented at the Salon of 1808. Nemesis drags in front of an enthroned *Justitia* a murderer, whose victims (mother and child) lie, lifeless, on the throne's majestic staircase. *Justitia*, seated high up on her *sella curulis*, looks downward, motionless,

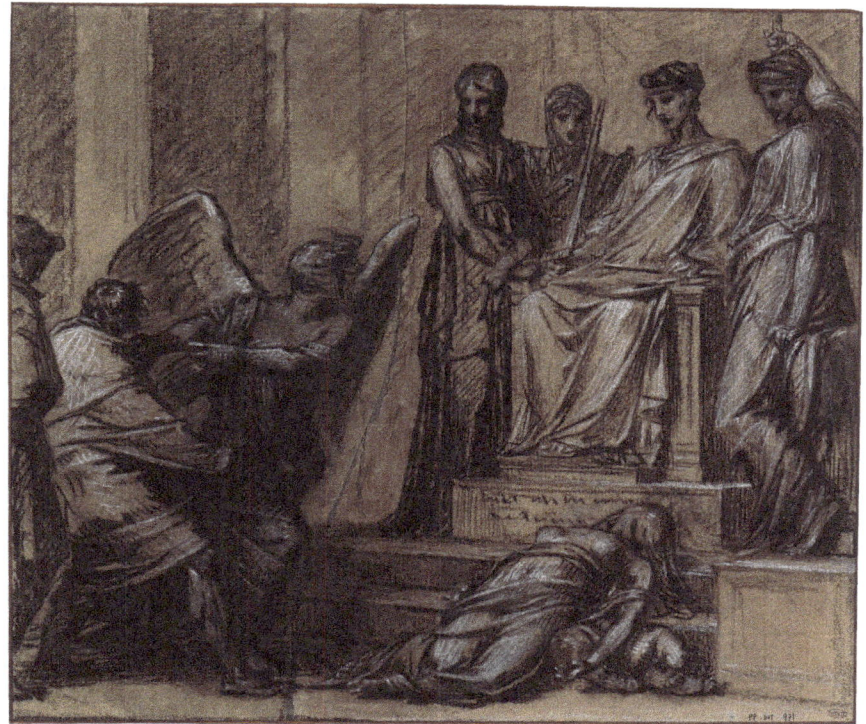

Figure 4.22: Pierre-Paul Prud'hon, *Themis and Nemesis*, 1805, drawing, 28.2 cm × 34.1 cm, inv. DDUT971. Petit Palais, Musée des Beaux-Arts de la ville de Paris

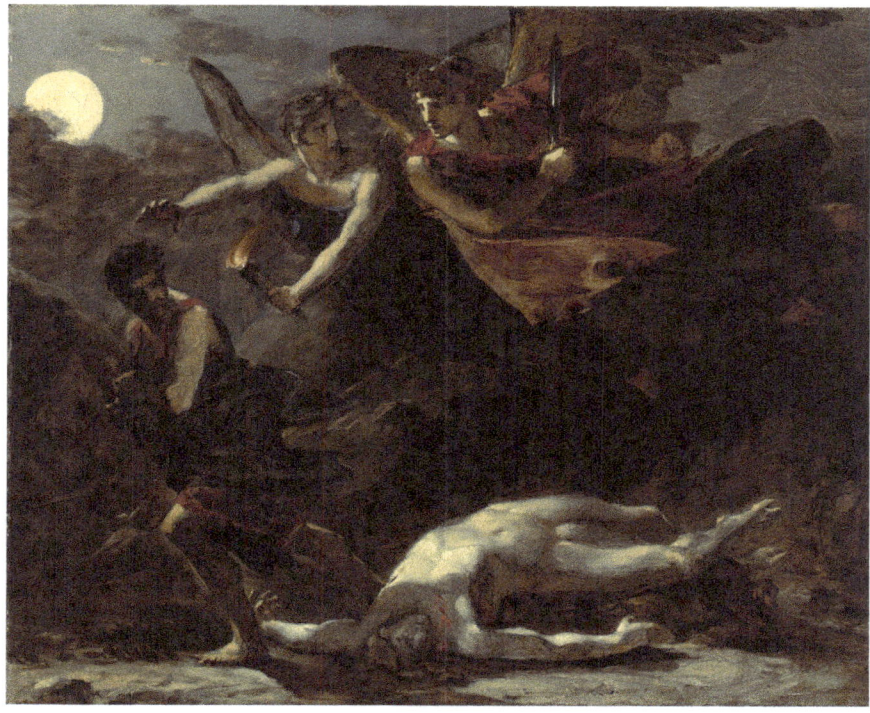

Figure 4.23: Pierre-Paul Prudhon, *Justice and Vengeance Pursuing Crime*, 1808, oil on canvas. J. Paul Getty Museum (the original is in the Louvre Museum)

flanked by the allegorical standing figures of wisdom, strength and moderation. Sitting in a calm and conventional posture, she is depicted with *dignitas* and majesty, at an ethical distance from what is happening *before* her. But the final version developed a more dramatic scene of action. Prud'hon depicts Nemesis acting out of *terribilitas*, swooping like a vulture on its prey, the devilish criminal covered by the veil of night (Figure 4.23). This sublime *concetto* seems to correspond better to an image of *Justitia* in motion and in action, capable of hitting hard and pursuing the criminal even beyond the frame of the painting.

Notes

1. See Bernard J. Hibbits, 'Making Motions: The Embodiment of Law in Gesture', *Journal of Contemporary Legal Issues* 6 (1995), pp. 51–81 (esp. p. 65).
2. Danielle Jacquart, *La médecine médiévale dans le cadre parisien, XIVe–XVe siècles* (Paris: Fayard, 1998), pp. 391–402; Chiara Beneduce, 'John Buridan on Complexion. Natural Philosophy and Medicine in the Fourteenth Century', in C. Beneduce and D. Vincenti (eds), *Œconomia Corporis: The Body's Normal and Pathological Constitution at the Intersection of Philosophy and Medicine* (Pisa: Edizioni ETS, 2018), pp. 41–9.
3. Jean Fernel, *The* Physiologia *of Jean Fernel (1567)*, trans. and annot. J. M. Forrester (Philadelphia, PA: American Philosophical Society, 2003), book 3, *The Temperaments*, p. 227.
4. Guillaume Maran, *Declaration et Manifeste de Maistre Guillaume Maran, Docteur Regent & Doyen des facultez des droicts en l'Université de Tolose, du cinquiesme May 1621* (Toulouse: Veuve de I. Colomiez, 1621), p. 10: 'J'advoue librement qu'il est bien mal aisé et comme impossible que parmy un procez espineux il ne se rencontre des picqueures & poinctures, & que là où il y a de l'émotion & contention il n'y aye de la chaleur & du feu, qui pousse & faict eschaper des paroles d'ardeur, & se treuvent contraires au style d'icelle, que Dieu nous a voulu marquer par son propre exemple (et par) la marque de la douceur & humilité cordiale que Jésus Christ nous a voulu enseigner de parole et de faict.'
5. Text written by Huigen Leeflang, no. 49.1–4, 'Jacob Cornelisz van Oostsanen en Lucas van Leyden, *Voorstellingen uit het leven van Christus met sibyllen, deugden en ondeugden* Ca. 1521–1523 [. . .] Amsterdam, Rijksmuseum, inv. RP -P-BI-6279-6282 [. . .] De verschijning van *Justitia* (Rechtvaaedigheid) tussen de *Bespotting* en de *Geseling van Christus* is haast ironisch te noemen', in Daantje D. Meuwissen, *Jacob Cornelisz van Oostsanen (ca. 1475–1533): De Renaissance in Amsterdam en Alkmaar* (Zwolle: Waanders Uitgevers, 2014), pp. 264–5.
6. Jean de Coras, *Petit discours des parties et office d'un bon et entier Juge* (Lyon: Barthélemy Vincent, 1596), p. 24: 'Il faut donc que le iuge se rende facile &

accessible aux parties playdantes avecques une honneste gravité, toutefois ne les admettant point en privée familiarité, d'où naist le mépris & contemnement, voyre en fin, comme Theophraste disoit, haine et inimitié. Voyla pourquoi Lacides Cyrenien appelé du Roy Attalus respondit qu'il falloit regarder les images, c'est-à-dire les Roys & Magistrats, de loing, d'autant que la familiarité continuée souventesfois diminue l'admiration de leur auctorité.'

7. See Antoine Garapon, Julie Allard and Frédéric Gros, *Les vertus du juge* (Paris: Dalloz, 2008), pp. 32–3: 'La distance entre la fonction de juge et la personne qui l'incarne: la vertu de dignité.'

8. Joos [Josse] de Damhouder, *Praxis rerum criminalium* (Venice: Ioannis Antonium Bertanum, 1572), ch. 154, p. 1666, col. 2: 'Justitia itaque in solio residens indicat omnem justitiæ administrationem debere sedere. [. . .] Hoc est, debere inferri censuram animo quieto, libero, et ab humanis affectibus desecato. [. . .] Et recte sedendo, debet judex sententiam pronunciare. In quiescendo enim et sedendo anima sit sciens et prudens, Aristotele teste.' See also Mario Sbriccoli, *Storia del diritto penale et della Giustizia* (Milan: Giuffrè Editore, 2009), p. 199.

9. The Dominican friar Antonino Pierozzi (1389–1459), Archbishop of Florence (1445/6–9) is the author of a *Summa sacræ theologiæ, juris pontifices, et cæsare* (Venice: apud Juntas, 1582) which is a pastoral manual and a compendium of theology, canon law and philosophy. See ch. 2, *De pertinentibus adjudicium*, p. 103: 'Jura statuerunt judicem in proferendo sententiam debere sedere ad judicandum mentis tranquilitatem.' On Antoninus' life, see Peter Francis Howard, *Beyond the Written Word: Preaching and Theology in the Florence of Archbishop of Antoninus 1427–1459* (Florence: Leo S. Olschki Editore, 1995).

10. For a recent overview of the uses of Pierre Bourdieu's theory, see Johann Lindell, 'Bourdieusian Media Studies: Returning Social Theory to Old and New Media', *Distinktion: Journal of Social Theory* 16 (2015), pp. 362–77. For a review essay of Pierre Bourdieu, *The Field of Cultural Production: Essays on Art and Literature*, ed. and intro. Randal Johnson (Cambridge: Polity Press, 1993), see Ian Maclean, 'Bourdieu's Field of Cultural Production', *French Cultural Studies* 3 (1993), pp. 283–9.

11. Andrea Alciato, *Emblemata cum commentariis* (Padua: Tozzi, 1621), fol. D1r, emblem 145. Thuilius' commentary of the emblem in the 1621 edition of the *Emblemata* includes two columns devoted to the question 'Iudices cur sedeant' (pp. 619–20).

12. *The Civil Law, including the Twelve Tables, the Institutes of Gaius, the Rules of Ulpian, the Opinions of Paulus, the Enactments of Justinian, and the Constitutions of Leo*, trans. and ed. S. P. Scott, 17 vols, vol. 16 (Cincinnati: The Central Trust Company, 1932). 'Sedebunt autem hi pedanei iudices continue, et nunc in regia basilica, in quibus et tunc domunculis iudicant.'

13. Ibid. 'quod datum est eis super hoc privilegium, ne cogantur aut sedere cum iudicibus cum iudicant aut stare rursus tamquam litigantes.'

14. 'Jus in castris sedens dicebat.'

15. 'Sedebant iudices centum et octoginta, [. . .] ingens utrimque advocatio et numerosa subsellia.'

16. 'Accusavi de pecuniis repetundis, iudex sedi, prætor quæsivi, defendi plurimos'; emphasis added.

17. 'Minos sedet arbiter Orci.'

18. Thuilius' commentary of Alciato's *Emblemata cum commentariis*, p. 619: 'Sedent autem vel ideo iudices, quia eos graves, quietos, et constantes esse oportet, nec facile commoveri.'

19. 'Sedit Moyses ut judicaret populum.'

20. Annette Ruelle, 'Sacrifice, énonciation et actes de langage en droit romain archaïque (*"agone", lege agere, cum populo agere*)', *Revue Internationale des Droits de l'Antiquité* 49, no. 1 (2002), pp. 203–39.

21. Damhouder, *Praxis rerum criminalium*, ch. 154, p. 1666, col. 2.

22. See the French translation by Pierre Pellegrin, *Physique* (Paris: Flammarion, 2002), p. 370: 'Car c'est par le fait que l'âme atteigne le calme en abandonnant son trouble naturel que l'on devient prudent et savant.'

23. Sigismondo Scaccia, *Tractatus de sententia et re iudicata* (Venice: Jacob Scalea, 1629), p. 232, glossa 8.6–7: 'Ratio huius conclusionis est, quia anima, sedendo, et quiescendo, fit prudentior [. . .] Nam cum movetur corpus, movetur anima, et ideo non est in soliditate rationis, sed cum sedet, anima laborat circa intellectum, et sic fit prudentior, quia non distrahitur intellectus ad aliam operationem.'

24. Ibid., pp. 232–3, glossa 8.8.

25. Bernard de La Roche Flavin, *Treize livres des parlements de France [. . .]* (Bordeaux: Simon Millanges, 1617), pp. 563–4: '*Les juges doivent ester assis en iugeant et opinant. Chapitre XII*. De tout temps, et en tous lieux, les Juges ont accoustumé de rendre la iustice, non debout, ny en se pourmenant, ains assis en des sièges, ou chaires à ce ordonnées en tous les tribunals où la justice a accoustumé d'estre rendue. [. . .]. C'est pourquoy par nos Mercuriales de l'an 1581, il est prohibé aux Conseillers [. . .] de permettre que les procureurs, ou les parties playdent devant eux en sortant du Palais, aux basses Cours d'iceluy, ny par les rues en sortant, ains qu'ils s'en aillent tenir leur audians dans la grande salle des Procureurs, assis en un des bancs des Procureurs, sur peine de nullité [. . .].'

26. *Œuvres de François Rabelais*, vol. 4, *Tiers Livre*, ed. Abel Lefranc (Paris: Champion, 1931), p. 310.

27. Boniface VIII, *Sextus decretalium liber* (Paris: Merlin, 1561), p. 396, col. 2: 'Anima enim sedendo et quiescendo sit prudentior. [. . .] Sedes describitur, ut maturitas sententiae sententiæ comprobetur. Unde si quid si in culo doleret, quod sedere non posset? Item qui si in ipsa sede nec sederet, nec staret: sed jaceret?' See J. Duncan M. Derrett, 'Rabelais' Legal Learning and the Trial of Bridoye', *Bibliothèque d'Humanisme et Renaissance* 25, no. 1 (1963), pp. 111–71 (p. 171).

28. Benoît Le Court, *Arresta Amorum* (Lyon: Sébastien Gryphe, 1533), p. 2: 'An vero iudex inter iudicandum debeat sedere? [. . .] Et quid si id non possit ob infirmitatem? And hanc vero rem Plautus in Mostellaria: Nimio plus sapio sedens.'

29. Priscian, *De Laude Anastasii Imperatoris*, trans. Patricia Coyne (Lewiston, NY: Edwin Mellen Press, 1991), p. 67.

30. Master Eckhart, Sermons 90 a–b (Sturlese 14 a–b), in *Sermons, traités, poèmes. Les écrits allemands*, trans. J. Ancelet-Hustache (Paris: Seuil, 2015), p. 145.

31. See Richard Begam, 'Beckett's Kinetic Aesthetics', *Journal of Beckett Studies*, special issue, 'Transnational Beckett', 16, nos 1 and 2 (2006–7), pp. 46–63.

32. 'To hold on to the claret' means abusing *clairet* wine (*claret, clairet*, by attraction of *cler*, is attested since the first half of the thirteenth century).

33. Pierre Coustau, *Pegma cum narrationibus philosophicis* (Lyon: Macé Bonhomme, 1555), p. 209: 'In perfunctoriè iudicantes. Μήδὲ δίκην δικάσῃς πρὶν ἀμφοῖν μῦθον ἀκούσῃς' (Against judges who are indifferent to the causes they defend. Don't give judgment until you have heard both sides of the case).

34. See Peter Goodrich, *Œdipus Lex: Psychoanalysis, History, Law* (Berkeley: University of California Press, 1995), p. 2, quoting Sir Edward Coke, *A book of Entries containing perfect and approved presidents of Courts, Declarations . . . and all other matters and proceedings (in effect) concerning the pratick part of the laws of England*, 2nd edn (1610; London: Streeter, 1671), fol. A 5 a: 'So too, even Sir Edward Coke, most usually an eulogist of the tradition and its perfections, was forced to admit that the student in the laws of the realm, "having sedentariam vitam, is not commonly longlived; the study is abstruse and difficult, the occasion sudden, the practice dangerous."'

35. Antoine Garapon, *Bien juger. Essai sur le rituel judiciaire* (Paris: Odile Jacob, 2001), p. 117: 'L'accusateur s'élève, se dresse, s'insurge, s'oppose; il accuse, montre du doigt, crée une rupture corporelle et scénique: c'est la magistrature debout. Le juge est assis, il écoute, prend des avis, ses gestes sont moins visibles, moins spectaculaires, il ne bouge pas, il délibère, il tourne la tête d'un côté et de l'autre, il est réfléchi: c'est la magistrature assise. L'image de l'homme debout évoque un affrontement, et d'ailleurs l'avocat se lèvera à son tour pour répliquer. Celle de l'homme assis évoque la tranquillité, la sérénité et la stabilité. On se lève pour s'affronter; on s'assoit pour échanger.'

36. Ernst H. Kantorowicz, 'ΣΥΝΘΡΟΝΟΣ ΔΙΚΗΙ', *American Journal of Archaeology* 57, no. 2 (1953), pp. 65–70.

37. *Questiones de juris subtilitatibus*, ed. Ginevra Zanetti (Florence: La Nuova Italia, 1958).

38. John Amos Comenius, *Orbis sensualium pictus* (Nuremberg: Michael Endter, 1658), p. 240.

39. Barthélemy de Chasseneuz, *Catalogus Gloriæ Mundi* (Geneva: Pierre Chouet, 1649), p. 627, col. 2.

40. John Case, *Sphæra Civitatis; Hoc est; Reipublicæ recte ac pie secundum leges administrandæ ratio* (Oxford: Josephus Barnesius, 1588), p. 61.

41. Guillaume Le Rouillé, *De Justitia et injustitia* (Lyon: Jean David, 1529), fol. 24, quarto: 'Et debet iudex immobilis esse: ut columna.'

42. See Frances Yates, 'Queen Elizabeth as Astræa', *Journal of the Warburg and Courtauld Institutes* 10 (1947), pp. 27–82; Frances A. Yates, *Astræa: The Imperial Theme in the Sixteenth Century* (London: Routledge, 1975).

43. Edmund Spenser, *The Faerie Queene: Book Five*, ed. Abraham Stoll (Indianapolis: Hackett, 2006), canto I, xi, p. 10.

44. David Rosand, *Myths of Venice: The Figuration of a State* (Chapel Hill: University of North Carolina Press, 2005).

45. L. B. T. Houghton, 'Maritime Maro: Virgil in Venice', in *Virgil's Fourth Eclogue in the Italian Renaissance* (Cambridge: Cambridge University Press, 2019), pp. 67–88.

46. Ellen Rosand, *Opera in Seventeenth-Century Venice: The Creation of a Genre* (Berkeley: University of California Press, 2007), p. 131.

47. Gianluca Belli, 'Un monumento per Cosimo I de' Medici. La Colonna della Giustizia a Firenze', *Annali di architettura. Rivista del Centro internazionale du Studi di Architettura Andrea Palladio di Vicenza* 16 (2004), pp. 57–78 (ill. 11, p. 67).

48. Henri Delaborde, *Marc-Antoine Raimondi; étude historique et critique suivie d'un catalogue raisonné des œuvres du maître* (Paris: Librairie de l'Art, 1888), pp. 188, 191.

49. Nicolas de Nancel, *Eisodus triomphalis/Triomphes et magnificiences faictes à l'entrée de Monseigneur filz de France et frere unicques du Doyen la ville de Tours, le vingthuictième jour d'aoult 1576*, Bibliothèque nationale de France, Ms. Fr. 848, fols 58r–71v (fol. 62r).

50. Ibid.

51. See 'Goddess *Justitia* and the paradoxes of *icones symbolicæ*' in Chapter 1.

52. E. H. Gombrich, '*Icones Symbolicæ*: The Visual Image in Neo-Platonic Thought', *Journal of the Warburg and Courtauld Institutes* 11 (1948), p. 179.

53. Jean de Vandenesse, *Collection des voyages des souverains des Pays-Bas*, vol. 2 (Brussels: Gachard Louis-Prosper, 1874), p. 569: 'Relation de l'entrée de Charles-Quint dans la ville de Mesine: 20 octobre 1536, 'Par ses loys paix règne, la déesse Astrea visite ses terres.'

54. Honoré d'Urfé, *Triomphante Entrée de très illustre dame Mme Magdeleine de la Rochefoucauld [. . .] Faicte en la ville et université de Tournon le dimanche vingt-quatrième du mois d'Avril 1583* (Lyon: Jean Pillehotte, 1583; reprinted as vol. 4 of *Images et témoins de l'âge classique*, ed. Maxime Gaume, Saint-Étienne: Presses de l'Université de Saint-Étienne, 1976), pp. 7–25.

55. Ibid., p. 59: 'Astrée tu le sais, ô Thémis, / Et toy Pere commun, Dieu puissant qui as mis / Dedans, l'esprit divin de ce Tournon amiable / De tes biens éternels trésor admirable.'

56. Ibid., pp. 61, 76.

57. Vincent Voiture, *Hymnus Virginis seu Astrææ. Ad illustrissimum Virum Dominum De Verdun, æquissimum Parisiensis Senatus Principem* (Paris: Julliot, 1612).

58. C. H. Rawski (ed.), *Petrarch's Remedies for Fortune Fair and Foul: A Modern English Translation of De remediis utriusque fortunæ*, 5 vols (Bloomington: Indiana University Press, 1991), vol. 1, p. 172, qtd in Walter S. Gibson, 'Festive Peasants before Bruegel: Three Case Studies and Their Implications', *Simiolus: Netherlands Quarterly for the History of Art* 21, no. 4 (2004–5), pp. 292–309 (p. 292).

59. Natalis Comes, *Mythologiæ, sive explicationis fabularum libri decem* (Padua: Tozzi, 1616), p. 58: '[. . .] ut scripserint pœtæ Justitiam e terris aufugisse, et in

cœlum convolasse: quæ naturæ fuit equitas in animis hominam insita, quæ paulatim crescentibus scriptis legibus ob hominum malitia ex animis mortalium deleta est. [. . .] Nam quanto simpliciores errant homines, tanto justiores errant natura: ubi legum volumina in civitatibus quasi Astrææ testamenta composita sunt, illa simplicitas paulatim ad rusticos homines extra civitatem recessit, ad horum testamentorum ignaros.'

60. Gibson, 'Festive Peasants before Bruegel', p. 292.

61. Joos [Josse] de Damhouder, *Opera omnia in quibus Praxis rerum criminalium [. . .] pertractantur* (Antwerp: Petrus Bellerus, 1646), ch. 158, p. 235: 'Sub Justitiæ pedibus substratam vides, sub persona rustici, miseram, calamitosamque plebeculam, cui Unusquisque nomen imponitur. Huic cum cæteris calamitosis hominibus appictus est cælestis paradisus, cuius hi omnes post has ærumnas, post multa injusta dure quidem, sed patienti animo perpessa, cum fide bona, & spe æquioris Iustitiæ percipiendæ, in futura eaque vita vera, sese fore participes sperant.'

62. Richard W. Wallace, 'Salvator Rosa's "Justice Appearing to the Peasants"', *Journal of the Warburg and the Courtauld Institutes* 30 (1967), pp. 431–4.

63. Pierre Wachenheim, 'Emblèmes de la Robe: les représentations de la Justice dans l'imagerie pro-parlementaire sous le règne de Louis XV', *Sociétés & Représentations* 18, no. 2 (2004), pp. 233–49.

64. Luc-Vincent Thiéry, *Guide des amateurs et des étrangers voyageurs à Paris ou Description raisonnée de cette Ville [. . .]*, vol. 2 (Paris: Hardouin et Gattey, 1787), p. 28: 'En rentrant dans la galerie Mercière, on trouve dans son milieu l'entrée qui monte à la Cour des Aides: elle est annoncée par deux colonnes ioniques, couronnées par l'entablement de cette galerie, et surmontée des armes du Roi. [. . .] L'escalier éclairé par le haut produit un grand effet [. . .]. A la bifurcation de l'escalier, se voit la statue de la Justice par M. Gois, Sculpteur du Roi: elle est placée dans une niche couronnée d'un fronton.'

65. Honoré Lacombe de Prezel, *Dictionnaire iconologique ou introduction à la connoissance des peintures, sculptures, médailles, estampes, pierres gravées, emblèmes, devises [. . .]*, vol. 2 (Paris: Hardouin, 1779), p. 45: 'LOI: On l'a représentée sous le symbole d'une femme majestueuse, assise sur un Tribunal avec un diadème sur la tête, un sceptre en main et un livre ouvert à ses pieds, sur lequel on voir écrit cette sentence, *In Legibus salus*.'

66. Jean-Raymond de Petity, *Le Manuel des artistes et des amateurs, ou Dictionnaire historique et mythologique des emblèmes, allégories, énigmes, devises, attributs et symboles*, vol. 2 (Paris: J. P. Costard, 1770), pp. 526–7: 'LOI: [. . .] Elle a un diadème rayonnant pour marquer que son origine est sainte. Le Sceptre qu'elle tient dénote son autorité; et le Livre ouvert avec les paroles, *In Legibus Salus*, signifie la récompense qu'elle promet à ceux qui lui obéissent.'

67. These highly finished sheets belong to a series executed for the Academy of Poetry and Music created during the reign of Charles IX, in November 1570. See Per Bjurström, 'Etienne Delaune and the Academy of Poetry and Music', *Master Drawings* 34, no. 4 (1996), pp. 351–64.

68. Michael Baxandall, *The Limewood Sculptors of Renaissance Germany* (New Haven, CT: Yale University Press, 1980), p. 78.

69. Christian-Nils Robert, *Une allégorie parfaite. La Justice: vertu, courtisane et bourreau* (Geneva: Georg Éditeur, 1993).

70. Paul Hofer, *Die Kunstdenkmäler des Kantons Bern, Band I, Die Stadt Bern* (Basel: Verlag Birkhäuser, 1952), pp. 314–17.

71. Ursula Schneeberger, 'Zuo beschirmen die gerechtikeÿtt, [. . .] un wer es allen fürsten leÿtt. Staat, Krieg und Moral im Program der Berner Brunnenfiguren', in André Holenstein (ed.), *Berns mächtige Zeit. Das 16. und 17. Jahrhundert neu entdeckt*, vol. 3 (Bern: Berner Zeiten, 2006), pp. 157–62.

72. See ibid., p. 159.

73. See <https://vitrosearch.ch/en/objects/2246359>.

74. Another example of the influence of this iconography is a roundel of stained and painted glass from an unknown artist, dated 1586, kept today at the Victoria and Albert Museum (C. 63-1919. A blindfolded, standing Lady Justice, dressed in a red cloak, dominates the figures of a Pope, an emperor and three other potentates. The coat of arms depicted on the roundel are those of the magistrates of the regional court of Wetzikon, near Zurich.

75. Denis Diderot, *Salons*, ed. J. Seznec and J. Adhémar, vol. 3 (Oxford: Clarendon, 1963), p. 289.

76. For a penetrating study of Reynolds's *Justitia*, commenting on *Justitia*'s erected posture, see Desmond Manderson and Cristina S. Martinez, 'Justice and Art, Face to Face', *Yale Journal of Law & Humanities* 28, no. 2 (2016), pp. 241–63 (p. 257): 'In contrast with the staunch stability, legs apart and arms akimbo, of the Portrait of *Fortitude* (1778–9, Private collection), Reynolds depicts *Justice* in a life-like *contrapposto* stance, one leg straight and the other slightly bent at the knee. In a pose that affirms the decorum and dignity of his classical subject, *Justice* is neither walking not standing but poised for action. This fine balance between composure and alertness establishes her constant disposition to judge, and cleverly underlines the message of the scales she holds.'

Chapter 5

Lady Justice and the judge's body: maimed hands, bare knee

This chapter aims at confronting two problematic renderings of Lady Justice's limbs. The hitherto understudied links between Lady Justice's anatomy and the judge's body will then become visible and legible. The severed hands and the undressed knee are linked here because they may both be studied as metastases. The shifting of these motifs from the male body of the judge to the female body of allegory is not without significance. The analysis of body parts, which Desmond Manderson terms 'incarnadine jurisprudence,'[1] will help to define Justice as a praxis in response to and embodiment of polymorphous and sometimes perverse pursuits. This chapter aims at recovering the materiality and the corporeality of *Justitia*, her image being first and foremost her corporeal apparition and in varied senses her tellurian presence. *Justitia* is not only an ethereal emanation, she also belongs to the here and now of judicial praxis, to the terrestrial universe of legal satire, opening up a world of flesh, plasticity and desire.

The first motif is the bizarre depiction of maimed hands. Lady Justice is sometimes depicted as a *puella manca*: the motif derives from Plutarch (*De Iside et Osiride* 10.27) where the statues of Theban judges are said to have no hands, in order to signify that Justice is incorruptible. On the fresco displayed at the Baudet Tower in the City Town Hall of Geneva, Cesare Giglio is not content with reproducing an image of a judge without hands (Figure 5.1). He depicts the judges' amputated hands in an extremely lifelike manner, covering their bleeding stumps with red pigment. This is probably an attempt to emphasise the imaginary nature of the image in the mind (*eidolon*), if we recall that the

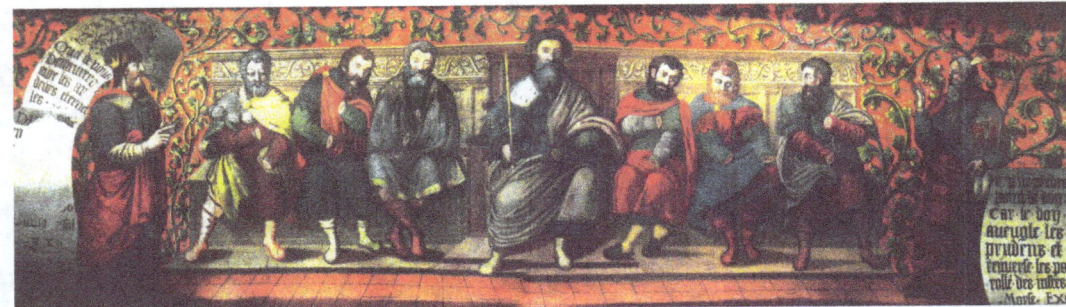

Figure 5.1: Hugues Bolard?, before 1523/Cesare Giglio?, c. 1541–72 or 1604?, *The Theban Judges between David and Moses*, Baudet Tower, City Town Hall of Geneva. Photograph by Sandra Pointet. Courtesy of the Centre d'iconographie genevoise

amputation of hands was above all one of the punishments which judges could inflict on the convicts of the time. It primarily focuses on a visual paradox: the 'naturalistic' depiction of the stumps clashes with the illusory character of artistic representation. The amputation of the hands migrates from the judicial figure to that of Justice portrayed as an amputated body. I will examine this transmission by means of a case study of a sculpted group preserved at the museum of Cambrai. Between the description of a mutilated statue and the realistic vision of a body without hands, the motif has a variable effect on the viewer.

The second iconographical problem which follows a similar metastasis concerns the knee. From the sovereign gesture (a sign of clemency) to the exhibition of Lady Justice's knee, the motif changes its meaning, inducing quite different reactions. The contamination of Lady Justice's anatomy with the judge's body (via the sovereign's body) shows how an apparently identical formula can morph into different forms. This chapter is an attempt to correlate the dramatic visual effects of truncated hands or noticeable knee gestures on both bodies. An increased attentiveness to these two features is noticeable from the end of the medieval period to the end of the seventeenth century. The nature of these anatomical emblems reveals a richer symbolism than the straightforward denotation of judicial attributes.

These patterns can be analysed through the Warburgian notion of energetic inversion. Collected under a common motif (severed hand or exposed knee), their visual correspondence will help to show the migration of a gesture from one configuration to another. In his notes to the *Mnemosyne Atlas*, Aby Warburg coined the idea of an 'iconology of interspace' (*Zwischenraum*), capable of uniting 'art historical material for a developmental physiology of the pendulous movement (*Pendelgang*) between stating a cause (*Ursachensetzung*) by means of images and doing this by means of signs.'[2] It is no coincidence that Aby Warburg used the kneeling position to define his *Pathosformel*:[3] a motif that is efficient enough in its movement (the energetic potential of its lines and contours) and its psychological content (the affective and emotional charge it contains) to have an immediate meaning and, therefore, to be able to exist in isolation. This chapter aims at investigating these two anatomical schemas in their propensity to become *pathos formulae* – images of gestures and memory capable of playing a considerable role in the transmission and migration of judicial ethics. The judge's body as well as *Justitia's* anatomy are used here as an archive of dynamic figures available for depicting judicial rituals.

The effigy of the amputated judge

A case study: Lady Justice standing in front of the penitent judge

The first moment of the inquiry will be rooted in the examination of the double image of the penitent judge paying *amende honorable* to Lady Justice, preserved today in the Musée Municipal of Cambrai (Figure 5.2). The artwork has been described as the remaining wooden *modello* of a judge kneeling before Lady Justice. The group had been set on the front façade of the courthouse of Cambrai in memory of the judicial error committed by the judge. The condemnation of the erring judge and his damnation is the usual paradigm of the time. A corrupt judge will be punished severely for failing in his overarching role of rendering to each their due. The interesting thing here is that the double effigy remains ambivalent and becomes the focal point of several narratives for the admission of guilt. I will try to reconstruct what might have been their fate in 1551 and then show how the sculpture was used to perpetuate the memory of the judge's crime. This contextual approach will explain how the motif of maimed hands is reworked with great sophistication.

The two sculptures are carved in oak: the kneeling judge 93 cm high, and Lady Justice 127 cm. Lady Justice holds in her left hand a pair of

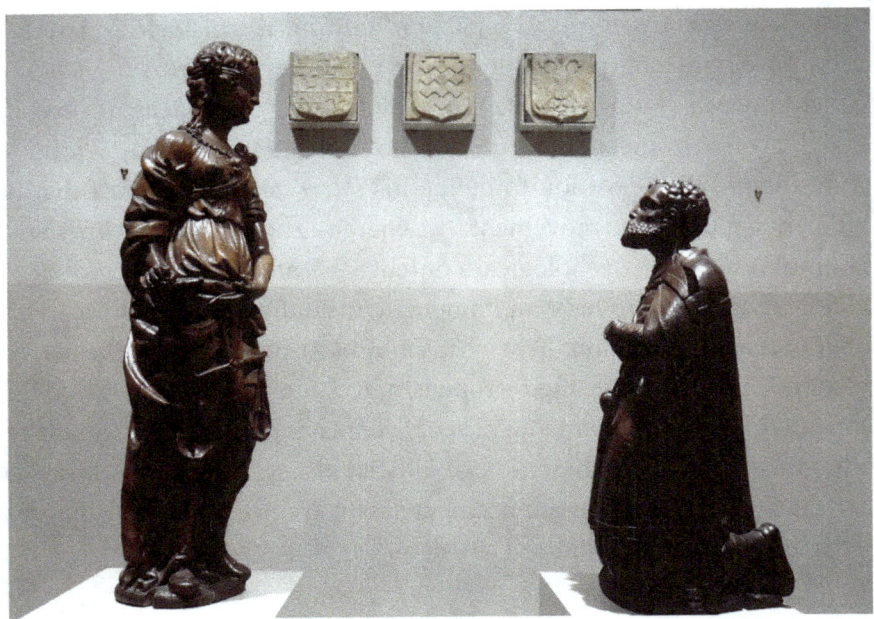

Figure 5.2: Guillaume Dannolle, *Jehan de Boves Kneeling in Front of Lady Justice*, c. 1551. Musée Municipal de Cambrai. Photograph by the author

scales; her right hand is slightly broken but a close examination shows that she used to lean on a downward-pointing sword. In front of her, the effigy of the penitent bailiff is bareheaded, kneeling, in a typical gesture of *amende honorable*. His hands are amputated.

One way of seeing this group is to use René Girard's theory of mimetic desire: Girard regards mimesis as the structure by which humans open themselves to the world and he believes that there must be a deep biological basis for it.[4] The vicious bailiff is an example of the scapegoat mechanism, in Girard's terms: unveiling his fault enables the community to achieve the restoration of peace, but it comes at the expense of the victim. But before settling on such an interpretation, we need to recall its original context: a sixteenth-century French bailiff was sentenced to public humiliation. The artwork was designed to be prominently displayed in public, on the Grand' Place or central marketplace of the town, the figures integrated into the façade of the town hall (Figure 5.3). It is useful to reconstruct its setting in the *longue durée*, from its creation, sometime around 1551, until its destruction during the French Revolution. For several centuries, the statues were seen by a variety of individuals and groups.

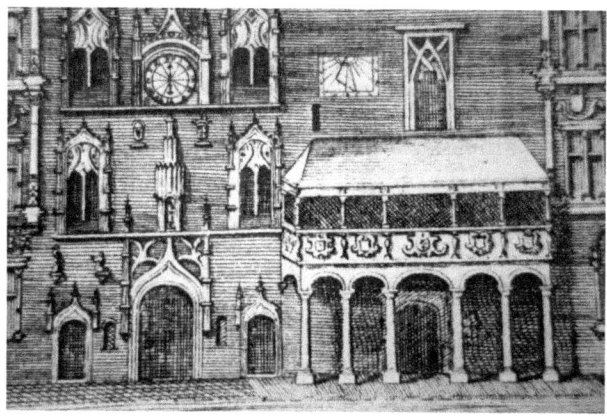

Figure 5.3: Original setting of both sculptures on the façade of the town hall of Cambrai, showing the *bretèque*. In P. Foppens, J.-B. Chrystin and F. Foppens, *Les Délices des Pays-bas ou Description générale de ses dix-sept provinces, de ses principales villes et de ses lieux les plus renommez* (Brussels: F. Foppens, 1697), p. 466. Photograph by the author

Cambrai was one of the twelve fortified cities of the Spanish Low Countries. The city had a strategic role due to its position on the frontier: it was ruled by a Count Bishop, who was the visible kin of the *imperium*. The intricate network of jurisdictions (at imperial and local levels) caused political and judicial tensions. This case may be described as an example of the Goldoni problem of serving two masters. The French bailiff of Marcoing, Jehan de Boves, was trapped between two conflicting authorities. He was condemned to pay a fine of 300 florins and ordered to commission an effigy of his public humiliation from the sculptor Guillaume Dannolle, executed in 1552 along with the inscription 'Jehan de Bove, bailli de Marcoing, demande merchy à la Justice' (Jehan de Bove, bailiff of Marcoing, asks Lady Justice for mercy). The bronze version was placed above the entrance of the courthouse of Cambrai to perpetuate the memory of his failure and punishment. In the archives, his kneeling posture is insisted on. On 28 May 1551, 'Jehan de Boves fut condamné à prier merchy à Dieu et à faire sa statue d'airain à genoux' (Jehan de Boves was condemned to pray to God for his grace and to have his kneeling statue fashioned in bronze).

The archives also tell the nature of his crime and the reason for his trial. In 1550, Jehan de Boves had his tax collector, Jehan de Tournay, arrested, without referring his arrest to the higher magistrate. Here we have the juridical character of his sentence: *poena usurpationis*. He was tried because he had not referred the matter to the Count Bishop. From 1550 to 1560, Philip II ordained a reorganisation of all jurisdictions; the presence of Reformers in the North was a constant bone of contention. This decade is characterised by political and religious instability, just before confessionalisation tore apart distinctive clans. The bailiff Jehan de Boves opposed his judicial power to the privileges of the town and this – not because he accepted bribes (the usual scheme for the corrupted judge) – is the principal reason for his conviction. This might explain why the bailiff was granted a reprieve in equity. Instead of being sentenced to infamous death (by wheel, gallows, rack or press), he was executed . . . but only in effigy.

The maimed hands of the bailiff

The Cambrai sculpture is made of wood, and one of its main features is to transform the original motif (a statue of the judge in isolation) into a lively pair. From the statuesque to the animate, the duet performs a genuine interaction – goddess and worshipper, idol and idolater, an icon of platonic desire. Viewed as a compositional whole, they form a symbolic dyad personifying earthly and divine justice, which seems to come to life. This sculptural group had a greater visibility to the general public than a statue hidden in the courthouse precincts, being close to the eye level of passers-by, enabling a detailed observation of the image.

The statue's severed hands were probably part of the sculpture's original design. It derives from Andrea Alciato's influential legal emblem 'In Senatum boni Principis' (In the Senate of a Good Prince), where judges are depicted handless, lest they be swayed by gifts or promises.[5] In 1551, the sculptor Guillaume Dannolle produced an early reference to the iconographic development of the Theban judges' motif, more than fifty years before the version painted by Cesare Giglio in Geneva, before Pierio Valeriano's account of the motif in his *Hieroglyphica* (Basel, 1556), or that of Vincenzo Cartari in *Imagini degli dei antichi* (Venice, 1556). Before them all a humanist sculptor born in Cambrai, who had travelled in Italy, had already designed an original sculpture alluding to the antique source of the Theban judges. The novelty of his creation should not be underestimated. It is worth noting that the motif of the maimed hands is associated with a kneeling posture. This unique combination is significant: praying hands are turned into maimed hands, preventing the corrupt judge from praying.

If we look at the original setting of the sculpture on the façade of the town hall, two points should be noticed. First, the original group is conceived as a pair, exhibited on two pedestals situated at the same level. The standing Lady Justice is located at the same level as Jehan de Boves. They face each other, and belong alike to the urban landscape of the 'Grand' Place'. Second, they are not included in any predefined visual hierarchy of values. The tradition usually represents *Justitia* alongside her siblings: Temperance, Prudence and Force, the other three cardinal virtues. But here the two figures are removed from such a framework. The devilish judge, in his unequal encounter with Lady Justice, is the object of personification and becomes a legal entity enacting a struggle *per se*. He stands between the *bretèque* (an outdoor tribune), the judges' loggia and the main door.

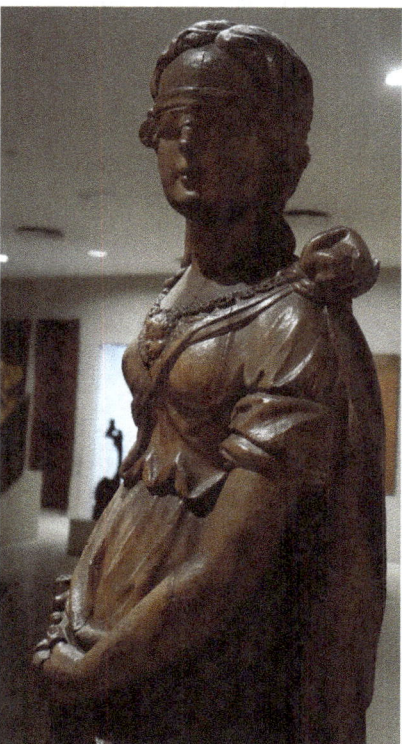

Figure 5.4: Guillaume Dannolle, detail of Lady Justice, c. 1551. Musée Municipal de Cambrai. Photograph by the author

As a typical *exemplum justitiæ*, this sculptural pair was first intended to connect the magistrates with the dangers and pitfalls of their daily practice. In the wooden group, Jehan de Boves is bareheaded, with maimed hands. Imploringly, he looks up at Justice. Lady Justice wears a kind of peplum tied at her waist. The penitent judge is forced to pay homage to Lady Justice and in return her blindfold makes her look as if she is implacable and merciless – he cannot look into her eyes (Figure 5.4). The scene is above all an allegory of public humiliation, an unequal dialogue between authority and submission which shows blatantly and painfully the limitations of earthly legal officials.

The missing hands: a shaming ritual?

The nineteenth-century interpretation of the scene treats the handless gesture as a sign of prayer, without acknowledging that the hands were missing.[6] The hypothesis, however, of pre-existing praying hands, perhaps in another material (silver, for instance), is unlikely, as the space between the two stumps is not far enough to contain extended hands in prayer (Figure 5.5). The stumps show no indication of the graft of silver hands onto them. The neat truncation of both hands suggests that the cut-off state of the sculpture reflects the original design, rather than loss or destruction. Religious scholars of the nineteenth century had long been aware of

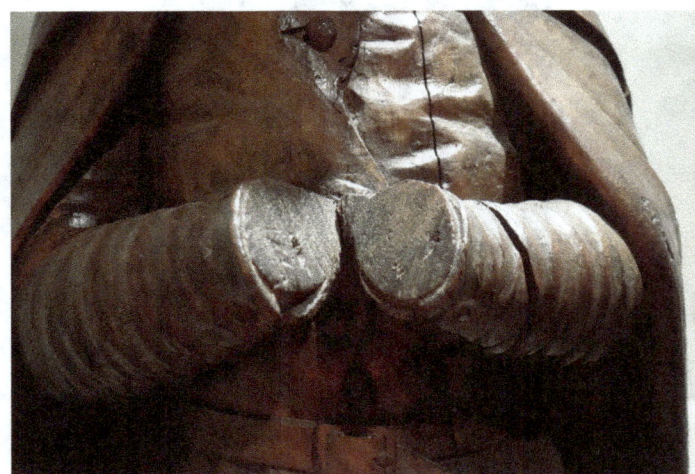

Figure 5.5: Guillaume Dannolle, detail of the bailiff's maimed hands, c. 1551. Musée Municipal de Cambrai. Photograph by the author

the ritual practice of the *amende honorable*; if the effigy of the bailiff is indeed represented in prayer, the motif of the maimed hands changes its meaning, as it suggests that the judge is paying for his forfeitures.

A licentious tale about the double effigy, written in 1763, mocks 'le vieux Jérôme,'[7] a fictive elaboration on the theme of the sexually vicious judge. The kneeling judge's genitals (Figure 5.6) were carved with special attention to its *braguette*, a codpiece which was appended to the front of the breeches during the late fifteenth and sixteenth centuries.[8] The treatment of the judge's codpiece is crude and oversized, and it prompted moral indignation and licentious verses. In front of this uninhibited exhibition, Lady Justice seems to cover up her intimate parts with her scales in a gesture of modesty. In the 1763 poetic account of the judge's trial, his phallus was mocked as a proof of his sexual deviance and his organ was submitted to a parodic ordeal. In the build-up to the Revolution, then, the sculpture's meaning changed dramatically: it became a public staging of the judge's sexual feebleness. The image of the vicious

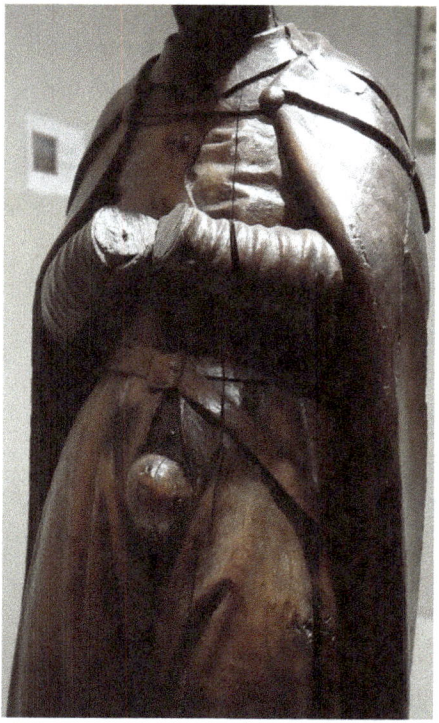

Figure 5.6: Guillaume Dannolle, detail of the bailiff's codpiece. Musée Municipal de Cambrai. Photograph by the author

judge became a focal point for different shaming practices, perhaps serving as a ritual scapegoat, perhaps as a kind of figurative outlet for growing public discontent. Finally, during the French Revolution, the bronze sculptures were carried to the Arsenal of Douai where they were melted down and converted into canon parts.

A double effigy of Justice

The common saying about effigies during early modern times is coined as *vera imago et effigies*: the effigy, as an incarnate form, can be used as a substitute for *persona* and it has a judicial function of real presence. Jehan de Boves' effigy acts more as a site of interpretative plurality. The representation of Lady Justice immediately next to a judicial figure is an unusual visual strategy. Their intimate interaction might be perceived as sadomasochistic, the maiming of the hands suggestive of castration, which takes phantasmagoric residence in the public eye. Somewhere between charivari and fictive trials, it brings to the fore a vision far removed from prejudices against obscenity. The mutilation of a body is of little use if there are no viewers. The figure of the amputated bailiff exemplifies the symmetry between divine and earthly justice, the corporal punishment inflicted on the judge paralleling the justice meted out by local rulers.[9] Dannolle combined the judge's penitential humility with the specific stigmata of corrupted judges. This association appears to stage an inversion of good and evil, highlighting the responsibility of the wicked judge facing damnation. The judge's posture, an expression of submissive humility, is similar to religious *proskynesis*, a concrete hierarchical prostration of an inferior to a superior rather than an abstract veneration. In front of the dominating figure of a standing Lady Justice, the kneeling judge adopts a posture of *adoratio*, performing an asymmetrical gesture of obeisance (a genuflection). The image of the damned bailiff exhorts our submission to the judicial institution.

Marten de Vos's *Adorodokia*

The iconography of maimed Justice has received great scholarly attention.[10] Michael Evans has stressed the originality of this theme, its medieval antecedents, its revival during the early modern period and the surprising coincidences that led to the reappearance of the Plutarchian image without establishing a historical filiation between the two periods.[11] In two fifteenth-century German manuscripts studied by Evans, Lady Justice is blind and her arms are maimed below the shoulders.[12] The image is glossed by a Latin text, which links the truncated hands to her incorruptibility. On her left, a man holding a parchment scroll claims that she would be more beautiful if she had hands and eyes whilst on her left, another one holds a scroll saying that, on the contrary, if she had hands and eyes, she would be very unsightly or unseemly (*turpissima*).

The Greek word for bribery illustrates this concept very neatly (*dorodokia* 'receiving gifts'). Hesiod's 'gift-swallowing nobles' (*basilêes dôrophagoi*) are strongly condemned as they pervert justice (*Work and Days*, ll. 37–9, 220–1, 261–4). A man who refuses to take bribes is *adoros* (Thucydides 2.65.8[13]) or *adorodoketos* (Demosthenes 19.274). In the *Laws*, Plato considers the matter with great severity: any official of the state who accepts a bribe, whether with good intentions or bad, is to be put to death (955c–d). The Supreme Court, he says, is to be 'as incorruptible as human power can make it' (768b). Quoting the oath of the archons, Aristotle reports that 'they climb on the stone, and swear that they will justly govern according to the laws, and will not accept bribes on account of their office', and that if they should accept any bribes, they would dedicate a golden statue (*Athenaion Politeia* 7.1).[14] It should be noted that no such golden statue as mentioned in the oath, as far as we know, was ever erected.[15]

Evans noted that an allegorical drawing by Marten de Vos, bearing the Greek title *Adorodokia*, is a close pictorial analogue of the medieval maimed Justices (Figure 5.7).[16] The case of the allegorical depiction of *Adorodokia* needs to be read here with a Warburgian eye, offering an interval for thinking, interpreting and sensing the history of images aside from the historical relationship between a model and its probable archetypes. Marten de Vos's allegory of integrity draws heavily on the motif of the Theban judges, but it also invents afresh a new form of female allegory. The surviving motif of maimed hands applies here to a statue of a new abstraction. Marten de Vos seems to combine two first-hand sources, drawn from a precise knowledge of antiquity. First, Plutarch's *Concerning Isis and Osiris* (*De Iside et Osiride* 10.27): 'In Thebes there were set up statues of judges without hands, and the statue

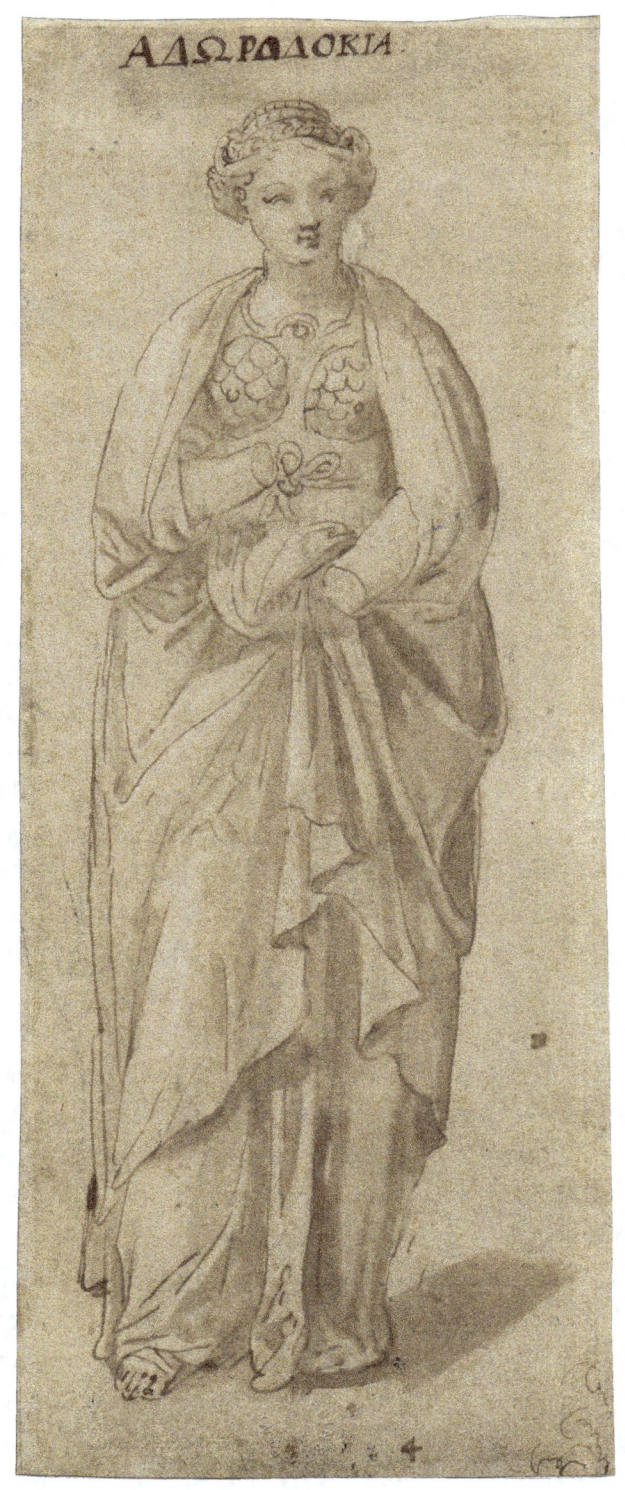

Figure 5.7: Marten de Vos, *Adorodokia* (Integrity), c. 1593–4, drawing, paper, 32.5 cm × 13.5 cm, inv. PK.OT.00017. Courtesy of the Museum Plantin-Moretus, Antwerp

of the chief justice had its eyes closed, to indicate that justice is not influenced by gifts or by intercession.' But the detail of the 'figure of Truth hanging from his neck' only appears in Diodorus Siculus' *Library of History* (1.48.6):

> In this hall there are many wooden statues representing parties in litigation, whose eyes are fixed upon the judges who decide their cases; and these, in turn, are shown in relief on one of the walls, to the number of thirty and without any hands, and in their midst the chief justice, *with a figure of Truth hanging from his neck* and holding his eyes closed, and at his side a great number of books. And these figures show by their attitude that the judges shall receive no gift and that the chief justice shall have his eyes upon the truth alone.[17]

The statues described by Diodorus Siculus were made of wood. Marten de Vos imagined a marble female statue with maimed hands, adding what seems to be an eyed necklace around her neck. The motif of the

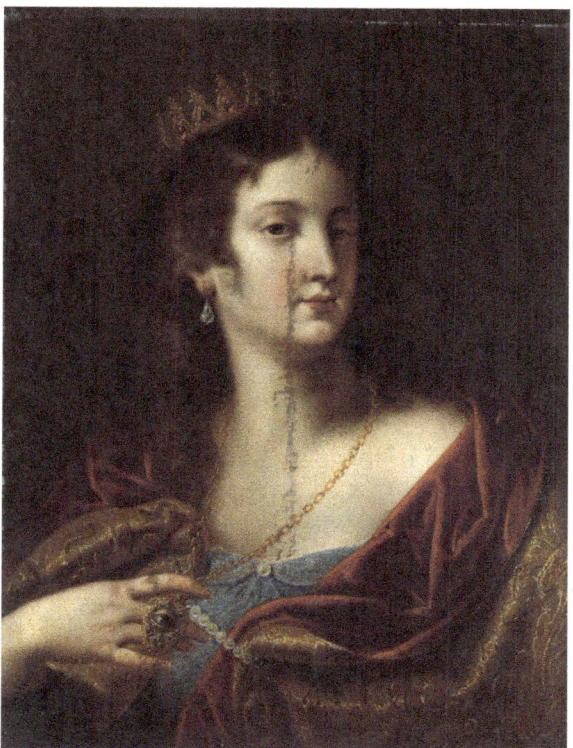

Figure 5.8: Anonymous painting, *Justice*, Florence, 1650–1720, oil on canvas, 74 cm × 57 cm, SK-A-1220. Courtesy of the Rijksmuseum, Amsterdam

eyed necklace of truth (*veritas*) appears in an anonymous Florentine painting (c. 1650–1720) preserved at the Rijksmuseum, Amsterdam (Figure 5.8). In Marten de Vos's drawing, the figure's maimed limbs are those of a statue, not of a living body. The idealised stone figure with its smooth surface, empty sockets and lack of expression indicates a body devoid of envy. Among *Adorodokia*'s more inventive aspects are the large knot of her cloak, simply tied on the belly, emphasising even more the stumps' infirmity, and the rendering of her eyes, a strikingly calm countenance. Instead of describing a brutal image of *Invidia*, begrudging, grasping or snatching a purse out of avarice, greed or envy, often depicted with a distended belly, the artist represents a potent exemplum of a virtue defined by its sense of restraint, and underlined by the tight knot of her cloak. Marten de Vos's figure is a bold invention. He extracts the motif of mutilated hands from its strictly judicial context in order to essentialise the abstract quality of integrity, giving it a broader resonance.

Most of the other uses of the Theban judges' motif insist on its juristic context. In Henry Peacham's manuscript emblem books (c. 1610), his 'Iustitiæ Symbolum' focuses on the oratorical gestures, coloured robes (red for the judge and violet for the presiding judge) and exotic white turbans of the maimed statues of the Theban judges (Figure 5.9).[18] Peacham's symbol of Justice is a representation of three male judges, two of whom are shown with their severed hands protruding from ermine-hemmed sleeves. In the pose of the judges' figures, Peacham has not only transposed Plutarch's text (referenced in the margin); rather, what we see is a *performed* representation that echoes his own symbolisation of judicial ethics. The maimed hands have become a *pathos formula* (a figure that enables affectivity to be stored and transmitted) for judicial ethics, the signature of a powerful dynamic of the body.

The innovative motif of the judge's maimed hands, though odd and somehow iconoclastic, introduces an important shift if we think of the use of judicial symbols in early medieval sources. In the Netherlands and in other Northern European countries, next to the seat of the judge stood the Rod of Justice.[19] Such rods were made of wood, sometimes debarked, painted or made of precious metals. Originally, they were handed to the judge by the monarch as the judge would hold the rod in his right hand when executing his office. In later periods, the rod could be held by an officer of the court or placed into a hand fixed to the wall

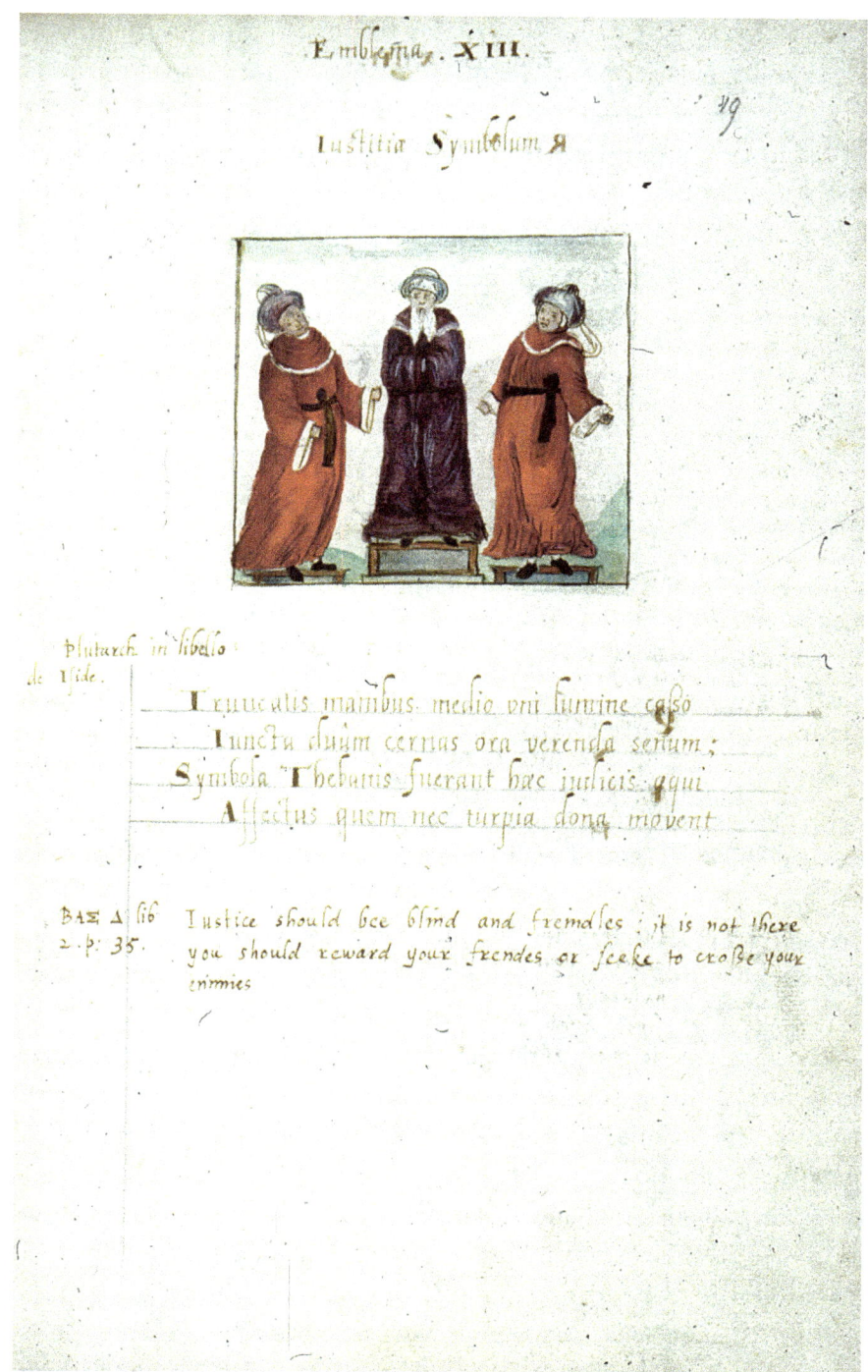

Emblema. XIII.

Iustitiæ Symbolum R

Plutarch. in libello
de Iside.

Truncas manibus medio vni fumine caso
Iuncta duum cernas ora verenda senum;
Symbola Thebanis fuerant hæc iudicis æqui
Affectus quem nec turpia dona movent

ΒΑΣ Δ lib
2. p. 35.

Iustice should bee blind and friendles; it is not there
you should reward your frendes or seeke to crosse your
enimies

Figure 5.9: Henry Peacham, 'Iustitiæ Symbolum', in *Three books of emblems*, London, c. 1610, Royal 12 A LXVI, emblem 13. British Library

(*manus justitiæ*). Cesare Ripa claims that the rod in the right hand signifies the judges' power over the criminal. Thus, the insistence on the crippled body of the failed judge bears witness to the epoch's difficulties in fixing a complacent, decorous image of criminal justice. Beyond the office's decorum, one catches a glimpse of the energetic inversions which may hide underneath the seemingly ridiculous narrative of the corrupted judge. A similar complexity can be demonstrated with knee gestures.

Clemency

Knee gestures

An uncovered knee is a very common feature in the representation of Lady Justice's body. There are many examples of Justices displaying a knee (usually the right one) in an unnatural way. The robe of Lady Justice is adapted so that her knee is protruding, becoming the principal focus of the body. Mario Sbriccoli introduces the exposed knee into *Justitia*'s canonical ensemble of attributes and interprets it as a sign of clemency.[20] From Homer to the historiographers and the Greek and Latin poets, the classical tradition overflows with examples of the knees as signs of sovereigns' *pietas*, *magnanimitas* and *clementia*. Sergio Bertelli writes that clemency is above all a royal virtue.[21] Kings are often depicted with knees exposed precisely because subjects who ask for mercy or intercession embrace their knees.

Our analysis of this bodily gesture may involve different processes (subordination, engagement, proximity) rather than attempting to subsume them under a single narrative. The abbreviated, almost lexico-graphic, attribution of a single meaning to a complex gesture risks falling into the iconographic fallacy.[22] Uncovering one's knee involves a *reciprocal* agency (a gesture of mercy answering a gesture of supplica-tion) belonging to a dense nexus of associations.[23] It proves useful to distinguish here between symptoms and warning signals, each channel-ling a different type of non-verbal communication.[24] Moreover, a similar gesture performed by a male or a female agent may reveal the differ-ences (or similarities) between gendered roles. The meaning of *Justitia*'s knee was not uniform but varied, part of a symbolic constellation, depending on moral values and specific contexts.

The knee as 'seat of clemency'

In his rhetorical and ethical treatise in 1616, *L'Arte de' cenni*, the jurisconsult and man of letters Giovanni Bonifacio (1547–1635) argues that gestures are more natural to the mind than words. The first part of the book is a comprehensive verbal description of around six hundred bodily gestures, moving from head to toe. The knee, he argues, is said to be 'consecrated to the goddess Mercy',[25] quoting Pliny (*Natural History* 11.103):

> The knees of a human being also possess a sort of religious sanctity in the usage of the nations. Suppliants touch the knees and stretch out their hands towards them, and pray at them as at altars, perhaps because they contain a certain vital principle.[26]

Pliny's quote echoes the Homeric epic, in which life was described by the mobility of the knees, death by the slackening of the knees.[27] Bonifacio's argument follows a passage from Servius' commentary on the *Aeneid* 3.607, dedicating each part of the body to a special virtue:

> Naturalists say that each part of the body is consecrated to deities, such as the ear to Memory [. . .], the forehead to Genius [. . .] our knees to Pity (*Misericordia*), hence the fact that supplicants touch them.[28]

For the Romans, the invocation of a man by his knees was also a form of emphatic supplication: *per tua genua te obsecro*.

No doubt the ability of genuflection to move to tears explains the symbolism of kneeling as an awakening of mercy. Isidore of Seville (early seventh century CE) claims that the etymology of *genua* ('knees') is derived from *genæ* ('eye-sockets') because the knees of the curled foetus press against the eyes, forming the hollows in which the eyes will later grow. Vestiges of this earlier state of existence, according to Isidore, can be found in tears:

> The knees are so called because within the womb they are opposed to the eye-sockets. In fact, they rest against them and are in close contact with

the eyes through tears and pity: indeed, we say knees (*genua*) because of the eye-sockets (*genæ*). In conclusion, it is said that man is engendered and formed in a curled position so that his knees are drawn up; by them are formed the eyes, in such a way that they are hollow and sunken. Ennius: And the narrow sockets compress the knees: hence men, when they sink to their knees, immediately begin to weep. For Nature makes them remember their mother's womb.[29]

The Bishop of Seville drew the etymological connection between the terms *genæ* (eye-sockets) and *genua* (knees) from the works of the Roman physician Helvius Vindicianus, author of a textbook about human anatomy, the *Gynaecia* (end of the fourth century CE).[30] Anatomists reworked the wordplay *genæ/genua* frequently in their treatises or handbooks. Though fanciful, it highlights a symbolic constellation between knee/pity/gaze which will be elaborated further.

The power of the knee to grant mercy was thus well established in antiquity, and actively revived by Renaissance mythographers and humanists. In his *Hieroglyphica*, Pierio Valeriano devotes an entire chapter to the knees (*De Genibus*), where they are associated with *misericordia*: the knee, he writes, 'is the seat of mercy' ('genu misericordiae sedem esse'),[31] as knees were dedicated in the Temple of Mercy. Lilio Gregorio Giraldi, in his *De Deis gentium*, quotes similar sources, adding that the right hand is consecrated to the goddess *Fides*, the fingers to Minerva and the knee to the goddess of Mercy.[32] Erasmus mentions Servius' reference to the 'genua Misericordiae' in the adage *Aurem vellere* ('to pluck by the ear') (*Adagia* 1.7.40). In his commentary on the *Geniales dies* of Alessandro d'Alessandria, the French jurist André Tiraqueau draws similar links, quoting Greek and Latin sources alike.[33] Alessandro d'Alessandria considers the knee to be 'numen and sedem miserationis' (the power and the seat of commiseration). The idea that a body part may act as *numen* and *sedem* of a virtue is particularly telling, as it anchors allegorical notions in sensory perception, making them more apt to strike the senses of the viewer.

Lady Justice's knee gesture as an index of clemency

In compositions where Lady Justice appears on the fringes of a narrative, her knee may act as a commentary enabling the viewer to see things from another perspective. Lady Justice's protruding knee appears in a design for stained glass executed in 1583 by Tobias Stimmer (1539–84) and copied by Christoph Murer in 1585 (Figure 5.10). The scene depicted in an oval frame of pierced strapwork is the Judgment of Solomon, between an allegory of Justice in the upper left corner, facing an allegory of rectitude, in the upper right corner. Lady Justice's uncovered knee appears as her major attribute, her sword unsheathed, her scales disorderly. Her gown lets us see her knee uncovered up to her thigh. Her posture echoes the mother of the disputed child who kneels in front of King Solomon on his throne. The knee gesture intensifies the plea for clemency, echoing and deepening the narrative of Solomon's judgment.

The salient gesture is construed as a visual signal rather than a uniform indication. The visual form of the bare knee may generate multiple interpretations, upon which the viewer may pause. It can signify simultaneously diverse and distinct polarities, not necessarily antithetical. As an example of mercy or a sign challenging strict

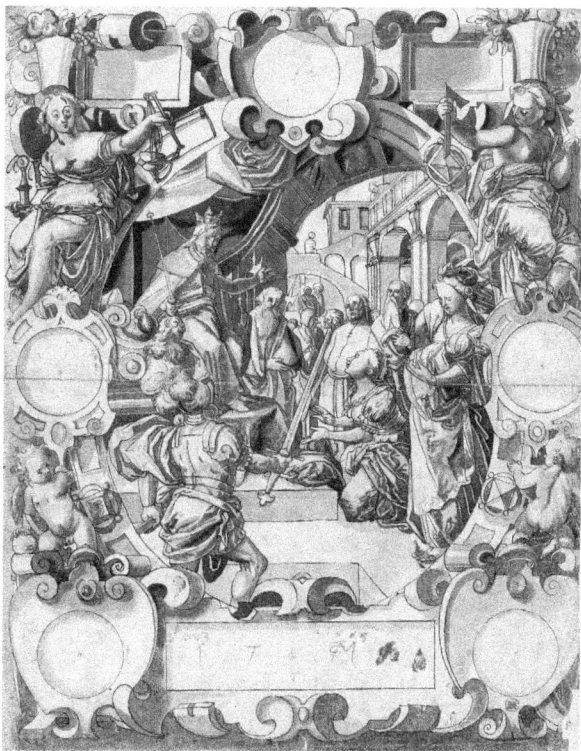

Figure 5.10: Tobias Stimmer (design 1583), Christoph Murer (execution 1585), *Lady Justice and the Judgement of Solomon.* By permission of the Victoria and Albert Museum, London

judgment, it might encourage the viewer to ponder the intricacies of a judgment in equity. Here, the allegorical device constitutes the sharing of a thought, of a point of view from which things are seen differently (*allos*).

In a drawing by Christoph Murer's father, Jos, produced between 1545 and 1580, the uncovered knee of Dame Justice also appears in relation to a judgment scene: Christ shows mercy towards the woman taken in adultery (John 8:1–11) (Figure 5.11). A group of scribes and Pharisees confronts Jesus. They ask whether she should be stoned, as prescribed in the Mosaic Law. Instead, Jesus shows mercy, arguing that he who is without sin should cast the first stone. In the lower part of the drawing, Lady Justice is seated before a curtain and ornamental ledge. She looks awry, balanced by a pronounced *contrapposto* which underlines her uncovered right knee, in a highly dynamic pose. Here, the protruding knee acts as a warning signal, introducing to the viewer the necessities of the Christian virtue of *misericordia*. Echoing Jesus'

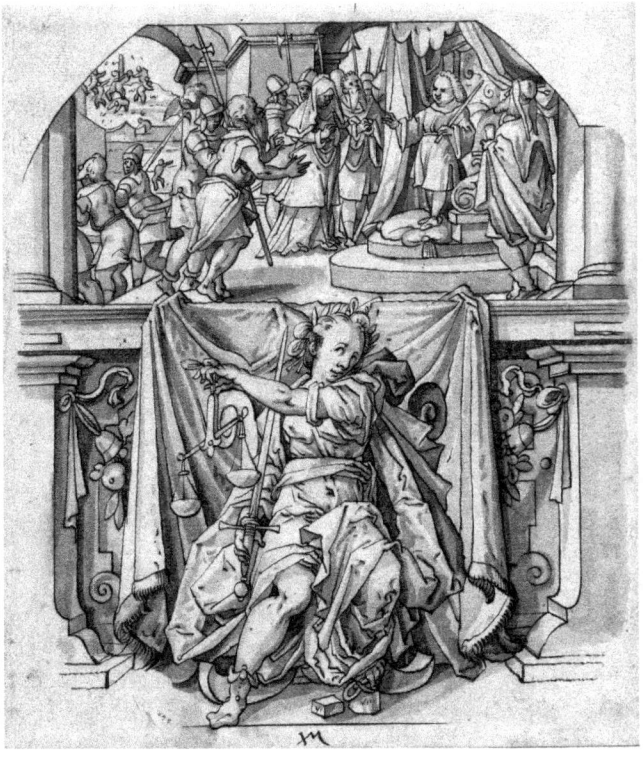

Figure 5.11: Jos Murer, 1545–80, *Lady Justice below the Christ and the Adulteress*, drawing on paper, 21.5 cm × 18.6 cm, inv. 1883,0714.79. © The Trustees of the British Museum

merciful judgment, Lady Justice invites the viewer to ruminate on the implications of the biblical word. Her posture provides the model for a merciful state of mind and visually anticipates Christ's *misericordia*. A gesture which might seem arbitrary at first glance indicates tangibly the vital role of merciful Justice in a Christian life.

Justus Oldekop's frontispiece as a judicial manifesto

It comes as no surprise that the frontispiece of Justus Oldekop's 1639 treatise of criminal law shows *Justitia* and *Clementia* in nearly identical poses, their right knees prominently bared (Figure 5.12).[34] The *genus misericordiae* conflates the attributes of both virtues. *Justitia* stands above a cartouche which reads 'Lex si non defendantur, 19 §§. De Poenis'. In this law, Ulpian specifies that if slaves are not defended by their

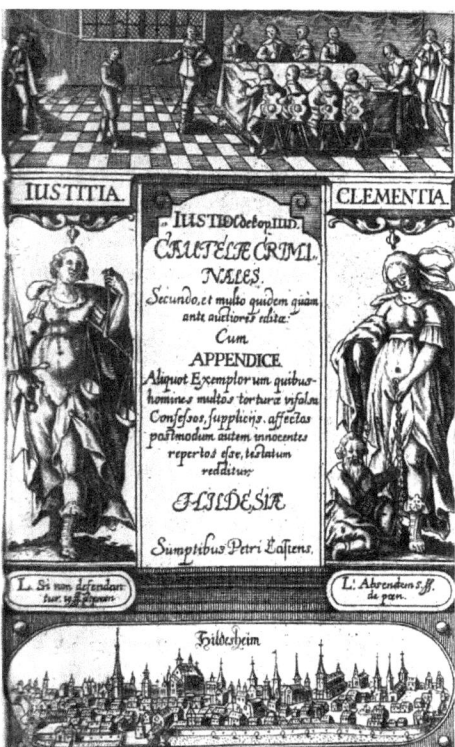

Figure 5.12: Justus Oldekop, *Cautelae criminales consiliariis, maleficiorum judicibus, advocatis, inquisitoribus & actuariis*, published by the heirs of P. Castens and printed by J. Gösselius in 1639, frontispiece. Private collection. Photograph by the author

masters, they are not immediately sent to torture but are allowed to justify themselves or to be defended by another. *Clementia* stands above a similar cartouche, 'Lex Absentem 5. D. de Poenis': a person accused of a crime should not be convicted on the basis of conjecture. Thus, in the midst of uncertainty, judges should incline towards acquittal rather than conviction, because it is better for a crime to go unpunished than for an innocent person to suffer. At the feet of *Clementia*, the engraver depicted a kneeling figure, undoubtedly the unjustly accused, whom she has freed from his chains.

Oldekop (1597–1667) was a protestant lawyer and diplomat. He called for caution and prevention in criminal proceedings, emphasising the need for a fundamental improvement in the entire criminal justice system. He played a leading role in the abolition of torture in witchcraft trials in Lower Saxony.[35] His insistence on the virtue of clemency is a constant feature of his works. The frontispiece is thus an eloquent visualisation of his own judicial philosophy. The use of the knee motif demonstrates the engraver's awareness of its function as an index of clemency, its affective power, and its sign value *pars pro toto* for the entire corpus of Oldekop's writings.

The bare knee as a sign of virtue in general

The eye-catching gesture of revealing one's knee may indicate the accessibility of virtue in general. It invites the viewer to imagine reaching forward to touch the allegorical body, as the gesture is directed outside the engraving, towards the spectator. In a 1579 drawing by Jost Amman, a bare knee serves as a visual index for virtue in general (Figure 5.13). The composition depicts the allegories of good government: Charity, Prudence, Peace and Common Good. At the centre, towering above them, stands Lady Justice, *regina virtutum*, queen of virtues. A chain holds them tightly together. The circle of virtues is closed by the handshake of *Pax* with *Respublica*, as a gesture of contract and unity. Above *Justitia*, in a cloud, the name of Jehovah sanctifies the union. Lady Justice shows a bare left knee. But the other four civic virtues all follow the same pattern, reinforcing their interdependence as a precondition of their efficacy: Justice, Prudence and Common Good uncover their left knee, whilst Charity and Peace uncover their right knee. As an

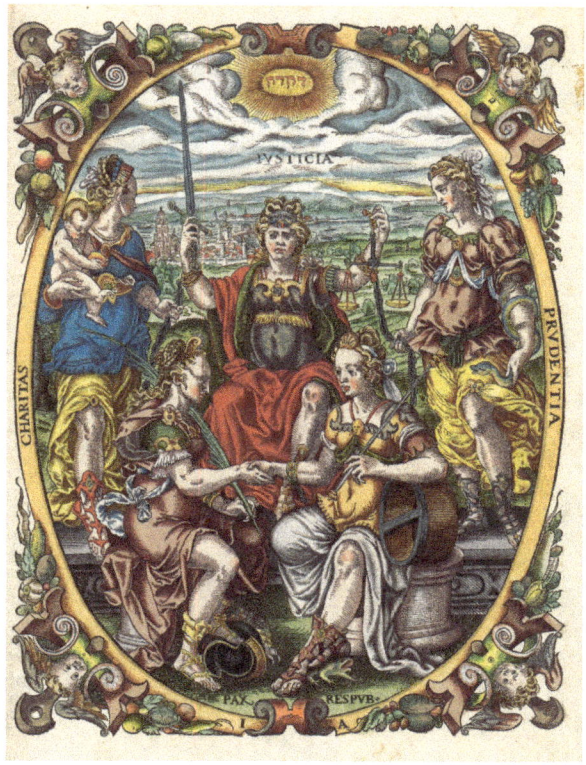

Figure 5.13: Jost Amman, *Allegories of the Good Government, Justitia/Prudentia/Charitas/ Pax/Respublica*, 1579, inv. RP-P-1964-482. Courtesy of the Rijksmuseum, Amsterdam

entreaty for the virtues' intercession, the uncovered knee encourages the viewer to sense the virtues' availability and proximity.

George Reverdy's allegory of injustice

A drawing attributed to Georges Reverdy (d. 1565) depicts Lady Justice in an oval medallion (Figure 5.14). She sits on a donkey and not on a throne. Her right arm grasps a sword pointing to the sky, and the hooked and spread fingers of her left hand, forming an ominous crab, cover the cord from which hangs her unbalanced scales. Did 'sitting on a donkey' merit mention in our discussion of sitting? Both knees are exposed and out of proportion to the narrow bust that surmounts them, suggesting a perverted Justice. Instead of a single bare knee indicating mercy, the engraver depicted the heaviness of an excessive strength untempered by wisdom.

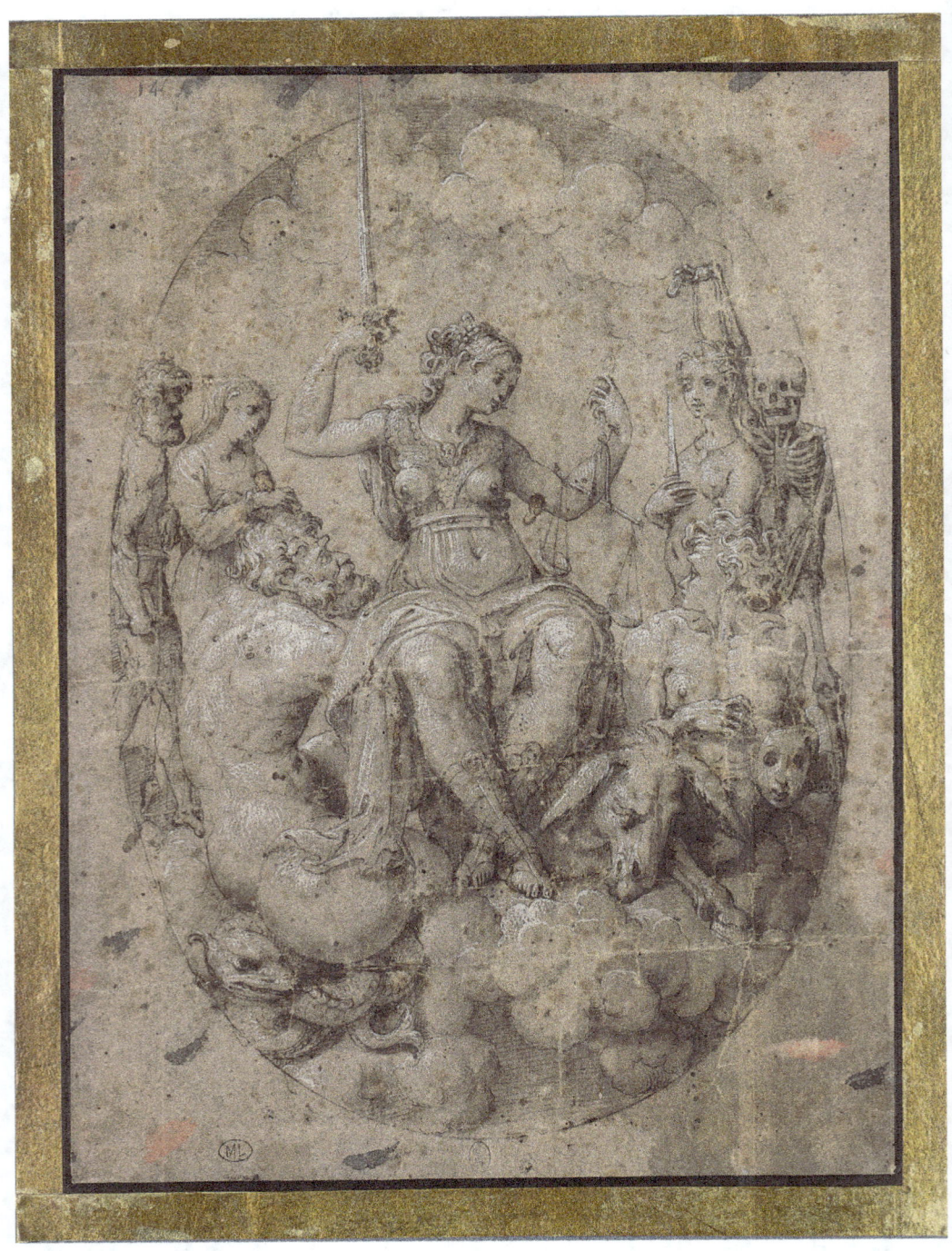

Figure 5.14: Georges Reverdy, *Lady Justice Enthroned, Sitting on a Donkey, with Fraud, Felony and Death*. Louvre Museum, Department of Graphic Arts

In the list of meanings associated with the knee, Bonifacio had noted that 'the firmness of the knees is a sign of strength and fortitude.'[36] Waldemar Deonna claims that since antiquity, the Greeks had considered the knee to be the seat of strength, even of man's vital power. In Homer, the valour of the fighter depended on it; the gods gave heroes strong and agile knees, which enabled them to defeat their enemies or escape from them.[37] The Romans likewise thought the knee 'the seat of paternity, of life and generative power.'[38]

Reverdy's is an allegory of injustice, of Force devoid of Wisdom. She leans towards three harmful allegorical figures: Fraud feverishly holds her mask and looks down, while Felony raises a dagger and Death honours her with a canopy. To her right, two other figures stand: the first one bows his head and implores. He embodies Mercy, seeking in vain to move her to pity. Behind her stands a man with a snarling look, his right hand clutching a stingray, the instrument of the devil. Her two bare knees, distorted and enlarged, show how bestiality may await even Justice, should she fall prey to vicious passions.

Nudity

Justitia meretrix: Lady Justice as a courtesan

Lady Justice sometimes allows us to glimpse more than just her bare knee, shifting its usual moral meaning to a more ambiguous, erotic sign. How does this comport with notions of decorum and norms in allegorical art? When Dame Justice is depicted with a bare knee and exposed breasts, she appears with the typical signs of prostituted women.[39] The Swiss artist Urs Graf (c. 1485–c. 1529), one of the most rumbustious artists of his time, served as a mercenary (*Reislaufer*) between 1510 and 1521 and authored several etchings depicting sexually alluring young women.[40] *Dirne mit Waage* (Prostitute Holding Scales, 1516), shows a harlot with a gathered garment, a beret adorned with a feather and jewellery (Figure 5.15). Along with her naked breasts, she exposes her legs, up to the thigh. The woman appears in profile, holding a pair of scales in her hand, the initial letters of Graf's name inscribed on the pans. She stands as a personalised version of *Justitia*, weighing 'V' and

'G', the letters of the artist's monogram. Since Urs Graf often played wittily with the insertion of his monogram into his drawings, the weighing of the two letters here suggests another monogrammed joke.[41] His version of Lady Justice as *Justitia meretrix* holds an unbalanced scale with one finger. He places his signature at the very place where one has to be to glimpse under her skirt. The monogram serves as a scopic delegate for the spectator as voyeur. The allegory of Justice is transformed here into a portrait of lust. In Urs Graf's drawings, lust is represented with great sensuality but, at the same time, undercut by satire or persiflage. In drawings such as *Dirne, das kleid anhebend* (Harlot, Raising Her Dress, 1516), lust is frequently suggested by hitched-up skirts showing bare knees or legs. In this case, we see an artist capable of interpreting allegorical figures in a satirical and personal way.

A drawing by Hans von Kulmbach depicts two standing female allegorical figures: on the left, a nude woman holds a pair of scales in which a feather outweighs two clasped hands (a symbol of *fides*, i.e. fidelity) (Figure 5.16). She manipulates the balance needle with one hand,

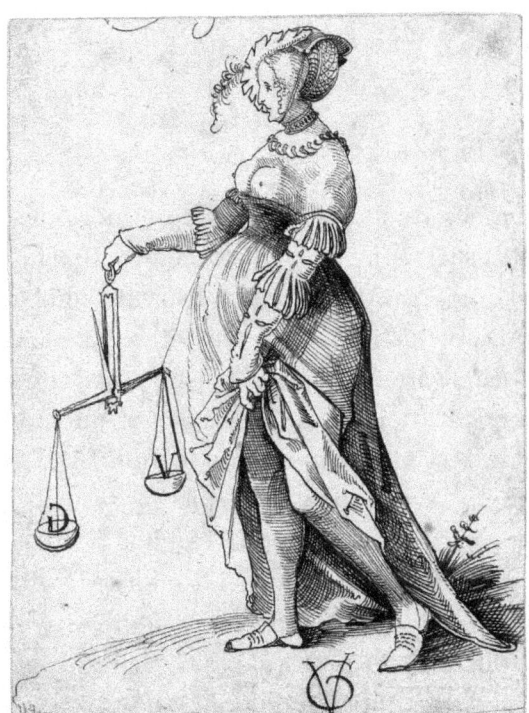

Figure 5.15: Urs Graf, 1516, *Dirne mit Waage* (Prostitute Holding Scales). Kunstmuseum, Basel

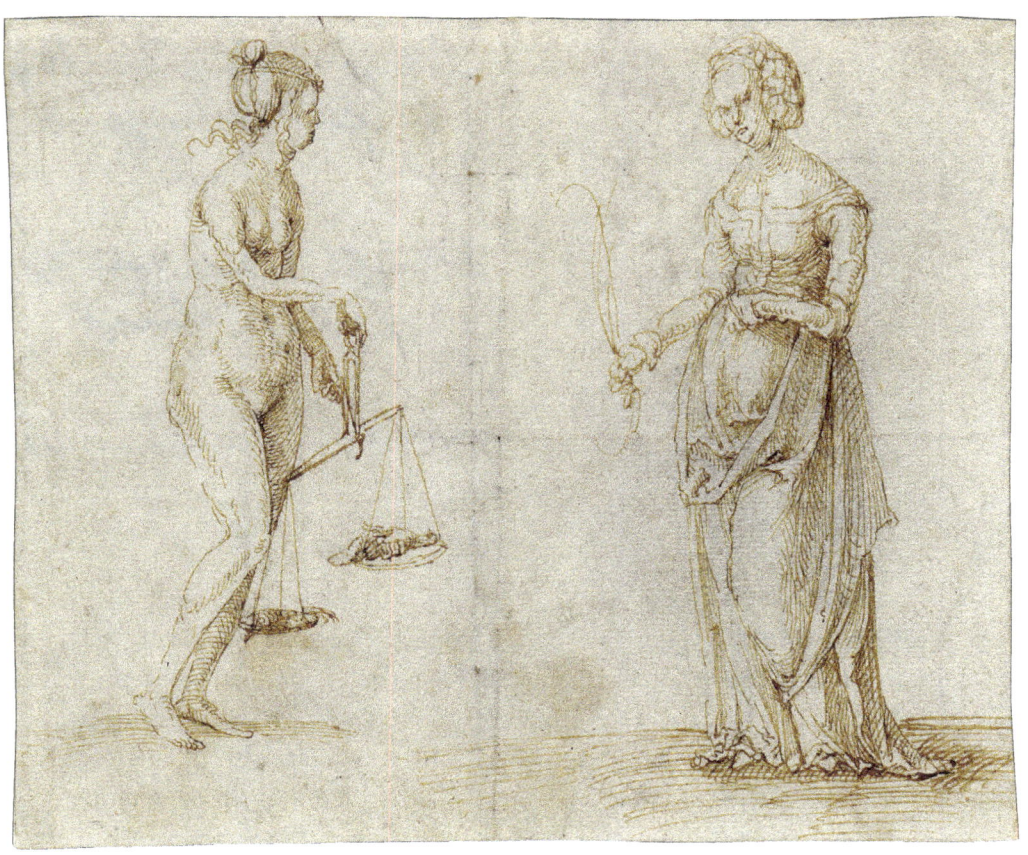

Figure 5.16: Hans von Kulmbach, *Two Standing Allegorical Figures*, c. 1514, inv. SL,5218.113. © The Trustees of the British Museum

preventing it from weighing accurately. On the right, a dressed woman holds what seems to be a harness. The pair contrasts inconstancy with the honest woman who restrains her desires with a harness. John Rowlands argues that the figure on the left represents '"fair-weather" friendship, which fades with the onset of adversity' and adds that the 'idea of a feather possessing more weight than this worthless association is described in the book of emblems by Guillaume de La Perrière, *Le Theatre des bons engins*, no. 14'.[42] In Kulmbach's drawing, infidelity borrows the scales of Lady Justice and is depicted as a courtesan. La Perrière's emblem is also illustrated by an alluring young woman ('foy legiere'), with a vertiginous décolletage, raising her skirt with her left hand to uncover her knee up to the top of her thigh, holding a gigantic scale, and fixing with a melancholic air the heavyweight feather (Figure 5.17).[43]

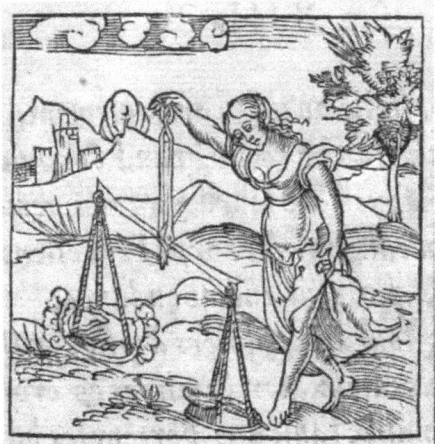

Figure 5.17: Guillaume de la Perrière, *Le Theatre des bons engins*, Paris, Denis Janot, 1544, C3v, emblem 14, 'Pour peu de cas trebuche foy legiere'. By permission of the University of Glasgow Archives & Special Collections, Stirling Maxwell collection

An exquisite allegorical portrait kept at Brussels town hall, today attributed to Hermann tom Ring (1521–96), a Westphalian painter from Münster, deploys the same tropes (Figure 5.18).[44] Designed for private viewing, it depicts a young woman half-bodied, seen from the front, with bare breasts, holding a balance in her left hand. On the higher pan are two united hands, while the lower contains a feather, to which the young woman points with a curious gesture, in which her spread index finger is separated from her other fingers. Her slender hands, a highly mannerist and conspicuously elegant gesture, are at least as articulate as her face. They might be read here to show invitation or an activity that has happened or will happen. The erotic effect is intensified by the directness of her gaze. In the lower right-hand corner, the painter added an inscription, fixed to the wall with a red wax pastille but now illegible. Her arms are bare, her breasts completely exposed. She is richly dressed, adorned with a necklace, three bracelets and a lace headdress, which supports a pearl-embroidered veil whose drapery unfolds voluptuously. Her alabaster breasts emerge from delicate lace ruffles worn as a shoulder strap on her chest. The panel carries a beguiling power. The clasped-hands device implies betrothal and was a common feature of engagement rings throughout the early modern period,[45] copying the very gesture (*mani di fede*) made by the bride and groom during the wedding ceremony while the priest blessed their union by tying their hands with a white cloth. The hand clasp featured in the left pan is depicted in front of a globe surmounted by a cross, a Christianised version of the antique *dextrarum junctio*, indicating a contractual obligation. The courtesan's dismissal of a marriage promise is underlined by erotic wit. The conspicuous feather can be associated through the word 'pennes' to pain (sorrow,[46] punishment and torture) or penis.[47] These puns were common in the world of Renaissance erotica. The seductive woman deliberately teases out the feathery associations of the white ostrich plume. The mask she wears on her belly suggests gluttony and lust. Unwilling to submit to the perpetual servitude of marriage, her gaze defies the viewer.

The theme of female subordination is made explicit in another iteration of the same motifs, this time in relation to an ill-matched couple (Figure 5.19). In a Swiss glass-painting c. 1515, a courtesan dressed in luxurious garments, wearing a beret adorned with an ostrich feather

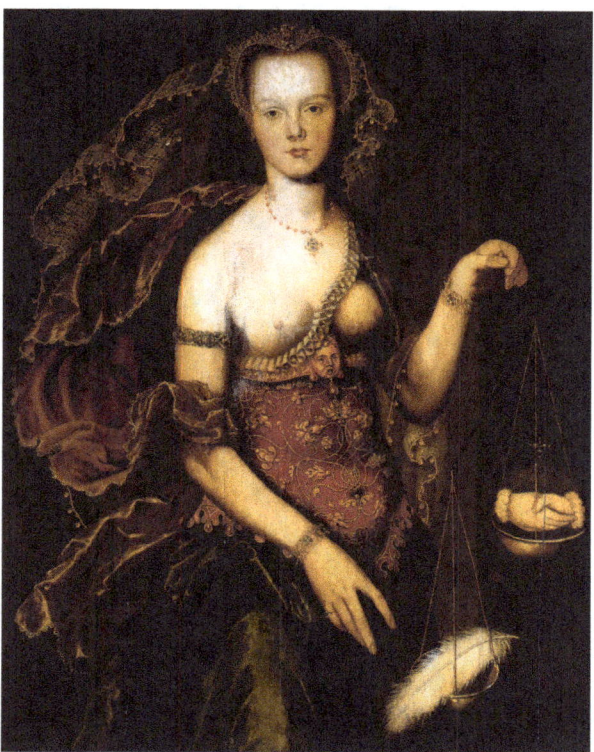

Figure 5.18: Hermann tom Ring, *Lady Justice as a Courtesan*, oil on panel, 8.7 cm × 6.7 cm. Formerly attributed to Hubertus Goltzius and depicted as a satirical portrait of Diane de Poitiers. Courtesy of the Brussels City Museum

and a golden necklace plunging into a vertiginous décolletage, faces a bearded old man gazing at her lasciviously. With a full money bag at his side, the client also presses the pan of the scale containing a feather with his hand. Here, the artist has adopted all the conventions of the usual portrait of the prostitute (loose hair, yellow dress and slightly unravelled corset).

Taken together, these examples vividly show how the allegorical language of Lady Justice can undergo surprising metamorphoses. Amorous law as practised by these courtesans offers a parodic image of Justice, grounded in deception and inconstancy (the handling of the scales in *mala fide*). Scales are used to measure abstract qualities; they might impair judgement and obstruct reason. In borrowing the attributes of legal officials, these figures reveal the troubling evidence of the senses and the whimsical powers of the flesh, under the auspices of

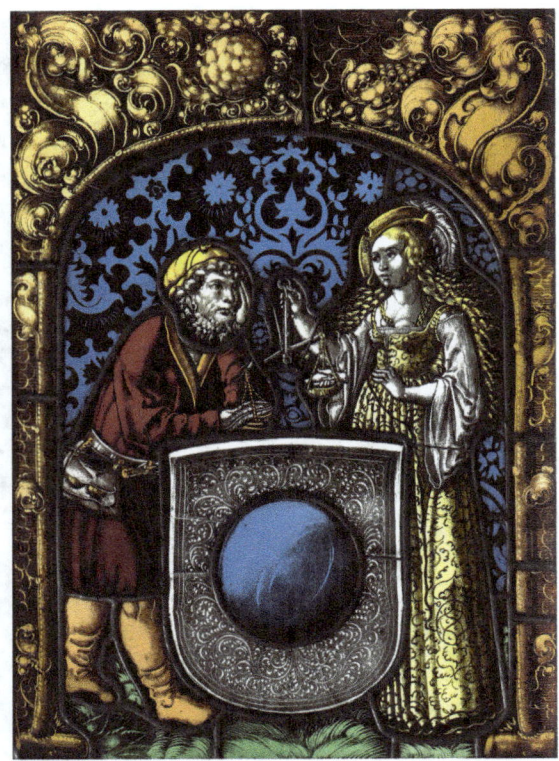

Figure 5.19: Anonymous artist, Swiss glass-painting, c. 1515, a woman holding scales containing a feather and clasped hands, facing an old man, inv. no. LM6432. By permission of Schweizerisches Landesmuseum, Zürich

Fortuna (the veil worn by tom Ring's lady seems almost blown away by unnatural winds).

In a 1614 drawing by Dietrich Krüger and Gabriel Weyer, Lady Justice is figured with bare breasts and a seductively posed leg with bare knee (Figure 5.20). The erotic elements of the allegory unfold Dame Justice's seductive powers and cast a paradoxical light on the inscription below: 'Aequa judicij suspendo singula lance, Nec me divitiae, nec me data munera flectunt' (On the scales of just judgment, I hold individual things in abeyance. Neither riches nor offerings bend me).

Lady Justice depicted as a courtesan seems to warn against the contrary: her beauty is not an expression of truth but mere appearance. She might, after all, be bought by riches or offerings, sold to the highest bidder. Another hint is present in Pieter Brueghel's famous depiction of Justice, standing on a raised pedestal in the middle of a scene of torture

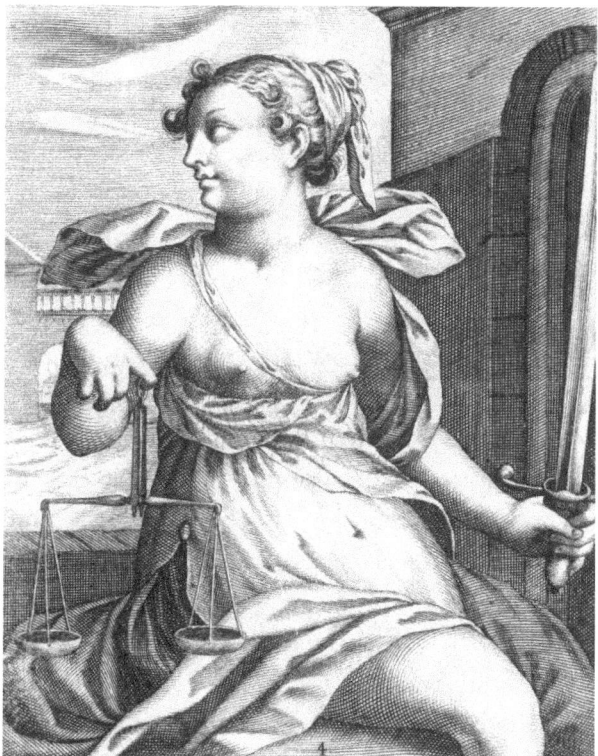

Figure 5.20: Dietrich Krüger (engraver), Balthazar Calmox (printer) and Gabriel Weyer (inventor), *Lady Justice with Bare Breasts*, 1614. By permission of the Herzog Anton Ultrich Museum

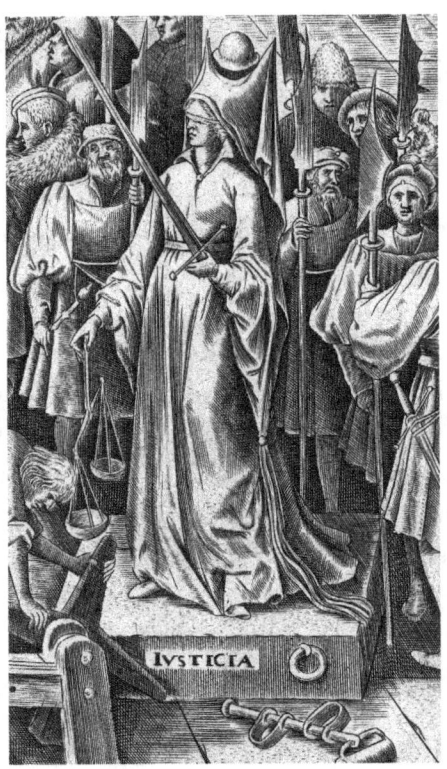

Figure 5.21: Pieter Brueghel (design), Philips Galle (printer) and Hieronymus Cock (publisher), *Justicia*, 1559, 24.5 cm × 29.2 cm. Series *The Seven Virtues*, detail of *Justitia*'s hat, inv. 1868,0328.367. © The Trustees of the British Museum

and punishment. The paradoxical tableau was probably intended to be a criticism of contemporary legal practice. In the middle of this theatre of cruelty, the allegory of *Justitia* wears a two-pointed headdress, which has been interpreted by Irving L. Zupnick as a sign of prostitution, on the basis of other Netherlandish sources (Figure 5.21).[48]

The image of *Justitia meretrix* appears frequently in the legal literature of the seventeenth century. The German jurist and pedagogue Joachim Schnobel (1602–71) uses the image twice in his *De pace Germaniae dissertationes quinque* (1641), depicting 'Justitia ex matrona meretrix sit', assisted by 'Judicum et assessorum dorophagia' (Justice is turned into a prostitute, assisted by judges and assessors 'eating presents').[49] Later, he claims that 'pro Justitia matrona meretricem tribunalibus praeesse & Jura' (in place of Lady Justice, a prostitute presides over the laws and courts). She is here depicted as a *matrona* – the socially respectable *mater familias* – turned into a *meretrix*.

Theologians also depict the profanation of the sacred temple of Themis by evil judges. The Dominican theologian Hyacinthe de Chalvet (1605–83) gives a vivid account of her reversed portrait, playing on the words *templum/prostibulum* (temple/brothel): 'The sacred temple of Themis is desecrated every day. The judicial forum among the gentiles once had a bad reputation, because it was not called the temple of the goddess Themis, but rather the brothel of Themis.'[50] Speaking of the greedy judges, he adds, 'We must distance ourselves from such men who are like swallows and harpies; for those whom we call priests of the sacred goddess Themis, we should rather call pimps (*lenones*) who sell Justice by an unholy and shameless contract.'[51] The desecration of *Domina Justitia* by a pimp draws a sharp contrast, operating at the level of both cult and ritual. Lady Justice is outlawed and socially disparaged in her own abode and temple.

In the series *Cognition and the Seven Virtues* by Harmen Jansz Muller (1567–70), engraved after designs by Gerard van Groeningen, *Justitia* is paired with Temperance. Temperance, on the right, is seated on a drunken, vomiting king, pouring water from a jar into a chalice of wine. Justice, on the left, is seated on a bearded man, holding a sword and scales. In the background, on the other hand, Christ is shown giving drink to the thirsty and driving the money changers from the temple. Below the images, verses from the Lord's Prayer are inscribed. This curious *Justitia* seems to reproduce the satirical posture of Phyllis riding Aristotle: a woman beguiling a wise man and persuading him to let her ride upon his back with a whip in her hand. It is an illustration of the triumph of female seduction over masculine intellect.

Vanquishing nudes

Justitia's bared breast is not always sexualised or erotic. The visual precedent is the Amazonian warrior, whose uncovered breast reveals her valour, her readiness to face the enemy without armour. In his *Justitia Vanquishes the Seven Capital Sins*, Antoon Claeissins (c. 1601) painted Justice as a bare-breasted Amazonian figure in the middle of just such a scene of combat (Figure 5.22).[52] She embodies the martial valour and bravery of a female warrior, with a metal girdle around her waist from which depictions of the seven deadly sins are chained. Her muscular arms are androgynous, but, at the same time, her bare breast is not depicted amputated (Amazons were said to maim their right breasts in order to shoot better). The Amazonian prototype of *Justitia* offers a warlike image, as well as a transgression of gender boundaries.

Breast milk has strong theological and political connotations. The sovereign was often depicted as a nursing father. The rare figure of a breast-feeding Justice appears at the opening of Pierre Coustau's emblem book: 'In simulachrum Iustitiæ. Ex Chrysippo' (Figure 5.23). Since such an image cannot be found in Chrysippus, it is better to translate 'Ex Chrysippo' as 'In response to Chrysippus'. Coustau would thus coin here

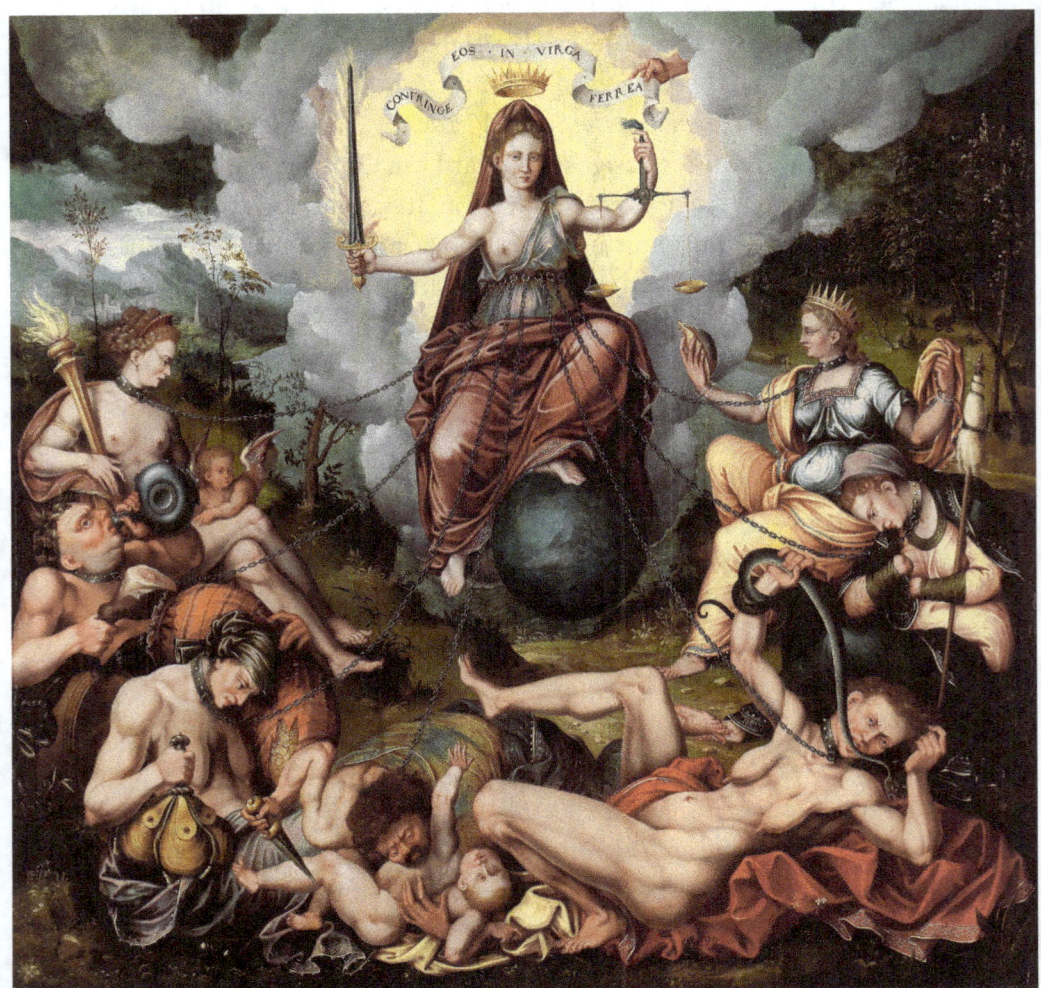

Figure 5.22: Antoon Claeissins (Bruges, c. 1536–1613), *Justitia Vanquishes the Seven Capital Sins*, oil on panel, 99.5 cm × 104.5 cm. Catalogue of the Dorotheum Auction Old Master Paintings, 30 April 2019. Private collection

something new: *Justitia duplex* 'nursing twin babies on her two breasts', 'her right breast nurturing warfare, her left, the law'.[53] Justice is depicted in the form of *Caritas*, a nursing loving mother. The symbol surely draws on one of the most familiar tropes of Rome and its foundation: the she-wolf that nourished the abandoned twins Romulus and Remus, and by extension, all future Romans, with the virtue of courage and martial spirit. So too Coustau's emblem nourishes all citizens with two paradoxical virtues, combining in one figure *Justitia victrix* and *Justitia genetrix*, able to preserve peace thanks to her military valour. Coustau's suckling Justice also hints at natural law and indeed wild judgment.

Bare leg or bare breast cannot be reduced to a univocal signifier; neither are the maternal or nurturing implications of Justice consistent. Judith, who triumphed over Nebuchadnezzar's general, the giant Holofernes, was often chosen to personify Justice. Already in the four-teenth century, in the *Allegory of Good Government* fresco of the Palazzo Pubblico in Siena, Ambrogio Lorenzetti made explicit reference to Judith, representing *Justitia* as an imposing seated female figure, with her hand brandishing a sword resting on a bearded man's severed head. In a dry fresco c. 1508, originally set above the side entrance of the Fondaco dei Tedeschi, the German merchants' trading post in Venice,

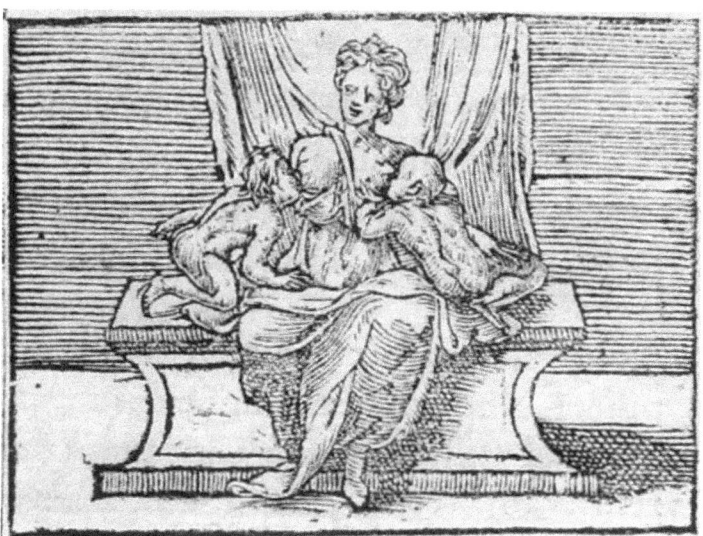

Figure 5.23: Pierre Coustau, *Pegma cum narrationibus philosophicis*, Lyon, Macé Bonhomme, 1555, emblem 'In simulachrum Iustitiæ. Ex Chrysippo'. By permission of the University of Glasgow Archives & Special Collections, Stirling Maxwell collection

Titian likewise painted Judith as Justice. She brandishes an upward sword in her right hand while trampling with her left foot Holofernes' severed head. As E. H. Gombrich noted, this pose follows an 'age-old formula, that for triumph which shows the victorious ruler trampling on his defeated foe'.[54] His understanding of gesture assumes that the schema used by artists is generally pre-formed in a ritual. This ritualised gesture of submission tends to reverse completely the association of the knee gesture with mercy, since the defeated foe displays instead the signs of his humiliation. Judith's bare knee is neither erotic nor compassionate. It emphasises her coercive power and military pride. Indeed, her naked leg crushing the head of her defeated enemy becomes the central energising nexus of the composition. Lady Justice is capable of the most strenuous feats of arms. Her powerful knee is in line with the sword she brandishes. If this seems inappropriate to the ethos of a cardinal virtue, her exposed breast and knee appear in other Venetian images of Justice. They are the signs of a dominant punitive Justice,[55] where the

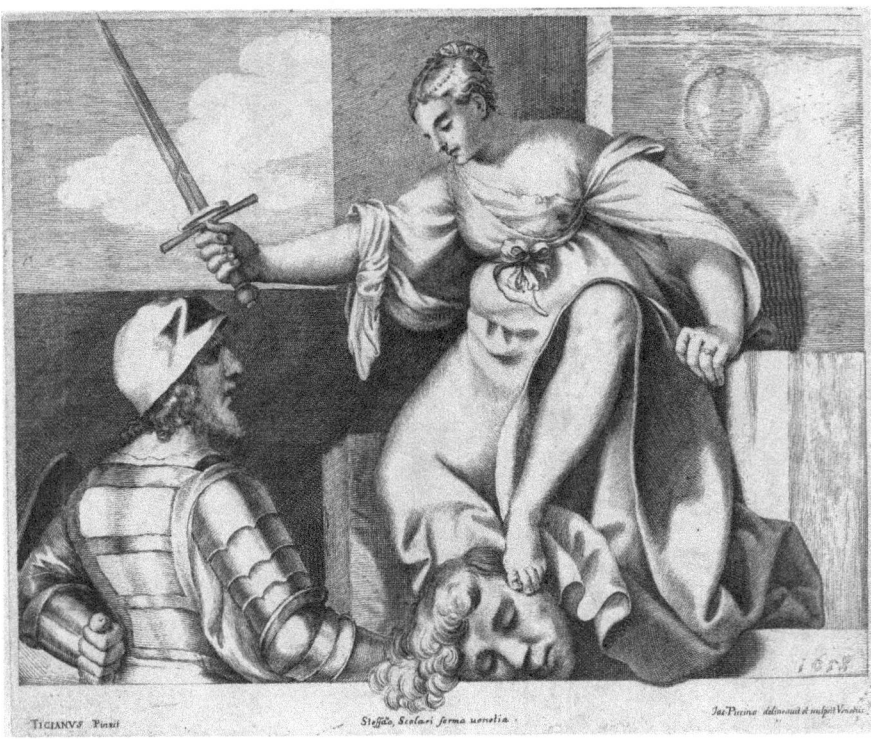

Figure 5.24: Jacopo Piccini, *Judith as Justice* (after Giorgione or Titian, from the Fondaco dei Tedeschi, Venice), 1658. Courtesy of the Rijksmuseum, Amsterdam

republic is, more than anything, an 'unconquered Amazon Venice'.[56] Judith therefore appears as a figure of Liberty-Justice, but also of hope in liberation, proclaiming victory over tyrants.

In his *Arte de' cenni*, Bonifacio points out the strongly derogatory connotation of the gesture of 'Haver alcuna cosa sotto i piedi' (to have something under one's feet). 'This is an act of having absolute power over it, and thus of despising it', he comments. So too he argued that '*Calcar co' piedi* [. . .] is an act of having conquered and overcome the enemy'.[57] Titian's fresco has been badly damaged and survives as a scarcely legible fragment. Many of its original details are only known from Jacopo Piccini's (1658) and Antonio Maria Zanetti's (1760) later reproductions. But even in the Fondaco fresco in the Galleria Franchetti in the Ca' d'Oro Museum, the prominent bare knee is still visible as the main focus point of *Justitia*'s body (Figure 5.24).

Conclusion

Hands, knees or breasts – the fragmented body of Lady Justice brings to the fore powerful anatomical schemes, leading to interpretative multivalence. Are these missing hands mutilated or accidentally lost? The pattern resonates differently on the walls of a courtroom than when it becomes the mark of a new female allegorical creation, *Adorodokia*. Is an exposed knee an invitation to eroticism, a sign of clemency or a mark of domination? Hands and knees imply an interaction with the viewer, a mute dialogue or a performative encounter. These interactions often create symbolic inversions. Gender aspects likewise open up diverse interpretations ranging from knightly domination to sensual arousal.

Lady Justice's kinesics are part of a variegated constellation. Dialectics between authority and submission, mercy and victory, mutism and gesticulation all play their part. The examination of *Justitia*'s body parts introduces us to the material manifestations of her corporeality, allowing for a free interchange between allegory and satire, vision and touch, *pathos formulae* involving mercy, punishment or the excitements of the flesh. Corporeal signs gain depth and weight, colour and grace, their iterative patterns producing numerous connections that bring to life the conventional postures of allegorical coding. But the whole is greater than the sum of the parts. The appearance of *Justitia*, fully formed and embodied, opens up dynamic graphical formulas that tear asunder the boundaries of gender and power.

Notes

1. Desmond Manderson, *Danse Macabre: Temporalities of Law in the Visual Arts* (Cambridge: Cambridge University Press, 2019). I would like to thank Peter Goodrich for pointing this out to me.

2. Aby Warburg, *Mnemosyne I*, in *Werke in einem Band*, ed. Martin Treml, Sigrid Weigel and Perdita Ladwig (Frankfurt: Surkhamp Verlag, 2010), p. 643, qtd in Sigrid Weigel, 'Epistemology of Wandering, Tree and Taxonomy. The System Figuré in Warburg's *Mnemosyne* Project within the History of Cartographic and Encyclopaedic Knowledge', *Images Re-vues*, special issue, 'Survivance d'Aby Warburg', 4 (2013), art. 15.

3. Aby Warburg, 'Der Tod des Orpheus', in *Ausgewählte Schriften und Würdigungen*, ed. Dieter Wuttke (Baden-Baden: Verlag Valentin Koerner, 1980), p. 87 n. 9.

4. René Girard, *Violence and the Sacred* (Baltimore, MD: Johns Hopkins University Press, 1977).

5. Waldemar Deonna, 'La Justice à l'Hôtel de Ville de Genève et la fresque des juges aux mains coupées', *Zeitschrift für schweizerische Archäologie und Kunstgeschichte/Revue suisse d'art et d'archéologie*, 11 (1950), pp. 144–9; Judith Resnik and Dennis Curtis, *Representing Justice: Invention, Controversy, and Rights in City-States and Democratic Courtrooms* (New Haven, CT: Yale University Press, 2011), pp. 45, 417 nn. 65–8; Frédéric Elsig and Nicolas Schätti (eds), *Peindre à Genève au XVIe siècle: le décor peint de la salle du conseil d'État à l'Hôtel de Ville* (Geneva: Georg, 2012), esp. Isabelle Brunier, 'La salle du Conseil, l'apport des sources écrites (XVe–XVIIe siècles)', pp. 21–38 and Naïma Jornod, 'Observations iconographiques', pp. 97–110; José M. González García, *The Eyes of Justice: Blindfolds and Farsightedness, Vision and Blindness in the Aesthetics of the Law* (Frankfurt: Vittorio Klostermann, 2017), pp. 134–9.

6. Achille Durieux, 'Les artistes cambrésiens du IXe au XIXe siècles et l'école de dessin de Cambrai', in *Mémoires de la Société d'émulation de Cambrai: agriculture, sciences et arts, Cambrai*, vol. 32 (16 November 1873), pt 2, pp. 69–70: 'Le registre des comptes de 1552–1553, nous apprend que le sculpteur Guillaume Dannel a taillé en bois les modèles des deux personnages que Jean de Bove, bailli de Marcoing, en punition d'une usurpation de pouvoir, avait été condamné, outre une amende de 300 florins, à faire exécuter en cuivre pour être placés au-dessus de la porte latérale gauche de la grande halle de l'hôtel de ville.'

7. *Le Vieux Jérôme, histoire véritable dédiée à M. le marquis d'Armentières, lieutenant général des armées du Roi* (Cambrai: Hurez, 1763).

8. Thomas Lüttenberg, 'The Cod-piece – A Renaissance Fashion between Sign and Artefact', *The Medieval History Journal* 8, no. 1 (2005), pp. 49–81.

9. However, this does not mean that the ways punishments are visualised in artworks of the time are necessarily literal enactments of the real treatment. See Madeline H. Caviness, 'Giving "the Middle Ages" a Bad Name: Blood Punishments in the *Sachsenspiegel* and Town Lawbooks', *Studies in Iconography* 34 (2013), pp. 175–235.

10. For a juristic treatment of the theme, see Peter Goodrich, 'The Missing Hand of the Law', in *Legal Emblems and the Art of Law: Obiter Depicta as the Vision of Governance* (Cambridge: Cambridge University Press, 2014), pp. 167–206.

11. Michael Evans, 'Two Sources for Maimed Justice', *Notes in the History of Art* 2, no. 1 (1982), pp. 12–15.

12. Ibid., p. 13: *Justice*, Rome Bibl. Casanatense Ms. 1404, fol. 33r, and *Justice*, Rome, Vat. Pal. lat. 1066, fol. 232 v.

13. Thucydides, *History of the Peloponnesian War*, trans. R. Warner (London: Harmondsworth, 1972).

14. Also Pollux 8.86, which contains the same account as in *Athenaion Politeia*.

15. Mogens Herman Hansen, *The Athenian Democracy in the Age of Demosthenes: Structures, Principles and Ideology* (Oxford: Blackwell, 1991), p. 228.

16. Evans, 'Two Sources for Maimed Justice', p. 14. The drawing might have belonged to a series of designs for the allegorical statues for the entry of Archduke Ernest of Austria into Antwerp in 1594.

17. Diodorus Siculus, *Library of History, Volume I: Books 1–2.34*, trans. C. H. Oldfather (Cambridge, MA: Harvard University Press, 1933), emphasis added.

18. Henry Peacham, *Three books of emblems*, manuscript written and illustrated by him, prefaced by a letter from Henry Peacham addressed to Henry Frederick, prince of Wales, and based on the Basilikon Doron (Royal Gift), James I's book of advice to his son and heir, London, c. 1610, British Library, Royal 12 A LXVI, emblem 13, 'Iustitiæ Symbolum'. For bibliographical details, see Alan R. Young, *The English Emblem Tradition, Volume 5: Henry Peacham's Manuscript Emblem Books* (Toronto: University of Toronto Press, 1998), pp. xviii–xix, 127–205, 233–4.

19. See M. A. Moelands and J. Th. de Smidt, *Weegschaal & Zwaard. De Verbeelding van Recht en Gerechtigheid in Nederland* (The Hague: Jongbloed Juridische Boekhandel en Uitgeverij, 1999), p. 101.

20. Mario Sbriccoli, 'La triade, le bandeau, le genou. Droit et procès pénal dans les allégories de la Justice du Moyen-âge à l'âge moderne', *Crime, Histoire et Sociétés* 9, no. 1 (2005), pp. 33–78.

21. Sergio Bertelli, *Il Re, la vergine, la sposa* (Rome: Donzelli, 2002), p. 25, qtd in ibid.

22. E. H. Gombrich, *Symbolic Images* (London: Phaidon Press, 1972), pp. 11–13.

23. For a discussion on methods and problems associated with the interpretation of gestures in art, see E. H. Gombrich, 'Ritualized Gesture and Expression in Art', *Philosophical Transactions of the Royal Society of London*, Series B, Biological Sciences, 251, no. 772 (1966), pp. 391–401; Jean-Claude Schmitt, *La raison*

des gestes dans l'Occident médiéval (Paris: Gallimard, 1990); K. Thomas, 'Introduction', in J. Bremmer and H. Roodenburg (eds), *A Cultural History of Gesture* (Ithaca, NY: Cornell University Press, 1992), pp. 1–14.

24. E. H. Gombrich, Review of *Gestures of Despair in Medieval and Early Renaissance Art* by Moshe Barasch, *The Burlington Magazine* 120, no. 908 (1978), pp. 762–3.

25. Giovanni Bonifacio, 'Delle ginocchia', in *L'arte de' cenni: con la quale formandosi favela visibile, si tratta della muta eloquenza, che non e' altro che un facondo silentio [. . .]* (Vicenza: Francesco Grossi, 1616), ch. 40, pt 1, p. 401: 'Delle ginocchia. [. . .] cosi le ginocchia sono consecrate alla Misericordia.'

26. Pliny, *Natural History, Volume III: Books 8–11*, trans. H. Rackham (Cambridge, MA: Harvard University Press, 1938). 'Hominis genibus quædam et religio inest observatione gentium. Hæc supplices attingunt, ad haec manus tendunt, hæc ut aras adorant, fortassis qui inest iis vitalitas.'

27. Homer, *Odyssey* 1.267.

28. 'Physici dicunt esse consecratas numinibus singulas corporis partes, ut aurem Memoriæ, frontem Genio [. . .] genua Misericordiae, unde hæc tangent rogantes.' *Servii Grammatici in Vergilii Carmina Commentarii*, ed. Georg Thilo and Hermann Hagen (Leipzig: Teubner, 1881).

29. Isidore of Sevilla, *Etymologies*, trans. W. M. Lindsay (Oxford: Oxford University Press, 1911), 11.1.108–9, qtd in Marie-Christine Pouchelle, *The Body and Surgery in the Middle Ages*, trans. Rosemary Morris (Cambridge: Polity Press, 1990), p. 186: 'Genua sunt commissiones femorum et crurium: et dicta genua, eo quod in utero sint genis opposite. Cohærant enim ibi sibi, et cognata sunt oculis, lacrymarum indiciis et misericordiæ [. . .].'

30. Louise Cilliers, 'Vindicianus' *Gynaecia*: Text and Translation of the Codex Monacensis (Clm 4622)', *The Journal of Medieval Latin* 15 (2005), pp. 153–236 (p. 186), 'Chapter 26: "An etymological connection between the terms 'genæ' and 'genua' and a physical connection between the eyes and the knees"'.

31. Pierio Valeriano, *Hieroglyphica sive De Sacris ægyptiorum aliarumque gentium literis commentarii* (Basel: Isengrin, 1556), book 35, p. 259.

32. Lilio Gregorio Giraldi, *De Deis gentium varia et multiplex historia* (Basel: Oporin, 1548), p. 21: 'Dextra fideo consecrata est [. . .] Digiti Minervæ, genua Misericordiæ.'

33. André Tiraqueau, *Semestria in Genialium Dierum Alexandri ab Alexandro Jurisperiti Neapolitano Libri VI* (Lyon: Guillaume Rouillé, 1586), p. 209: 'Servius scribit Physicos genua misericordiæ consecravisse' (Servius wrote that naturalists have consecrated the knee to Mercy).

34. See Justus Oldekop, *Cautelæ criminales consiliariis, maleficiorum judicibus, advocatis, inquisitoribus et actuariis* (Hildesheim: Heirs of P. Castens, printed by J. Gösselius, 1639), qtd in González García, *Eyes of Justice*, p. 190.

35. Joachim Lehrmann, 'Justus Oldekop (1597 bis 1667). Die Flucht Niedersachsens Streiter wider den Hexenwahn an den Wolfenbütteler Hof', in *Heimatbuch für den Landkreis Wolfenbüttel* (Braunschweig: Oeding, 2005).

36. Bonifacio, *L'arte de' cenni*, p. 402: 'La fermezza delle ginocchia e segno di vigore et di Fortezza.'

37. Waldemar Deonna, 'Le genou, siège de force et de vie et sa protection magique', *Revue Archéologique* 6th series, 13 (January–June 1939), pp. 224–35.

38. Richard Broxton Onians, *The Origins of European Thought about the Body, the Mind, the Soul, the World, Time, and Fate* (Cambridge: Cambridge University Press, 1951), p. 175.

39. See Christian-Nils Robert, *Une allégorie parfaite. La Justice: vertu, courtisane et bourreau* (Geneva: Georg Éditeur, 1993).

40. See Christiane Andersson, 'Harlots and Camp Followers. Swiss Renaissance Drawings of Young Women circa 1520', in E. S. Cohen and M. Reeves (eds), *The Youth of Early Modern Women* (Amsterdam: Amsterdam University Press, 2012), pp. 117–34.

41. Andersson, ibid., p. 127, notes that in a drawing dating c. 1514, a young nude woman wearing only slippers, a beret, a curry comb and some jewellery, followed by a lecherous *senex stultus*, holds a rope forming loops and a love knot in which the artist has inscribed his monogram. She interprets the insertion, saying that 'the artist demonstrates with malicious pleasure that he, not the old fool, is the object of her attention and her curry comb'.

42. John Rowlands, *Drawings by German Artists and Artists from German-Speaking Regions of Europe in the Department of Prints and Drawings in the British Museum: The 15thC & 16thC by Artists Born before 1530* (London: British Museum Press, 1993), p. 407. See also the same emblem translated into English by Thomas Combe, *The theater of fine devices containing an hundred morall emblems. First penned in French by Guillaume de la Perriere* (London: Richard Field, 1614), emblem 14: 'False faith is ouer-peisd with smallest weight, / The ballance yeelds vnto the lightest fether [. . .]'.

43. Guillaume La Perrière, *Le Theatre des bons engins* (Paris: Denis Janot, 1544), C3v, emblem 14: 'Pour peu de cas trebuche foy legiere'. One of the most popular and influential French emblem books, the first edition of the *Theatre* was published early in 1540, but the work was completed in 1536 and was presented in an incomplete manuscript version to Marguerite de Navarre when she visited Toulouse in 1535. For full bibliographical details, see the Glasgow Emblem Website, <https://www.emblems.arts.gla.ac.uk/french/books.php?id=FLPa>.

44. See Didier Martens, 'Ni Hubertus Goltzius, ni Diane de Poitiers: une "Allégorie de l'Infidélité" de Hermann tom Ring à l'Hôtel de Ville de Bruxelles', *Annales d'Histoire de l'Art et d'Archéologie* 18 (1996), pp. 23–34. Martens attributes the painting to Hermann tom Ring, after recalling that it had previously been attributed to Hubertus Goltzius (1526–83) by the English patron John Waterloo Wilson, who donated it to the city of Brussels in 1878.

45. In his *Apologie de Raimond Sebond* (*Essais*, II, 12, 599A), Montaigne describes precisely a type of ring bearing feather motifs and their paradoxical appearance, since the design of the feathers creates an optical illusion: 'Ces bagues qui sont entaillées en forme de plumes, qu'on appelle en devise, pennes sans fin, il n'y a œil qui en puisse discerner la largeur, et qui se sût défendre de cette piperie, que d'un côté elle n'aille en élargissant, et s'appointant et étrécissant par l'autre, même quand on la roule autour du doigt: toutefois au maniement elle vous semble équable en largeur et toute pareille' (Those rings which are

cut in the form of feathers, and which they call *pennes sans fin*, the eye cannot determine their size, or help being deceived by the imagination that on one side they are not larger, and on the other side become gradually narrower, and this even when you have them round the finger; yet when the touch comes to test them, it finds them of equal size and alike throughout). *Essays of Montaigne*, trans. Charles Cotton (London: Reeves and Turner, 1877), p. 366.

46. See Claude d'Expilly, 'Sur un don d'une bague de Pennes sans fin', in *Les Poemes de Messire Claude Expilly, Conseiller du Roy an son Conseil d'Etat & Prezidant au Parlemant de Grenoble* (Grenoble: Pierre Verdier, 1624), p. 116: 'Je tiens que mon tourmant ne finira jamais [. . .] Donne-moy d'un anneau l'antidote asseuré, / Qui fait croire l'amour & fait mourir la crainte. [. . .] Pren cetuy-ci de moy, qui bien mieux qu'un tableau / Marque en ses plis retors mes peines infinies. [. . .].'

47. In the second edition of his dictionary, John Florio adds to the meaning of 'penna' (*feather, quill* or *writing pen*) the following: 'Penne, used for the privities of a man, of the Latin word *Penis*.' John Florio, *Queen Anna's New World of Words* (1611; Menston: Scolar Press, 1968), p. 366, qtd in Patricia Simons, 'Annibale Carracci's Visual Wit', *Notes in the History of Art* 30, no. 2 (2011), pp. 26–31 (p. 30 n. 6).

48. Irving L. Zupnick, 'Appearance and Reality in Bruegel's Virtues', in *Évolution générale et développements régionaux en histoire de l'art*, Acts of the International Congress of the History of Art, Budapest, 1969, vol. 1 (Budapest: Akadémiai Kiadó, 1972), pp. 745–53. See also Gerd Schwerhoff, 'Virtue or Tyranny? Pieter Bruegel, *Justitia* and the Myth of the Inquisition', in Bertram Kaschek, Jürgen Müller and Jessica Buskirk (eds), *Pieter Bruegel the Elder and Religion* (Leiden: Brill, 2018), pp. 79–113.

49. Joachim Schnobel, *De pace Germaniæ dissertationes quinque* (Rostock: Johannes Haller, 1641), pp. 120, 140.

50. Hyacinthe de Chalvet, 'De Justitia', in *Theologus Ecclesiastes. De quatuor virtutibus cardinalibus*, vol. 8 (Cadomi: Jean le Jeune, 1676), p. 122: 'Sacra Themidis templum quotidie prophanatur [. . .] Forum Judiciale, apud Gentiles etiam olim male audiebat, ut non deæ Themidis templum, sed potius prostibulum diceretur.' A Dominican friar born in Toulouse, de Chalvet was sent on a military expedition against the Turkish army in Crete, during the siege of Candia, visited the Holy Land and was captured. His main work, the *Theologus Ecclesiastes*, was first published in 1653. He was a famed preacher and taught theology in Caen.

51. Ibid., p. 122: 'Has humani generis hirudines, ac harpyas absit, inquit, ut sacræ Themidis Sacerdotes appellemus, sed potius lenones, qui nefario, & incestuoso contractu Iustitiam vendunt.'

52. See A. van Oosterwijk, in Stefan Huygebaert, Georges Martyn, Vanessa Paumen and Tine Van Poucke (eds), *The Art of Law: Three Centuries of Justice Depicted* (Tielt: Lannoo, 2016), pp. 165–9.

53. Pierre Coustau, *Pegma cum narrationibus philosophicis* (Lyon: Macé Bonhomme, 1555), at a4r, *In Simulachrum Iustitiæ* (On the statue of Justice), verse 4: 'Dextra fovet bellum mamma, sinistra togam' (Her right breast nurtures warfare, her left, the law).

54. Gombrich, 'Ritualized Gesture and Expression in Art', p. 396.
55. In Valeriano's *Hieroglyphica* (1556), book 42, p. 315, the figure of an adamant punitive justice (with scales and *fasces*) is collocated between the hieroglyph of *Periculosus* (the dangerous soul) and the hieroglyph of *Irritatio* (Rage), and the author discusses the dangers of wrath, adding that the hieroglyph of God's wrath is the double-handed sword (*gladium ancipites*).
56. Vincenzo Marostica, *Venetia Trionfante* (Venice: Domenica Farri, 1572), qtd in Karen-edis Barzman, *The Limits of Identity: Early Modern Venice, Dalmatia, and the Representation of Difference* (Leiden: Brill, 2017), p. 104.
57. Bonifacio, *L'Arte de' cenni*, p. 409: '*Calcar co' piedi*. E Atto d'aver vinto, e superato il nemico [. . .]'

Chapter 6

Justitia's body movements: a sensual lesson in symbolic *fascinatio*

Even the *Mona Lisa,* even *Las Meninas* can be seen, not as immobile and eternal forms, but as fragments of a gesture or as photograms of a lost film, which alone could restore their true meaning. For always, in every image, there is a kind of *ligatio* at work, a paralyzing power that must be exorcised; and it is as if from the whole history of art there rises a silent call to restore the image to the freedom of gesture.

Giorgio Agamben, 'Notes on Gesture'[1]

A fascinating introduction

A mere disparate accumulation of attributes glued together in a more or less haphazard fashion will never result in a good allegory: this is why the physiological structure of the allegorical body helps to articulate them with verisimilitude, which is what Momus, in the *De Justitia pingenda*, mordantly reminds us. The more Lady Justice is encumbered with contradictory attributes, the more likely she becomes the target of mockery: *Justitia unimanum,* certainly, but without arms, how can she weigh? *Justitia multiocula* perhaps, but how can she keep all her eyes open? *Justitia* weighing with efficient scales, why not, but how can she not appear to be a small-time grocer? Momus makes *Justitia* a body full of knots. The dialogue reveals the most vivid aporias of this dilemma: *Justitia,* because of her divine and human nature, female and male appearance, with or without a masked eye, with or without a naked body, is perhaps only one face of the limits of faith in allegory. Her constitutive ambivalence (to some extent, *Justitia* is always depicted as Janus-faced, *duplex*) is certainly the stigmata of an unbroken sceptical gaze, but it is also a visible sign of her plasticity. The Carmelite consulted by Mantegna says as much: Justice is of another order, it is probably better to refrain from representing her. Momus' robust common sense makes us see this impasse with great acuity. In order to convince, and possibly to move the viewer's affects, the allegorical creation must combine the effects of verisimilitude of a genuine weighing up of good and evil with the articulation of the divine in man and the human in God. This is why the artist must also be attentive to the combination of gestures with each other. It is a perfect indication of the effectiveness of her theatrical presence. Judicial allegories are yet to be rescued from the various teleological discourses of narrow aesthetic norms sometimes projected onto them. The patient dismantling of devout or puritanical readings of *Justitia*'s avatars revive the ironic, somehow absurd, faces of this curious lady, dispensing her blows blindly, wearing a blindfold, with cumbersome attributes or with a dangerously tilted scale. Sometimes, the puzzling lady was looked on by contemporaries as a not very successful allegory: a piece of nonsense or gibberish ('galimatias').[2]

Justitia's images serve to connect many polarities, beyond the iconological norms set up by Cesare Ripa in the work whose full title reads:

> Iconologia di Cesare Ripa Cavaliere De S.ti Mauritio, et Lazzaro, Nella quale si descrivono diverse Imagini, di Virtù, Vizi, Affetti, Passioni humane, Arti, Discipline, Humori, Elementi, Corpi Celesti, Provincie d'Italia, Fiumi, Tutte le parti del Mondo, ed altre infinite materie. Opera utile ad oratori, predicatori, poeti, pittori, scultori, Disegnatori, e ad ogni studioso, per inventar Concetti, Emblemi, ed Imprese, per divisare qualsivoglia apparato nuttiale, funerale, humano. Ampliata ultimamente dallo stesso autore di CC imagini, e arricchita di molti discorsi pieni di varia erudizione; e con nuovi intagli, e con Indici copiosi nel fine. Dedicata all' Illustrissimo Signor Filippo Salviati, Siena; her. Matteo Florini, 1613.

To scholars who would be tempted to shorten this prolix title, a word of warning.[3] It might appear to careless scholars unnecessarily long and almost unreadable, but it is crucial to dissipate some of the most common misunderstandings about Ripa's oeuvre. It is wrong to consider the *Iconologia* a simple thesaurus, a rag-bag accumulation of visual metaphors, putting together such oddities as *Corpi Celesti* (Heavenly bodies) and *Provincie d'Italia* (Provinces of Italy). His intentions, set out in the prolegomena, are explicit: a manifesto claiming the epistemic quality of a 'science of images' (*iconologia*), the rational expression of a fully-fledged humanist programme, an encyclopedic work in the spirit of the Counter-Reformation. The many users of the book (imaginative minds, sculptors, painters but also orators and preachers) may have distorted, fragmented and divergently circulated the wealth of erudition contained in the book. It nevertheless has a purpose, in Aristotelian parlance, of distinguishing between definition, genre and accident. While most scholars have laid emphasis on the correspondence between iconological norms and allegorical metamorphoses, the observations made so far on the variegated stances and manifestations of *Justitia*'s avatars show that gestures cannot be reduced to prior textual translations, trapping the transient nature of her multiple axes, into a taxonomy of fixed signs. Animated by signs that are in essence mutable, *Justitia* may be perceived as an allegory in motion. Scholars who pretend to master the intricacies of this science of images forget an important fact: allegories disseminate through a wide panel of outward patterns (cultural appropriation, voluntarist symbolic acts, self-presentation) but also through the unknown rules of the psyche (engrams, fantasies, sonic images,[4] synaesthesia).

Ripa's preamble folds together visual and rhetorical images according to the *ut pictura poesis* doctrine: 'The rhetorical image will not be dealt with here, only the visual image. Despite the difference in their means, they have a great conformity to each other and the same anthropological basis.'[5] The purpose is to 'declare each image in its verisimilitude' as 'fables are a means of communication' which is 'both exoteric and esoteric.'[6] The immediate context of this programme of *eruditio* goes back to the primary sense of the word, which is to educate the *rudis* (ignorant), to strip him of the dross of ignorance and initiate him into the science of images. Ripa's intentions stand at the crossroads between 'The Plebian' and the initiated, exoteric and esoteric allegoresis, God's unfathomable Ideas and human *concetti simbolici*.

At the beginning of his book *Une allégorie parfaite. La Justice: vertu, courtisane et bourreau* (1993), Christian-Nils Robert highlights the reversibility of the image of Lady Justice that is split into an oxymoronic combination between an awe-inspiring goddess and a bloodthirsty prostitute. When facing Gieng's fountain of Justice, his viewing experience is said to stem from an openly stated fascination.[7] It bears note that in Latin, *fascinatio* has connotations of trapping the gaze. As Victor I. Stoichita insightfully remarks:

> at the time when Giotto was working in Padua, in the same city in which Pietro d'Albano was discoursing on the nature of magical arts, fascination had an important place in the panoply of *maleficia*. The work of the fascinating eye (*opus oculi fascinantis*) Pietro d'Albano argued, modifies bodies, depriving them of their strength, in particular by striking their generative capacities.[8]

A similar belief in the agency of the *maleficia* appears in the depiction of emblematic objects. The word *fascinum* means a 'phallic charm used against evil spells', sometimes hung around the necks of children as a talisman.[9]

Beyond the normative textual order of the science of images, allegories of Justice generate various inventions in *allegoresis*, from works by Georg Pencz (1533), Germain Pilon (1585) and Hendrick Goltzius (c. 1578–82). The three-dimensional geometries of *Justitia*'s bodies in the early modern period articulate a new sense of perception, rooted in a triangular physiological scheme (eye movements/ambidextrous ability/ synaesthetic agency). This chapter will also explore the challenges faced by scholars trying to go beyond the *ocularcentric* approach to allegory.[10] Taking a multisensory approach to embodiments of *Justitia*, we will look at works that contemporary beholders would have encountered, not primarily as online reproductions or photographic reductions but rather in the flesh. Lady Justice adorning clockwork encourages an exploration of acoustic jurisprudence whereas the act of kissing reveals the implication of kinetic aspects in the experience of contemporary beholders.

In his emblem 'Nec igni, nec ferro cedit' (It yields neither to the fire nor to the sword),[11] Hadrianus Junius uses the iconic motif of a signet ring (*anullus sigillarius*) to invent a new emblematic sign in which an inserted diamond is clasped in a bezel and held crosswise with a burning iron crucible, on one side, as a talisman 'against the spiteful'. On

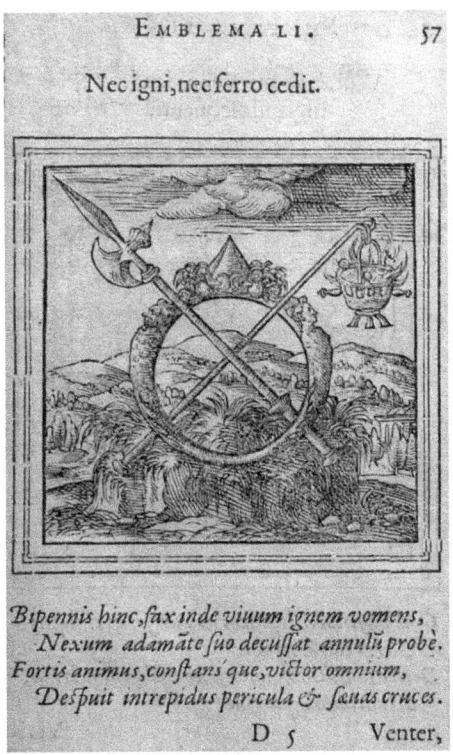

E MBLEMA LI.　57

Nec igni, nec ferro cedit.

Bipennis hinc, fax inde viuum ignem vomens,
Nexum adamāte ſuo decuſſat annulū probè.
Fortis animus, conſtans´ que, victor omnium,
Deſpuit intrepidus pericula & ſanas cruces.

D 5　　　　Venter,

Figure 6.1: Hadrianus Junius, *Emblemata* (1565), emblem LI *Nec igni, nec ferro cedit.* By permission of the University of Glasgow Archives & Special Collections, Stirling Maxwell collection

the other side stands a *bipennis*, an impressive piece of weaponry, a double-headed battle axe, requiring the use of both hands (Figure 6.1). This emblematic montage is not simply a 'picture'; it stands as a flag, a weaponised tool to wage symbolic war on those who try to steal his emblematic *persona*. Using one of the iconic attributes of war, the *lansquenet*, Junius associates his own device with the campaign he fought as a champion of humanist letters. Moreover, Junius explicitly states the provenance of his emblematic creation, so as to protect it from plagiarism by publishing it as a token of his method of advancing the recovery of humanist letters.[12] This example of a talismanic use of emblematic material sheds new light on how to understand the agency of symbolic objects in the early modern visual context, especially the ways in which images of a certain kind could trigger responses other than the purely aesthetic ones we attach to them in our post-Enlightenment societies.

If we want to understand the eschatological dimension of the imaginal, Lady Justice's attributes serve as an intriguing case. This is controversial; we need to distance ourselves from the idea of a 'power of images' contained in images themselves. Images are always fragments of imaging processes, part of rituals, and in the case of *Justitia*, situated at the interface of natural and institutional signs.

When a viewer encounters an embodied image of Justice, he presumably addresses the artifact with his own cognitive and affective style. We have to take into account the 'periodicity of the eye',[13] but also the entire body as involved in a viewing process. Perception is a nexus of interlocking senses (eye movements, prehensile movements, circumnavigation movements). To fulfil persuasive, mnemonic or deontological functions, allegories of Justice use a wide panel of sensory arousal traps. Are Lady Justice's attributes to be considered as types of magical instruments? As noted by Robert, two-pan scales were generally perceived as a complicated and expensive instrument because public use was granted upon the payment of a tax. This device was frequently subject to falsification and inspired distrust.[14] Its use was reserved to a small number of professions (money-changers, jewellers, chemists). Viewers beholding these wondrously decorated instruments would not necessarily perceive them as symbols of equitable judgments or efficient decisions. To many viewers, weighing is not judging, but an external affirmation of destiny – scales are not only an indication of what will happen but a symbolic representation of *what is fated to happen*. Setting out the scales is an action that can only be operated by a goddess, that is, a transcendent order, whose effects remain undetermined.

Hadrianus Junius' ring displays a diamond (referring to the Greek *adamas*), the gemstone *par excellence*, according to Pliny's *auctoritas*. It is possessed of superior strength (his *singulari praerogativa*), 'disdainful of two of the most destructive things in nature, iron and fire' ('contemptricem vim duarum violentissimae naturæ rerum, ferri ignisque'). Junius explains further that its talismanic power originates, according to the authority of the ancients, in a *mancipatio*. He purposely uses the legal phrase *atque auctoritate scriptorum veluti mancipi tenet*. The Roman legal procedure of *mancipatio* entails a verbal contract by which the ownership of certain valuable goods, called *res mancipi*, can be transferred. As an object coined to protect its bearer, the emblem is therefore treated as a valuable asset. Junius goes back, figuratively, to the etymological root of the word, *manus* (hand) and *capio* (to take), indicating, imagistically, that coining and bearing an *emblema* are acts of taking with the hand the thing which one is acquiring. In Roman times, this formality was accompanied by symbolic rituals which empowered them with efficacy. Junius publishes his emblematic invention in a context of fierce rivalry with those who would dare to misuse it for their own ends.

Michel Pastoureau's definition of the heraldic seal returns to the same judicial understanding of signs. The seal transmits the '*imago* of the sigillant, that is, his personal image, the one to whom he transmits his *auctoritas*, the one who legally represents him and prolongs him, emblematizes him and symbolizes him, who is both himself and the double of himself'.[15] If the individual bearer of a seal coined especially for him is perceived as a doubling of his own *persona*, it is worth asking how Lady Justice uses the semiotics of her own avatars. Her allegorical body is not simply an image of female physiology, but stands as a curiously weaponised envelope using devices such as *fascinatio* (as a magical art of the gaze) combined with other sensuous appeals, such as the *basium* or kiss. The aims of this chapter are thus threefold: first, to interrogate the triangular relationship between gaze, sword and scales, through which the 'augmented' body of Lady Justice is seen as an avatar of the judge; second, to recover the spatial dimension of an interpretative plurality through the analysis of the allegorical association of *Justitia/Lex* with a monumental representation of clockwork; and third, to retrace the blossoming of *Justitia*'s kisses. The juxtaposition of these themes will help us to move from a semiotics to an aesthetics of Justice. The first example shows how the allegorical medium can be a tool for the exposure of acoustic Justice. Second, the allegorical nexus of the kissing theme reveals the ways in which viewers' responses remain very diverse, depending on where these paintings were placed and who would be affected by the erotic force of *Justitia*'s incorporations.

Justitia will be considered here as an imaginal crossroads of contradictory affects. These affective processes are to be thought of as major constituents of *Justitia* as an apparatus (*dispositif*). The power of the gaze, whether beneficial or malefic, cannot be dismissed as unthinkingly superstitious. As numerous sources attest (at least until the eighteenth century), the practice of execution in effigy, commented on by jurists as well as by commentators on the Church Fathers, implied that the jurists and preachers who made use of these practices lent *real effect* to these rituals of death by image.[16] But the manifold allegorical iterations of *Justitia* are also manifested in her visual complexion, her facial colouring, physical features and sartorial habits. As we saw with the tradition of judicial *ekphrasis* at the opening of the book, *Justitia* draws on the *auctoritas* of Chrysippus to mould an *imago* of judicial ethics. On the one hand, physiognomy is used by judges as a practical skill for adjudicative assessment.[17] On the other hand, allegory is used symmetrically by early modern artists to convey an aesthetic and ethical metaphor of the Law. It functioned simultaneously as the judge's daimon and a protection for litigants. The triumph of Lady Justice was, at least in part, a triumph of representation. The early modern treatment of the kiss of *Justitia* and *Pax* shows how the exegetical tradition of biblical allegory is completely reworked during the early modern era, playing a crucial role in establishing new visual formulas for an irenic and amorous fusion between Justice and Peace.

Triangle

Georg Pencz's *Automaton* (1533)

Beyond formal convention and subsequent decay, *Justitia*'s 'instruments' were mediated through early modern technological inventions, such as scales, clockworks or automata, placing both the judges and litigants under her auratic power. Her gigantic sword or oversized scales conflated two types of *fascinum*, beyond logos and nomos, pointing towards the need to ward off *anomia*, which, according to Thucydides and Plato, provokes the displacement of democracy into ochlocracy. In one of the most imaginative and fascinating effigies of Lady Justice, Georg Pencz offers a striking vision of the unknowing knowledge of the legal subject, which can only be apprehended through the enigmatic holding of the magical instrument (Figure 6.2). Captured at the pivotal moment of a symbolic task, a powerful nude in profile manipulates with extreme care the two instruments of sword and scales as if they had

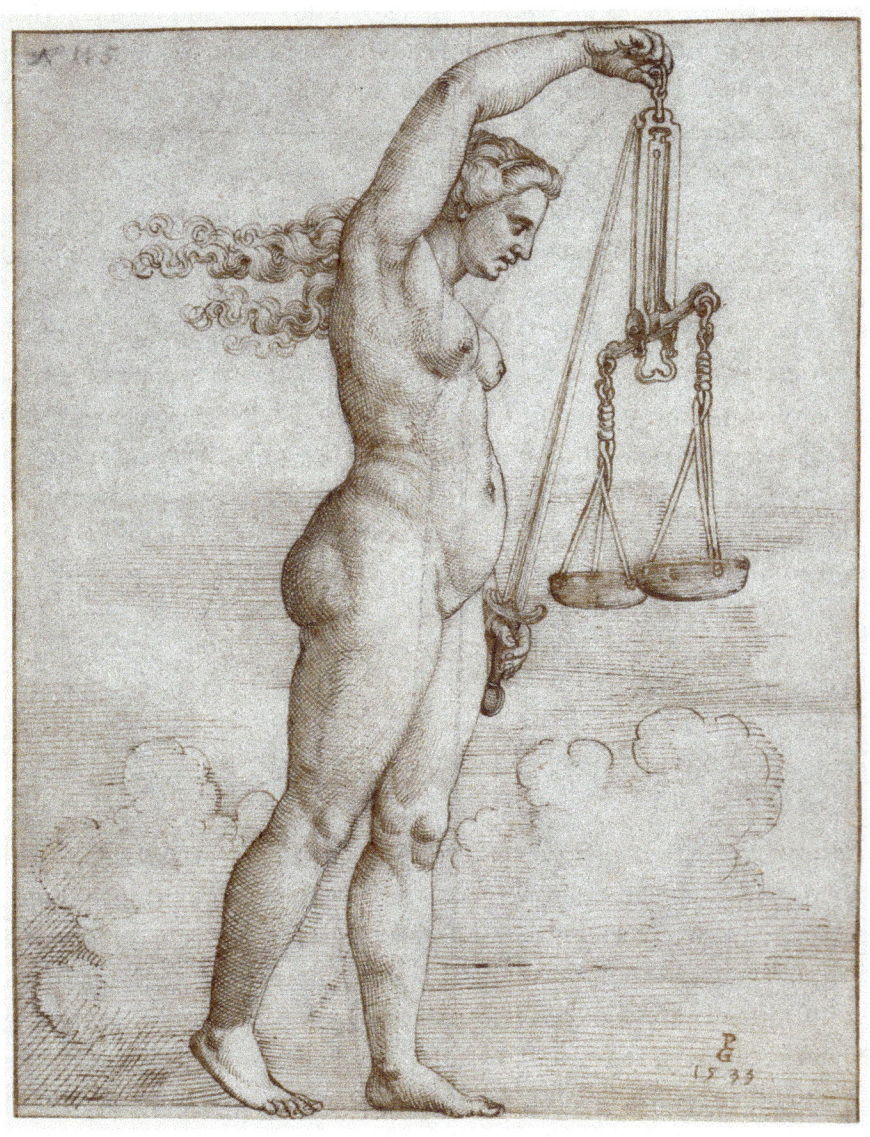

Figure 6.2: Georg Pencz, *Allegory of Justice*, 1533, pen and brown ink over black chalk, 7 3/5 inches × 5 9/10 inches (19.2 cm × 14.9 cm). Getty Research Institute

been bewitched by the *fascinum* of her own gaze. Her outstretched right arm holds a type of scales like those depicted in Dürer's *Melencolia*. Her line of sight goes through the fulcrum which cause the pans to be balanced. The sword's edge is purposely drawn so as to measure by touch the half-body length of the gigantic scales she manipulates. Her tiptoed right foot indicates a sequence of movements, corroborated by life-sketching lines in fine black chalk. Lady Justice is here depicted as a living being, an animated heroic nude. Above all, the geometrical premises of her body are prosthetically enhanced by her command of both instruments.

As noted by several scholars, this is Pencz's answer to Dürer's *Nemesis*, based on a carefully delineated canon of proportions derived from Vitruvius.[18] The latter had used simple numerical relationships to depict the correct proportions of human bodies: for instance, the height of a man is measured by the height of eight heads, or of ten faces from chin to hairline, with similar relationships for other parts of the body. The fruit of Dürer's research appeared in two of his treatises, *Instruction in Measurement with the Compass and Straightedge of Lines, Planes and Solid Bodies* (1525) and *Four Books on Human Proportion*, published posthumously. Pencz's drawing follows the same theory: beauty in a drawn figure depends on a system of measurement and geometry with all its developments in physics. Geometry serves as an experimental laboratory for drawing.[19] Pencz's drawing is first and foremost a practical exercise in the geometry of movement. But the harmonious triangle construed by *Justitia*'s gaze, staring narcotically at some imaginal perspectival point between an upward pointing sword and the fulcrum of the scales, seems to indicate that measurement itself may be bewitching.

Pencz's invention answers the dilemma once posed by Momus: 'For how can you represent Justice both with one eye and many eyes; and how can you depict her one-handed, and yet measuring, at the same time weighing and simultaneously brandishing a sword?'[20]

Pencz's response to this challenge is to use the temporal nature of drawing to suggest a mobile automaton, indicating much more than a simple nexus of odd gestures.[21] Rather than fixing her allegorical stances into a two-dimensional still image, the outstretched arm emphasises the process of weighing through a shift of orientation and the unusual articulation of the limbs. The artist invites viewers to interpret his composition by adopting a spatial perception of the drawing. Instead of drawing a sequence of movements broken into several steps, Pencz conflates three movements: the *fascinum* that captivates the eye, the prehensile movement of supporting the scales, and the lifted right foot indicative of walking and of rotation. With her left foot grounded, *Justitia* will presumably turn around as if she were a pillar able to lift the gigantic scales. This highly sophisticated automaton points to a visual methodology through which percepts meet concepts.

At this point, we need to come back to the concept of automaton, recovered by Andrea Alciato in his *Parerga*.[22] His elucidation of the Greek word restores its classical meanings and corrects the misunderstandings of the glossators.[23] Quoting Hero of Alexandria's *Pneumatics* (first century CE) and other first-hand Greek manuscript sources, Alciato pioneers an early modern understanding of how these self-propelled devices rolled on wheels.[24] Georg Pencz's *Justitia* is therefore a kind of automaton. He transforms the two-dimensional drawing into an illusion in which Lady Justice's animated body acts by itself. Her body in motion seems about to be manoeuvred so as to make both scales and sword coincide. She seems to slowly lift the weight of the gigantic scales, counterbalancing the weight of her enormous sword as if she were a machine.

In his depiction of a muscular nude against a cloudy background, Pencz hints at the untold nature of mathematical Justice. If mathematical proportions for the female nude are emphasised with hatched lines creating a greater sense of volume, the handling of both instruments under the fierce gaze is of another nature, suggesting a different aspect of space-time on a scale tied to a vanishing point situated outside the frame of the drawing. Pencz's erect *Justitia* explicitly introduces movement into a normally static allegorical stance. The use of a linear perspective is framed in such a way that the focal point is situated beyond the human agency of measuring scales, suggesting another agency, beyond the reach of humans. Instead of separating two distinct symbolic systems – the geometrical proportions of the body and the mechanical agency of the measuring instrument – Pencz unites them, creating a harmonious and dazzling representation of a Nemesis staring at the technical possibilities of her 'sword–scales' apparatus. Beyond conventional attributes conceived as definitional tools, her automated body is not ill-ordered and subject to mockery. It suggests instead a substantial, richly articulated automaton, able to move by itself, leaving human wit free to explore other purposes and applications. The allegory does not entail any teleological discourse. No attempt is made to link the gestural ethics of Lady Justice to a broader system of reasoning. More importantly, the invention of *Justitia* as an automaton opens up *Justitia*'s gestures to a new semiological process through which legal science hides an evident character of initiation.

According to recent findings in cognitive science, one way to assess *Justitia*'s symbolic gestures is to address the ways in which her instruments act as an extension of her own body, enabling what Maurice Merleau-Ponty termed a 'palpation par le regard'.[25] Alain Berthoz has likewise forged the concept of 'perçaction' to explain that perception is not just an interpretation of sensory messages but an internal simulation of action.[26] Perception and action are strongly intertwined. Half-sword and half-scales, Pencz's *Justitia* has completely integrated both of her attributes into the functioning of her own body. Taking into account the embodiment of Lady Justice allows us to evaluate allegoresis by appealing to the viewer's own postural sensations (visual, haptic and proprioceptive). Pencz's drawing is a sublime response to Momus' sarcasm. He renders it possible to handle great complexity (three diverging body movements) through 'simplexity': allegory defined as a physiological phenomenon converts discursive issues into an imaging process, without reducing their complexity.

Aristotle had considered two kinds of scales in his second mechanical problem, according to the position of the rotation above or below the beam. According to Aristotle (*Mechanical Problems* 849a6–17), large scales would be more precise than smaller ones. Aristotle's argument is that for larger scales, the relation between natural movement and unnatural movement is bigger than for smaller scales, therefore the weights on it move more easily, and consequently, large scales are more sensitive and thus more precise. In this example, the gigantic size of the sword and scales and the unusual handling of *Justitia*'s attributes hint at the latest inventions in the field of *artes mechanicae*.

Justitia's spatial apparatus

The implication is that gestural ethics are not a by-product of legal symbolism, nor are they an oversimplification. On the contrary, gestures are to be treated explicitly as a key expressive mode and conduit of agency, through which the subject innovates and departs from the script. Gesture, because of its transitive nature between natural and institutional signs, is able to restore the enigma necessary for the functioning of the judicial apparatus. Aside from the centrality given to linear perspective, Lady Justice's symbolic transience offers a geometrical anatomy rooted in the spatiality of multiple points of view. Her attributes are thought by Renaissance artists as a genuine extension of her body. Is the intended viewer necessarily forced into the preformatted role of voyeur versus censor? When the viewer is gendered as male or female, what about his or her perception of this fleshy creature, encumbered with bizarre attributes? In our analysis of gestures as signs combining features inherited from a physiological symbolical grammar *and* signs of institution, we will bear in mind an important caveat: because gestures are 'means without ends', they do not imply a teleology of action.[27]

Attracted by the sensuality of her gestures, baffled by the handling of her instruments, the viewer, whatever his degree of literacy, cannot fail to observe that Justice sometimes bears the distinctive signs of the courtesan. Her finery (feathered hat, expensive jewellery, deep cleavage) is combined, as we have seen, with deliberately erotic gestures. Allegorical art manages to flesh out the convention at the heart of its claim to meaning. Lady Justice, when she appears as a bloodthirsty prostitute, enters the resonance chamber of affects, and thus welcomes the cry of the litigant, the fear of any viewer trapped into her *maleficia* – before any semiotic reduction has occurred, beyond logos, in the foreground of our emotional responses. The efficacy of such images of Justice, together with other objects such as amulets or talismans, is often denied in rational discourses, but as Ian Maclean shows, it remains an important piece of the cabbalistic discourse in which 'images and verbal formulae are believed to bear inherent force which can be harnessed for healing purposes.'[28] These ideas formed the background for thinking about the representation of Justice in the early modern era. But the vividness of what is called *motif* left an enduring legacy which still inhabits literary texts today.

Victor Hugo, remembering the long genealogy of images of Justice, saw this with great acuity. In his tireless and ironical charge against the death penalty, Victor Hugo underlines the slow dehumanisation that presides over the spectacle of the guillotine, the hideous key to a collapsing vault, while the pillars of the *Ancien Régime*, the priest, the king and the executioner, have disappeared:

> Yes, the horrible and voracious Themis of Farinace and Vouglans, of Delancre and Isaac Loisel, of Oppède and Machault, is withering away. She is losing weight. She is dying. The [place de] Grève[29] no longer wants her. La Grève discharges itself. The old blood-drinker behaved well in July.[30] She wants to lead a better life from now on and to remain worthy of her last great deed. She who had been a prostitute for three centuries on all the scaffolds, is overcome by modesty. She is ashamed of her former profession. She wants to lose her ugly name. She repudiates the executioner.[31]

The symbolic efficacy of allegory is not confined to the rigid personification of an outdated codification, as Victor Hugo extends it to the place of memory: the Place de Grève itself becomes an allegory of arbitrary and bloody Justice: what count are not the attributes, which sound false, but the *genius loci*, the mental image of all the tragic executions that have been committed on the Place de Grève so far. In contrast to the self-righteous stories of the docile image of Themis, it is appropriate to revive here the muted ambiguity of this bloodthirsty figure. For Victor Hugo, this unbearable motif of the female executioner prostituted to kings is nothing more than a slut, a decrepit old woman, a bigot on the comeback trail, in short, a hypocrite. Themis is no better than the Erinyes, an unbearable image of the violence of judicial murder.

A redefinition of the spatial apparatus of *Justitia*'s body is therefore welcome, if we want to assess the polarities triangulated by the three key elements of her bodily agency: the gaze, the power grip of the sword and the precision handling of her scales. Henceforth, allegories of Justice should no longer be thought of as immobile forms, trapped into the teleological grammar of a linear and one-way path. Instead, they are mutable and mobile *automata*. This novelty allows for the realignment of agency and gesture according to a new set of technological instruments.

Mechanical Justice

Let us now bring Lady Justice back to her spatial incarnations within urban space. The double effigy of *Justitia/Lex* that surrounds the Horloge du Palais in Paris, to the north-east of the Palais de la Cité, is still visible today *in situ* (Figure 6.3). Instruments of measurement are often associated with the equilibrium between just punishments and just laws, which is a fundamental element of theories of law.[32] Bearing an instrument of time measurement visible to everyone, the allegorical clock invented by Germain Pilon to adorn the Tour de l'Horloge is a bold invention. The viewer can effectively recollect the idea of Justice by hearing and beholding the equal and regular measurement of the hours. Here we have a telling example of a symbolic process opened up to synaesthesia. The monumental clock, situated above eye level, on the façade of the second highest tower of the Palais de la Cité enclosure, was topped by a bell which sounded the alarm in the event of a city-wide emergency (fire, massacre or war). Not only visible to lawyers and officers of the courthouse precincts, the clock is located at a pivotal point of the urban landscape, outside the enclosure: it aims to regulate all sorts of temporalities across the city. It was built by Charles V around 1370 so as to embellish the city of Paris,[33] enabling the *gens du Parlement* as well as its citizens to regulate their activities. During the fifteenth century, the office of the Governor of the Clock, a royal office,

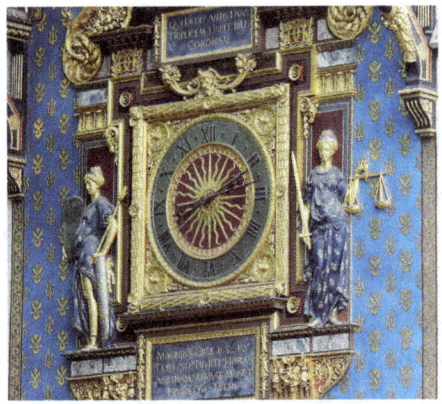

Figure 6.3: View of the Horloge du Palais de la Cité, Paris. Photograph by the author

was a theatre of iterative litigations between the royal representatives of the parliament and the greedy monetary pretentions of successive office-holders.

Still visible today at the crossroads of the Boulevard du Palais and the Quai de l'Horloge, the clock was adorned in 1585 with an allegorical setting by the French sculptor Germain Pilon (*fl.* 1540–90). He was a faithful inhabitant of the sanctuary, and the creator of a famous *Mater dolorosa*, whose most popular version was placed in the Sainte-Chapelle, at the most sacred centre of the entire Île de la Cité. The new allegorical clock face was then visible at the corner of the Pont-au-Change with the Quai des Morfondus and the rue de la Barillerie and would have stood at a symbolically charged location. The clock overlooked one of the most active double bridges in Paris, on the southern bank of the Seine. The monument was visible from three main axes at the same time (Figure 6.4).

The two allegorical figures framing the clock quadrant present a double effigy of *Justitia* and *Lex*, inserted into a genuinely emblematic montage containing verses created by the poet Jean Passerat (Figure 6.5). The *inscriptio* written into the upper cartouche reads, 'QUI DEDIT ANTE DUAS TRIPLICEM DABIT ILLE CORONAM' (He who has already given him two crowns will give him a third).[34] The bottom

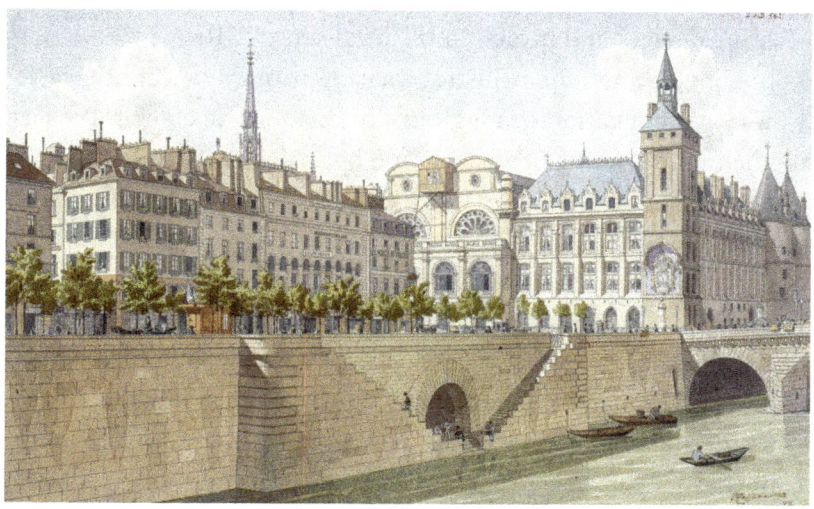

Figure 6.4: View of the location of the Tour de l'Horloge. Painting by Fedor Hoffbauer, *Le quai de la cité et la tour de l'horloge en 1855*, inv. D.5821. Courtesy of the Musée Carnavalet, Paris

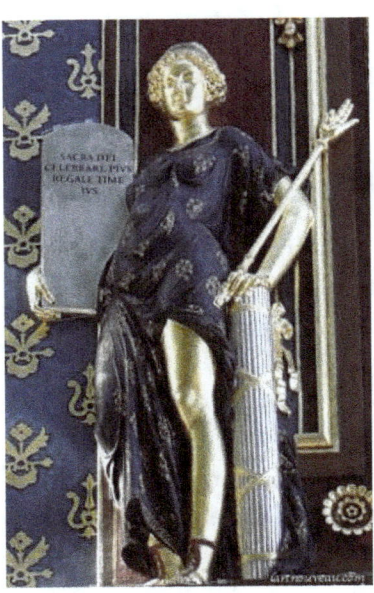

Figure 6.5: View of *Lex* and *Justitia* in the allegorical setting of the clockwork by Germain Pilon, after restoration. Photograph by the author

subscriptio instructs us, 'MACHINA QUÆ BIS SEX TAM JUSTE DIVIDIT HORAS JUSTITIAM SERVARE MONET LEGES TUERI' (This machine which divides twelve parts so equitably teaches us to safeguard Justice and to observe/defend the laws). The verb *tueri* signifies first 'to see', 'to observe' and in a second sense 'to safeguard, to protect'. Both figures are thus, at the same time, objects to be seen, protecting devices and tutors (in the legal sense of the word).

Pilon's divine and *duplex* Justice was not primarily meant to lay down any monastic obligation or religious profession. The clock served as an embodied reawakening of what should be understood as true Justice, in which everyone is enjoined to make virtuous use of time. If the message communicated here provides a visible archetype of *oikonomia*, aiming to impact all sorts of everyday practices, what remains ambivalent is the binary effigy of *Justitia* and *Lex*. The tradition of adding ethical mottos to sundials or public clocks is well documented.[35] Just as the dials on mosques are intended to remind the faithful of the schedule of their prayers, or sundials fixed on churches refer to the canonical hours of prayer, lawyers and magistrates are reminded of their duties, having in front of them a pointer towards the colossal clock facing the Place de Grève and opposite the Pont-au-Change, where public executions took place. But citizens, merchants on the Pont au Change and passers-by were also affected by the totemic presence of this automaton, whose bell chimed when *Securitas* was under siege. Here the allegorical pair *Justitia/Lex* not only serves as a frame for a three-dimensional monument; both figures are set in the four-dimensional geometrical space of the automaton, mobile not just in space but in time.

On the mechanism of the clock itself, Julien Le Roy, born in Tours (1686–1759) and Louis XV's clockmaker, describes a clock with cogwheels and a pendulum, 'very roughly made' and driven by a motor weighing 500 pounds, which was far too heavy for it.[36] At a time when the gnomon of public clocks aimed at giving the best possible measure of time, it is worth noting that this impressive machine was presumably still far from our contemporary standards of exactitude. In his *Règle artificielle du temps*, Le Roy says that the quadrant of this clockwork would only mark hours (not minutes or even seconds) by bell-ringing.[37] The associational chain between *Justitia/Lex* and the revolutions of the clock, operated by a highly visible monumental clockwork built at the corner of the judicial enclosure, was designed as a *machina judiciale*, a tool for thinking the links between Justice and measurement, opening up the vision of a city and a judicial world that can resonate in memory.

What about Germain Pilon's allegorical setting?[38] In 1585, the situation in France was uneasy. Often compared to Herod in contemporary protestant pamphlets, Charles IX was held responsible for the continuous revival of the Hydra of war since he had publicly admitted his role in the Saint Bartholomew massacre. The allegorical setting of the clock may have been meant to ward off the bad omen of an infamous king. The former allegorical contract (Charles IX as the union of *Pietas* and *Justitia*) now looks as if it were void. Instead, Pilon offers a new formula: *Justitia* and *Lex* protecting the symbolic order with the promise of all the reliability and efficiency of a machine – an engram of reliability, trustworthiness and vigilance.

Thus, *Justitia* meets *Lex* around the impressive square dial (1.5 metres in diameter) with a radiant sun at its centre, placed on the royal mantle of France against a background of *azur fleurdelisé*. The radiant sun adorning the clock face seems commonplace, but it might also revive the dynastic memories of the Christian paradigm of the king's

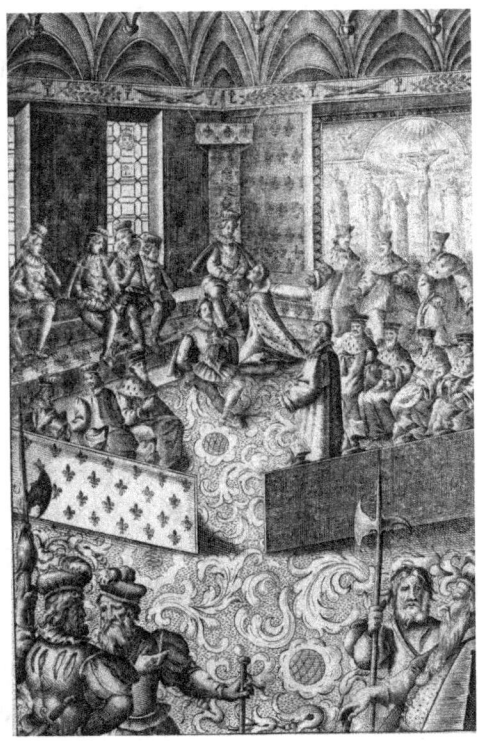

Figure 6.6: Anonymous, *Lit de justice tenu par le jeune Louis XIII au lendemain de la mort de son père*. Archives Nationales, Paris AE-II-3890. Note the king's seat located at a tierce position, in the corner of the Chambre dorée. Wikimedia commons

persona as *Sol Justitiæ*. The alluring posture of *Lex*, with a slit skirt revealing her upper thigh, contrasts with the fully clothed *Justitia*. *Lex* leans on a lictor's *fasces*, holding in her right arm the tablets of the Law (*sacratissima leges*) and in her left hand an upward rod of Justice, whilst *Justitia* holds a set of equilibrated scales in her left arm and an upward sword tucked into her right wrist. The king's emblematic portrait has vanished. Both female allegories occupy a similar position to soldiers guaranteeing the security of the *parquet* inside the *oikonomia* of the courthouse's *lits de Justice* (Figure 6.6). A dual figure of the threshold, *Justitia/Lex* frames the mechanical apparatus of the metrics of Justice in order to secure the sanctified locus of the *parquet*, its most holy see.[39]

During the Revolutionary period, both allegorical figures were defaced. These iconoclastic destructions dismantled the pompous apparatus of the royal insignia. *Justitia* supported by *Lex*, protected by a

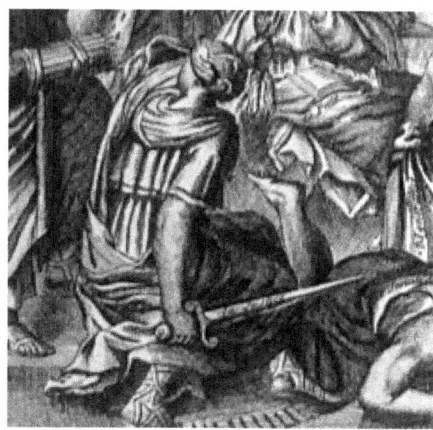

Figure 6.7: Anonymous engraving, 1762, *Arrêts du Parlement rendus contre les Jésuites*. Detail of *Justitia* seen from the back, kneeling in front of the Parliamentarians. Archives Nationales, Paris. Photograph by the author

canopy, would have stood out as visible dynastic emblems, asserting their sphinx-like presence against a blue background strewn with fleurs-de-lis. This formula appears in an engraving of parliamentarians (1762) in conflict with the Jesuits (see Chapter 7), where *Justitia* is seen from behind, serving as a scopic delegate to the scene of conflict depicted in the background (Figure 6.7). Her role is to protect the parliamentary session with her drawn sword, which bears the inscription 'La Justice'.

According to Albert Krantz, in Bohemia, at the beginning of the fifteenth century, a Hussite leader, Ziska, close to death, asked that a war drum be covered with his own skin, the sound of which would scare off the enemy.[40] Similar stories are reported in Africa, but there the skin is that of an adversary, or his mummified hand is turned into a drumstick. This symbolic ritual recalls Cambyses' painful *damnatio*, a visual engram showing that the failing ruler must pay with his own flesh. It also brings to the fore the synaesthetic emblem of the war drum, half musical instrument, half relic, whose sound was thought to ward off bad luck. Likewise, the clockwork pairing *Justitia* and *Lex* shows how much the visual dimension is enhanced by sonic experience. The drum would have encouraged observers of these rituals to think of the sacred soundscape of Justice as a physical memento of the pains of inflicting judgments.

Kisses

Justitia et Pax osculatæ sunt

The ambivalent threshold character of *Justitia*, subservient to the French kings, is certainly a relevant example for framing the question of positive and negative perceptions of the judicial apparatus through images of *Justitia*. But we now need to reconsider a further enduring visual motif: the kiss of *Pax* and *Justitia*. This survey, spanning more than five centuries, is not conceived as a practical *osculologia*, such as the encyclopedic entries written on the subject in the seventeenth century. The goal is to combine a study of the biblical allegorical kiss with a new understanding of Lady Justice's imagery, highlighting the manifold roles her gestures of embrace play in proposing a symbolic pact between the human and the divine. The rise of the allegorical theme of the kiss of *Justitia* and *Pax* owes its great longevity to its constant reinvention and appropriation by a shared community of influential artists, enlightened patrons and wealthy amateurs. The influence of the allegorical medium cannot, however, be judged solely by these high-culture parameters. If allegorical artworks are undeniably designed to cater for certain categories of viewers, they may also trigger unpredictable aesthetic responses. The motive of two women kissing was a long-lasting early modern formula, a polyphonous device meant to endure a wild growth outside iconological codes, set beyond the sometimes narrow corset of aesthetic norms. We certainly must acknowledge the central and productive role of Cesare Ripa's *Iconologia* and his followers, but we must not overlook other allegorical formulas that shape a wider understanding and appreciation of allegory in practice.

In his commentary on the four-fold depiction of Justice ('Justice/Justice inviolable/Justice rigoureuse/Justice divine'), Ripa insists on equating *Justitia*'s chastity with the assumed moral purity of the judge: 'Like the most chaste virgins, they must be free from all kinds of passion.'[41] The body of the judge is thus dreamt of as anaesthetised, a blinker against pathos and terror. We are reminded that in Descartes' theory of passions, one of the affects under study is the 'passion de la fuite'. Escaping out of fear is considered a passion. Ripa's injunction, too, in endeavouring to shun the affects of the judge's body, seems to forget the nomos of nature and the humours of biopolitics. In Chapter 4, we saw that the glossator Giovanni d'Andrea examined the legal validity of a judge proclaiming his sentence astride a horse, so as to be able to flee immediately after proclaiming the sentence. Ripa's codification is meant to settle Justice in a temple of sacred norms. We will now see how these norms fluctuate in other settings, in which the treatment of a biblical narrative, based on a centuries-old tradition of allegorical commentary, is reinvented by sensuous gestures more attuned to the Counter-Reformation's bold affirmation of the senses.

The erotic kiss

To understand the theological substratum of the allegory of the kiss of Justice and Peace it is necessary to elaborate on the haptic dimension of Lady Justice's symbolic acts. The scheme was built on influential medieval theological readings and was mobilised to convey political significance (as is the case in the use of the motif in Richelieu's castle[42]). One aspect, however, is rarely discussed. When *Justitia* kisses Peace in an overly intimate impulse, as is the case with the sexualised rendition by Goltzius which is the focus of the discussion here, the women depicted suddenly descend from the pedestal on which centuries of allegorical dignity had placed them. The aesthetic norms of the allegorical genre are exploited to depict something obscene. With the Counter-Reformation, the sexual aspect of pictorial works – especially when they were placed in the church – became highly problematic. From its origins in the Psalms, seen firstly as part of a centuries-old biblical tradition of patristic hermeneutics, the female kiss gradually traverses amorous islands and political maps of desire.

Since medieval times, the meeting and kissing of Justice and Peace in Psalm 85 had provided an authoritative justification for representing female desire through allegorical lovemaking. In the third plate of his series of 'Allied Virtues' (*De verenigde deugden*), dating from c. 1578–82, Hendrick Goltzius depicts the embrace of Justice (with her sword attached to her scales) and Prudence (instead of *Pax*), wielding a pair of entwined snakes (Figure 6.8). The intimate embrace of these two full-bodied and sexualised nude figures enables a bold invention: the representation of same-sex desire. Goltzius's emphasis on volumes and torsions and *Prudentia*'s pose from the rear are particularly noticeable.

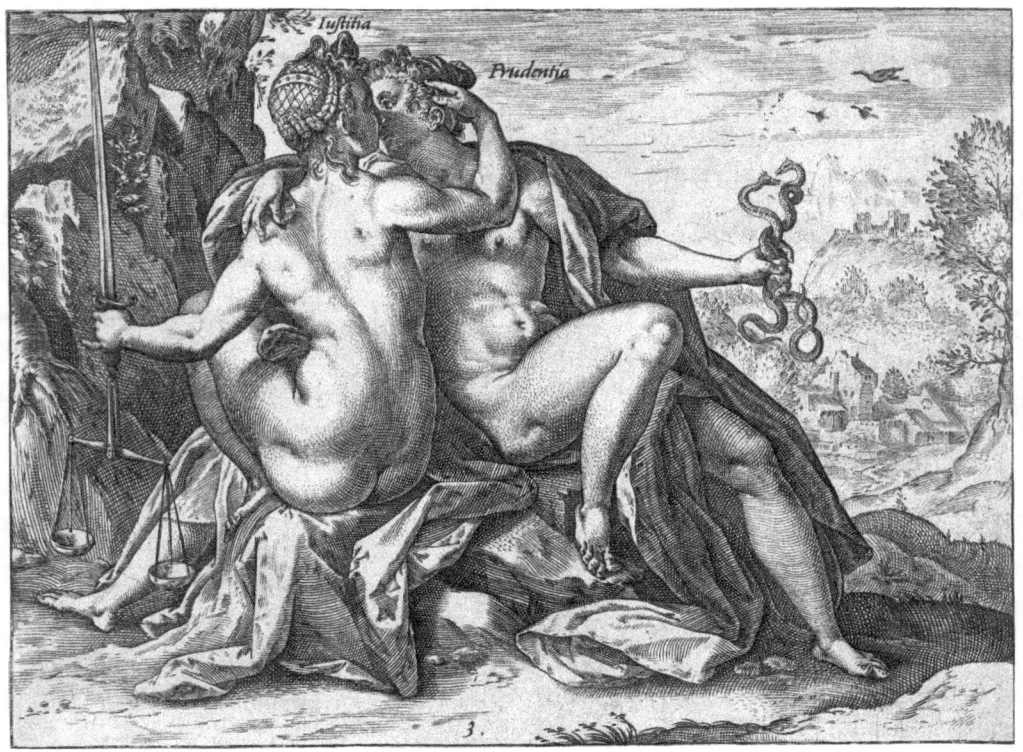

Figure 6.8: Hendrick Goltzius, *Prudentia & Justitia*, from series of *Allied Virtues* (*De verenigde deugden*), dating from c. 1578–82. Courtesy of the Rijksmuseum, Amsterdam

The Latin motto precisely connects the image to its erotic undercurrent: 'Ardua Justitiæ venerans Prudentia limen, Quid poterit vasto sanctius orbe coli' (If the sublime Prudence honours the threshold of Justice, what is the most sacred thing that can be glorified in the vastness of the world?). The threshold of Justice is a metaphor of the vagina, a gateway to paradise. 'The most sacred thing that can be glorified in the vastness of the world' is neither Justice nor Prudence (which stand as explicit metaphors for desire) but erotic love.[43] Goltzius has dramatically heightened the erotic contact between the two figures, athletically built and scantily clad, clasping one another in a vigorous *basium*. Despite their formal dignity, their full-bodied, fleshy sensuality connotes the global dominion of carnal passion. The sensual embrace makes the bodies turn, twist and drift along a serpentine line, keeping the travelling gaze of the beholder in motion. The engraving not only depicts a scene of concord between two civic virtues but mobilises the viewer's desire for it.

The erotic tension of Lady Justice's pose echoes stories of a Spaniard overcome by lust when he saw the irresistibly enticing, naked figure of Justice on Guglielmo della Porta's tomb for Paul III in Saint Peter's, completed in 1574. Indeed, the Spaniard allegedly satisfied himself on the statue, after spending a night making love to it.[44] In 1595, by order of Pope Clement VIII, the figure was covered with a metal robe crafted by Guglielmo's son, Teodoro. It was a notorious instance of Counter-Reformation censorship.[45]

Around 1575, an oil on canvas attributed to Marten de Vos provides another amorous version of this embrace (Figure 6.9).[46] The diffuse eroticism of the scene explains why the painting, lacking identification, has also been entitled *Bellone Disarmed by Venus*. Here two women are seated, and their exquisite beauty lends them the features of Venus. The theme was popular at the time; several compositions by Flemish masters

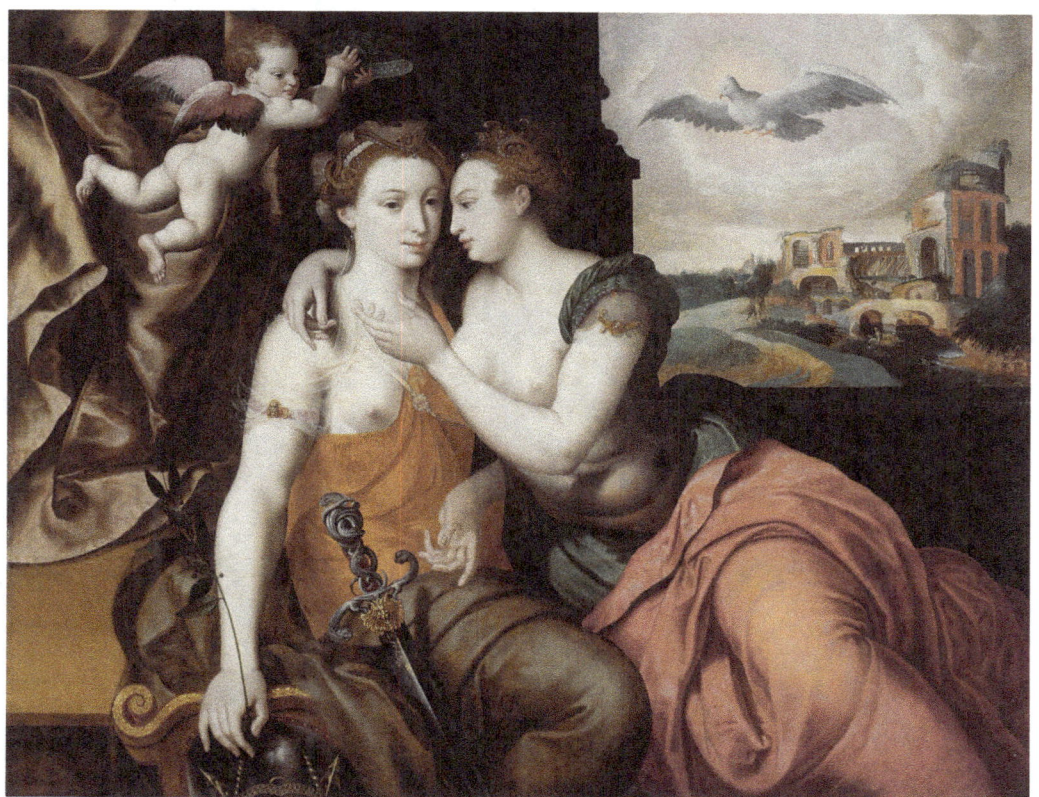

Figure 6.9: Attributed to Marten de Vos, *Allegory of Peace and Justice*, also called *Bellone Disarmed by Venus* and *Diane de Poitiers Crowned by Venus*, inv. 7999.1.2.363. By permission of the Museum of Fine Arts and Archeology, Châlons-en-Champagne

are known. Justice and Peace, lightly dressed in precious robes and cloths, are in the foreground. The handle of Justice's sword is decorated with snakes. Peace turns lovingly towards Justice, looks at her, embraces her, inclines to kiss her. Justice looks out of the picture. Below them, a river flows peacefully, by a path, a bridge, a ruin. All represent the fruitful consequences of the kiss of Justice and Peace.

The scene's perspective changes when the figures are depicted standing, their bodies animated by a gesture of fraternal embrace. This is the choice adopted by Jacopo Palma the younger (1544–1628) in a painting kept at the Estense Gallery in Modena, dating from c. 1620 (Figure 6.10). The verse of the Psalm is inscribed in a rock in the lower left-hand corner. The intimacy of the kiss is preserved by a play of

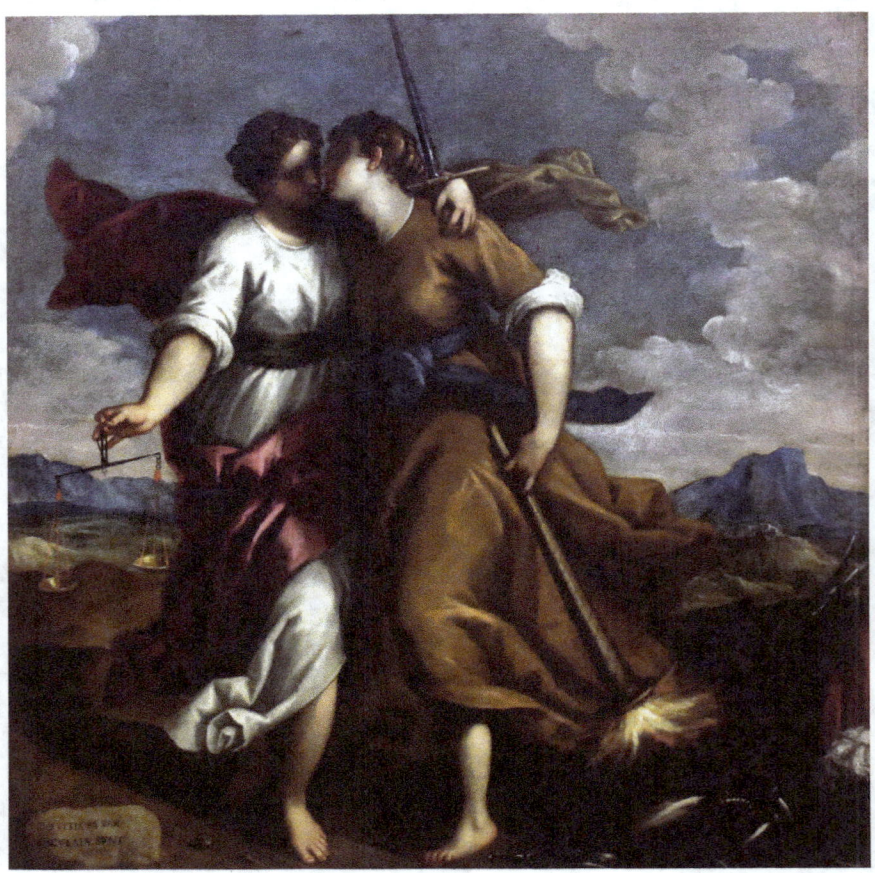

Figure 6.10: Jacopo Palma the Younger (1544–1628), *Justitia et Pax osculatæ sunt*, c. 1620. Estense Gallery and Museum, Modena. ALG78316. By permission of Wiki Loves Monuments 2017, Wikimedia Creative Commons

chiaroscuro that keeps the closed eyes of the two women in shadow. The painter emphatically underlines the emotional register of the embrace. In a similar vein, an anonymous allegorical painting from the first half of the seventeenth century presents the theme of the kiss as one of a *consolatio* between two friends (Figure 6.11). Justice, dressed in yellow and blue, blindfolded, warmly shakes Peace's hand while approaching her cheek in a gesture of empathy and sisterhood. The sword of Justice is laid aside.

When the treatment of the kiss becomes the occasion of a touching gesture, one woman grasping the breast of the other, as in the anonymous version kept at the Pinacoteca Tosio Martinengo in Brescia, the kissing schema receives further connotations of terrestrial love. The theme is interpreted in a much more chaste manner in a composition by Egbert Jansz, engraved by Johann Theodor and Johann Israel de Bry (1588–1608) (Figure 6.12). The Latin inscription below the print, 'JUSTITIAM PAX amplexatur honestam' (Peace embraces honourable Justice), underlines the chaste encounter of the two virtues. In

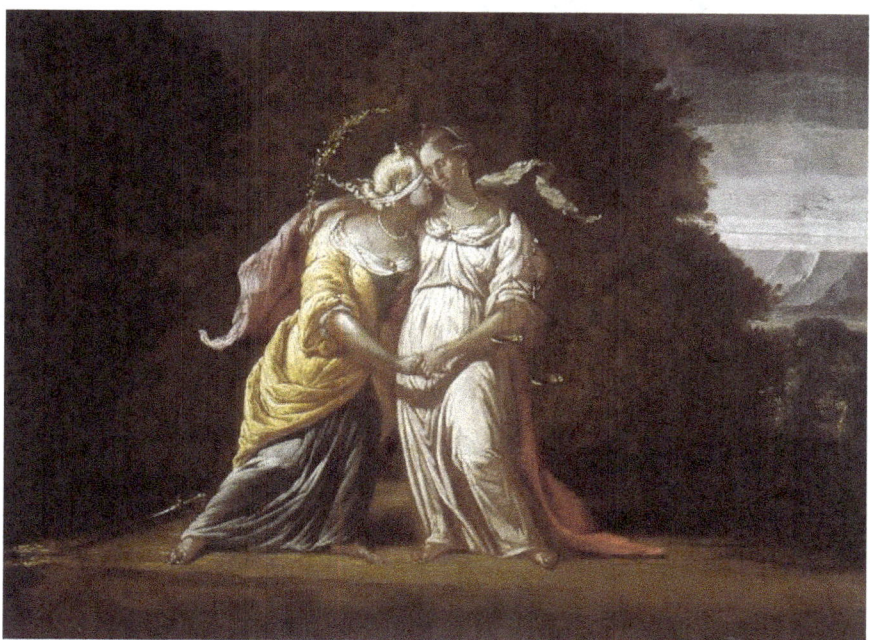

Figure 6.11: Anonymous painter, *Allegory of Peace and Justice*, France, first half of the seventeenth century, inv. C. 992.558.1. By permission of the Departmental Museum of Flanders, Cassel. Photograph by Jacques Quecq d'Henripret

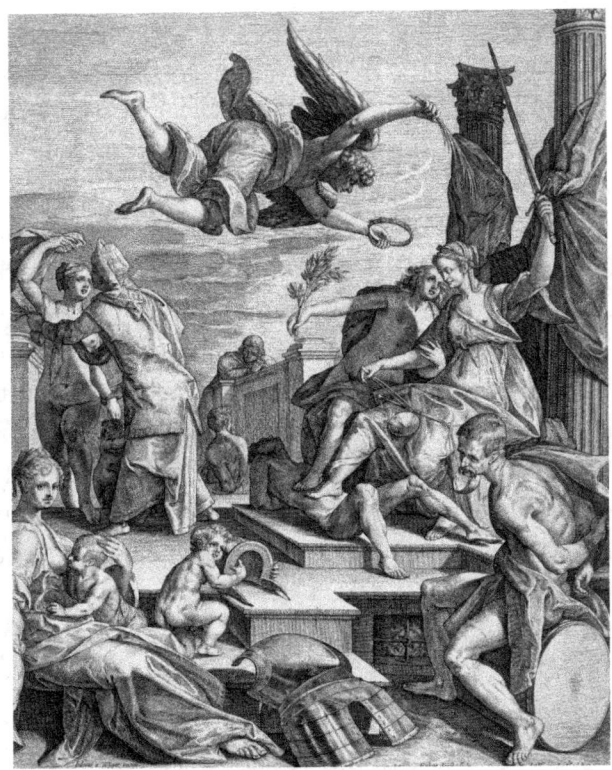

Figure 6.12: Egbert Jansz, after Joos van Winghe, published by Johann Theodor and Johann Israel de Bry, *Allegory of Justice, Peace and Charity*, copperplate engraving, 45 cm × 35.7 cm, 1588–1608, inv. RP-P-1878-1-1126. Courtesy of the Rijksmuseum, Amsterdam

accordance with moral decency, *osculatur* is replaced by *amplexatur* and Peace only timidly grasps the arm of Justice.

The kiss in theology

In the seventeenth century, several authors eagerly embarked on voluminous treatises on the history of the kiss. The subject was of interest to theology, jurisprudence and medicine. Martinus Kempius compiled an extensive encyclopedia on the subject.[47] He starts from the origins and different meanings of the word *os* ('mouth', 'face'), the root of the word *osculum*, which means at the same time 'small mouth' and 'kiss'. Adopting an extensive classification of kisses, divided into sacred and profane kisses, he lists, among the mystical kisses, Psalm 85, verse 11: Justice and Peace have kissed each other (*Justitia et Pax osculatæ sunt*). But well before the various modalities of the kiss became the subject of extensive 'osculologia', paintings often depicted a wide variety of kisses.

The study of the motif of the kiss of Peace and Justice, taken from sacred scripture, makes it possible to analyse a significant range of cases as well as to read the allegory from a dialectical perspective: a practical meditation between Justice and peace links the judge and the litigant to the exercise of moral judgment in any given situation. In his lecture *Love and Justice*, Paul Ricœur evokes the poetics of the imperative underlying the discourse of love (praise, blessing, macarism).[48] In the same way, the discourse of Justice is part of a prayer, a call for help, which has an exegetical basis. In the sixteenth and seventeenth centuries, the subject became a frequent theme in paintings and prints, and also in emblems, seals and medals. The theological readings of the Psalm, firmly established by medieval patristics, were gradually grafted onto more openly political interpretations, reminding us that the cardinal virtues of Peace and Justice were indispensable to the proper functioning of the state.

The kiss in Psalm 85 refers explicitly to a collective prayer or appeal for help, containing praise of the powerful and just Lord, the supreme benefactor. It has its origin in a situation of distress and serves as a community lament, written during the period of Israel's return from Babylonian exile. Supplication, trust and gratitude are very closely associated: the prayer is a covenant that emanates from a community gathered for a liturgical ceremony: 'Mercy and Truth come together; Justice (Righteousness) and Peace have kissed each other; / Truth shall spring out of the earth; and righteousness shall look down from heaven.' Just as the psalmist in turn evokes, begs, acknowledges, implores or expresses personal or collective devotion, so the allegory of the kiss of Peace and Justice offers an embodied form of lyrical outpouring, adaptable to many different situations.

At heart, *Justitia et Pax osculatæ sunt* is a love song, an *epithalam*. Within the quartet of the four virtues, the kiss has already taken place (*osculatæ sunt*), it has been given. The graphic and iconic possibilities deployed around this theme range from the most chaste kiss to the most lascivious embrace. When the text of the Psalm is transposed into an allegory, Justice does not merely unfold a whole range of affects in an unequivocal movement; the couple creates an ascending and descending spiral that gravitates in both directions. Justice and Peace embrace each other, but this gesture does not exclude their differences; in a sense, it pre-supposes them: through this analogy and this process of metaphorisation, Justice increases the value of the Peace it grasps, Justice helps Peace to become higher than it in terms of values, and vice versa. The kiss is a sign of true cooperation, where both parties admit to being mutually indebted.

The verse *Justitia et Pax osculatæ sunt* is widely commented upon in theology, for example in texts by Saint Augustine, Hugh of Saint Victor and Saint Bernard. If we want to understand the novelty of Goltzius's creation, we need to recover the main lines of patristic transmission of the schema. In 1630, the Lutheran theologian Jacob Herrenschmid (1578–1641) wrote a treatise on theological-philological osculology in which he established an extensive typology of kisses.[49] Chapter 7 is entirely devoted to the interpretation of the kiss of Peace and Justice, and the author begins by affirming its holy and mystical character. Herrenschmid then quotes part of Augustine's commentary:

> Mercy and Truth came together; Justice and Peace embraced each other. Do justice and you will have peace, so that justice and peace may embrace. If you do not love justice you will not have peace, for the two love and embrace each other. He who does justice finds peace; peace embraces justice. They are friends. Perhaps you love one and not the other, for there is no one who does not love peace, but not everyone wants to act justly. If you ask all men, 'Do you love peace?' all the human race answers together, 'I love it, I desire it, I long for it.' Therefore, they must love justice, for they are friends and embrace each other. If you do not love the friend of peace, it will not love you and will not come to you. Do you think it is a great thing to desire peace? Any perverse man desires it. Well, it is a good thing, peace. But do justice, for Justice and Peace embrace each other and do not fight.[50]

Augustine emphasises the friendship between the two virtues. The kiss is fraternal and the friendship between the two sisters transitive – to love one is necessarily to love the other. In 1697, in his Sermons and Christian instructions on various subjects, the Jesuit father Pierre Joseph d'Orléans underlined the contractual nature of the kiss:

> Saint Augustine, moralizing on the last of these passages, particularly on these words: Peace and Justice have kissed, says, following the figure of the

Prophet, that Peace and Justice have made a treaty, by which peace obliged itself not to enter the heart of the sinner, unless Justice has preceded it.[51]

The theologian Johann Daniel Prangen also points out that the kiss of Justice and Peace is holy and spiritual. He lists an extensive taxonomy of kisses: *oscula reverentia, oscula adorantium, oscula diabolica, oscula idololatrica, oscula civilitatis, oscula amoris, oscula reconciliationis, oscula favori*. He again cites Augustine in defining the spiritual kiss. It belongs only to friends who live under the law of friendship. It is not given by the contact of the mouth, but through the affection of the soul; not by the joining of the lips, but through the union of the spirits, under the inspiration of the Holy Spirit who purifies everything and who communicates to all a fragrance of heavenly chastity.[52]

The kiss of *Justitia* and *Pax* serves frequently as a vehicle to voice the conjunction of souls.[53] As such, it was a leitmotiv of funeral court practices. Peace, says Father Jean-François Senault in his funeral oration for Henriette-Marie of France, Queen of Great Britain, is

assisted by the Justice that reigns with her and makes her reign too. For these two sisters hold each other's hand in defence, and they embrace each other so closely that they cannot be separated without making them both die together: *Justitia & Pax osculatæ sunt.*[54]

Bernard of Clairvaux, in his first Sermon on the Annunciation, offers a second theological reading. He highlights the rivalry between the two virtues, who, before agreeing to a kiss of peace, engage in a merciless struggle. Justice, before being tempered by Peace, follows its zeal for vengeance and strikes its victims with affliction. In a very lively and alert style, Bernard writes here a kind of little opera on an almost mythological theme involving the four virtues quoted in Psalm 85: Mercy, Truth, Justice and Peace. The medieval commentators, following in his footsteps and those of Hugh of Saint Victor, interpret the virtues as the 'four daughters of God'. The battle between them was quickly developed in numerous mysteries, moral homilies and theatrical plays. Bernard situates the action in heaven, at a time when God had not yet decided to send his son to save mankind. The whole sermon is devoted to the controversy of the four virtues that are fighting over how to save a mankind lost to sin. God ended their controversy when he decided to make his son man and sacrifice him to redeem humanity.

Finally, I come to a third theological reading of the kiss, as a symbol of the mystery of incarnation. In his commentary on the Psalms, Isaac-Louis Le Maistre de Sacy interprets verse 11 of Psalm 85 in this way:

> This all-divine kiss of Justice and Peace is properly understood as the mystery of the Incarnation of the Adorable Word [. . .] this Peace and Justice have given each other the kiss through the covenant they have made with each other. For the righteousness of the Father required the punishment of the sinful man. And the peace of the Son required reconciliation. So, what did the incarnation of the Word do? It combined these two things together for our salvation. [. . .] The Peace of the Son disarmed the Justice of the Father. The ancient psalters prefer to replace *osculatæ sunt* by *amplexae sunt*, because the verb suggests an embrace and not a kiss of the lips.[55]

We must therefore discern, under the unstable equilibrium expressed by the patterning of the kiss, the various possibilities it contains. It stages a whole range of situations, from the touching of the lips to a fraternal embrace. A kiss is sometimes the site of an unstable relationship that must be established and protected. Kissing is certainly an erotic or emotional sign, but it can also regulate social relationships. It can be a sign of submission (feudal kiss), of reconciliation or the seal of a promise. In most of the early modern and classical visual representations of the scheme, the theological content of the Psalm was no doubt unmistakable. It was a direct reference to the central Christian idea of redemption. But conversely, the scheme was also used, ironically, in the prolix literature of the Mazarinades as a counter-model, a topical locus for the depiction of a *mundus inversus*.[56] Until the sixteenth century, the kiss of Justice and Peace was active in the field of Mariology; the two virtues were juxtaposed with the meeting of Mary and Elizabeth. This is the way the motif is understood in Cardinal Alessandro Farnese's Book of Hours from 1546. At the same time, however, the meaning of the kiss was consistently associated with political messages. It would soon become ubiquitous as an expression of the idea of a peaceful state. This allegorical nexus formed the background for iconotexts, pleas, emblematic prints and genre paintings throughout medieval and early modern times, but also survived well into the nineteenth century.

The kiss in law

The very nature of the kiss is also a legal question. The humanist jurist Benoît Le Court defined three degrees of kissing in his commentary on the *Arrêts d'Amour* by Martial d'Auvergne.[57] This commentary is a work of youth, bold and playful, published in the judicial style that was supposed to be characteristic of love courts. These courts, in the tradition of the ethics of chivalry, were made up of priests, nobles and ladies, and judged matters of love as if they were matters of state.[58] Le Court's lexicological remarks often take the form of digressions: 'In order to depart a little from this subject', he says, 'we shall distinguish between *basium, osculum* and *suavium*. According to Ælius Donat, in his commentary on the Eunuch by Terence, *osculus* is the kiss offered for convenience, *basium* refers to the modest affections between parents and *suavium* is the lascivious kiss.'[59] Servius, on the contrary, in his commentary on the *Aeneid*, identifies *osculus* as the religious kiss and the latter, *basium*, as lascivious.

This distinction was of interest to the law and in particular to the nature of presumptions in cases of adultery. If a cleric kissed a woman, a careless judge might say that such a kiss should be interpreted as a blessing. Le Court reported how the jurist Antoine Favre saw no futility in posing the problem.[60] In his commentary on the *Digest* (9.25.3), he asks 'if because of a kiss, a woman may be deprived of a dowry'.[61] The same case is defended by Giovanni di Ripa against Giasone de Maino and Filippo Decio. Ripa believed that punishment should vary according to the customs of the regions or nations concerned. According to Ovid (*Elegy* 4.5.56), the lover considers the kiss as an act: 'If you gave me a kiss, I would immediately declare myself your lover.'

The gesture of the kiss, according to Le Court, constitutes the true semiotics of amorous jurisprudence. Therefore, it calls for an interpretation that is not self-evident. As a potentially ambiguous sign, the kiss becomes the object of a *vis permittandi* (a will to authorise) or a *vis vetandi* (a will to deny), as in a sense, every act of kissing is performative of the desiring body. When it is depicted by an allegorical rendition, does the *osculum Justitiæ* turn into a *basium* or a *suavium*? Is it a sensual embrace or a sign of consolation? Moreover, legal texts constantly remind us that the kiss is an oath; it has the value of a performative statement. The iconographical scheme of the kiss of Justice allows us to question its perlocutionary force.

The kiss in politics

From the outset, the allegory of kissing was associated with living persons. One of the main features of the political narratives that developed around *Justitia/Pax*, whether as a good or bad omen, was to build a triangular space where a sovereign, king, emperor, Pope or other figure of governance attends the allegorical ritual in which the two virtues kiss each other.

The image of the kiss of Justice and Peace was often used to glorify princes by reference to biblical authority. A manuscript of the poems of Eloy Costentin (1530–1) shows François I holding the hands of both virtues as they kiss (Figure 6.13). The poem itself emphasises the leading role of the King in fulfilling David's prophecy.[62] The illuminator has represented Justice, with sword and scales in her right hand, an olive branch in her left, trampling on Iniquity and crushing War underfoot. There is a clear sense here of the auratic power of the king, whose gesture aims at making explicit claims for his prophetic role.

In the iconography of the sixteenth century, it is rare to find a representation of the four virtues together. One example is a copper engraving by Agostino Carracci (1556–1602) after a drawing by the Bolognese mannerist painter and draughtsman Orazio Samacchini (1532–77) at the Albertina in Vienna (Figure 6.14). The engraving was executed in 1579 and contains in its lower margin the full quotation of verses 10–11 of the Psalm, with the mention of the scriptural source: 'Misericordia et veritas obiaverunt sibi Justitia et Pax osculatæ sunt'. The engraving was later copied by Theodore de Bry in 1598. On the left, below, Samacchini has represented Mercy expressing milk into a cup or bowl, her breast overflowing with the milk of human kindness. Facing Mercy, Truth is seated to the right, nude, her foot resting on a globe, holding an open book and a radiant sun disc on her head. Justice stands in the background, holding *fasces* in her right hand and a pair of scales in her left hand. She embraces Peace, who stands to the right, holding a caduceus. The engraver has

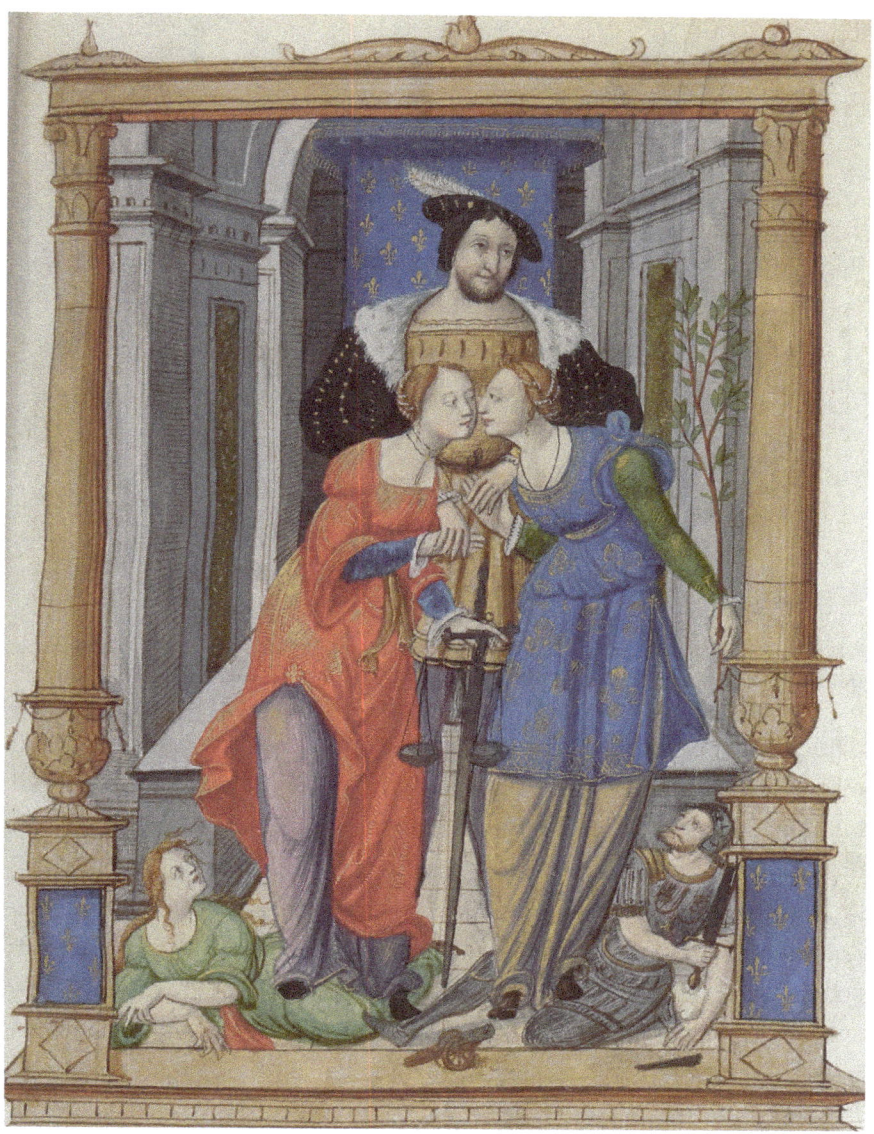

Figure 6.13: Eloy du Mont dit Costentin, illuminated manuscript, *François 1er Holding the Hands of Justitia and Pax Kissing Each Other*, 1530–1. By permission of the Bibliothèque nationale de France, manuscrits français 2237, fol. 2r

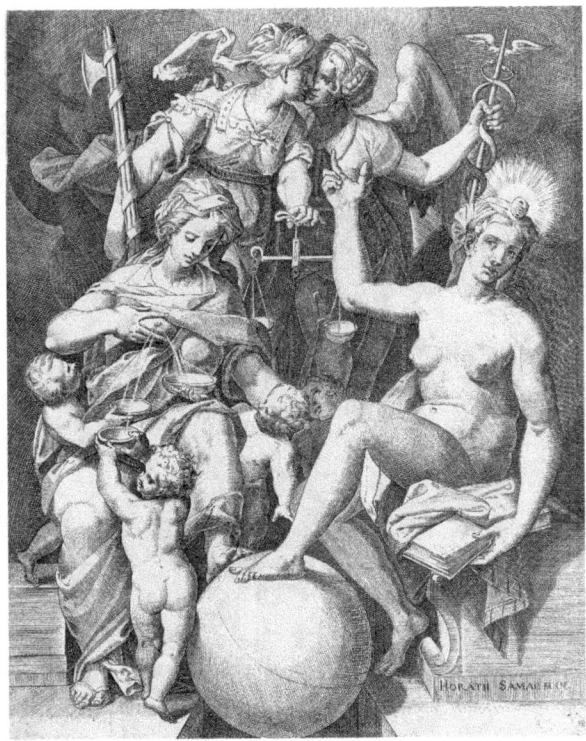

Figure 6.14: Orazio Samacchini, *Justitia & Pax with Mercy and Truth*, 1579, copper engraving by Agostino Carracci, inv. 2032. By permission of the Albertina Museum, Vienna

depicted the moment of the kiss on the lips, cheek to cheek and eye to eye. The fact that Peace is adorned with wings underlines the hieroglyphic abstraction of the scene: two powerful women embody two abstract ideas and the kiss is mystical rather than carnal.

In the course of the sixteenth and seventeenth centuries, the two allegories of Justice and Peace freed themselves from this quaternary schema. The kiss of Justice and Peace becomes a widely disseminated subject, especially as it distanced itself from previous theological readings to take on a more clearly ideological and political meaning.[63] Representations in which the concept of salvation is central are no longer recognisable. The pairs *Misericordia et Veritas* and *Justitia et Pax* often appear separately. Indeed, increasingly the biblical tradition provides no more than a pretext.

An engraving dating from 1580, attributed to Ambrosius Francken I, develops an interesting treatment of the theme (Figure 6.15). The print accompanies the New Year's greetings (*xenia*) of the Provosts of

Antwerp to Archduke Matthias of Habsburg (1557–1619). *Pax* has placed her right leg over the thigh of Justice, as a supplementary sign of loving affection. The allegorical kiss is associated with two major figures of revolt: David and Judith. Both are clearly identified by their attributes and inscriptions: David stands like a peasant holding a slingshot, a sword and the head of Goliath. With his sling he also symbolises life in faith. Judith, with the severed head of the enemy commander under her left arm, points up to the camp of the Assyrian army, in front of the besieged city of Bethulia. In the centre, the kiss of the two virtues is placed under a radiant dove, signifying the Holy Spirit, itself beneath the name of Yahweh inscribed in a radiant cloud. Again, the dove reminds us that the kiss of the virtues is spiritual. The coats of arms of the Duchy of Brabant (top left) and the city of Antwerp (top right) are a regional reference to the specific context of the print. The texts in Latin, Flemish and French above and below the image are a message of New

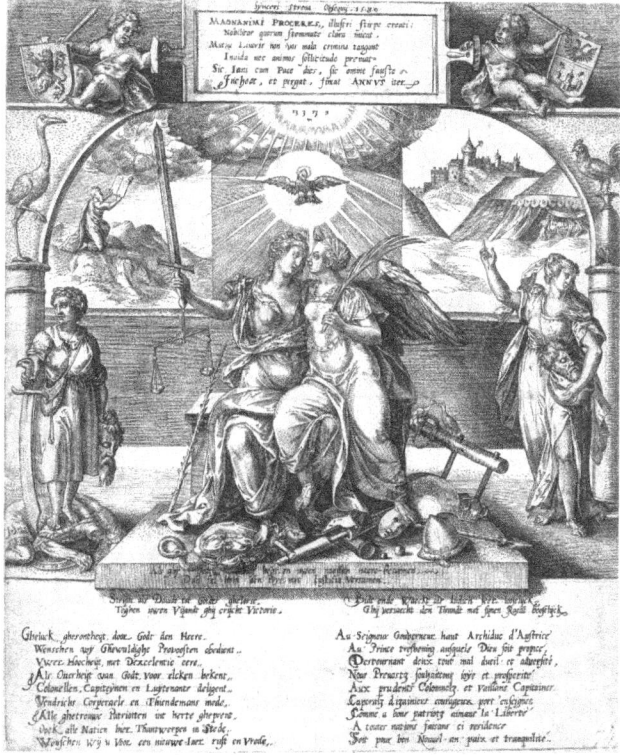

Figure 6.15: Ambrosius Francken I, print designed for the New Year's greetings of the Provosts of Antwerp to Archduke Matthias of Habsburg (1580). Courtesy of the Rijksmuseum, Amsterdam

Year's greetings in which Antwerp expresses its hope for a just reign and a peaceful year.

The kiss in economy

In 1659, the Dutch painter Theodor van Thulden (1606–69) reworked the theme in a stunning baroque composition, drawing together many of the allegory's now-familiar political tropes in a scene of triumph and abundance (Figure 6.16). Two female figures lean towards each other. *Justitia* is dressed in a blue gown and red cape, holding the raised sword in her right hand. She holds a purse from which coins fall out at her feet. Beside her, a putto holds her scales up, pointing his index finger towards the evenly balanced pans. Peace approaches her as a beautiful young woman, almost completely naked, loosely surrounded by a green cloak. She holds a cornucopia as well as a caduceus in reference to the arts, sciences and trade which flourish in times of Peace. At her feet are weapons and pieces of armour, while in the background, a putto is burning other weapons in a blazing fire. *Justitia* turns completely towards *Pax* and by embracing her grants her the protection she desires. Van Thulden revives the *locus classicus* of the Psalm, allowing the figures to interact strongly with each other. Inspired by Rubens's particularly dynamic treatment of allegorical figures, van Thulden nevertheless only hints at

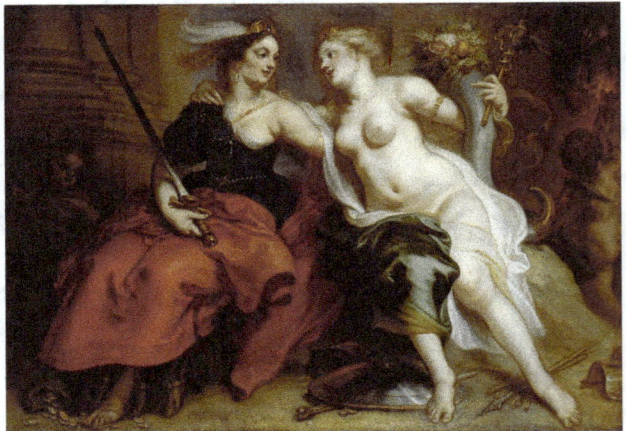

Figure 6.16: Theodor van Thulden, *Allegory of Peace and Justice*, 1659, oil on canvas, 109 cm × 162 cm, inv. 1540LG, Münster. By permission of the Westphalian Landesmuseum for Art and Cultural History

the kiss the two exchange. The two women do not make contact with each other; instead, they look directly at the viewer. The theological context of the Psalm is relegated in favour of a secular political context, more attuned to the eyes of wealthy citizens, merchants, judges and governors.

Over time, then, the theological and even the erotic foundations of the image ceded their place to a paean to civic prosperity, increasingly generic in character. It calls to mind a global description and taxonomy of cities, enriched with allegorical motifs aimed at displaying ideas of good governance across the world. Daniel Meisner's *Sciographia Cosmica* is a case in point.[64] It consisted in a series of 830 emblematic topographical prints, seeking to combine *moralia politica* with city views from around the world in order to give to each an easily memorable dictum. An engraving of the Dutch city of Leuwarden in Friesland is accompanied by the German motto 'Fried und Gerechtigkeit kussen sich' (Peace and Justice kissing each other) (Figure 6.17). The two virtues, identified by their attributes (scales for Justice and palm leaf for Peace), are seated on a cloud beside each other, and the *inscriptio* states that the kiss is a symbol of civil prosperity ('symbola civilis

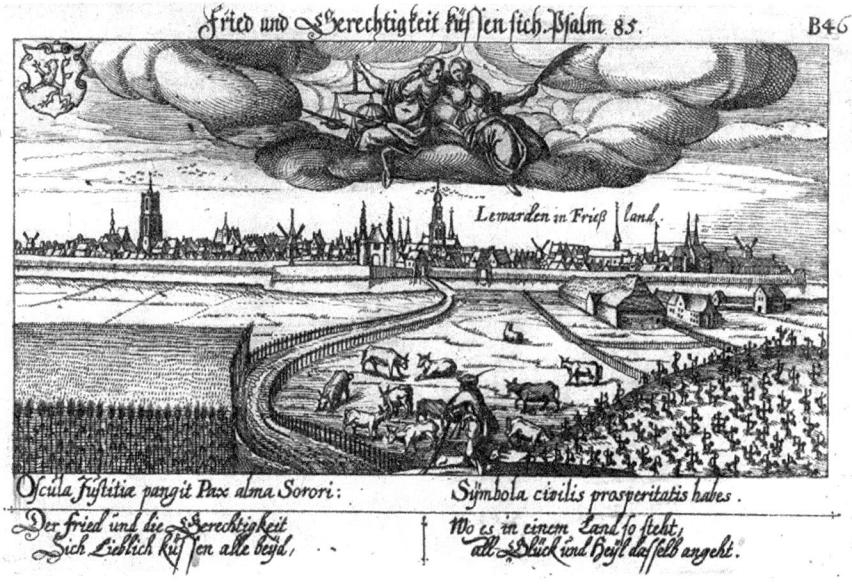

Figure 6.17: Daniel Meisner, *Sciographia Cosmica. Das ist newes Emblematisches Büchlein: darinen in acht Centuriis die Vornembsten Stätt Vestung, Schlosser etc.* (Nuremberg: Paul Fürst, 1638), second volume, emblem B 46. Wikimedia Creative Commons

prosperitatis'). The *subscriptio* in German written below reads: 'Peace and Justice kiss each other sweetly. When it is so in a country, peace and happiness flourish abundantly.' The bird's-eye view of the city in the background is linked to the peaceful landscape in the foreground, where a shepherd grazes his flock.

Polyglot and mystical kisses

The kissing scheme was anthologised in different ways and drawn upon to support a variegated *tableau vivant* of symbolic constructions. One of the most striking syntheses of all these paths are the *eikones mysticae* (mystical icons) as a sub-category of the *icones symbolicæ* of the time. Combining theological and political uses of the schema, they aimed to assert the theology of images through the use of hieroglyphical signs, that is, sacred iterations of divine symbolism. For example, Jacob de Zetter's trilingual *Kosmographia Iconica Moralis* adapts Ambrosius Francken's print to a political and religious emblematic poem. Below the engraving, an epigram in three idioms (Latin, German and French) reads, 'When Justice and Peace kiss each other without being feigned / There is more wealth in the world and fewer complaints / Too strict a Law brings only fear / But the Holy Gospel causes our hearts to rejoice.'[65]

The ninety-eight emblems of this collection are reproduced in their entirety in the work of the German theologian Heinrich Oraeus, the *Aeroplastes Theosophicus, sive Eikones Mysticæ.*[66] Emblem 86, devoted to the kiss of the Psalm, is accompanied by a two-page scholarly commentary (Figure 6.18). Oraeus' version bears the title 'Mutua Justitiæ ac Pacis oscula.' Justice and Peace, cheek to cheek, are sitting on the same throne, about to be crowned by two angels brandishing a single crown from which scales are suspended. Two putti are trampling on weapons and pieces of armour. The background scenes depict, on the left, Moses receiving the Tables of the Law and, on the right, the crucifixion of Christ. Oraeus' explanation begins by returning to the full quotation of the Psalm, asserting that the print describes the best possible state of a Republic: the association of the two cardinal virtues brings multiple riches and good governance. If Justice is depicted as the bronze wall of the kingdom, it must be tempered by Clemency, Mercy and

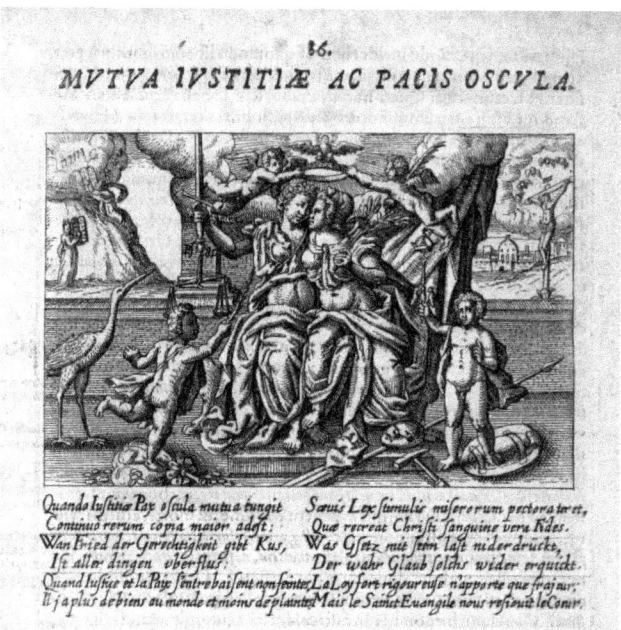

Figure 6.18: Heinrich Oraeus, the *Aeroplastes Theosophicus, sive Eikones Mysticæ*, published twice in Frankfurt by Bry (1620 and 1644), emblem 86. Wikimedia Creative Commons

Meekness. Excessive rigour and austerity are undesirable. Oraeus then links his political reading of the theme to the biblical figures of Moses and Christ, who put these virtues into practice, allowing mercy to temper the excesses of strict law.

These examples show that by 1650 the kissing schema had absorbed the visual apparatus of many different traditions. In their long and sustained rivalry with theological elaborations of the kiss, Renaissance artists had proven that they could rework and reappropriate the Psalm in unexpectedly imaginative ways. Freed from the injunction to signify theologically, Lady Justice was invited to kiss Lady Pax in an overtly sexual, indeed even obscene affirmation of anatomical embodiment. The smooth polished skin of both Ladies, the palpable embrace of the lips, the sound of the clockwork adorned with *Justitia* and *Lex* studied above: these were all experienced by the early modern beholders through a number of multisensory experiences. Unlike the static displays of allegorical prints mediated by online reproductions or photographic media, the analysis of these examples opens up new ways of questioning the ocularcentric regime of art.

Conclusion

To conclude this chapter, we need to come back to what the juxtaposition of two allegorical entities may tell us. *Justitia* and *Pax* kissing, as well as the pairing of *Justitia* and *Lex* on the sides of the monumental Paris clockwork, are particularly significant. Their gestural connection provides an example of physical encounter grounded in a syncretic unity. This is quite different from what Erwin Panofsky called the '*numen mixtum*' (mixed deity), a formula initially proposed by Lucan in *Pharsalia* 5.73–4.[67] Panofsky implies a blending of Gods, a unifying force made up of the conjunction of more than one divinity in which standard attributes of two or more allegorical conventions are brought together in order to synthesise diverse meanings. For instance, the famous figure of Nemesis/Fortuna by Albrecht Dürer borrows several elements from the thesaurus of classical attributes associated with several entities (Victory/Chastity/Moderation/Fortuna) in order to show how the spiritual essence of all gods closely resemble each other.

But the doctrine of the *numen mixtum* should not be rigidly applied to fixed attributes. The most important aspect of the allegorical pairs studied here lies in the importance of the art of gesturing. Allegories of divine justice do not simply *bear* their attributes in a more or less composite way. Their expressive kissing (whether a friendly or feudal *osculum*, a tender or consoling *suavium* or an ardent *basium*) is also a *numen*; the Latin word can suggest both an entity or a sort of state or activity. The power of this second type of *numen* lies in the eye of the beholder.

These gestures combine the effects of fascination, desire and voluptuousness. *Justitia* bewitches, kisses, and entices. Her animated stances invite us to look beyond the dogma of allegorical discursivity. Nonverbal communication restores multiple gestural games, pervasive formulas and the realm of the unconscious. Because of its nature of embodied representation, the allegorical vehicle has a special interest in using expressive gestures that introduce a sensual component to the composition, arousing the body of the spectator in order to move the soul. In a sense, what remains vivid in the viewer's memory is a world where gestures have overcome discourses, as if we were to observe judicial rites as pure pantomimes.

Notes

1. Giorgio Agamben, 'Notes on Gesture', in *Means Without End: Notes on Politics*, trans. Vincenzo Binetti and Cesare Casarino (Minneapolis: University of Minnesota Press, 2000), pp. 49–59 (p. 56).
2. In his *Réflexions critiques sur la poésie et la peinture* (1719; Utrecht: Étienne Neaulme, 1732), p. 107, Jean-Baptiste Dubos explains the rules of allegorical intelligibility: 'Si l'on n'entend pas l'allégorie aisément, on la laisse comme un vain galimatias. Il est des galimatias en peinture aussi bien qu'en poésie' (If we do not understand allegory easily, we abandon it as if it were nothing but gibberish. Gibberish exists in painting as well as in poetry).
3. Peter Goodrich, *Schreber's Law: Jurisprudence and Judgment in Transition* (Edinburgh: Edinburgh University Press, 2020), printed in elegant Adobe Garamond Pro font, unpacks the gynaecocratic roles of failed Judge Schreber with unparallel morosophical wit. The emphasis laid upon the affects of the male judge are the point of departure of this chapter.
4. See Gary Watt, 'Oyez, oyez!', in Peter Goodrich and Shaun McVeigh (eds), *Diversities of Office* (forthcoming).
5. Cesare Ripa, *Iconologia* (Siena: Heirs of Matteo Florini, 1613), advertised as containing 200 woodcuts. I worked with the two copies preserved at the Biblioteca Nazionale Centrale, Florence, one of them being mutilated.
6. Ibid., *liminary prolegomena*; my translations.
7. Christian-Nils Robert, *Une allégorie parfaite. La Justice: vertu, courtisane et bourreau* (Geneva: Georg Éditeur, 1993), p. 7: 'Depuis plusieurs années, fasciné par la Justice, celle de Berne évidemment, puis par l'allégorie en général, je ne pus résister aux sirènes de l'histoire de l'art, pauvre autour de ce thème, et j'ouvrais alors un chantier qui n'est qu'à peine balisé' (For several years, fascinated by Justice, that of Berne obviously, then by allegory in general, I could not resist the sirens of art history, poor around this theme, and I opened a site which is only just marked out).
8. Victor I. Stoichita, *Des corps. Anatomies, défenses, fantasmes* (Geneva: Droz, 2019), pp. 127–8: 'à l'époque où Giotto travaillait à Padoue, dans la même ville, Pietro D'Abano, revenu de Paris, dissertait sur les arts magiques, en donnant, dans la panoplie des *maleficia* une place importante à la *fascinatio*. Le travail de l'œil fascinateur (*opus oculi fascinantis*) dit-il, peut modifier les corps, les priver de leurs forces, en frappant notamment leurs capacités génératives.'
9. See Pascal Quignard, *Le sexe et l'effroi* (Paris: Gallimard, 1994).
10. See Geraldine A. Johnson, 'Embodying Devotion: Multisensory Encounters with Donatello's Crucifix in S. Croce', *Renaissance Quarterly* 73, no. 4 (2020), pp. 1179–234.
11. Hadrianus Junius, *Emblemata* (Antwerp: Christophe Plantin, 1565), p. 57, emblem 51.
12. See <https://www.emblems.arts.gla.ac.uk/french/emblem.php?id=FJUb051> and the English translation provided for this fragment: 'The emblem is taken (lest

anyone steal our talisman against the spiteful, when we have openly and honestly offered the fruit of our labours to the public) from the frontispiece of books printed in Prague, which is far and away the richest city in Bohemia and the one most famous for its learning.'

13. See Michael Baxandall, *Painting and Experience in Fifteenth Century Italy: A Primer in the Social History of Pictorial Style*, 2nd edn (Oxford: Oxford University Press, 1988).

14. Robert, *Une allégorie parfaite*, p. 60.

15. Michel Pastoureau, *Les sceaux* (Turnhout: Brepols, 1981): 'l'*imago* du sigillant, c'est à dire son image personnelle, celle à qui il transmet son *auctoritas*, celle qui juridiquement le représente et le prolonge, l'emblématise et le symbolise, elle est à la fois lui-même et le double de lui-même', quoted as the third definition of what 'seal' means, according to a cultural history perspective, in the digital database of the seals preserved in France, <http://www.sigilla.org/fr>.

16. For a fuller account of the role of executions in effigy and their ritual agencies, see Valérie Hayaert, 'Le rituel judiciaire d'Ancien régime et ses images face à la mort', in Ilona Hans-Collas, Fabienne Le Bars, Danielle Quéruel, Nathalie Rollet-Bricklin, Yann Sordet and Anne Weber (eds), *Le Livre et la Mort (XIVe–XVIIIe siècles)* (Paris: Bibliothèques Mazarine & Sainte-Geneviève – Éditions des cendres, 2019), pp. 181–204, especially the eighteenth-century survival of these issues through the writings of Protestant theologians.

17. Manuela Bragagnolo, 'Fisiognomica e profezia nel pensiero giuridico tra Cinque e Seicento. Alcune considerazioni', *Laboratoire Italien* 21 (2018).

18. See George R. Goldner, Lee Hendrix and Kelly Pask, *European Drawings 2: Catalogue of the Collections* (Los Angeles: Getty Publications, 1992), p. 306, for full provenance, exhibition and bibliographical details.

19. Renaud Chabrier, 'From Sketches to Morphing: New Geometric Views on the Epistemological Role of Drawing', in Tamar Flash and Alain Berthoz (eds), *Space-Time Geometries for Motion and Perception in the Brain and the Arts* (Cham: Springer, 2021), pp. 151–83.

20. Battista Fiera, *De Justicia Pingenda Fieræ Mantuani Dialogus. Interloquutores Mantynias Momus*, in *Hymni Divini. Sylve Melanisius* (Mantua: Francesco Bruschi, 1515). The copy consulted is that of the Biblioteca Communale, Mantua: 'Quomodo enim et unioculam et multioculam pariter pinxeris? Quomodo et unimanum tantum et metientem tamen et librantem simul et pariter ense minantem?'

21. See Jessica Riskin, 'Machines in the Garden', in Charlene Villaseñor Black and Mari-Tere Álvarez (eds), *Renaissance Futurities: Science, Art, Invention* (Oakland: University of California Press, 2020), pp. 19–40.

22. Andrea Alciato, *Parerga* (Lyon: Jacobus Giuncta, 1539), book 1, ch. 19, p. 31: 'Quid sit automaton apud Paulum Iurisconsult. quid cantari vel catarrhi, quid salientes: quid enim catadromus' and esp. 'automata dicuncur a mechanicis ea opera, quæ sponte sua moventur, qualia sunt horologia'.

23. Alarico Barbagli, *A Chapter about the Automaton in Andrea Alciato's* Parerga, RSA Virtual 2021, paper presented 20 April 2021.

24. See Philip Steadman, *Renaissance Fun: The Machines behind the Scenes* (London: UCL Press, 2021), especially ch. 3, 'The Automata of Hero of Alexandria'.

25. Maurice Merleau-Ponty, *Le visible et l'invisible suivi de Notes de travail*, ed. Claude Lefort (Paris: Gallimard, 1964), p. 175.

26. Alain Berthoz, *Le sens du mouvement* (Paris: Odile Jacob, 1997). See also Mark Franko, 'The Conduct of Contemplation and the Gestural Ethics of Interpretation in Walter Benjamin's "Epistemo-Critical Prologue"', *Performance Philosophy* 3, no. 1 (2017): 'There is no mentality without motility and the question of movement reconstruction concerns the possibility that thought would capture itself in and through its affinities with its own movement. As Samuel Weber has said: "[W]hat Benjamin seeks to articulate in that Preface is not simply another form of cognitive investigation, but rather a form of interpretation that does not take cognition for granted"', quoting Samuel Weber, 'Genealogy of Modernity. History, Myth and Allegory in Benjamin's Origin of the German Mourning Play', *MLN* 106, no. 3 (1991), pp. 465–500 (p. 467).

27. Giorgio Agamben, *Means Without End: Notes on Politics*, trans. Binetti Vincenzo and Cesare Casarino (Minneapolis: University of Minnesota Press, 2000).

28. Ian Maclean, *Logic, Signs and Nature in the Renaissance: The Case of Learned Medicine* (Cambridge: Cambridge University Press, 2002), p. 112.

29. Physical place where all the executions were staged in pre-Revolutionary Paris during the *Ancien Régime*.

30. Allusion to the historical period of the July Monarchy (Monarchie de Juillet).

31. Victor Hugo, 'Le dernier jour d'un condamné' (preface for the 1829 novel), in *Écrits sur la peine de mort*, ed. Marie Salavert (Arles: Actes Sud, 1992), pp. 36–7: 'Oui, l'horrible Thémis dentue et vorace de Farinace et de Vouglans, de Delancre et d'Isaac Loisel, de d'Oppède et de Machault, dépérit. Elle maigrit. Elle se meurt. Voilà déjà la Grève qui n'en veut plus. La Grève se réhabilite. La vieille buveuse de sang s'est bien conduite en juillet. Elle veut mener désormais meilleure vie et rester digne de sa dernière belle action. Elle qui s'était prostituée depuis trois siècles à tous les échafauds, la pudeur la prend. Elle a honte de son ancien métier. Elle veut perdre son vilain nom. Elle répudie le bourreau. Elle lave son pavé.'

32. See Carolin Behrmann, 'Metrics of Justice. A Sundial's Nomological Figuration', *Nuncius* 30 (2015), pp. 161–94.

33. André Bossuat, 'Documents inédits sur l'horloge du Palais et sur les gouverneurs du XVe siècle', *Bulletin de la Société de l'histoire de Paris et de l'Ile -de-France* 56 (1929), pp. 91–102, esp. n. 4, quoting Henri Moranvillé, *Chronographia regum francorum* (Paris: Librairie Renouard, 1891), vol. 2, pp. 396–418 (p. 396); and also quoting 'Pièces justificatives': Arch. nat. X1a 4792, fol. 119v. Plaidoiries. Matinées: 'ladicte horloge est située et assise ou milieu de Paris et sert à toute la ville, et y est tres nécessaire pour le fait des habitans et de la chose publicque de Paris'.

34. At the time King Henri III comes back from Poland, God has already given him the royal crown of Poland, so the future tense (*dabit*) indicates a good omen, the positive advent of a *corona cælestis*, sign of his divine election.

35. Margaret Gatty, *The Book of Sun-dials* (London: Bell and Daldy, 1872). The author includes the example of the motto invented by Jean Passerat for the Horloge du Palais de Justice de Paris (p. 60, no. 153).

36. Bossuat, 'Documents inédits', p. 96.

37. Henry Sully, *Règle artificielle du temps par Henry Sully, nouvelle édition corrigée et augmentée par M. Julien Leroy* (Paris: Grégoire Dupuis, 1737).

38. On Germain Pilon, who was commissioned to produce the funerary monument of Henri II and the Valois Chapel in the shape of a rotunda at the Saint-Denis Basilica modelled on the Medici Chapel of San Lorenzo, Florence (destroyed after 1719), see Geneviève Bresc-Bautier, 'Le monument funéraire de Henri II et la Chapelle des Valois à Saint-Denis (1560–1585)', in Dominique Cordellier, assisted by Bernadette Py, exhibition catalogue, *Primatice: Maître de Fontainebleau*, Paris, Musée du Louvre, 22 September 2004–3 January 2005. Pilon had sculpted two allegorical figures for the tomb of Henri II, Force and Justice, melted by the artillery iron-caster Benoît Le Boucher. Primaticcio's favourite sculptor, Pilon was also commissioned to sculpt the recumbent figure of King Henri II.

39. Behrmann, 'Metrics of Justice'.

40. Albrecht Krantz, *Wandalia in qua de Wandalorum populis, et eorum patrio solo, ac in Italiam, Galliam, Hispanias, Aphricam, et Dalmatiam, migratione* (Coloniæ: Agrippinæ, 1519), book 11, ch. 9.

41. Cesare Ripa, *Iconologia* (Padua: Tozzi, 1611), pp. 246–7.

42. See Valérie Hayaert, 'Le Baiser de Justice et de Paix: à propos d'une allégorie politique peinte pour le château de Richelieu par Nicolas Prévost', *Histoire de la Justice* 33, no. 1 (2022), pp. 91–101.

43. I owe this interpretation to Desmond Manderson, who helped me to clarify the argument of this chapter.

44. This episode is retraced by Hans Körner, *Statuenliebe in St Peter. Rompilger und Romtouristen vor Guglielmo della Portas Grabmal für Papst Paul III* (Düsseldorf: Kreis der Freunde des Seminars für Kunstgeschichte, Heinrich-Heine-Universität Düsseldorf, 1999).

45. Opher Mansour, 'Censure and Censorship in Rome, c. 1600: The visitation of Clement VIII and the Visual Arts', in Marcia B. Hall and Tracy E. Cooper (eds), *The Sensuous in the Counter-Reformation Church* (New York: Cambridge University Press, 2013), pp. 136–60 (p. 145).

46. This version is very similar to the composition attributed to Jacob de Backer, *Allegory of the Kiss of Justice and Peace*, c. 1580, Kunstpalast, Düsseldorf, inv. M 209.

47. Martinus Kempius, *Opus polyhistoricum dissertationibus XXV de osculis, subnexisque de Judæ ingenio, vita et fine scaris epiphyllidibus* (Frankfurt: M. and A. Hallerword, 1680).

48. Paul Ricœur, *Amour et Justice* (1989; Paris: Seuil, 2008).

49. Jacob Herrenschmid, *Osculologia Theologo-Philologica sive De variis variorum Osculis Patriarchum, Prophetarum Impp. Regum, Episcoporum Academicorum, Christianorum, Gentilium, Exoticorum, etc. Commentariolus* (Wittenberg: Heirs of Clément Berget, 1630).

50. Augustine, *Expositions of the Psalms, Volume 4: Psalms 73–98*, trans. Maria Boulding (Hyde Park, NY: New City, 2002), p. 215.

51. Pierre Joseph d'Orléans, *Sermons et instruction chrétienne sur diverses matières* (Paris: Jean Anisson, 1697). The text quoted is drawn from the 'Sermon on Love and Truth', p. 14.

52. Johann Daniel Prangen, *Oscula sacra et profana* (Minda: Pilerian, 1688), p. 6.

53. In his scholarly essay *De mutuo justitiæ pacisque osculo, ex Psalmo 85,11* (Dresden: J. G. Harpeter, 1755), pp. 21–2, Christoph Kretzschmar later stresses that if the meaning of the verse in Hebrew initially designates a literal kiss, it then denotes, by metonymy, the conjunction of souls, whose physical sign is the kiss of the lips.

54. Jean-François Senault, *Oraison funèbre de Henriette-Marie de France, reine de la Grande-Bretagne* (Paris: P. Le Petit, 1670), p. 8.

55. Isaac-Louis Le Maistre de Sacy, *Les Pseaumes de David, traduits en français avec une explication tirée des Saints Pères et des Auteurs Ecclésiastiques*, vol. 2 (Brussels: Henry Fricx, 1710), p. 382: 'Ce baiser tout divin de la justice et de la paix s'entend proprement du mystère de l'Incarnation du Verbe adorable [. . .] cette paix et cette justice se sont donné mutuellement le baiser par l'alliance qu'elles ont faite l'une avec l'autre. Car la justice du Père demandait la punition de l'homme pécheur. Et la paix du Fils demandait la réconciliation. Qu'a donc fait l'Incarnation du Verbe? Elle a allié ensemble ces deux choses pour notre salut. [. . .] La paix du Fils a désarmé la justice du Père.'

56. 'Mazarinades' are violent pamphlets against Cardinal Mazarin. See Pierre Ronzeaud, 'Usages polémiques de l'allégorie en contexte pamphlétaire: les *Mazarinades*', in Marie-Christine Pioffet and Anne-Élisabeth Spica (eds), *S'exprimer autrement: poétiques et enjeux de l'allégorie à l'Âge classique* (Tübingen: Narr, 2016), pp. 215–26.

57. Benoît Le Court, *Arresta Amorum* (Lyon: Sébastien Gryphe, 1538).

58. Peter Goodrich, *The Laws of Love: A Brief Historical and Practical Manual* (London: Palgrave Macmillan, 2007).

59. Le Court, *Arresta Amorum* (1538), p. 183 (the text by Martial d'Auvergne dates from c. 1520): 'Ut paululum a materia divertamus, quid sit discriminandi inter basium, osculum et suavium dicamus. Alius Donatus, in Eunucho Terentiano tria osculandi genera ponit, osculum scilicet, basium & suavium. Oscula officiorum sunt, basia vero pudicorum affectuum, suavia libidinum vel amorum.'

60. Ibid., p. 233.

61. Antoine Favre [Antonius Faber], *Opera omnia*, vol. 2 (Lyon: Borde, Arnaud et Rigaud, 1658–61), p. 451: 'Propter osculum quis dote privari potest.'

62. Poems by 'Eloy du Mont dit Costentin', Bibliothèque nationale de France, manuscrits français 2237, fol. 2r: 'Avecques Paix le Roy maintient / Iustice, et es deux la main tient / La prophétie davidique / Est accomplie ou David dict que / Iustice et Paix on faict accords / en baisant mieulx que corps a corps / Iustice iniquite corrompt / Et paix a guerre le col rompt.'

63. Rainer Wohlfeil, 'Pax antwerpiensis. Eine Fallstudie zu Verbildlichungen der Friedensidee im 16. Jahrhundert am Beispiel der Allegorie "Kuss von

Gerechtigkeit und Friede"', in Brigitte Tolkemitt and Rainer Wohlfeil (eds), *Historische Bildkunde: Probleme* (Berlin: Duncker & Humbolt, 1991), pp. 211–58.

64. Daniel Meisner, *Sciographia Cosmica. Das ist newes Emblematisches Büchlein: darinen in acht Centuriis die Vornembsten Stätt Vestung, Schlosser etc.*, vol. 2 (Nuremberg: Paul Fürst, 1638), emblem B 46.

65. Jacob de Zetter, *Kosmographia Iconica Moralis* (Frankfurt: Johan Theodor de Bry and Hendrick Laurensz, 1614), emblem 52.

66. Heinrich Oraeus, *Aeroplastes Theosophicus, sive Eikones Mysticæ* (Frankfurt: Johann Theodor de Bry, 1620; 2nd edn, 1644).

67. Erwin Panofsky, *A Mythological Painting by Poussin in the Nationalmuseum Stockholm* (Stockholm: Nationalmusei skriftserie, 1960), pp. 36–8, qtd in Behrmann, 'Metrics of Justice', p. 191 n. 65.

Chapter 7

Lady Justice's fragility

The early modern tradition of depicting Lady Justice oscillates between images of divine justice as an immobile goddess in the empyrean of fixed forms and a tellurian woman, performing judicial gestures in the here and now of the diurnal sphere. As a cardinal political virtue, *Justitia* often defines herself by the overthrow of her victims, a victorious virgin trampling trespassers and evildoers. Before finishing this book, it seems useful to question this propensity of Lady Justice to fight vice with such ardour. The preceding chapters have, in turn and in their own way, underlined the variety of her struggles, the subtlety of her gestures, the stakes of her vocation which animate her body with tumultuous or tranquil movements, violence or restraint. What remains to be examined now is her passivity and inertia, in other words, her fragility and melancholy. Lady Justice's performative gestures interrupt the quotidian world. Perceiving her iterative gestures, the manifold patterns of her gestural ethics, weighing causes or making sword-brandishing threats, involves consideration of the ways in which a female body takes hold of a sword and a pair of scales. The consequences of apprehending *Justitia* as an assemblage of body parts (maimed hand, exposed knee or elbow, breast or thigh) is another fruitful method of analysis, as it brings us to a further vantage point for investigating the role of bodily semiotics within a conventional allegory. If we now look at the ways in which artists imagine Lady Justice being assaulted, injured, raped or shackled, the use of allegory now differs radically from a mere encomium. Her intrinsic fragility has a more intriguing side; it implies a contrasting perception of Justice, where norms of allegorical decorum may also be denied. Often depicted as a dragon-slayer trampling some vanquished enemy, Lady Justice may also represent the ability of humanity to judge, when she exhibits the wounds of judgment themselves. Her flesh has become vulnerable, she now leans or sleeps as if needing to be rescued from her earthly woes: these *pathos formulae* may even symbolise more by inversion than their victorious counterparts.

The technology of inflicting death

A threshold figure, Lady Justice occupies an extremely sensitive zone, between the judge's gaze and the litigant's expectations, where the judicial apparatus supervises its own mechanisms. Her allegorical vessel is a privileged site for affective responses. However, in an exceptional situation, against an extraordinary evil, she may be reduced to a dystopian character, thus becoming the emblem of a cruel and ingenious prison of the senses. In so doing, she is turned into a dispassionate puppet, immune to the many offences, crimes, mistakes or infamies committed right in front of her blindfolded eyes.

Brueghel's *Justitia*

I will start from the famous print by Pieter Brueghel, dated c. 1559, where a blindfolded Justice, wearing a curious two-horned hat, stands motionless and apparently unconcerned by the spectacle of the dreadful torments that are carried out in front of and around her (Figure 7.1).[1] *Justitia* is portrayed as an immobile allegory, powerless in the face of the tortures that saturate the entire landscape. Scholars who have studied this engraving have debated the supposed intention of the author, without reaching a consensus. While some see it as a 'naturalistic' depiction of the administration of early modern criminal justice, a legitimation of the use of extreme violence in the name of divine and earthly justice, others point out that Brueghel depicted quite the opposite, a satiric delineation of her powerlessness, a harsh criticism against an excessive carnage unaccountable to any spiritual or earthly power. Unable to see the many tortures imposed in her name, Lady Justice stands, incapacitated, mute and static, lacking the power to curb those who invoke her authority. The inscription which is supposed to guide the exegesis of the engraving reminds us that 'the aim of the law is to either correct him whom it punishes, or that his punishment should improve others, or that, once the evil ones are removed, the rest should live more securely'. This *sententia* comes from a long tradition originating in Seneca's *De Clementia* and Plato (*Gorgias* 525a–b): correction, in order to be effective, calls for a measured punishment (to leave the punished something to lose) and the prince, if he wants to keep his *auctoritas*, must use it sparingly.[2] This idea was also shared by Plato in the *Laws*, with the aim, however, of making people love justice, and of only coming to the death penalty when someone is judged incurable. What Brueghel conspicuously depicts is precisely the contrary: Lady Justice does not appear to have much authority over the spectacle of ruthless cruelty she seems forced to witness. Completely ignored by the surrounding protagonists, she appears to be playing a 'game of blind man's bluff'.[3] In his thorough study of the print, Karl Heinz Burmeister has emphasised an important detail: *Justitia* 'climbs onto the blue stone that was used as pillory or gallows. Evidently, she is placed on the pillory and must be executed.'[4] Instead of representing a 'village fool' such as the *Justitia* blindfolded by a fool as depicted by Sebastian Brandt, Brueghel's *Justitia* is depicted as

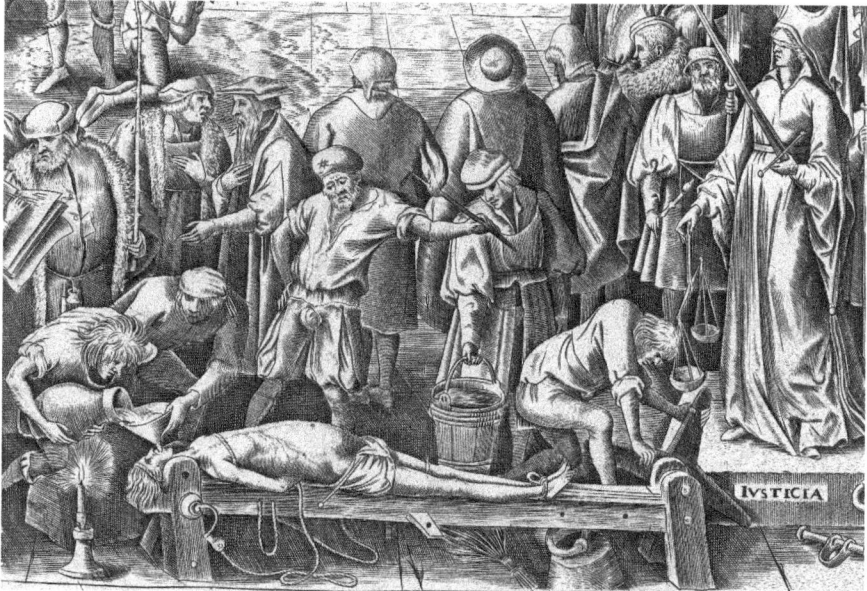

Figure 7.1: Pieter Brueghel (design), Philips Galle (printer) and Hieronymus Cock (publisher), *Justicia*, 1559, 24.5 cm × 29.2 cm. Series *The Seven Virtues*, inv. 1868,0328.367. © The Trustees of the British Museum

a bitter figure, whose execution is the blind spot of her own theatre of criminal justice. The supreme irony is to witness her elimination as a tiny detail in the *tableau vivant* surrounding her, as none of the characters depicted around her appears to care about her fate.[5]

The question of Brueghel's intention must be left open for the time being. For present purposes, the ambiguity problematises the very possibility of any action on the part of Lady Justice. This constrained figure, as if suffering from some kind of locked-in syndrome, presents an autistic Justice, unable or unwilling to act for her neighbour. We will explore *Justitia*'s bitterness, the affectless detachment with which she sometimes appears. Justice is denied when her attributes are trampled or dispersed, when she is handcuffed, gagged, raped, disarmed or defeated.

Sleeping Justice

Under the motto 'Der Welt Lauf' (The way of the world), Barthel Beham depicts a naked *Justitia* asleep, chained in iron handcuffs and shackles (Figure 7.2). A child has snuggled into the crook of her left arm and has fallen asleep. At her feet, a lamb has settled down to rest as well. Her scales have slipped away from her powerless hand and a fox has carried off her sword, driving a goose-like bird before him. A large castle, perhaps Nuremberg, can be seen in the background (the view is inverted). Several scholars have interpreted the engraving biographically, as 1525 was the year in which Barthel Beham, his brother Sebald and Georg Pencz were banished from Nuremberg. They had been tried as 'godless painters' for asserting that they did not believe in baptism, Christ or transubstantiation. Barthel also refused to recognise the city council as the highest temporal authority. Herbert Zschelletzschky further suggests a connection to the peasants' revolt of the same year and interprets the engraving as a critique of Luther's position in these disputes.[6]

The German motto 'Der Welt Lauf' (The way of the world) is a commonplace in the early modern period, and has a very broad meaning, alluding to the vicissitudes of human existence or the natural order of things, such as the succession of seasons.[7] According to Jean Wirth, Beham's *Justitia* reproduces a nude by Agostino Veneziano which shows Cleopatra facing in the opposite direction.[8] Only the first state of the engraving bears the date 1525 and a rather vague motto replaces it in

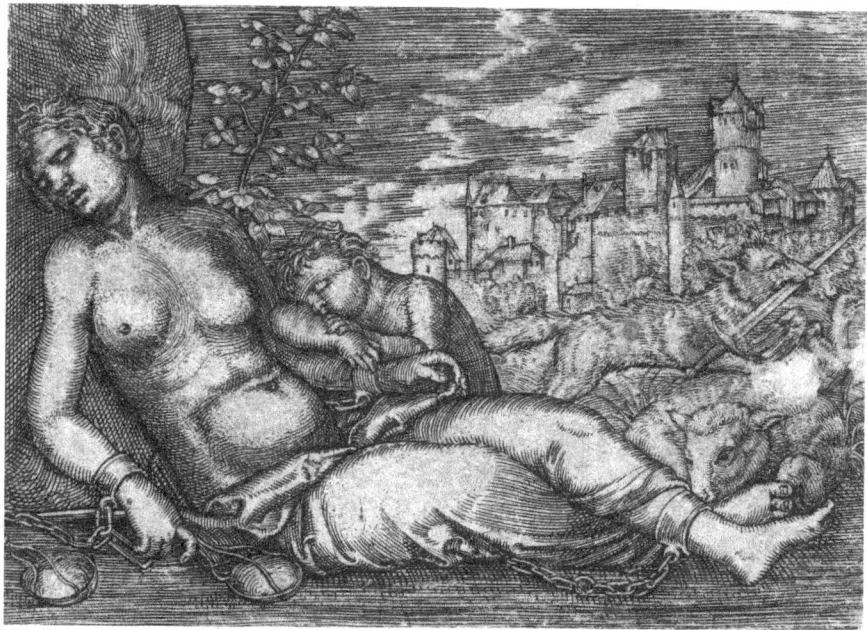

Figure 7.2: Barthel Beham, *Der Welt Lauf* (The Way of the World), engraving on paper, 1525, inv. 1852,0424.166. © The Trustees of the British Museum

the second. Since the second version is significantly more frequent than the first, Wirth concludes that the direct topical allusion had to be transformed into a pessimistic and vague commonplace so as not to incite polemics.

Many details of the drawing remain paradoxical.[9] Why has the fox, who does not need a sword to hunt a goose, stolen *Justitia*'s sword? Are the figures of the boy and the sheep allusions to Christ? Jan-David Mentzel suggests that the image is a call for patience.[10] Beham offers a pessimistic assessment of his own fate around 1525. Above all, the sleep of Justice is perplexing. Is she resting or exhausted? Her languid pose is reminiscent of similar compositions, showing a slumbering nymph or a resting Venus. But her face seems tense and her frowning eyebrows suggest that she is in the grip of a nightmare.

A later depiction of an allegory of a bound sleeping Justice by Matthias Gerung (1543) lets us perceive her creatureliness (Figure 7.3).[11] Staged as an earthly justice in a sensuous pose, her body is offered to us as a human being: here sleep may be regarded as a relative of death. An inscription reads 'Justicia dormit', and Gerung follows Beham in

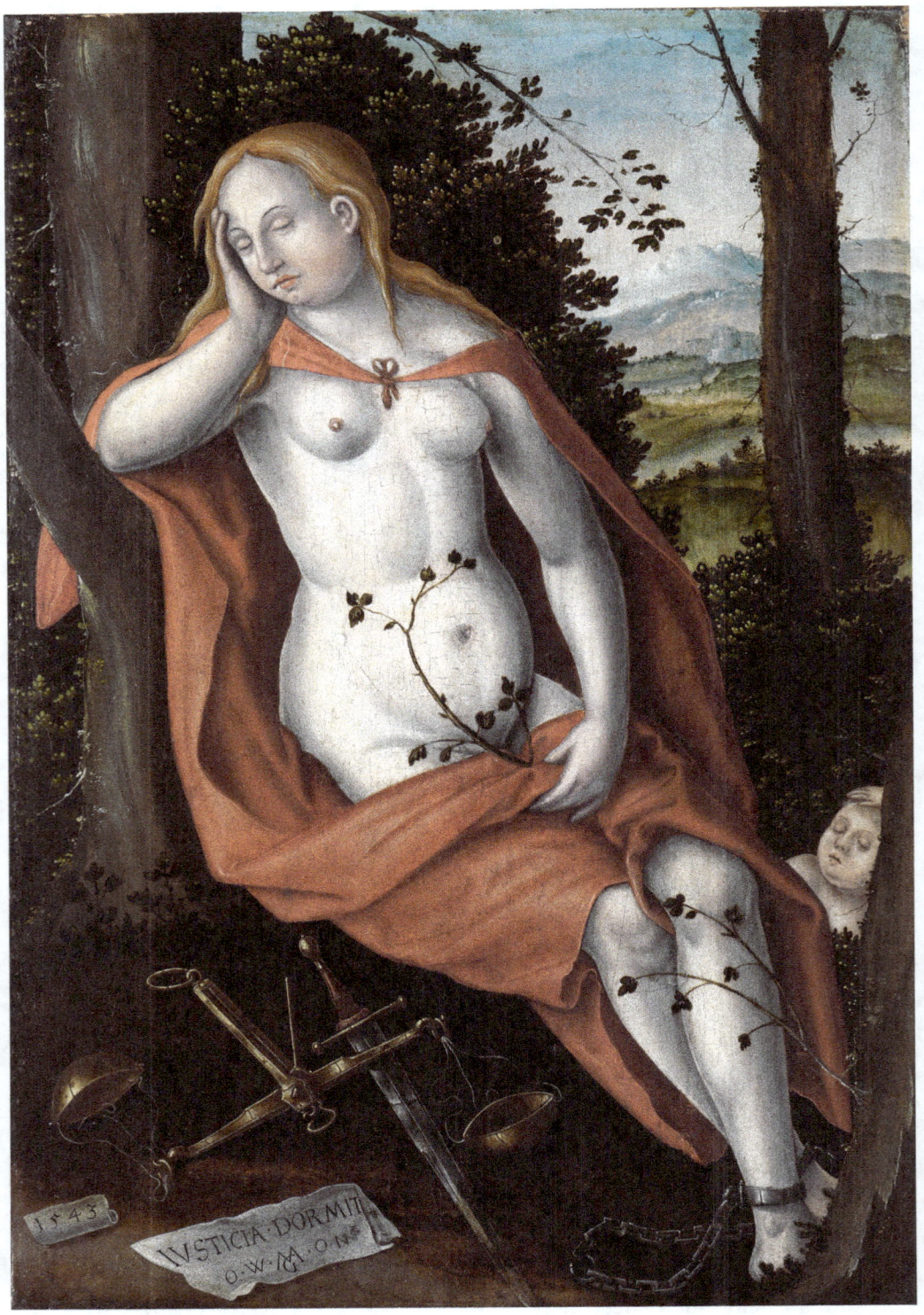

Figure 7.3: Matthias Gerung, *Allegory of Bound Justice Sleeping*, 1543, oil on lime wood, inv. 105. Staatliche Kunsthalle Karlsruhe

depicting her leaning against a tree trunk and shackled. He adds a detail borrowed from Albrecht Dürer's *Melencolia*; *Justitia* rests her head in her right hand. Her cross-legged posture also hints at a reflective state of mind, a type of inward gaze.

Gerung's portrait of *Justitia* probably reflects the influence of Luther's Reformation with its emphasis on the individual conscience as ultimate moral authority. Dressed in *porpora*, Gerung's *Justitia* prefigures the promised advent of divine justice, imprisoned in its earthly form. Since life on earth is considered to be a test of human nature, *Justitia*'s sleep reflects the anguish of human existence and the misery of postlapsarian life. The relatively rare motif of the sleeping infant Jesus appears in Marian paintings around 1500 and is thought to be an indication of the Passion. Luther, however, interprets the sleeping child in this religious context as the future judge, who suspends punishment, whose youth grants the sinner a little more time.[12]

A common feature of both Beham's and Gerung's treatments of the sleeping Justice is to portray her leaning against a tree trunk. In both artworks, the tree (the hawthorn is a familiar medieval threshold symbol[13]) is fully grown and its extended branches cover the young boy. As a plant used to make Christ's crown of thorns, *Justitia*'s hawthorn is coherent with the crimson mantle covering her body. The allusion to *spinas* (thorns) refers to symbols of pain and affliction, a sign of humankind's alienation from God. Gerung correlates a biblical symbol of martyrdom with a plant linked to carnality and eroticism, in a particularly compelling way.

In Gerung's oil panel, *Justitia*'s body is ostensibly covered by two branches of the same tree, one of which, at the bottom, is an outgrowth of the trunk on the right, while the other, a branch that the young woman holds through the fabric of her cloak, covers her crotch and belly. This double branch could symbolise the two paths of the *arbor virtutum* and the *arbor vitiorum*, a common Christian interpretation of the dimensions of the Cross.[14] But here, instead of depicting a tree of virtues on a model that orders vices and virtues, Gerung has painted the anarchic foliage of two hawthorn branches that evolve according to the laws of pure nature. The sacred site hedged by the hawthorn, where *Justitia*'s body seems trapped, sheds a pessimistic light over earthly justice: carnal justice is spiritually barren, suffering from insomnia rather than enjoying a celestial rest. Her fragile body lives in a thicket of thorns and must endure the sharp discomforts of anguish and temptation. Gerung adds another layer to his depiction of a sleeping Justice: the physiognomy of *Justitia* is that of *Melancholia*, 'main à la maisselle', echoing a collective form of bitterness or dispassion, on the edge of *acedia*.[15] Gerung exposes Justice to melancholy's wounds and tears, a continuum between front and rear, between anger and black spleen. Legal processes are strewn with the buried sores of error, the arcane mysteries of arbitrary dice games and the illogical roots of legal violence.

Justitia's dispassion in the stage management of capital punishment

Throughout the Late Middle Ages and the early modern period, mobile images (*tavolette*, crucifixes) accompanied the condemned to the scaffold. In Bologna and other northern Italian towns, mobile representations of Christ's Passion or saints' martyrdoms – little portable panels or in the shape of mobile crucifixes – were held by criminals in front of their eyes to help guide their soul to redemption. In Italy, novel types of *tavolette* were invented which further accentuated the visual constraint: the idea was to present an image on which the condemned man's gaze had to be so focused that he could not see anything else.[16]

In an anonymous Netherlandish engraving, Lady Justice tramples one of the reversed pans of the scales at her feet (Figure 7.4).[17] Instead of holding them in balance, her left arm embraces a downturned executioner's sword and her right hand holds a *tavoletta*. Her melancholic expression seems to raise the question of the justification of the violence inflicted by the sword. She directs her *tavoletta*, affixed to a short handle, towards the blade of her sword. Many are wrongly punished, but still die thanks to the combined action of the sword and the *tavoletta*, which is supposed to force them to accept their execution. In using the tricks of a misleading image, *Justitia* seems to lend herself to a cruel sleight of hand.

During his stay in Rome, on the morning of 1 January 1581, Michel de Montaigne – while riding his horse, not far from the Tor di Nona prison – came across the Company of San Giovanni Decollato accompanying a condemned man to the scaffold. The testimony is recorded by Montaigne's secretary:

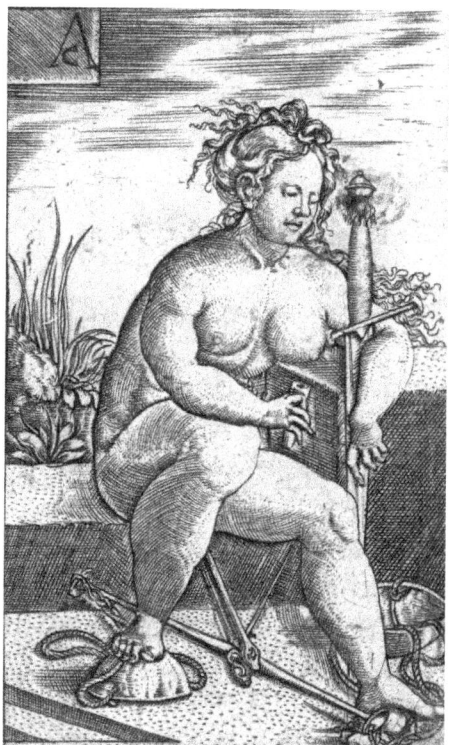

Figure 7.4: Anonymous artist (monogrammist AC), c. 1520–30, *Justice Seated with a Sword and Trampling on Manacles*, engraving, inv. 1866,0623.20. © The Trustees of the British Museum

In contrast to the practices in France, they have the criminal walk behind a large crucifix covered with a black curtain, and a large number of men on foot, dressed and masked in cloth. There are two of them, or monks, dressed and covered in this way, who assist the criminal on the cart and press him, and one of them continually presents him with a picture of the image of Our Lord on his face and makes him kiss it over and over again; this makes it impossible to see the criminal's face in the street. At the gallows [. . .] he was always held up against the image until he was executed.[18]

Montaigne does not think that the *tavoletta* is there primarily for the benefit of the condemned man but in order to conceal his face from the crowd. In creating an exclusive pictorial space just for the condemned, a space into which the sinner was withdrawn from the world before his execution, the *tavoletta* would stop the spectators seeing his face. Through the artifice of the forced kiss, the officiant turns the image of devotion inscribed on the *tavoletta* into a powerful narcotic, to 'prepare' the sinner's affliction. The comforters would use the gory close-ups of the pictures of martyrdoms to whip up the devotion of the criminals. *Tavolette* were used as triggers of remembrance as these visual dying aids would urge the poor sinners to focus on the sight of drops of blood as a symbolic anticipation of their own suffering. The repeated insistence with which the painting was placed next to the faces of the condemned turned the unrepentant criminal into a faceless effigy. Since the *tavoletta* was also used to shield the criminal's eyes from the instruments of death,[19] the gesture of *Justitia*, here holding the *tavoletta* up to the sword, suggests an apology for the technique of inflicting death. Not only is *Justitia* trampling on her scales, she also seems to meditate on her weighty sentences, while staring at the attributes used for the staging of capital punishment.

In a roundel from the North Lowlands (c. 1510), *Justitia* appears blindfolded, handling an enormous double-bladed sword in her right hand, manipulating scales in her left, in front of two bound prisoners (the rich sinner is well dressed whereas the poor one is in rags) (Figure 7.5).[20] Lady Justice's blindfold is used as a blinker, protecting her from the gaze of the rich sinner who, instead of looking at the comforting crucifix he clutches, stares defiantly and angrily at her. Instead of offering visual solace, Lady Justice offers nothing but dispassion. No priests are present. Her detachment is strikingly different from the expected pity for the dead Christ usually expressed through the crucifix. Lady Justice wields a double-bladed sword, while a richly dressed older man watching the scene from a nearby loggia touches her scales to influence her judgment.

The motif of the two-edged sword (*gladius anceps* or in Greek *distomos*, literally 'double-mouthed') has a long exegetical history. It refers to the texts of the Apocalypse (John 1:16) and the Epistle to the Hebrews (4:12) which describe Christ in his judicial office, thus armed, separating in each individual what is God and what is man. The mystical sword of Jesus Christ pierces the most hidden folds, the deepest secrets of the soul. It will be sharpened, says Ezekiel, 'to kill the victims, it will be polished to cast a sharp shine' (Ezekiel 30:9). This mystical *gladius anceps* is situated in God's mouth, says Ezekiel. Its double-sidedness is often depicted by the conjunction of the sword and the lily, symbols of justice and grace. But here, in the hands of a blindfolded Justice, this

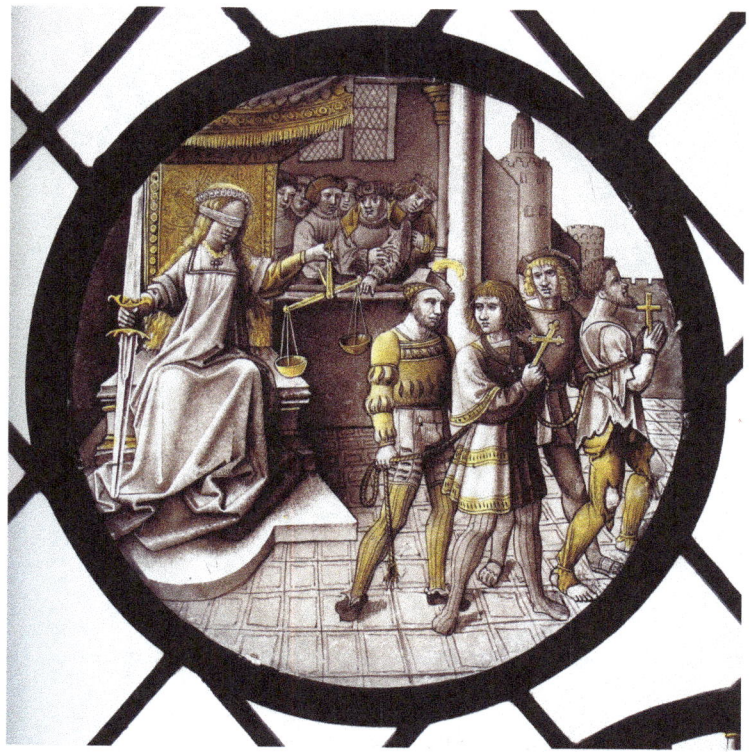

Figure 7.5: Anonymous artist, *Roundel with Justice*, North Lowlands, c. 1510, colourless glass, silver stain and vitreous paint: diameter 22.5 cm. The Cloisters Collection, 1983, inv. 1983.418. The Metropolitan Museum of Art, New York. Public domain

oversized weapon, a lethal device as sophisticated as it is nightmarish, seems to caricature the *gladius anceps* of the apocalypse. The proliferation of uneasy to handle attributes, combined with the blindfold device, leaves us with a rare oneiric image. The two-sided sword seems to apply the same fatal equation to rich and poor criminals alike. The opaque bandage that covers Lady Justice's eyes, however, and the gigantic, quasi-fabulous weapon, do not augur well.

The two swords of Lady Justice

The double-bladed sword motif also stands for the potency of speech. In Hebrew, Aramaic and Greek, the double-edged sword is literally a 'sword of mouths'.[21] As can be seen in a manuscript miniature decorating a French book of hours (c. 1430–5), the dilemma faced by Justice in the execution of capital punishment is figuratively evoked by the

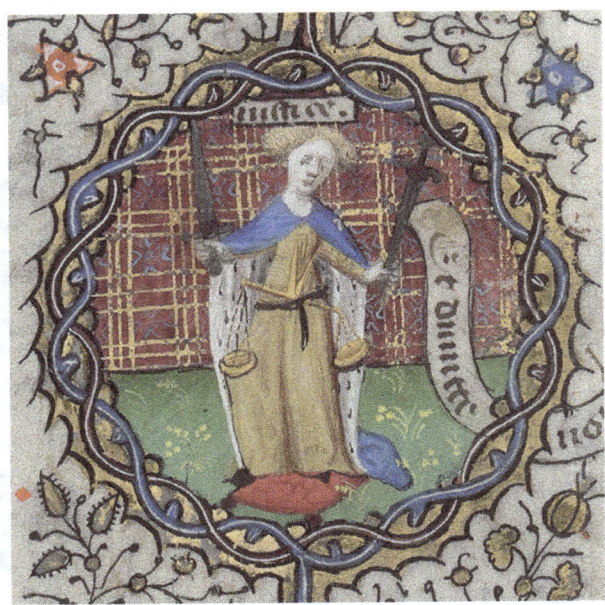

Figure 7.6: Ms. M. 359, fol. 118r, *Book of Hours*, Paris, France, 1430–5, 174 leaves (1 column, 16 lines), bound: vellum, ill.; 25.4 cm × 17.5 cm. By permission of the Pierpont Morgan Library, New York

representation of two swords (Figure 7.6). In a medallion with ivy-*rinceaux*, foliate and vinescroll ornament, a personification of Justice, standing on a cushion, wears an ermine-lined mantle, with scales tucked in her belt; her arms extended are holding two swords, by the hilt in her right hand and by the blade in her left hand. Above her is a label inscribed 'IUSTICE'. To the right and extending into the margin is a scroll inscribed 'Et dimitte nobis debita nostra' (Forgive us our trespasses, Matthew 6:12). Lady Justice handles two swords, one for evildoers, the other for the just, which is held by the blade, reversing and annulling its lethal effect. These two ways of holding the sword are reminiscent of heraldry. A 'sword pendant' is a non-active form, considered as defensive, whereas a 'sword ascendant' is active and offensive. Holding a weapon by the tip is a custom in funerals, so as to commemorate the sacrifice of the dead.

The allegorical Justice decorating the tomb of Juan II of Castile and Isabel of Portugal (1489–93) also holds a sword in each hand (Figure 7.7).[22] The right hand holds a lowered sword, while the left grasps a sword raised in the air, and the scales are held by the left arm. Presumably, with her lowered sword Justice spares the vanquished, while with the other she subdues the arrogant. *Justitia* is both master of her weapon

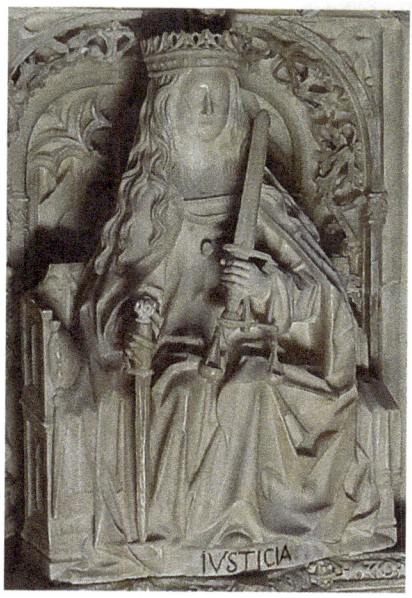

Figure 7.7: Gil de Siloe, Burgos, Sepulchre of Juan II of Castille and Isabel of Portugal (Miraflores Charterhouse). Photograph by the author

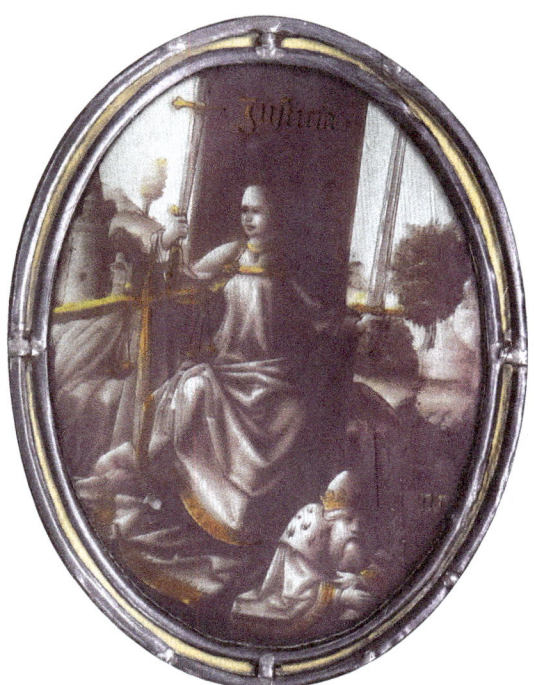

Figure 7.8: Allegory of Justice and bust of French King Louis IX, roundel, coloured glass, 140 cm × 85 cm, bearing an inscription 'Jehan Jaques Borgoy de Visé, 1584', inv. MX. 1583, 10132003. Liège Musée du Verre. Photograph by IRPA, 1959

and subject to its blade. Wielding two swords at the same time, one by the blade, at the risk of cutting oneself, is a particularly eloquent way of expressing the dialectics of strength and fragility. The body of Lady Justice is not only the warlike envelope of a dragon-slayer, but the weakened body of a *Justitia dolorosa*, sister of the holy martyrs and suffering icons of a *mater dolorosa*. A similar formula appears later on (1584) in an oval glass roundel from an unknown artist, depicting *Justitia* above the bust of the French King Louis IX. *Justicia* sits, enthroned, holding one sword by the blade in her right hand and another by the hilt in her left hand (Figure 7.8). The conflict between cruelty and mercy is implied by the bifurcated handling of two swords; the spiritual tone is introduced by the sword held by the blade with the hilt uppermost, which in this position presents the sign of the cross. A sword has morphed into a cross: here again is testimony to *Justitia*'s mysterious alchemy.

Justice assaulted

How is Lady Justice paradoxically strengthened by her courage and resilience? *Justitia*'s body, with its strange composite, material and corporeal presence, may have been a perfectly decorous icon for the judicial officers; she nevertheless unlocks several subversive narratives when she lends her body to the public display of sexual violence.

Justice raped

Allegory is sometimes an opportunity for bold inversions. The trope of personification makes it possible to subject a body, and in particular a female body, to a whole range of abuses.[23] The fragility of human justice is brought to a head here, as *Justitia*'s sacrosanct vessel is violated. A coloured print dating from c. 1535–50 depicts a knight threatening to rape and kill *Justitia* (Figure 7.9). Standing with his sword unsheathed over the figure of a fallen woman, the warrior with his high-plumed headgear tries with his left foot to lift the ruby robe and reach her crotch. *Justitia*, blindfolded and with her arms folded (a gesture she borrows from personified *Patientia*), lies helplessly on the ground. The assailant has grabbed her sword, and her scales lie next to her torn clothes. On the right, a clearly visible slit in the trunk of a tree, sprouting a short branch with a phallic shape, suggests that rape is imminent. The outright display of sexual violence towards an allegorical body inserts the ideal of Justice into a dramatic narrative. Her flesh-and-blood body is stretched out on the ground. Her powerlessness questions the chivalric codes of war and its warrior ideals through a frightening depiction of a fierce kind of swashbuckling masculinity. In sixteenth-century Germany, sexual misconduct by mercenaries and itinerant soldiers was a crucial issue.[24] Artists such as Urs Graf (who, as noted in Chapter 5, was himself a Swiss mercenary, a *Reislaufer*) painted these disorders in a harshly satirical style. Here, too, *Justitia* is imagined as a woman susceptible to rape, a suitable allegorical reflection on the limitations of earthly justice. Her passivity is underlined by her blindfold. Her mouth is closed, unable to raise any 'hue and cry' which would help her to build a successful case against her assailant. *Justitia* is painted as an unfortunate and prostrate maiden, passively enduring her sufferings, beset by hardship, her clothes

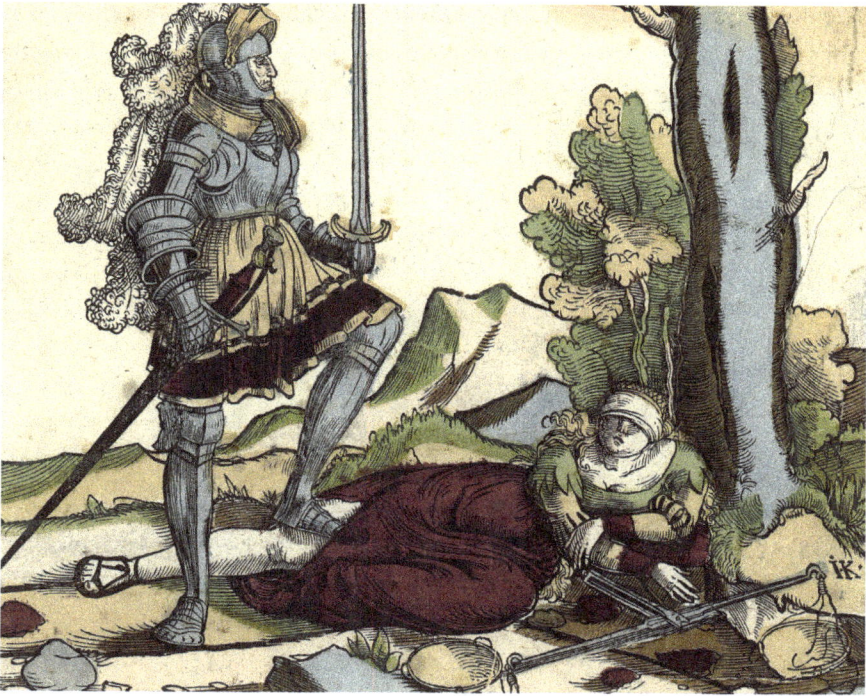

Figure 7.9: Anonymous German artist, *Knight Threatening to Rape and Kill Justitia*, print made by monogrammist IK, c. 1535–50, woodcut on paper, 19.9 cm × 24.7 cm, inv. 1982, U.2206. © The Trustees of the British Museum

torn apart by a cruel *Landsknecht*. She lies tearfully ravished, a spectacle to move her beholders to pity and her advocates to vengeful ire.

Justice shackled and dishevelled

One of the most striking representations of the pains inflicted on Dame Justice appears in the depiction of Malgoverno in Ambrogio Lorenzetti's *Allegory of Bad Government* (1338–9), in the Palazzo Pubblico in Siena.[25] Instead of rehearsing the abundant scholarship dealing with the textual sources of the *pictor doctus*, we will focus primarily on the iconological details of the frescoes themselves, and especially a rarely discussed figure of shackled *Justitia* (Figure 7.10).[26] We will refrain from trying to 'explain' this strange allegory through textual categories, resolving in advance and without really engaging with the problems raised by genuinely pictorial processes of creating meaning.

The famous frescoes of the Sala dei Nove extend over three walls: on the west wall is the *Allegory of Bad Government* and its consequences, on the north wall, the *Allegory of Good Government* and on the east wall, the effects of Good Government on town and countryside. Below the monstrous figure of a tyrant with a goat lies a woman, dressed only in an undergarment, tied up, her hair dishevelled. The inscription names her

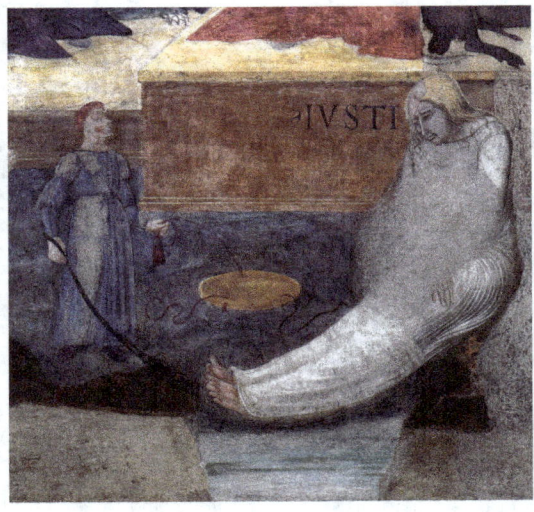

Figure 7.10: Ambrogio Lorenzetti, 'Shackled Justice', *Allegory of Bad Government*, 1338–9, Palazzo Pubblico, Sala dei Nove. Wikipedia Creative Commons

as *Justitia*; the scales with their pans lie smashed on the ground to her right and left. The figure is damaged in the upper part and heavily over-painted in the lower part. Gerhard Wolf describes her as a 'dame blanche';[27] her expression reveals her despair, her semi-nudity in contrast to the red cloak of tyranny signifies deprivation, an embarrassment of a figure that is otherwise positively conceived. Wolf adds that she is the only positive personification on this wall, a metonymic figure whose deprivation symbolises the overthrow of Good Government. Bound *Justitia* represents a break in the pictorial order of Bad Government, which has no counterpart in the depiction of Good Government.

In pictorial terms, Wolf argues that the alter ego of the despairing *Justitia* under the rule of Bad Government is to be found in the other woman in white appearing with her head bowed: the eroticised figure of *Pax* central to the *Allegory of Good Government* on the adjacent wall (Figure 7.11). She relaxes on a divan. The analogous inclination of the two women contributes to this invitation on the part of the artist. Rather than disembodying the allegorical body by reducing it to a predefined conceptual signified, which merely enumerates, by isolating them, each

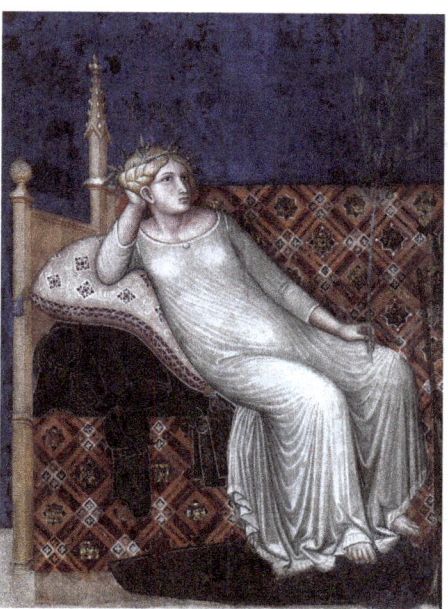

Figure 7.11: Ambrogio Lorenzetti, 'Pax', *Allegory of Good Government*, 1338–9, Palazzo Pubblico, Sala dei Nove. Wikipedia Creative Commons

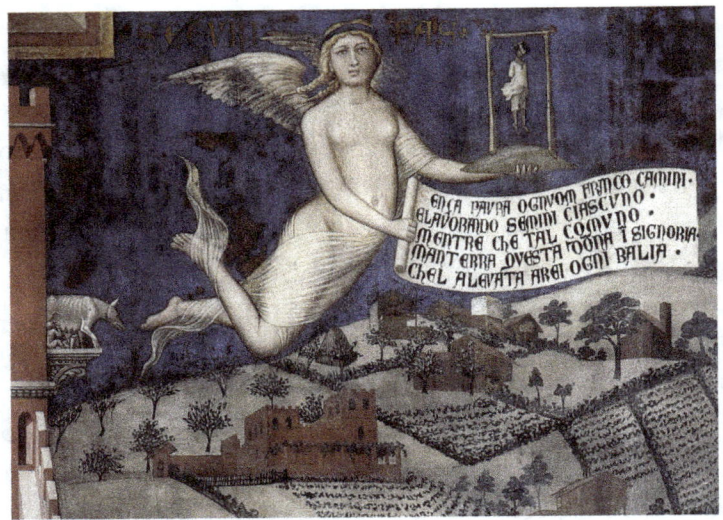

Figure 7.12: Ambrogio Lorenzetti, 'Securitas', *Allegory of Good Government*, 1338–9, Palazzo Pubblico, Sala dei Nove. Wikipedia Creative Commons

of the figures according to their *tituli*, it is a question of restoring to the gestures and postures their full capacity to signify by themselves. Allegory, because it is incarnated according to expressive bodily patterns, cannot be reduced to a univocal and textualist explanation. The analogy of the two 'dames blanches' invites the viewer to consider that *Pax* is not a distinct virtue but the true effect of Justice. *Justitia* and *Pax*, as we saw in Chapter 6, have a strong reciprocal relationship. This articulation is made all the more visible if we bear in mind that the original name of this room was the Sala della Pace.

The irruption of a handcuffed woman, deprived of her scales and her freedom, at the feet of a tyrant, in a fresco dedicated to the question of good government is disturbing. Many iconographic analyses of these frescoes tirelessly base their interpretations on the didactic labels surrounding the painting. In general, these inscriptions have undergone transformations, and it is therefore wrong to interpret the allegories exclusively on the basis of the *tituli* that are visible today. Moreover, there is no indication that all these legends were there from the beginning. If there is indeed an organic link between the *tituli* and the allegories, making the whole what Hans Belting calls a *Bildtext*,[28] the fact remains that the allegory also articulates pictorial processes that present an alternative syntax. It is not impossible, moreover, that the grammar of the postures leaves a stronger impression in the eye and body of spectators than the patient deciphering of their *tituli*.

The Sala della Pace was the meeting room of the Nine, the supreme governing body of Siena. The message delivered by the frescoes was first of all intended for the magistrates themselves, to whom the exhortation is addressed: 'Turn your eyes to admire, you who exercise power [. . .].' The Signori Nove sat on a platform against the north wall, directly beneath the allegorical painting of the virtues of good government. Under the figure of the hindered *Justitia*, a cartouche reads, 'Where Justice is tied up, no one ever agrees on the Common Good, nor does anyone pull the rope straight' ('Là dove sta legata la giustizia, nessuno al ben comun giammai s'accorda, né tira a dritta corda'). Through the motif of the rope, this shackled Justice signals towards the celebration of *Justitia* on the north wall. The theme of Justice is amply developed there. A representation of Justice in its dual Aristotelian nature (distributive and commutative) is inspired by *Sapientia*, which holds the scourge of the scales in the sky of ideas. If we follow the cords of the scales, which the allegory of Concord takes up, below that of Justice, we see a young woman, a carpenter's plane on her knees (a symbol of Aequitas). From the two strands of the scales, one red and the other white, she braids a rope, which she gives to a group of twenty-four citizens.

Lorenzetti's fresco provides a plurality of points of view, depending on whether one is in the place where the Nine were to sit, or facing them. The painted texts themselves invite one to move from one to the other: 'Volgiete gli occhi a rimirar costei, vo' che reggiete, ch'è qui figurata et per su eciellenzia coronata, la qual sempr a ciascun suo [dritto rende]' (Turn your eyes to admire who exercises power, who is portrayed here, crowned on account of her excellence, who always renders to each his due). The pathetic spectacle of this Justice afflicted and subjected to tyranny is meant to highlight the roots of evil. Through the motif of the rope Lorenzetti makes a striking contrast between the prisoners' submission, under the iron rule of *Securitas* – another woman in white, lightly dressed, holding gallows (Figure 7.12) – marking rigorous Justice, and at other times the voluntary bond that unites the citizens. The painting of vice is not merely the inverted double of a virtue; rather, it is by contemplating the pathetic portrait of a damaged and suffering Justice that Lorenzetti draws us towards an image of true Justice.[29]

The frescoes, then, do much more than illustrate the political pro-gramme of their inscriptions. They propose an *Imago Justitiæ* which draws its shattering force from this duplex, powerfully antinomic, *bifrons* shape. In Chapter 1, we argued that *Justitia* is, in essence, a binary image. In creating a particularly efficient use of contrasting visual entities, Lorenzetti succeeds in producing a nightmarish vision of *Justitia* dethroned, as a moral and cognitive counterpart to the ideal of Justice. The allegory of this broken, dishevelled and mistreated Justice strikes the spectator's eyes all the more in that it offers itself as one of the main pieces of an art of memory articulated by visual rhymes. Compared with *Pax* on her divan in an antique eroticised pose, and *Securitas*, floating in victory above the city, *Justitia*, tied and partially stripped, emerges as an effigy conveying an even more effective *pathos formula*. In this trinity of allegories all draped in white, the painter mixes eros, pathos and thanatos towards the unconscious substratum of disquieting images. *Justitia* appears as the unfortunate counterpart of a once victorious or erotic body. These three polarities invest the percep-tion of her body with a plural memory and provoke in the viewer a range of intense reactions from anger and erotic arousal to sympathy.

The Michelfeldt Tapestry

In addition to Lorenzetti's fresco, the object of almost uninterrupted exegesis since the nineteenth century, a group of engravings comment-ing on a late Gothic tapestry, most often attributed to Dürer, has caused much ink to flow. For a detailed study of the ensemble called *The Michelfeldt Tapestry* and the history of its attribution, we refer to the analysis by José M. González García.[30] Only the central panel of the set of three woodblocks will be discussed here as it offers a portrait of *Justitia* in the stocks (Figure 7.13). The entire work aims at describing the *mundus inversus* of corrupted Justice. The central woodblock bears an inscription explaining the context of the tapestry's design as a whole:

> These images and their accompanying rhymes were copied and reproduced from an old tapestry woven some one hundred years ago and found in Michelfeldt Castle in mid-Lent, in the year one thousand five hundred and twenty-four. They show how the old folk understood current events which occurred every day and which they kept secret.

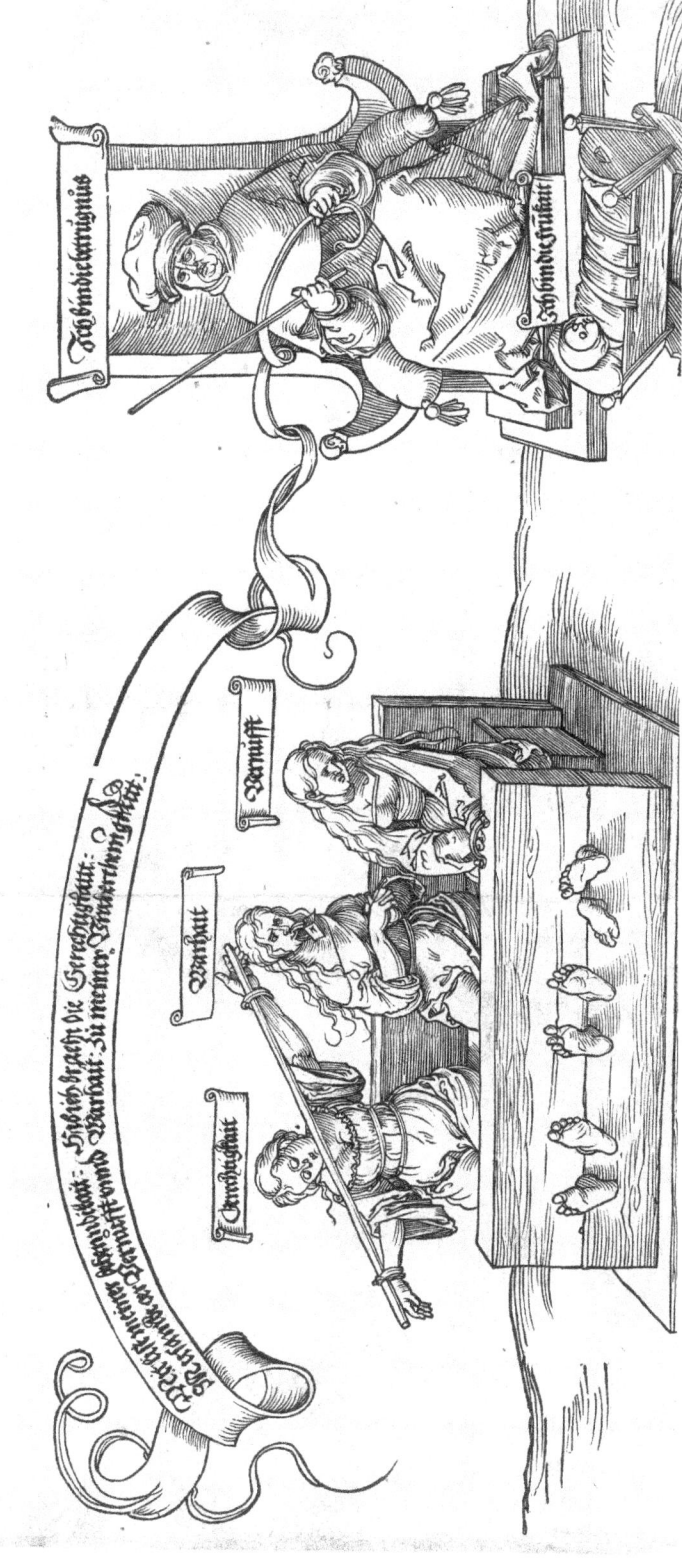

Figure 7.13: Albrecht Dürer (attributed to), *The Michelfeldt Tapestry*, central panel, 1524–6. © The Trustees of the British Museum

The print displays a portrait of an enthroned tyrannical and cheating judge: 'Ich bin die Betrügnüs'(I am Deceit) says the scroll above his head. At his feet, a powerless baby girl in a cradle figures Piety: 'Ich bin die Frommigkeit' (I am Piety). On the left, Justice, Reason and Truth are locked in wooden stocks. Their feet and ankles are fastened into the device so that their legs are straight. Since the stocks were designed as a shaming punishment, exposing the criminals to the public gaze, placards detailing their crimes were often placed nearby. Here, these placards have been turned into labels ironically denoting the names of each virtue: Gerechtigkeit' (Justice, Truth) and 'Vernunft' (Reason). Above them, a banner, which the deceiver holds like a whip, proclaims the victory of the unjust judge: 'With my deception and cunning, I have made Justice as well as Reason and Truth subservient to me.' Each of the three allegories receives special treatment. *Justitia's* outstretched arms are kept tied to a straight staff and her closed eyes indicate her exhaustion; Truth has her lips sealed with a padlock; and Reason has twisted feet and hands also trapped in the stocks. The corporal punishment inflicted on *Justitia* is directed against her arms, thus against her ability to handle a scale or to grasp a sword. Whereas the white lady in Lorenzetti's fresco was mainly characterised by her defeated look, her stiffened body in pain and her resigned gaze, Dürer's *Justitia* looks more like a disarticulated puppet. The stick that holds her arms in a cross prevents her from moving. Her sleepy eyes turn her into a laughable figure.

Dürer's woodcut reproduced an earlier work, dating from c. 1490–5, as a satirical comment on the decline of the reign of Emperor Charles V in the aftermath of the Peasants' War of 1525.[31] In using an existing tapestry as a model for an offensive political and social pamphlet directed against social injustice, Dürer was also establishing its value as a trustworthy and reliable historical document. His scathing critique of a pinioned Justice in the stocks is based on an acute observation of contemporary disorders.

Justitia inter arma

The image of *Justitia* as a martyred body is thus well anchored in the allegorical tradition. It is of particular intensity and effectiveness when taken as a witness of contemporary injustice. This is the case in a plea written by Advocate General Jacques Aubéry at the time of the Cabrières and Mérindol massacre, in the French region of Lubéron, in 1551. The case was of considerable notoriety. Copies of the pleadings and indictments that multiplied in the seventeenth and eighteenth centuries give a precise idea of the emotions that it continued to arouse.[32] This major crisis was part of the long period of persecution of the 'heretics' of Provence. On 30 July 1540, 'those of Mérindol' were summoned to appear before the parliament of Aix-en-Provence for the crime of divine *lèse-majesté*. Faced with their failure to appear, the parliament convicted twenty-two individuals and demanded that they be arrested, their property seized and their houses levelled. In the years that followed, the king's policy oscillated between a strict application of the ruling and edicts of pardon through abjuration. In the winter of 1544–5, the king eventually ordered the execution of the decree. A military campaign was ordered, resulting in many abuses: thefts, looting, rapes, murders and sackings. The country was devastated. Between 1545 and 1550, multiple complaints were addressed to Henri II, and in 1550, the case was referred to the Grand Chambre of the Parliament of Paris. The lawyer Jacques Aubéry investigated and pleaded the case on behalf of the king.[33] If the Cabrières and Mérindol affair made headlines, it was first of all because of the novelty that saw one sovereign court brought before another.

Aubéry's lengthy indictment lasted fifty sessions before the Parliament of Paris in 1551. In it, he uses an allegorical painting of Lady Justice to arouse emotion in the courtroom:

Who is so blind that he refuses to see twenty-four villages on fire? Who is so deaf that they cannot hear the cry and the noise of the destruction of Cabrières [. . .] women and children killed in front of the altar, wives abducted, daughters, mothers and husbands forced to watch their daughters and wives raped? [. . .] Can this be covered with the mantle of Justice, and four 'judgments': one against a village that was never informed of the charges nor called to the hearing; the other pronounced on the holy day of Sunday, by incompetent and inhibited judges, who were not sufficiently qualified to wield the power of judging; the other two at the sole discretion of the Chief Judge, ordering executions and persecutions of villages and unnamed communities without hearing them, without condemning them, on an unnamed people, designated neither by their names, nor by their houses, nor by their families, which is nothing else than to allow the whole country to fall prey to the whims of soldiers, as this pitiful event has monstrously shown? Can this pretend to have been weighed in the scales of prudent and delicate scales of justice, where even half an ounce, a scruple can make it turn where it should? I call to witness her portrait which is located above our heads, she holds a sword in one hand, scales in the other, to show that her sword follows the compass, and to the nearest quarter of an ounce, she kills the father, absolves the son, exterminates the wife, and saves the husband. Will you then let the sword of justice be turned into one of war, which cuts off everything without measure or discretion, a pair so contrary that the one only ever does its duty when the other is absent? *Silent enim leges inter arma* [in times of war, laws fall silent] said Cicero. The opposite is true, where Justice is present, war comes to an end.[34]

This piece of forensic eloquence takes into account the courtroom decor, making explicit reference to the allegory (here a painting) above the heads of the audience. It relies on vivid metaphors that correspond to iconographic motifs well anchored in the visual memory of the time, such as that of the mantle of Justice, which refers both to the *virgo mantellata* and the images of *Justitia* sheltering her flock under her mantle (Figure 7.14).[35] The conflating iconographic formula borrowed from Christian art with the idea of a legal duty to care for the Christian community. The specific allusion to an allegorical painting of *Justitia*

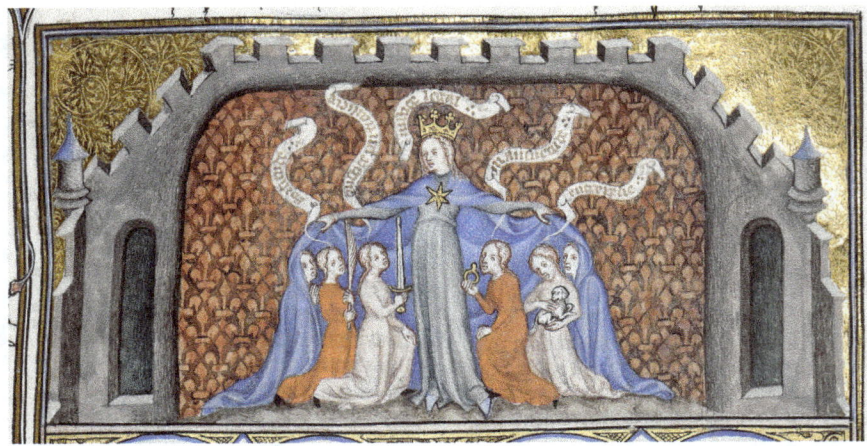

Figure 7.14: Anonymous artist, miniature from the manuscript of Nicole Oresme's French translation of Aristotle's *Nicomachean Ethics*, 1370–5, Ms. 9505, fol. 89r. Bibliothèque Royale de Belgique

present in the courtroom is remarkable: it serves as a *punctum* in which the sword of Justice becomes the climactic symbol of the injustices committed against the ransacked villages. How, the indignant orator asks, can the sword of a precise and reliable judicial machine take on such a vile and ungodly task? The sword of Justice has morphed into a lethal weapon. Bearing an indiscriminate rage, it has lost all positive valence to indicate only the clash of battle and the arbitrariness of war. The orator signals that it is nothing less than *Justitia* herself who has been attacked, her own weapon turned against her.

Justitia vulnerata

If Justice obstructed was the subject of several images in the sixteenth century, a new step is taken when *Justitia*'s body is wounded. Evoking the stigmata of Christ, new ways of exploring, venerating, imagining and experiencing the holy body of *Justitia*, holy wound in her side, are brought to the fore. The wounding of *Justitia* provides a new pictorial formula, introducing startling images, and generating devotional responses.

In 1646, the Dutch jurist Stephanus Nathen, also called Spormächer, a law professor at the Cologne Academy, wrote a long treatise called *Justitia Vulnerata, Christiane, Iuridice, Politice curate*, lavishly printed with an elegant frontispiece rich in symbolism (Figure 7.15).[36] At the top of the page, *Justitia* is sitting on a throne, her chest pierced by an arrow, her arms folded, her eyes blindfolded and her head bowed. On the ground, a laurel wreath and her sword and balance lie in disorder. Two angels fly to her rescue and make the aggressive crowd flee – a king armed with a bow, who has just shot an arrow, warriors and men in armour as well as other protagonists. In the din of battle, two books fly past the prostrate figure: *Libri interpretationum et Distinctionum* and *Opinionum et Exceptionum*. The rescuing angels represent divine justice, symbolised by a radiant sun marked with the Yahweh tetragrammaton in Hebrew lettering.

The frontispiece has a programmatic or even prefatory value. It announces figuratively some of the themes that are developed in Nathen's large volume: *Justitia* becomes the principal character of a new type of Passion play. Her wound is a synecdoche of numerous injuries; she is wounded by the administration of justice on earth, but also by

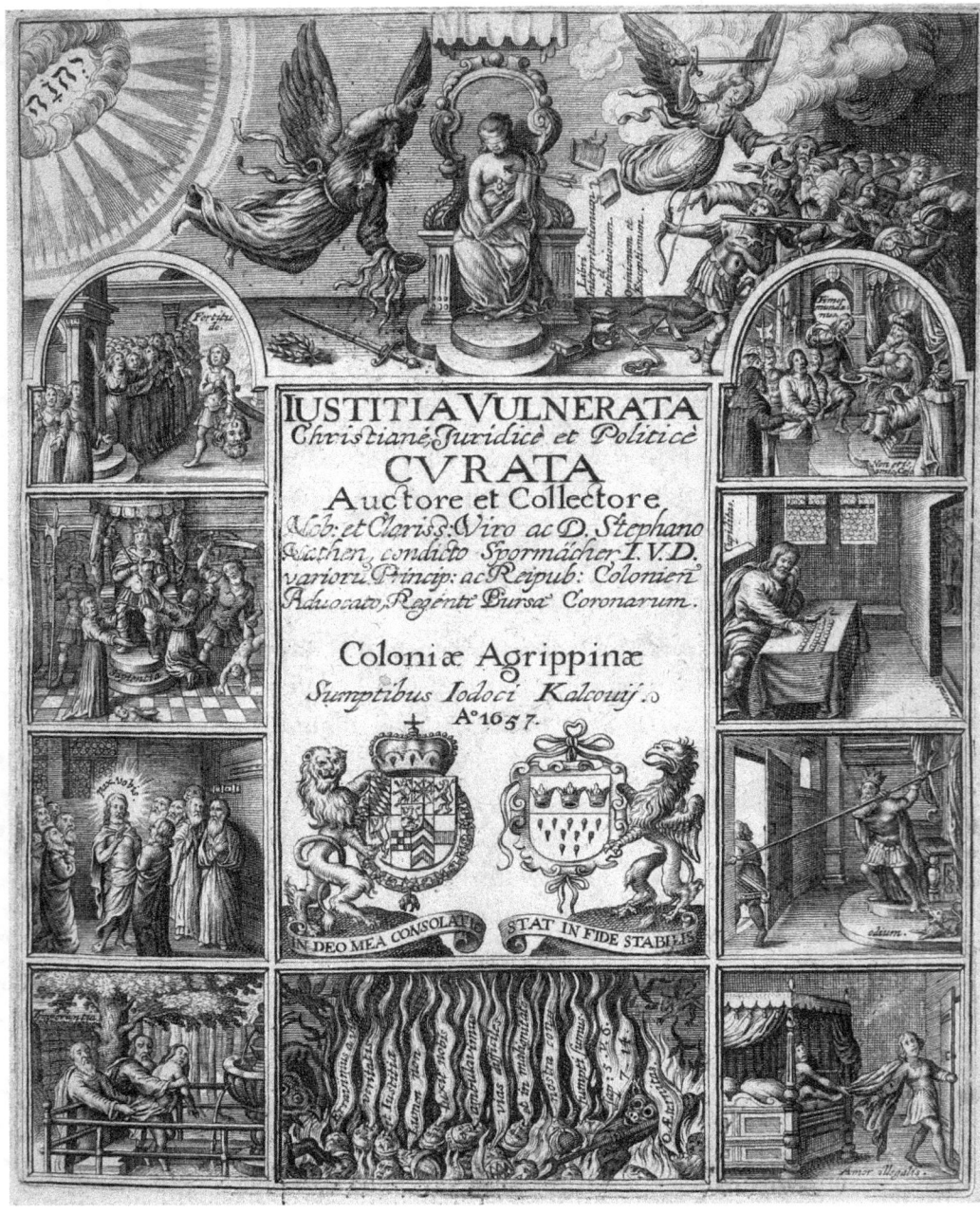

Figure 7.15: Stephanus Nathen, alias Spormächer, title page of *Justitia Vulnerata, Christiane, Iuridice, Politice curate* (Cologne: for lost Kalcoven, 1646). Photograph by the author

fear, greed, illicit love and hatred. In her struggle to heal earthly justice of its wounds, she relies on strength, wisdom, peace and temperance. On her right stand the virtues necessary for the proper exercise of justice, while on her left the vices that assail her. But perhaps the most important feature is carried on the axis that goes from the heavens of divine justice to the mouth of hell at the bottom of the print; *Justitia* serves as a mediator between the two orders, even though she herself is depicted suffering, pierced by an arrow like a martyr. Like the sermons that preach from the tried and tested model of the *imitatio Christi*, Nathen offers a secular counterpart, a kind of *imitatio Justitiæ* for apprentice lawyers, where the virtue receives more decisive concreteness and particularity in the depiction of her earthly vicissitudes.

Several poems accompany the publication of the book, including one by the author's relative, Christophorus Nathen, which underlines the pathos of the image: 'And now, the sublime Virgin goddess stands languishing, dislodged from her throne, while she bears, livid, a thousand wounds without complaint? Oh, what a monstrous shame! What an abominable unholy crime!'[37]

Of all the physical wounds inflicted on *Justitia*, the most curious comes from the books lying on the ground or flying, in scattered formation, to the left of her throne. One of the books has even been cut in half by a sword. These books of law, described as 'interpretations, distinctions, opinions and exceptions', refer to the logorrhea of legal hermeneutics, to an insatiable appetite for splitting hairs so as to drown Justice in labyrinthine quibbles. *Justitia* is wounded in her search for truth because legal interpretation fragments and dissipates it. What seems to be denied here is the value of textual hermeneutics, for usually the law book is handled with care or exhibited as an attribute that is at least as valuable as the sword and scales. In 'De l'expérience', Montaigne claims that this interpretative fury augments doubt and ignorance. The act of judging, he reasons, is always a matter of opinions, distinctions and variable interpretations rather than of knowledge.[38] *Justitia* is depicted here as a martyr who vainly searches for truth in law. Her withered, wounded and pierced body reveals the straying of opinion, the hazards of an oblique and limping knowledge. More importantly, by placing it at the opening of a practical law book, the image connects the wounding to the hermeneutic context of the art of law that it introduces.

Oppressed Justice

One of the privileged places for the staging of an assault on Justice is that of 'oppressed justice'.[39] It is another iteration of *Justitia vulnerata*, but this time it is the *judicial ritual itself* that is called into question. Here, Lady Justice becomes the central protagonist of a dramaturgic scene where magistrates and clergymen make their entrances and exits. During the reign of the French King Louis XV, marked by a series of parliamentary crises, the magistrates, and in particular the judges of the Parliament of Paris, went on strike. A war of attrition was waged by them, and despite repeated calls to order from the sovereign, it led to the definitive exile of the rebels and the installation of the Maupeou parliament.[40] In this fierce polemical context, an anonymous print of Oppressed Justice inserts the allegorical body of *Justitia* into the representation of a concrete event: the expulsion of the magistrates

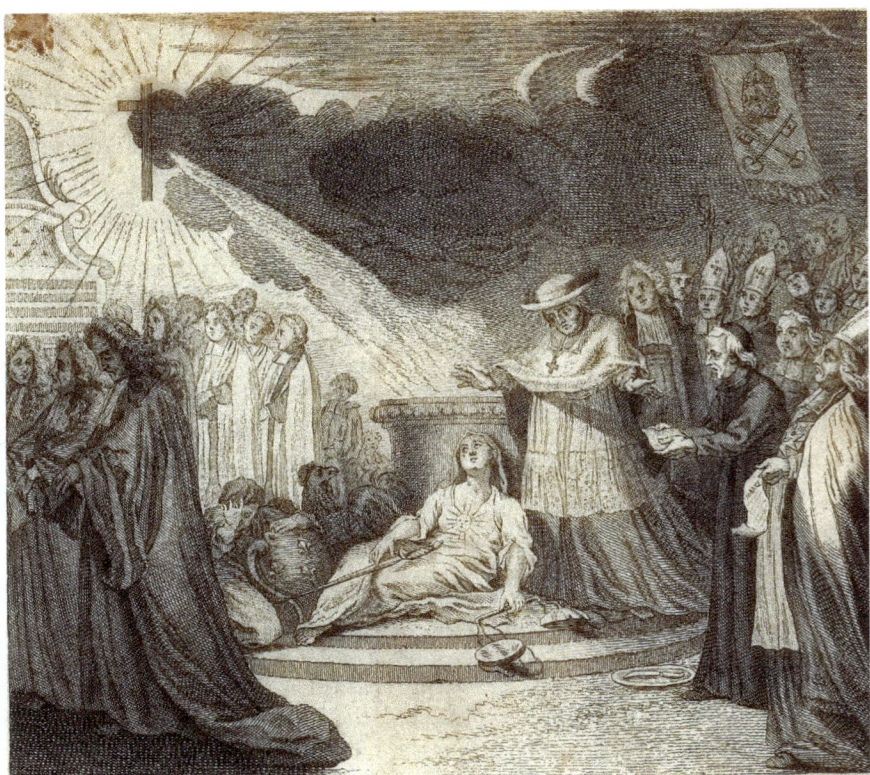

Figure 7.16: Anonymous print, *Justice opprimée*, 'Tous vos ennemis ont ouvert la bouche contre vous, ils ont sifflé, ils ont grincé des dents et ils ont dit nous la dévorerons [. . .]', c. 1732, engraving, 18 cm × 18.2 cm, inv. G.24137. By permission of the Musée Carnavalet, Paris

from the Palace in 1732 (Figure 7.16). In the centre of the composition, lying on the ground on the steps of an altar where she languishes, her eyes riveted on the cross in the sky, *Justitia* offers a distressing spectacle, amidst the disorder of attributes (sword and balance) that fall from her hands. By her side, France, kneeling in despair, can only lament her fate. On the right, we recognise an assemblage of clergymen, placed under the banner of the Holy See, as well as Cardinal Fleury, with a knife on a dish (presumably a eucharistic vessel) at his feet, signalling that the sacrifice of *Justitia* is imminent. The text underneath the engraving describes the anthropophagous and ungodly staging of an odious massacre: 'They said we will devour her! [. . .] you high priests, therefore, prostrate yourselves between the vestibule and the altar, weeping and crying to the Almighty [. . .].'[41] This highly theatrical representation of a moribund young woman, with vacant eyes, destined to be devoured, in the midst of a ritual with atheistic accents, is lent an apocalyptic hue by a cross whose sunny halo is eclipsed by heavy grey clouds, foreshadowing the dark night that descends on this unholy scene.

Lady Justice's oppression rises to a new level at the dawn of the Revolution, when pornography is mobilised as a picaresque political weapon against authority in general. In an anonymous late eighteenth-century engraving, dating from 1790, a magistrate attempts one last, perfectly obscene gesture in the face of the lack of cooperation from *Justitia*, who is here an emblem of royal authority (Figure 7.17). The ejaculative and hyperbolic exhibition is directed against hegemonic Justice, but it also seems to mock the tradition of allegorical decorum itself. Lady Justice, in a boudoir decorated with a *fleurdelisé* fabric, legs crossed, receives a suitor, while another magistrate runs away, ostensibly hiding his face in his hands. Her averted gaze is reinforced by a hand gesture that expresses her discomfort and parodies the hand of Justice placed between her downward-pointing sword and her scales. *Justitia* has no other choice but to participate in a picaresque sexual narrative, which desacralises her allegorical dignity.

Just below the hand of Justice, the engraver has incorporated a satirical bust of Louis XVI. In France, Lady Justice's effigy usually appears in miniature, as she may only be admitted in minor mode, in the background of the royal ceremonial portrait. An example of this telling visual hierarchy can be seen in the famous portrait of Louis XIV by Hyacinthe

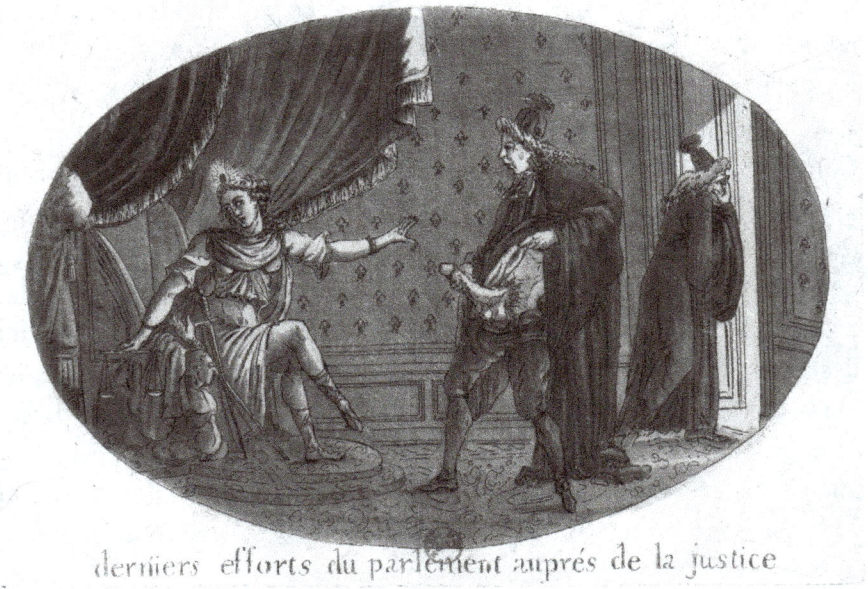

deriers efforts du parlément auprés de la justice

Figure 7.17: Anonymous print, *Derniers efforts du Parlement auprés de la justice*, 1790, satirical etching, RESERVE QB-370 (8)-FT 4. By permission of the Bibliothèque nationale de France

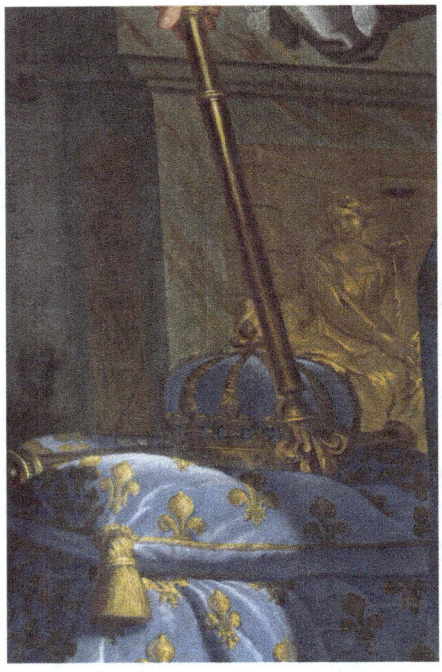

Figure 7.18: Nicolas-Guy Brenet, copy of the full-length portrait of Louis XIV aged 63 in full royal costume by Hyacinthe Rigaud (1659–1743), 1769. Parlement de Flandre, Douai, France. Photograph by the author

Rigaud, whose formula was so often copied (Figure 7.18). *Justitia* appears as the object of a *mise en abyme* in the official portrait of the monarch, an emblem of the divine right of kings. Not only has the engraving from 1790 removed the numinous portrait of the king, but it also ridicules the traditional visual device of *Justitia*'s submission to the king. Here the king appears only in the stunted form of the shadow of a miniature bust. Beyond its explicitly pornographic context and its humorous carnivalesque spirit, this provocative pamphlet also questions the age-old allegorical formulae of the *Ancien Régime*, degrading and inverting the prescribed norms of taste.[42] Regalia have been supplanted by genitalia.

Justitia at the crossroads

I must stress the political rationale which lies behind the desecration of the allegorical decorum. Far from being the ongoing norm of allegorical subtleness or sublimity which the legal officers steadily recommend, Lady Justice is often shown to be an easily mocked figure. This is why her image was tied to a set of rituals, doctrines and ceremonies which controlled its use and gave it a practical meaning.

These visions of a mishandled and weakened Justice do not correspond to the victorious image often deployed by sovereigns and judges. There is a good chance that judges and magistrates who are primarily interested in her noblest aspects will even displease the powerful. Insofar as they were primarily designed for such an audience, it is useful to give an account of what those concerned thought of it. Guillaume du Vair was a high-ranking magistrate and an exemplary figure of judicial eloquence in the first part of the seventeenth century.[43] After unravelling the genealogy of Themis, Astræa and Dike as the names of *Justitia*'s avatars, du Vair offers a meaningful selection. The three options he proposes are as follows:[44] the first, unsurprisingly, gives pride of place to Chrysippus' *ekphrasis*, showing all the strength of its ambivalence: 'a virgin flower adorned with its first modesty, armed however with a seriousness tempered by a pleasant serenity that shines in its eyes, who judges by her silence and by her sole gaze all the actions of men'. Modest but armed, serene-looking but watchful, she uses wisely the mute eloquence of her eyes. The second image, simpler according to him, comes from Aristotle and simply brings the matter back to the ornament of *Justitia*, which bears a star brighter than the evening and morning stars. This variation on the theme of the Sun of Justice is not encumbered by any of *Justitia*'s usual attributes. Finally, the last image, taken from Lactantius, focuses on her status as a *virgo mediatrix* between God and men. The last formula described by du Vair is a Cornucopian portrait of the virtues resulting from the good effects of *Justitia*. What is striking in the judgement of these different images by a high magistrate is the praise of beauty as such. This beauty is of the Platonic order; far from relegating Lady Justice to the rank of *Justitia vulgaris*, she is described as a *Justitia cælestis*, the keystone of a cosmological order, as without her, the world would collapse. This ideal of Justice actually corresponds to the image of decorum that legal professionals wish to imprint on the sacrosanct temple of civil justice. Du Vair presents *Justitia* in her best light; it is in fact a question of offering an image in accordance with the norms and the whims of the taste of these art lovers that are the magistrates. The broad question of giving body to *Justitia* has been reduced to its most praiseworthy aspects. On the contrary, the variety of images studied in this book has shown that *Justitia* does not only belong to the hushed interiors of the decorum of the sacrosanct Temple of Justice.

Classical Greco-Roman thought had in some way placed Justice as the exemplary virtue, the foundation of all human coexistence, and almost the meeting point and the knot between the natural world and the world of man, between the macrocosm and the microcosm. Brunetto Latini (1230?–1294) in the *Livres dou tresor* insisted on the noble appearance of her figure: 'Justice is the noblest thing, and the strongest virtue; and of all the virtues of which we are aware she is noblest.'[45] What later images of *Justitia* present is rather different from this encomium. As an immanent norm structuring every human existence, *Justitia* is susceptible to anguish as well. The processes of her visual embodiment strike us because they are more attuned to the historical vicissitudes of the unwritten laws of eros, pathos and thanatos. When she appears as an armoured virago, upholding a threatening sword as a symbol of violence and vengeful punishment, the allegorical decorum barely conceals the idea that Justice is a manifestation of armed violence, a display of terror intended to remind the viewers of the unrestrained power behind the law.

The temptation to solve the aporia of figuring Justice in terms of pure equality – and equality of goods – was easily inspired by mathematical explanations; and it was easy to pass from the idea of an order, a harmony and a balance, to the vision of a series of equal units. What the anatomy of Dame Justice teaches us, on the contrary, is the interplay between nomos and *physis*, the deep sense of the corporeality of good judgment, the need to constantly revive the arbitrariness of iconological codes and conventions in order to regain the strength of a symbolism anchored in the parts of the body. Justice is a worldly virtue: her epiphany reveals the aporias of civil justice. The fictional ideal of a mathematical entity, underlining the character of Justice as a proportional order, falls flat in front of the *Imago Justitiæ*, a heroic celebration of an unfortunate virtue. In the appeal to the laws of nature, to the laws from above, to the unwritten laws of images, and against the emptiness of juridical formalism, *Justitia* is perhaps located precisely in this aporia that constitutes it. Her flesh is prior to the Law. Allegories of Justice are the judicial legs of past symbolic practices. They let us see the forbidden knowledge of affects, penetrating into courthouse spaces, now and then interrupting the normal course of judicial procedures with mockery and parody. Even if they rarely have the corrosive nature of bringing a sense of satire within the precincts of law, their mere presence reveals the uneasiness of separating interpretive power from punitive power. Female allegories of Justice are always situated at the threshold of parallel worlds: between the judge's body and the female incarnation, between the promise of redemption and the threat of inferno, between measurable metrics and immense violence. The striking apparitions of Lady Justice are an integral part of the affective transmission of legal culture: their corporeality creates patterns of inversion, assimilation, overlap or even absorption.

The allegorical body of Lady Justice combines divergent attributes that hint at almost incompatible polarities. The difficulty is clearly apparent on the reverse of the medal of the jurisconsult Aurelio dall' Acqua, Doctor of Law, Knight and Count Palatine (Figure 7.19).[46] It shows a figure of *Justitia* whose ostensive arm gestures are contorted and well-nigh impossible. *Justitia*'s body provides a common ground for

Figure 7.19: Giulio di Girolamo della Torre, medal, bronze, depicting the bust of Aurelio dall' Acqua in profile to the left with inscription around, Italy, sixteenth century, diameter 11.76 cm. Inscriptions: (obverse) 'MAGN. AURELIVS. AB. AQUA. VICENTINVS IVRISCONSVLTVS. EXCEL. COMES. PAL. ET. EQUES'; (reverse) 'IN. MEMORIA. AETERNA. ERIT. IVSTVS. OP. IV. TVR', inv. 7133-1860. Victoria and Albert Museum, London

gestures that cannot a priori coincide. It can juxtapose in a single anatomy three or even four different and somehow incompatible gestural grammars, nevertheless allowing them to survive alongside or opposite one another. *Justitia*'s gesticulations create a necessary backdrop of 'mimethics' that subvert legal norms but also aesthetic norms and physiological constraints. In performing their judicial duties inside courtroom spaces, judges are constantly teased by these intriguing figures, while the public audience may deliver such diverse responses as apotropaic, numinous, sensuous or dispassionate gestures.

When her body is located above an urban fountain, passers-by may notice her curious gestural nexus, not far from the courthouse entrance. Her pivotal location is an attempt to communicate with citizens, a way of imagining the pervasive interpenetration of law and *nomos* in the entire spectrum of city life. As an alter ego of the judge, *Justitia*'s metamorphoses appear to embody the various avatars of judicial magic. Her body is a type of daimon, located at the crossroads of judgment, but it also acts as a sphinx, possessed of a mute and ambivalent eloquence. Her liminal status blurs the contrasts between honour and shame, life and death, vigilance and sleep, male and female. As a major constituent of the apparatus of punishment, she often appears on the frontline, but nevertheless turns her back on the world of horror to which she lends legitimacy without ever seeing it.

This tension and torsion is particularly evident in the engraving by Jacob de Gheyn II already discussed in Chapter 3 (Figure 7.20). Lady Justice stands under the orb of a radiant sun, sword and scales in hand, indicating with an apotropaic gesture of her left-hand fingers that she is trying to keep the evil eye away from the scenes of horror and punishment unfolding behind her. But what makes the engraving particularly noticeable are two elements that appear at her feet: the position of her

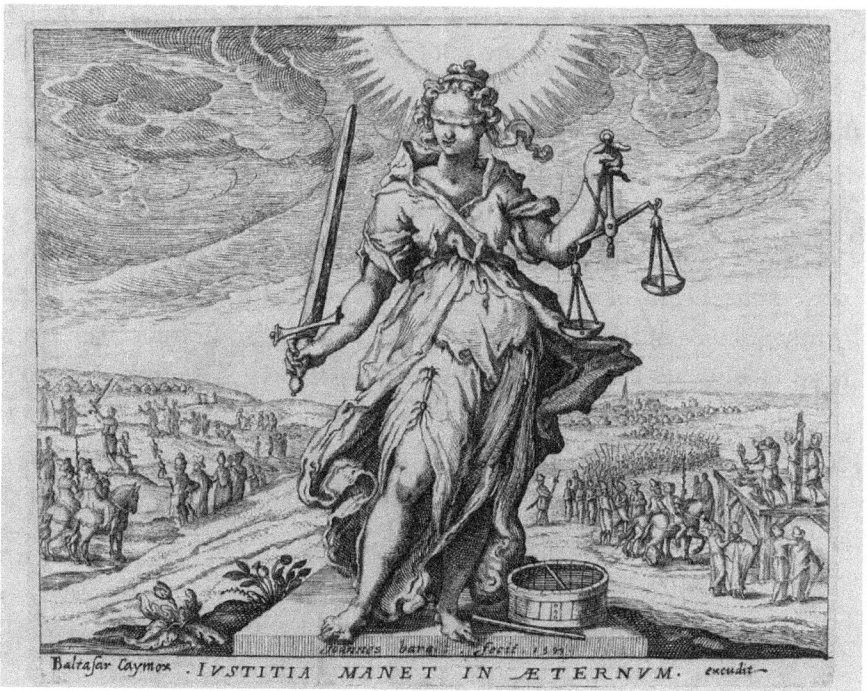

Figure 7.20: Johannes Bara/Baltazar Caymox (after an original drawing by Jacob de Gheyn II), *Justice Standing under the Orb of a Radiant Sun*, with the motto 'Iustitia manet in æternum', 1599. By permission of the Herzog August Bibliothek, Wolfenbüttel

toes, placed on the outer edge of the pedestal, indicate that she is above all a figure of the threshold, creating a link between divine justice and the accomplishment of punishment here on earth; while the role of the sieve next to her reminds us that she stands there to judge individuals. The sieve serves as a pictorial analogue to her sword – drawing distinctions, separating the just from the unjust. The pictorial syntax of the Last Judgement, which provided the chosen ones with an escape to more merciful heavens, has disappeared. We are left with a schizophrenic allegory, meant to insulate perpetrators and prisoners from comforting allies or compassionate witnesses. By ostensibly turning her back on what is happening in her name, Lady Justice reproduces in the space of her contrasted body an equivalent of the inner psychomachy that inhabits the judge's conscience.

Bodily details recur stubbornly, physical or physiognomical features are given symbolic salience. Between the judge and his allegorical counterpart, these signs act as reflections, doublets or multiplicities that cannot be explained by the simple chains of cause and effect. Rather, inversion, intertwinement, overlapping or dissemination suggest rich and varied modes of symbolic contamination. The present book has attempted to reveal some of these hidden genealogical laws. Some of these images remain disquieting; they trouble the domain of legal discourse. Allegories of *Justitia* expose legal procedures to disturbing reflections, sensuous bites or unexpected wounds. At the sight of the metaphoric abyss which gapes below her, judges may use her body as a convenient means of veiling the power of affects or the terror inflicted by the violence of their judgments. But the image soon frees itself from those who believe they can manipulate it. *Justitia*'s eye is often portrayed as a numinous gaze looking down: as Psalm 85:11 reads, 'Veritas de terra orta est, et iustitia de cœlo prospexit' (Truth shall spring out of the earth; and righteousness shall look down from heaven). It is therefore an image with an overhanging gaze, plunging or hovering above those who depend on her.

Notes

1. For a detailed and convincing examination of Brueghel the Elder's *Justitia*, see José M. González García, *The Eyes of Justice: Blindfolds and Farsightedness, Vision and Blindness in the Aesthetics of the Law* (Frankfurt: Vittorio Klostermann, 2017), pp. 118–24: 'The author emphasizes the theatrical nature of the composition of the engraving, showcasing with great detail torture scenes, trial scenes, scenes of court bureaucracy and execution or punishment scenes, all surrounding Lady Justice, standing in isolation in the middle of this bustling theater.'

2. Seneca, *De Clementia* I, ch. 22: 'In quibus vindicandis hæc tria lex secuta est, quæ princeps quoque sequi debet: aut ut eum, quem punit, emendet; aut ut poena ejus cæteros meliores reddat; aut ut, sublatis malis, securiores cæteri vivant.' *L. Annaeus Seneca. Moral Essays: Volume 1*, ed. John W. Basore (London: Heinemann, 1928).

3. Desmond Manderson, *Danse Macabre: Temporalities of Law in the Visual Arts* (Cambridge: Cambridge University Press, 2019), p. 47.

4. Karl Heinz Burmeister, 'La Justicia de 1559 de Pieter Brueghel el Viejo', *Pensamiento jurídico* 24 (2009), pp. 19–37 (p. 33), qtd in González García, *Eyes of Justice*, p. 124.

5. See Manderson, *Danse Macabre*, pp. 47ff.

6. Herbert Zschelletzschky, *Die 'drei gottlosen Maler' von Nürnberg. Sebald Beham, Barthel Beham und Georg Pencz. Historische Grundlagen und ikonologische Probleme ihrer Graphik zur Reformations und Bauernkriegszeit* (Leipzig: Seeman Verlag, 1975).

7. See Hans-Martin Kaulbach and Reinhart Schleier, *'Der Welt Lauf.' Allegorische Graphikserien des Manierismus*, exhibition catalogue, Stuttgart, 18 October 1997–25 January 1998 and Bochum, 17 May–6 July 1998.

8. Jean Wirth, *La jeune fille et la mort. Recherches sur les thèmes macabres dans l'art germanique de la Renaissance* (Geneva: Droz, 1979), p. 140. For a recent account of the interpretations of the engraving, see Jürgen Müller and Thomas Schauerte (eds), *Die Gottlosen Maler von Nürnberg. Konvention und Subversion in der Druckgrafik der Beham-Brüder* (Emsdetten: Edition Imorde, 2011).

9. See a full account of the drawing in Müller and Schauerte, *Die Gottlosen Maler von Nürnberg*, p. 239.

10. Jan-David Mentzel, 'Taufe im Sündenbad. Sebald Behams "Jungbrunnen" von 1531', in Müller and Schauerte, *Die Gottlosen Maler von Nürnberg*, pp. 98–114.

11. Gerung was a German painter, miniature painter, and woodcut and tapestry designer born in Nördlingen around 1500; he died in Lavingen in 1568 or 1570. His major patron was Otto Henry, later Elector Palatine of the Rhine. He was also employed from 1531 to 1567 as the town inspector of weights and measures. A supporter of the Lutheran Reformation, he produced several satirical works directed against the emperor and the Pope and the abuses of the Church (in 1546, an engraving shows devils boiling the Pope; in 1548, he

depicts the coronation of the Antichrist and the Whore of Babylon, topped with a tiara). See C. Dodgson, *Prussian Jahrbuch*, xxix (1908), pp. 195ff.; Dodgson, ii, pp. 212ff., 447; and C. Dodgson, *Graph. Künste*, NF, i, 1936, pp. 81–5, all held by the Department of Prints and Drawings at the British Museum. See also F. W. H. Hollstein, *German Engravings, Etchings and Woodcuts c. 1400–1700* (Amsterdam: M. Hertzberger, 1954–), x, pp. 15ff.; P. Roettig, *Reformation als Apokalypse: Die Holzschnitte von Matthias Gerung im Codex germanicus 6592* (Bern: der Bayerischen Staatsbibliothek in München, 1991).

12. See Susanne Zeunert, 'Bilder in Martin Luthers Tischreden. Argumente und Beispiele gegen die Laster Hochmut, Abgötterei und Betrug', unpublished thesis, University of Trier, 2016, p. 35.

13. Susan S. Eberly, 'A Thorn among the Lilies: The Hawthorn in Medieval Love Allegory', *Folklore* 100, no. 1 (1989), pp. 41–52. The author stresses that the hawthorn is a constant of medieval carnal love allegory; in the gardens of love where the hawthorn is found, dreams or heavenly visions are caused, leading to insomnia and erotic nightmares (p. 48).

14. See Eleanor Simmons Greenhill, 'The Child in the Tree: A Study of the Cosmological Tree in Christian Tradition', *Traditio* 10 (1954), pp. 323–71, and esp. p. 342, her quote of an Easter homily attributed to Saint Hippolytus of Rome (third century CE) where the Cross is described in cosmological terms: 'This wood belongs to me for my eternal salvation. I feed and nourish myself with it . . . For my hunger, I find delicate food; for my thirst, a fountain; for my nakedness, a garment; its leaves are an invigorating spirit . . . [. . .] This Tree, which extends as far as the sky, ascends from earth to heaven. An immortal plant, cosmic intertwining, comprising within itself all the variegation of human nature.'

15. Raymond Klibansky, Erwin Panofsky and Fritz Saxl, *Saturn and Melancholy: Studies in the History of Natural Philosophy, Religion and Art* (London: Nelson, 1964), pp. 125–214. The pensive head resting on the hand, beneath the jaw (*maisselle*) is the classical gesture of Saturn, a widespread expression of melancholic state. It famously appears in Albrecht Dürer's 1517 engraving *Melencolia I*.

16. See especially Nicholas Terpstra (ed.), *The Art of Executing Well: Rituals of Execution in Renaissance Italy* (Kirkville, MO: Truman State University Press, 2008).

17. Throughout the 1520s, a number of prints signed 'AC' have been attributed to Allert Claesz, without certainty. According to J. P. Filedt Kok, it is plausible that this monogram is not that of the artist but of his publisher. See J. Richard Judson, 'Jan Gossart North of the Rivers', *Netherlandish Kunsthistorisch Jaarboek* (NKJ)/*Netherlands Yearbook for History of Art* 38 (1987), pp. 128–35.

18. Michel de Montaigne, *Journal de voyage en Italie*, ed. M. Rat (Paris: Garnier, 1955), p. 101: 'Outre la forme de France, ils font marcher devant le criminel un grand crucifix couvert d'un rideau noir, et à pied un grand nombre d'homes vestus et masqués de toile [. . .] Il y en a deus de ceus-là, ou moines, ainsi vestus et couverts, qui assistent le criminel sur la charrette et le preschent, et l'un d'eux lui presente continuellement sur le visage et lui fait baiser sans cesse un

tableau où est l'image de Nostre Seigneur; cela faict que on ne puisse pas voir le visage du criminel par la rue. A la potence [. . .] on lui tenoit tous-jours cette image contre le visage jusques à ce qu'il fut élancé.'

19. See Terpstra, *Art of Executing Well.*
20. See Timothy B. Husband, Madeline H. Caviness and Marilyn Beaven, 'Monograph Series I: Stained Glass before 1700 in American Collections: Silver -Stained Roundels and Unipartite Panels (Corpus Vitrearum Checklist IV), *Studies in the History of Art* 39 (1991), pp. 3–277 (p. 139). See also William D. Wixom (ed.), *Mirror of the Medieval World* (New York: The Metropolitan Museum of Art, 1999), no. 295, p. 232: 'A satisfactory interpretation of the subject of this roundel has yet to be offered.' Another version of this roundel exists in Christ Church, Llanwarne (Herefordshire, UK).
21. Joshua Berman, 'The "Sword of Mouths" (Jud. III. 16; Ps. CXLIX, 6; Prov. V 4): A Metaphor and Its Ancient Near Eastern Context', *Vetus Testamentum* 52, no. 3 (2002), pp. 291–303.
22. See Didron Ainé, *Annales archéologiques*, vol. 20 (Paris: Librairie archéologique de Victor Didron, 1860), p. 72.
23. On the study of attitudes towards the notion of woman in the Renaissance, see Ian Maclean, *The Renaissance Notion of Woman: A Study in the Fortunes of Scholasticism and Medical Science in European Intellectual Life* (Cambridge: Cambridge University Press, 1980).
24. See Diane Wolfthal, *Images of Rape: The 'Heroic' Tradition and Its Alternatives* (Cambridge: Cambridge University Press, 1999), esp. ch. 3.
25. See Gerhard Wolf, 'Die frau in weiss visuelle strategien und künstlerische argumentation in Ambrogio Lorenzettis fresken in der Sala dei Nove', *Mitteilungen des Kunsthistorischen Institutes in Florenz* 55, no. 1 (2013), pp. 26–53.
26. The bibliography is vast. What follows is only a selection. Nicolai Rubinstein, 'Political Ideas in Sienese Art: The Frescoes by Ambrogio Lorenzetti and Taddeo di Bartolo in the Palazzo Pubblico', *Journal of the Warburg and Courtauld Institutes* 21 (1959), pp. 179–207; Quentin Skinner, 'Ambrogio Lorenzetti: "The Artist as political philosopher"', *Proceedings of the British Academy* 72 (1986), pp. 1–56; Quentin Skinner, 'Ambrogio Lorenzetti's *Buon Governo* Frescoes: Two Old Questions, Two New Answers', *Journal of the Warburg and Courtauld Institutes* 62 (1999), pp. 1–28; Maria Monica Donato, 'Dal "Comune rubato" di Giotto al "Comune sovrano" di Ambrogio Lorenzetti (con una proposta per la "canzone" del Buon Governo)', in A. Carlo Quintavalle (ed.), *Medioevo: Immagine e racconti. Atti del convegno internazionale di studi* (Milan: Parma, 2002); Patrick Boucheron, '"Tournez les yeux pour admirer, vous qui exercez le pouvoir, celle qui est peinte ici". La fresque du Bon Gouvernement d'Ambrogio Lorenzetti', *Annales. Histoire, Sciences Sociales* (2005–6), pp. 1137–99; Rosa Maria Dessi, 'L'invention du "Bon Gouvernement". Pour une histoire des anachronismes dans les fresques d'Ambrogio Lorenzetti (XIVe–XXe siècle)', *Bibliothèque de l'école des chartes* 165, no. 2 (2007), pp. 453–504; Patrick Boucheron, *Conjurer la peur: Sienne, 1338. Essai sur la force politique des images* (Paris: Seuil, 2013); Rosa Maria Dessi, *Les spectres du bon gouvernement* (Paris: Presses Universitaires de France, 2017).

27. Wolf, 'Die frau in weiss', p. 33.
28. Hans Belting, 'Das Bild als Text. Wandmalerei und Literatur im Zeitalter Dantes', in H. Belting and D. Blume (eds), *Malerei und Stadtkultur in der Dantezeit* (Munich: Hirmer Verlag, 1989), pp. 23–8.
29. Boucheron, '"Tournez les yeux"', pp. 1193–4.
30. González García, *Eyes of Justice*, pp. 309–13. See also Betty Kurth, 'Zwei unbekantte Fragmente des Michelfeldter Bildteppichs', *Die graphischen Künste* 2 (1937), pp. 27–31, where she documents fragments of the original tapestry; and Wim Hüsken, 'The Michelfeldt Tapestry and Contemporary European Literature. Moral Lessons on the Rule of Deceit', in Dagmar Eichberger and Charles Zika, *Dürer and His Culture* (Cambridge: Cambridge University Press, 1998), pp. 69–92.
31. Hanns Hubach, 'Tapestry to Woodcut: Albrecht Dürer's Representation of the Michelfeld-Tapestry (1526)', paper presented at a Study Day on the History of the Textile Image, German Centre for Art History, Paris, 24 June 2010.
32. See Gabriel Audisio, 'L'affaire Cabrières et Mérindol: de la valeur des témoignages (1545–1551)', in Amis de la Méjane (ed.), *Le Parlement de Provence (1501–1790)* (Aix-en-Provence: Presses Universitaires de Provence, 2002), pp. 41–53.
33. Jacques Aubéry, *Histoire de l'exécution de Cabrières et de Mérindol et d'autres lieux de Provence* (Paris: Cramoisy, 1645; reprinted with notes by Gabriel Audisio, Paris: Les éditions de Paris, 1995). The text dates from the opening of the trial on 18 September 1551 but was edited and published for the first time in 1645.
34. Ibid., p. 216: 'Qui fera l'aveugle qui ne verra le feu bruslant dans vint-quatre villages? Qui fera le sourd qui n'entendra le cry & le bruit de la défaite de Cabrières, [. . .] des femmes et des enfants tuez jusques sur l'Autel, des femmes & des filles ravies, & des mères & des maris qui virent forcer leurs filles & leurs femmes? [. . .] cela se peut-il couvrir du manteau de Iustice, & de quatres Arrests: l'un donne contre un village non appellé & non ouy: l'autre un saint jour de Dimanche, par des Juges incompetans & inhibez, & non suffisamment restituez du pouvoir de iuger: les deux autres à la seule suggestion de Messieurs les Presidens, contenans des executions & des persecutions sur des villages & sur des communautez non ouyes, non condamnées, sur un peuple non nommé, non désigné, ny par noms, ny par maisons, ny par familles, ce qui n'est autre chose que de bailler en proye & à la discretion du soldat tout un pays, comme le piteux evenement l'a monstré? Cela peut-il sembler avoir esté pesé à la balance de Justice, qui est si prudente & si delicate, qu'une demy-once, un scrupule la fait tourner où elle doit? J'appelle à témoin sa peinture que voilà sur nos testes, elle tient l'espée d'une main, la balance de l'autre, pour montrer que son espée ne va que par compas, & à un quart d'once près, elle fait mourir le père, absout le fils, elle extermine la femme, & sauve le mary. Permettez-vous donc que l'espée de la Justice soit changée à l'espée de la guerre, qui coupe tout sans balance et sans discretion, & qui sont si contraires, que jamais l'un ne fait son office que quand l'autre n'y est point. *Silent enim leges inter arma* dit Cicéron. Au contraire la guerre cesse ou est la Justice.'

35. See Claire Richter Sherman, 'Some Visual Definitions in the Illustrations of Aristotle's *Nicomachean Ethics* and *Politics* in the French Translations of Nicole Oresme', *The Art Bulletin* 59, no. 3 (1977), pp. 320–30. In the upper part of the miniature, there is a depiction of *Justitia generalis*, represented as Our Lady of Mercy, crowned as her, queen of virtues, covering with her mantle (she is depicted as the *Virgo mantellata*) her six daughters, kneeling before her: *Fortitude*, holding a palm, *Justice particulière* (Individual Justice) with a sword, *Mansuétude* (Gentleness) offering a ring, and *Entrepesie* (Conciliation) cuddling a dog. For an extensive treatment of the iconographical theme of the Madonna of Misericordia, underlining the legal origins of the mantle motive, see V. Sussman, 'Maria mit dem Schutzmantel', *Marburger Jahrbuch für Kunstwissenschaft* 5 (1929), pp. 285–351.

36. Stephanus Nathen, alias Spormächer, *Justitia Vulnerata, Christiane, Iuridice, Politice curate* (Cologne: Iost Kalcoven, 1646). Each chapter describes a specific wound: Justitia vulnerata *1st part* (1) in administratione; (2) in bello; (3) in clementia; (4) in dubiis; (5) in æquitate; (6) de Justitia fori & poli vulnerate; (7) de Justitia in genere, specie & individuo vulnerata; (8) de justitia in honoribus vulnerate; *2nd part* (1) in jurisdictione; (2) in litibus; (3) in munerum acceptatione; (4) in negligentia; (5) in opinionibus; (6) in personarum acceptione; (7) in quæstionibus; (8) in ratione; (9) in stylo & statuto; (10) in tempore & prætextu temporis; (11) in veritate.

37. Ibid., liminary pieces, unpaginated: 'Panegyris in Librum Colendissimi Patris', a poem by Christophorus Nathen, verses 9–11: 'Et nunc diva throno sublimi Virgo iacebit / Detrusa? & livens vulnera mille ferret? Proh pudor immanis! Scelus heu crudele nefandum!'

38. Michel de Montaigne, 'De l'expérience', in *Essais*, ed. André Tournon, 3 vols (Paris: Imprimerie Nationale, 1998), vol. 3, ch. 13, p. 429.

39. Pierre Wachenheim, 'Emblèmes de la Robe: les représentations de la Justice dans l'imagerie pro-parlementaire sous le règne de Louis XV', *Sociétés & Représentations* 18, no. 2 (2004), pp. 233–49.

40. See Dale K. Van Kley, *The Jansenists and the Expulsion of the Jesuits* (New Haven, CT: Yale University Press, 1975); Dale K. Van Kley, *The Damiens Affair and the Unraveling of the Ancien Regime, 1750–1770* (Princeton, NJ: Princeton University Press, 1984); Julian Swann, *Politics and the Parlement of Paris under Louis XV, 1754–1774* (Cambridge: Cambridge University Press, 1995); John Rogister, *Louis XV and the Parlement of Paris, 1737–1754* (Cambridge: Cambridge University Press, 1995); Peter Campbell, *Power and Politics in Old Regime France, 1720–1745* (London: Routledge, 1996).

41. The text below the print reads: 'Justice opprimée. Tous vos ennemis ont ouvert la bouche contre vous, ils ont sifflé ils ont grincé les dents et ils ont dit nous la dévorerons / voici le jour que nous attendions nous l'avons trouvé, nous l'avons vu: vous donc prêtres du très haut, prosternez-vous entre les vestibule et l'autel / fondez en larmes et criez au tout puissant: lamant 2.v. 16, 1732.'

42. On the role of pornography as a force for revolution in late eighteenth-century France, see Robert Darnton, *The Corpus of Clandestine Literature in France, 1769–1789* (New York: W. W. Norton, 1995).

43. Guillaume du Vair (1556–1621), counsellor in the Parliament of Paris during the Catholic League crisis and friend of Pierre Pithou, Nicolas Le Fèvre and Jacques-Auguste de Thou, was strongly engaged in favour of the Gallican cause. A prolific writer and erudite lawyer, he became *garde des sceaux* under the King Louis XIII and Bishop of Lisieux. See Bruno Petey-Girard and Alexandre Tarrête (eds), *Guillaume du Vair, parlementaire et écrivain (1556–1621)* (Geneva: Droz, 2005), esp. Robert Descimon's contribution (pp. 17–77), for a social biography of du Vair, grounded in the study of many first-hand archival discoveries.

44. Guillaume du Vair, *Les Œuvres du Seigneur Guillaume du Vair* (1617; Geneva: Slatkine, 1970), pp. 209–10; my translation: 'Now, which hand do you want her painting with? For so many excellent workmen have worked to animate it with the delicate strokes of their rare brushes, that if I were to represent all the portraits they have drawn from it, the multitude would make the choice too difficult for you. I shall therefore deliver you from this trouble, and will show you only three of them, by the hand of three of the greatest masters of ancient wisdom, the first being that famous Stoic, Chrysippus, who escaped from the ruins of Athens, and found himself hidden in the *Attic Nights* of Aulus Gellius. Here is how he portrayed her *forma virginalis, adspectu vehementi & formidabili luminibus oculorum acribus, neque humilis neque atrocis sed reverendae cuiusdam tristitiae*. What could be more beautiful and more excellent? You see a virgin flower adorned with its first modesty, armed however with a seriousness tempered by a pleasant serenity that shines in its eyes, who judges by her silence and by her sole gaze all the actions of men. [. . .] But let us see if the painting of this great Aristotle, though simpler and not enhanced by the bright colours and varnish of Chrysippus, does not bring us such an august and venerable face, when he says in his *Politics*, that *neque Hesperus neque Lucifer adeo mirabilis atque iustitia*. Of what can she be adorned and made more beautiful than by the clearest and brightest stars in the firmament? This is something that we could not understand if we did not learn it from a painting by the erudite Porphyry, [. . .] where he explains why Justice is so beautiful and excellent [. . .] because she draws all her make-up and embellishment from true piety and religion. Also, the greatest effect that Lactantius attributes to her is to keep men united by respect, reverence and veneration to divinity, and to be like a bond that unites these two extremities so far apart, God and men. If you have seen her portrayed as a beautiful woman, you must not imagine she is less powerful or less useful and beneficial: she is the liberal hand that spreads peace, rest, friendship, concord, opulence, freedom over the earth. Without her nothing in the world can survive.'

45. 'Justice est la plus noble vertuz et la plus fors qui soit, [. . .] porce que ele est plus enterine et plus complie que nule des autres vertuz.' Brunetto Latini, *Li Livres dou Tresor* (1260–7; Paris: Polycarpe Chabaille, Imprimerie Nationale, 1853), book 2, pt 1, ch. 27, p. 293.

46. Aurelio dall' Acqua (1476–1539) was a prominent jurist from Vicenza. He was part of the solemn entry procession into the city of Emperor Maximilian of Hapsburg together with the other doctors of the College of Jurists in 1508.

Elected vicar in Verona in 1529, he became acquainted with Cardinal Pietro Bembo, offering him numerous services. He held many political offices and was at the centre of all events concerning the life of Vicenza. After his death on 13 March 1539, he was buried in Vicenza Cathedral at the foot of the high altar which he had built years before. Two medals were minted in his honour, the work of Giulio di Girolamo Della Torre, judge and lawyer in Verona, who also dabbled in the art of casting. The two medals depict dall' Acqua and both bear an engraved celebratory epigraph. See Raffaella Zaccaria, 'Dall'Acqua, Aurelio', in *Dizionario Biografico degli Italiani*, vol. 31 (Rome: Istituto della Enciclopedia italiana, 1985).

Epilogue: why has Lady Justice survived until now?

Allegory corrupts into allegorism (clumsy or far too frequent use of allegory) when the genre becomes locked into conventions whose meanings have been lost. Fiercely critical of the allegorical genre, the nineteenth century was spared none of its excesses: they would only be superficial illusions, heterogeneous assemblies of badly digested lessons, vehicles for a procession of outmoded norms, lame relics of a bygone era. This 'peinture de pointus' no longer corresponds to modern society.[1] Its traditions of aristocratic and esoteric exegesis ring hollow and, more seriously, fall flat. Because it is saturated with objects that have become unintelligible, it no longer functions in a democratic world that aspires to generalise public education.

Whereas the allegory of the *Ancien Régime* irremediably separated the initiated from the vulgar, the young republic can only detest this elitist painting, reserved for the instruction of the great and the good, which distinguishes 'the chosen' from 'the unworthy'. Instead of the codified lexicon of iconology, Pierre-Paul Prud'hon famously prefers a directly legible archetype: *Justice and Divine Vengeance Pursuing Crime* (c. 1805–6). The painter does not seek to initiate the eye of the spectator to another language: he wants to 'give the soul a commotion'.[2] Just as classical allegory at its best lies at the juncture of two regimes of imagination (dream and prophecy), the reception of these figures affects both body and soul. The iconological tradition is anchored in a long-term memory: it is because it changes little or not at all that allegory becomes necessary; necessary because it authorises institutions. Walter Benjamin insists on the 'inactuality' of allegory which provides this anachronic symbolic space.[3] It is by definition conservative, hoarding and accumulating, while constantly adapting to the gaze of its viewers.

Inventing new allegories for today's world is therefore not an easy task. It remains necessary to return to the reasons that explain the surprising vitality of Lady Justice through the centuries up to the present day, a vitality that appears as not-so-distant echoes of the early modern gestural grammar of *Justitia*. Three allegorical reinventions of *Justitia* (Damien Hirst, Banksy and Peter Greenaway) will be used to argue against those who prophesy her decline too quickly. Though these contemporary creations may seem completely disconnected from their early modern counterparts, it is worth considering the features they share with their distant ancestors.

First, the curious allegorical sculpture by Damien Hirst shows a naked, pregnant woman brandishing a sword pointing to the sky, and holding behind her, as if hidden, the trays of her scales (Figures E.1 and E.2). Situated facing the sea in the seaside resort of Ilfracombe in North

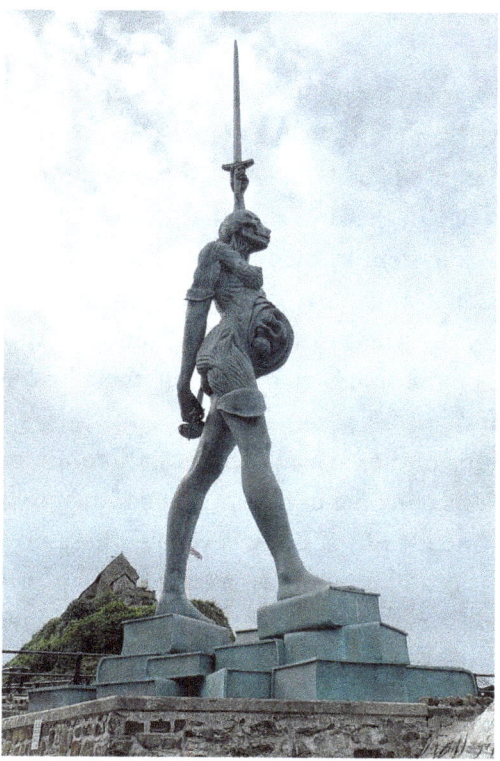

Figure E.1: Damien Hirst, *Verity and Justice*, from the right side. Wikimedia Commons

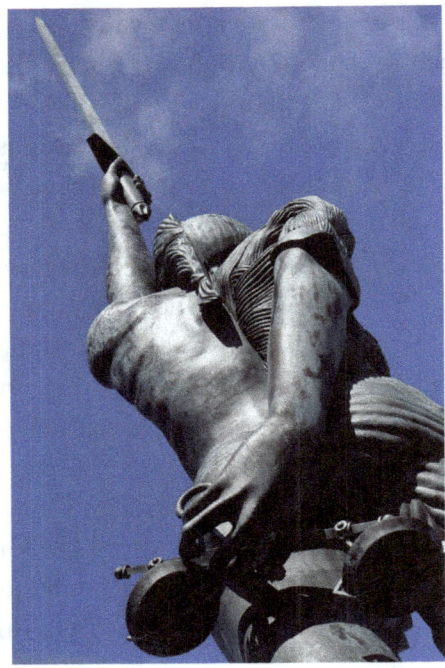

Figure E.2: Damien Hirst, *Verity and Justice,* close-up from behind. Wikimedia Commons

Devon, this monumental sculpture, 66.4 feet high, stands as a contemporary allegory of truth and Justice. Depicted as an antithetical figure, she balances on piles of law books that serve as her pedestal. If we first look at her right profile, her internal anatomy is fully exposed, from the complex muscular system to the foetus in her womb, in the manner of the Renaissance anatomical Eves or Venuses which were used to teach obstetrics. Half of the head is a smiling skull and its skin is in tatters, like that of the famous *écorchés* that pose in the illustrated treatises of Andreas Vesalius.[4]

At the beginning of the early modern era, three-dimensional anatomical representations emerged in Europe.[5] In contrast to ordinary statues, where only the outside of the body is visible, these polychrome works, usually made of wax and sometimes capable of being disassembled, show the inner parts of the body. Under the cover of scientific and didactic instruments, these Venuses or anatomical Eves served as supports for a meditation on Vanity, but above all they provided a pretext for a form of morose delectation which can be assimilated to a truly macabre pornography. One of these anatomical Eves, of Germanic origin and apparently

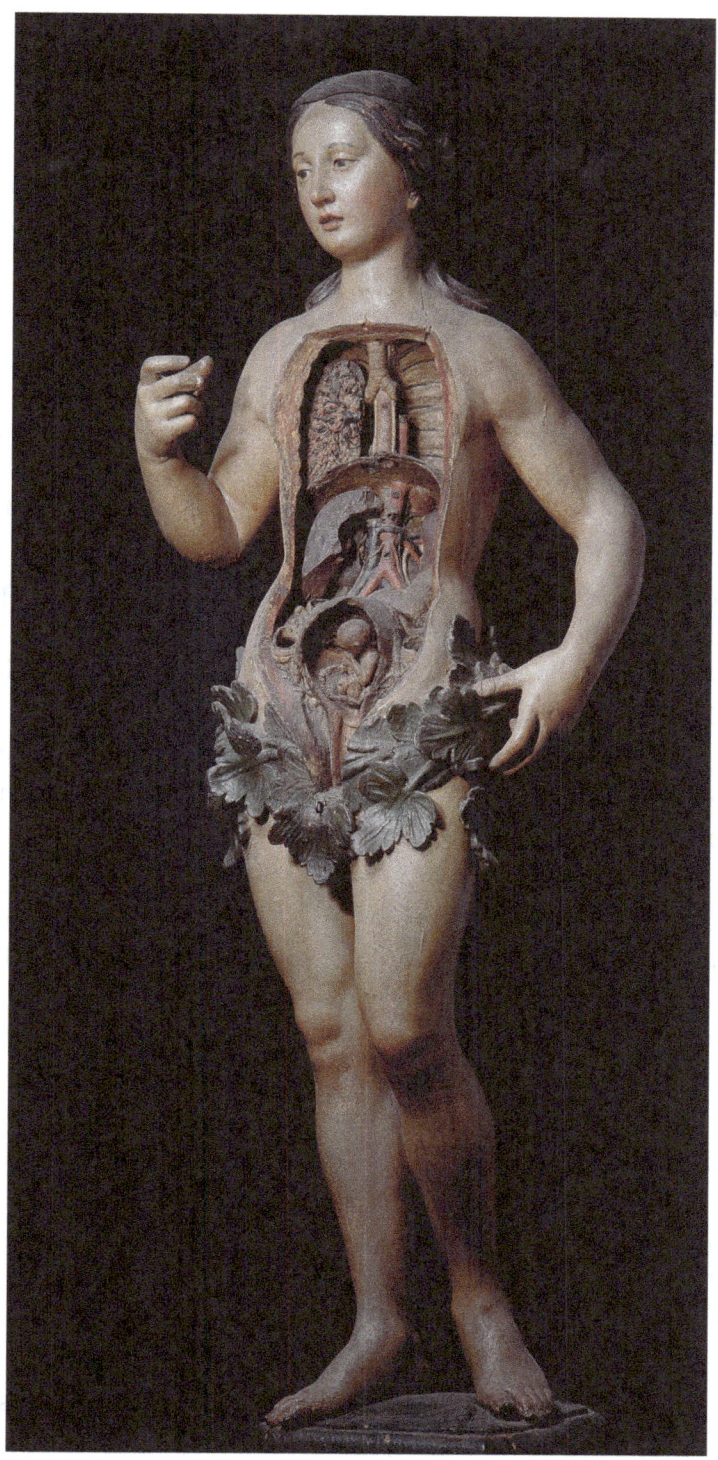

Figure E.3: *Anatomical Venus*, c. 1620. Ghent, private collection. Photograph by Paul Louis

made at the beginning of the seventeenth century, is an elegant, life-size (1.40 metre high), polychrome wooden statue, kept in Ghent in a private collection (Figure E.3). The thorax–abdomen part opens to reveal the arrangement of the internal organs, all removable (lungs, heart, stomach, liver, uterus). The uterus contains a foetus, which is also removable. The skull cap opens like a lid, allowing examination of the brain. This type of sculpture always follows the same pattern: a pregnant woman, whose stomach and sometimes head open. These female figures often had a male counterpart. In the guise of Adam and Eve, the ideal archetype of man and woman was represented. There is, however, a sexual differentiation in anatomical mannequins: men are usually skinned, portrayed as *écorchés* (possibly dismountable), while women always keep their skin intact.

Damien Hirst's sculpture combines both characteristics. The body of his allegory is represented both according to the aesthetic code specific to male anatomical mannequins, in the form of a skinned body, and according to the standard that suits female mannequins, that of leaving the skin smooth and intact. Here he applies to Lady Justice the dreadful observation once attributable to Christian morality: the feminine ideal is nothing but an illusory seduction, for Eve is, in the final analysis, nothing more than a heap of entrails or a bag of organs. Behind the vanity of Lady Justice's beauty lies the true nature of the female body. The gesture of this half-scorched woman, walking on the stacked volumes of legal knowledge, proposes an equivocal vision of Justice, subjected to a genuine medical evisceration.

The symbolic lateralisation that defines *Justitia*'s gestures – with her right hand she grasps her sword, with her left her scales – is here redoubled by one of the recurring features of the macabre art of anatomical statuary. Indeed, one of the effects sought after by ceroplastic sculptors who carved these kinds of figures is to surprise the spectator by first showing a part of the body full of life, a left and very handsome profile, but which, when you then go around the figure, turns into a terrifying spectacle: for example, the first sight is of a beautiful female profile, but a tear runs down her cheek. Turning around, the viewer discovers that half of the head is missing, sawn vertically to show the inner parts of the skull (e.g. André-Pierre Pinson's *La femme à la larme*, 1784). Of his own artwork, Hirst comments, 'without the perfect equilibrium enacted by the scales, the sword becomes a dangerous instrument of power, rather than justice.'[6] By taking up the anatomical tradition of the pregnant woman with an open belly that gives a glimpse of her foetus and combining it with the grimacing figure of a skeleton whose profile is straight out of a macabre dance, Hirst brings anatomy closer to pornography and shows that Justice is forever an evanescent thing. His paradoxical figure of Verity/Justice brings into existence the *coincidentia oppositorum*, a reality of contradictory essence that shows, once again, how the anatomy of Lady Justice's body can arouse fascination and repulsion, terror and morbid pleasure.

In a more satirical tone, Banksy's *Justice* renews in contemporary parlance the figure of *Justitia meretrix*, studied in Chapter 5 (Figure E.4). At its unveiling at Clerkenwell Green, once the site of England's largest and busiest courtroom, the statue spoke, through leaflets distributed that day, of a recent miscarriage of justice. The stunt was timed to coincide with the anniversary of the death of the lorry driver Kevin Callan, wrongly imprisoned in 1991 for the murder of a severely disabled four-year-old girl. Callan was finally able to prove that it was an accidental death, but his conviction was only overturned in 1995. As a 'monument for London', said Banksy, 'dedicated to thugs, to thieves, to bullies, to liars, to the corrupt, the arrogant and the stupid', the artist put in place his monumental sculpture (three and a half tons) without permission, transforming its erection into a collective protest against British legal institutions.[7] It is amusing to note that Banksy, an artist usually turned towards the ephemeral, chose to erect a monument: three tons of bronze, in the purest tradition of Horace's 'exegi monumentum aere perrenius' (I have raised a monument more permanent than bronze, *Ode* 3.30). He wanted it to remain in place, mimicking the commemorative rhetoric of the official monument. The statue takes up the allegorical sculpture of the Old Bailey at the top of the Royal Court of Justice and delivers a scathing pastiche. A blindfolded *Justitia* gives herself to the highest bidder with her garter holding a one-dollar note, thigh-booted in PVC, her skirt raised to the navel, her thong straight out of a sex shop.[8] On the pedestal, the ironical motto 'Trust no-one' makes this statue look like a form of public outlet, where passers-by can multiply irreverent talk or writings. The pedestal of the statue, at head height, invites all manner of satirical inscriptions.

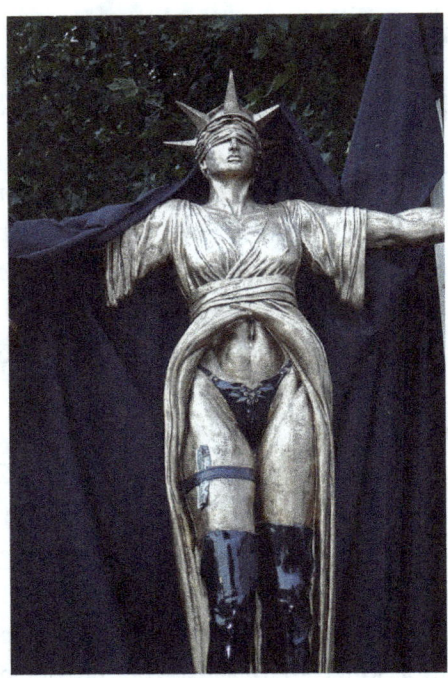

Figure E.4: Banksy, *Justice*. 'A monument for London'. Wikimedia Commons

By installing a monumental statue with a cumbersome presence in a place now open but once devoted to judicial activity, Banksy dislodges a statue originally designed to sit atop a building to literally work on the streets. As a pimp of earthly justice, his *Justitia* is not only discrediting the British system of justice. Banksy takes *Justitia* off her pedestal and puts her back on the street, as a potential medium for political protest and outspoken graffiti. There is a distant echo of Renaissance 'talking statues' such as *Pasquino*, a remnant of an antique marble figure group, which has stood since 1501 on piazza di Parione, a busy crossroads in downtown Rome in an area frequented by notaries and employees of the curia (Figure E.5).[9] Anonymous lampoons mocking the Pope and other powerful figures were posted on the statue, for the amusement of passers-by. Once a 'useless statue', a vile and despised trunk, Pasquino's grotesque form was often completely covered in satirical leaflets or obscene cartoons. Banksy's *Justitia* enables citizens to transform the unattainable crowning figure of the Old Bailey into a type of *pietra del vituperio* (a stone of ignomiy) where the public outcries of today's citizens are able to reinvent her.[10] The clandestine dressing of Lady Justice offers a telling example of how an allegory exhibited in a public place welcomes socially diverse and multiple voices or responses. The revival of Lady Justice through a semi-pornographic figure outside the threshold of a museum or a courthouse questions the ancient concept of decorum. Allegories of Justice may be more attuned to contemporary irony when they abandon their 'decent' and 'noble' appearance. Banksy's sculpture revives the alchemy of Lady Justice, the magical conception of the *simulacrum*, as well as her carnivalesque potential. *Justitia* in the public street continues to interact with a wider audience, arousing new interest from publics who are reluctant to acknowledge the vitality of allegory *per se*.

In his *100 Allegories to Represent the World*, Peter Greenaway pleaded for a new inventory of one hundred allegories, drawn from old or recent models and coinciding with the end of the last millennium.[11] Greenaway photographed non-professional models, academics and students (all inhabitants of Strasbourg) whose naked poses and attributes are copiously detailed. The images thus obtained were digitally processed on a

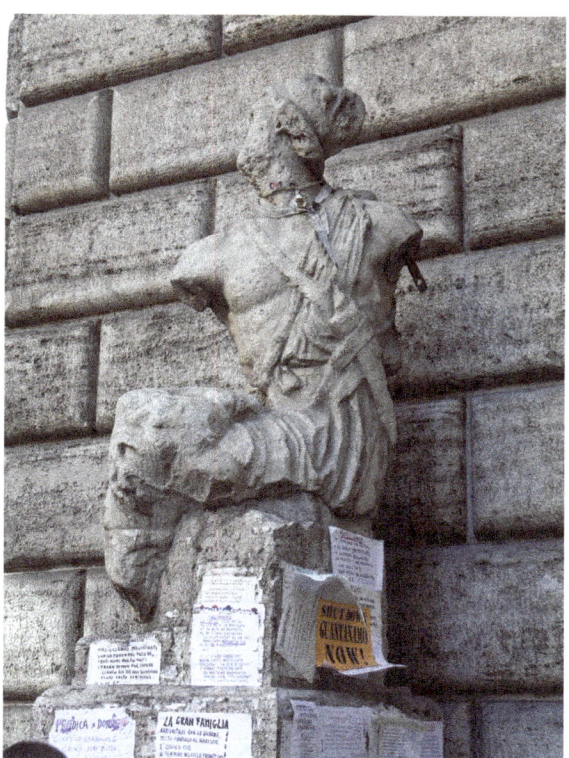

Figure E.5: *Pasquino*, piazza di Parione, Rome. Wikimedia Commons

computer, and Greenaway 'dressed' them by adding elements of his own work or borrowed from a long list of precursors. In order to 'inventory, decollate and regroup knowledge with a view to bringing the world to book', these photographs have graphic inlays that multiply the registers of meaning.[12] The total amount of one hundred items is grouped into twenty-two 'families'. The bilingual texts commenting on the images have been relegated to the end of the volume. The visual therefore takes precedence over the order of the discourse.

Greenaway's new classification is a feat of prestidigitation because although the allegory of Justice is mentioned in the introductory text as one of the surviving ancient forms, it does not appear in the book, at least not as such. Greenaway has dissolved it and redistributed its attributes. *Justitia* was probably too closely linked to the moral virtue or the institution. Perhaps the artist felt that her codified appearance was too obvious a poncifix to be broken down to retain some mystery and novelty. In any case, her scattered attributes haunt the book. Like the children's game of Happy Families, *Justitia* has initially scattered her attributes, redistributing them like cards. In her place, new allegories have appeared, showing that an alchemical operation is possible. In the family of the *Fool* (*Juggler, Simpleton, Pedant, Prig, Pimp* and *Drunk*), a figure reminds us that the role of *Justitia* is close to that of the Pedant – an uncanny reminder of Sebastian Brandt's *Ship of Fools*, discussed in Chapter 2. 'Blinded by text', the Pedant is described as 'a proud man of texts', 'covered in writings, but all the writings are bogus in some way, befitting the excessive pedagogue who traditionally respects sycophantic approval, is in awe of the official seal':[13]

> As a blindfold, he wears across his eyes a letter of admiration written in a script so elegant it knocks the content into incomprehensibility. He has a body-band of text from an empty Roman tomb, a loincloth made from a sophistical scribble of complete nonsense bought from a tramp on a London Underground station and an oriental script in reverse on the shin. [. . .] The tattooed sun of enlightenment on the pedant's left pectoral is aspirational, not illuminating.[14]

In the family of *Domestics*, the *ekphrasis* that accompanies the portrait of 'The Allegorists' offers a sort of instruction manual for the inventiveness of allegorical play, from the need to cultivate a form of *serio ludere* to frequenting good libraries: 'Allegory herself must be allegorized. She is undoubtedly female, impatient of too much official learning, and keen to promote alternative knowledge. [. . .] Their heroine is Frances Yates and their favorite library is the Warburg Institute.'[15]

Instead of the irenic and pacifying figures of *Justitia*, Greenaway prefers to allegorise a new entity, *The Executioner*. The 'allegory of judicial murder' is a couple of male figures, master and apprentice; the trade of executioner is advertised as a family business. We are told that the 'ideal executioner is an automaton using his axe excellently and elegantly with the greatest detachment – though Mary Queen of Scots suffered three blows before death and more than one hangman has struggled with the rope over the life and disfigurement of his victim.'[16] This ironic commentary is a stinging counterpoint to the moralistic discourse usually associated with iconological manuals. This allegory challenges the enjoyment of judicial murder.

Of course in a world where God existed, the question of judicial execution was not posed in the same terms as today, but again the resonances between Greenaway's contemporary image and the discourses of the early modern world are compelling. In early modern punishment rituals, giving death was based on a rite and a very rigorous symbolic form. The executioner only acts within the regulated framework of a binary regime of torture, assisted by a confessor. Infamy must be avoided at all costs. If the condemned man is a Christian, he should, in the last resort, only be concerned with his salvation. Otherwise, the judicial machine, which claims to be legitimate because it is entitled to kill under the double regime of delegation, accomplishes its work inexorably. Killing presupposes the alliance of Justice and force; the punitive logic relies on instruments, co-agents of the rite, that are worth meditating on.

The presence of Apelles' allegory of Calumny on the scabbards of swords used to execute criminals (*Richtschwert*) reminds us that the image of Justice could be represented on the lethal object itself. One of the swords of Justice preserved today in the Paris Musée de l'Armée (Invalides, inv. J. 353) is conceived as a *badelaire de Justice*, the blade evoking the profile of oriental scimitars. A note specifies that its decoration presents, on one side, the allegorical representation of Justice, and on the other, a shield enclosing the figure of a dragon and topped with a Greek cross. This weapon was probably designed for judicial use, as the symbolic figure engraved on the hilt could attest. The conduit at the end of the pommel was intended to hold in place a seal which was broken only when the device of death was to be used. The sword is strictly for judicial use, an instrument of capital punishment, and a tool made available to the executor of high justice, but it is also the vector of a symbolic act of dedication: its sacred function is often recalled by inscriptions on the edge of the iron. We often read, *Fiat justitia ruat cælum* (Let justice be done even if the world must perish). When Lady Justice is depicted, she is engraved from the point of view of the one who will take the sword; the orientation of her body is significant; she is not addressing the wretch whose neck will be cut. It is visible only to the executioner or the executioner's servant. So, if Lady Justice has any efficacy, she serves as a figure of redemption only for those performing the rite of killing. The image of Lady Justice, sanctified by a cross, becomes the mirror of the executioner's heavy burden. When decapitation requires three, four or five attempts, this derisory symbol becomes the distorting mirror of his defeat, of an execution that turns into gratuitous violence, into infamy.

Peter Greenaway's allegory of *The Executioners* (Figure E.6) has seven famous decapitated heads at their feet: 'Charles I, John the Baptist, Goliath, Saint Catherine, Robespierre, Orpheus and Danton'. All the heads are 'partially draped in an execution sack', which is 'part blindfolded to anaesthetize the unfortunate victim, part body-bag to contain the corpse, part shroud to bury it'.[17] The attribute of the execution sack brings together all the polarities of the staging of capital punishment discussed in Chapter 7: the use of the double-bladed sword, the narcotic-salvific function of the *tavoletta* and the ambivalence of the blindfold. The author's commentary on the allegory takes these issues and pushes them to their sharpest edges, to the point of black humour: 'Since the executioner maims judicially as well as kills legally, here are the breasts of Saint Agatha and the genitals of the Philosopher from allegory 12 who could always argue against all forms of capital punishment'.[18]

In Greenaway's thesaurus, Agatha is one of the three allegories of the family. She is 'The Saint' chosen because she has her 'breasts publicly removed by the executioner's surgery'; she allegorises 'female suffering in the name of masculine sadism or prurience legitimated in the name

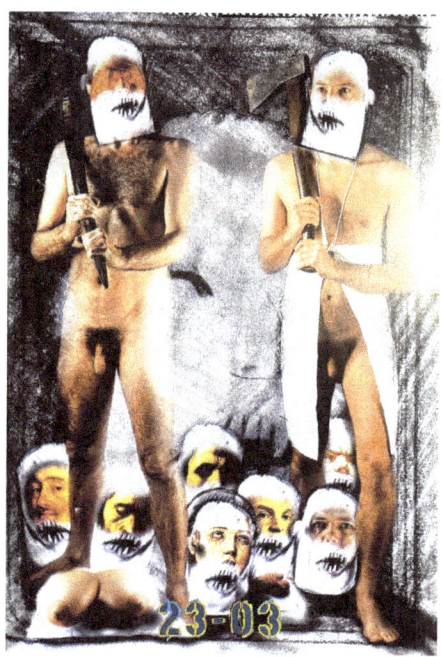

Figure E.6: Peter Greenaway, *The Executioners*, in *100 Allegories to Represent the World/100 Allégories pour représenter le monde* (Paris: Adam Biro, USHS, 1998)

of Christ.'[19] Early modern images of *Justitia* located on executioners' swords were still concerned, in a haunting manner, with one of the primordial questions of humanism: an executioner, however strong he may be, is never safe from the blows of Fate; his justice by the sword, however solemn and regulated, is not immune from the setbacks of Fortune. Greenaway's bold invention reflects another attitude, a gory manifestation of nightmarish killings, peppered with a new history of 'the art of beheading well'.

These contemporary reiterations of *Justitia* demonstrate the survival of the allegorical genre, its ability to serve militant causes and its openness to contemporary forms of creativity. The vitality of the allegorical image of *Justitia* is perhaps a sign of a wider evolution, which does not necessarily respond to the conclusions of Craig Owens's influential work, *The Allegorical Impulse* (1984).[20] Drawing heavily on a famous text by Walter Benjamin, Owens celebrates the return of allegory in force.[21] He argues convincingly that allegory is as much an impulse as a technique, a perception as much as a process; but he also highlights that every allegory is resolutely turned towards the past and that its humour of predilection is melancholy.[22] Benjamin eagerly emphasised the melancholic gaze of the allegorist (this was also Erwin Panofsky's point in his reading of Dürer's *Melencolia*), and he is followed on this point by Owens, who describes the *facies hippocratica* of history as being conveyed in the mode of allegory.[23] The very diversity of the faces of Lady Justice showed that her image did more than arouse a tone of *gravitas*. A second point concerns the relationship between allegory and writing, which Owens has termed a defining component of visual allegory:

> What [the reciprocity that allegory establishes between the visual and the verbal] reveals is the essentially pictographic nature of the allegorical work. In the allegory, the image is a hieroglyph, the allegory is a rebus, a writing composed of concrete images.[24]

My study leads to an entirely different conclusion. The allegory cannot be reduced to scriptural form if we approach it, as this study has done, from the point of view of the phenomenology of gestures. If allegory touches us, it is first and foremost because it invents a pictorial compositional process peculiar to the image as such. For the judges who comment on it in their courthouse precincts, the painted image of *Justitia* is a *visual apparatus*, an artefact placed above or behind them, drawing some of its numinous force from the *genius loci*. Rather than conceiving of the allegory as a palimpsest, a device for rewriting, elaborated from a primary textual canvas towards its figurative senses, we have to give back to allegory all the performative force of its gestures, faces and bodily expressions. Lady Justice's epiphanies question the seemingly obvious assumption that *Justitia* derives from *Jus*. Justice is first and foremost an image, a major constituent of the birth of judgment in Europe, just as images of the Annunciation or the Crucifixion have primarily evolved in relation to other images. This argument has been stressed methodologically in the works of Aby Warburg, Ernst Cassirer and Edgar Wind, through the study of Renaissance art. In their attempts to describe how symbolic images convey meaning, they aimed at removing the privilege of discourse as a primary way to assess visuality. In a paradoxical rephrasing of the *Digest* (1.1.1), this book is an attempt to argue that it is in fact *Jus* (as a text ossified into a code of law) that derives from *Justitia* (the embodiment of Justice, its living principle). Originally, therefore, the interest in allegory was not verbal but optical.

Why has the allegory of Justice survived so well through the centuries?[25] The first response, physiological and anthropological, was mentioned in Chapter 3. It is because her body is animated by two founding gestures, identified by the paleoanthropologist John Russell Napier, namely power grip and precision handling, through which she performs a gestural grammar that defines our biological humanity in all its anthropological depth. There is therefore a strong physiological component to her allegorical schemata which explains her survival by virtue of the fact that these two gestures are the primordial signs of all human prehension.

The second answer relates to the specificity of the allegorical medium. It lies in her relationship with her most frequent attributes, sword and balance. These attributes are not arbitrary objects but instruments that she manipulates with a degree of plausibility. This is an aspect that Gotthold Ephraim Lessing saw clearly:

> among the attributes that artists use to distinguish their abstractions, there is a kind that is more susceptible and more worthy of being used by the poet. I am referring to those which, strictly speaking, have nothing allegorical about them, but which must be considered as instruments which the beings to whom they are attributed would or could use if they acted like real people. The bit in the hand of *Moderation*, the column on which *Firmness* rests, are entirely allegorical and are therefore of no use to the poet. The balance in the hand of Justice is already less so, because the fair use of the balance is indeed a part of Justice.[26]

Moderation does not have the same kind of relationship with the 'bit' as Justice has with her scales. The bit is valid only for what it means, argues Lessing, because the allegorical bit is not real but merely a material translation of the idea of temperance. On the contrary, *Justitia*'s scales are a real instrument, which refers to the field of perception of an activity that can be transposed to real life. Johannes Vermeer's painting *Woman Holding a Balance* (1664) maintains precisely this ambiguity (Figure E.7). Her balance is indeed a weighing instrument used to weigh real-life objects, such as the gold and pearl necklaces displayed on the table, even if the pans of the scales are empty. It is the insertion of a picture of Christ in Majesty with raised arms within a nimbus on the Day of the Last Judgement which hangs on the wall above her, in the semi-darkness, that illuminates the whole picture in an allegorical sense.[27]

The third answer concerns the relationship between allegory and the reality of the social world. Unlike her siblings (Temperance, Prudence, etc.), *Justitia* is both a virtue and the image of an institution.[28] As an earthly institution that can be parodied, Justice lends herself more to allegorical games that give pride of place to satire. Justice even takes up its own caricature so as to become a pedagogical instrument.[29] The allegorical image of Justice carries within herself a propensity for inversion, and it is this cathartic effect of judicial comedy that is one of the guarantees of her longevity. The desire for a system of justice which is close to the social body has never dissipated.

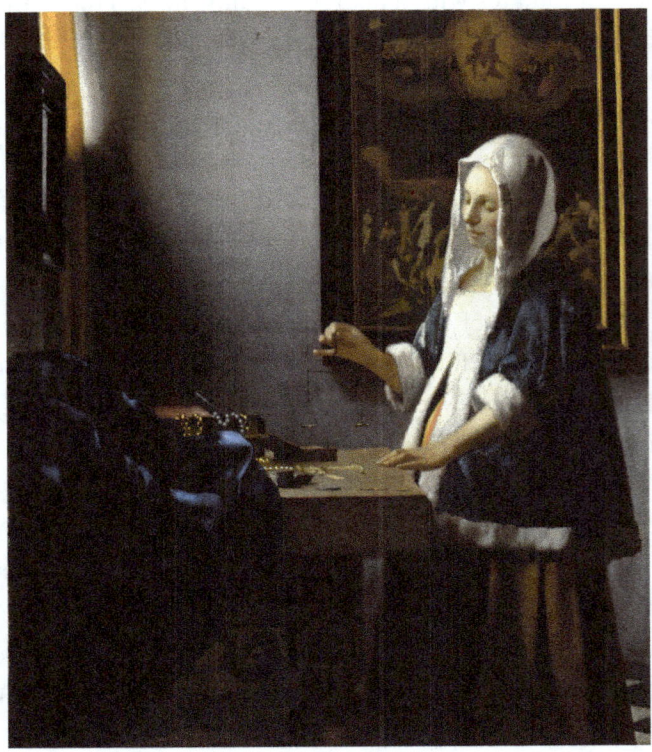

Figure E.7: Johannes Vermeer, *Woman Holding a Balance*, oil panel, c. 1662–5. Courtesy National Gallery of Art, Washington DC

At a time when a growing abstraction pervades our contemporary courthouses,[30] giving body to Justice by reviving the gestures of *Justitia* is perhaps more than a purely artistic choice. It is a bulwark against the ambient formalism that dismisses the affects and jolts of the body. If the contemporary period is often perceived as anti-allegorical, the present study shows that allegory still has work to do, critical and crucial functions to perform. Looking back to the early modern period as an era contributing to the formation of a reflection on symbolic practices, today's crisis of representation may be addressed through the revival of *Justitia*'s fragility. The allegorical processes surveyed in this book attempt to show the value of gestures as a source for art historical research as well as for the cultural history of Law. Because of their intrinsic polysemy, allegories of Justice have remained profoundly discontinuous and heterogeneous, somehow creating a utopian or dystopian interval beyond strict historical periodisation. This methodological choice questions modes of judicial portrayal in order to reveal the fundamental features of affective Justice. The contemporary salience of allegory is fully coeval with our urgent need to revive the fruitful dialogue between art and law throughout public space.

Notes

1. Charles Baudelaire, *Curiosités esthétiques* (Paris: Michel Lévy frère, 1868), p. 290.
2. Letter from Pierre-Paul Prud'hon to Nicolas-Thérèse-Benoît Frochot, 3 May 1805, *Gazette des Beaux-Arts* 6 (1860), p. 311.
3. Walter Benjamin, *The Origin of German Tragic Drama*, trans. John Osborne (1977; London: Verso, 2003), pp. 160–5.
4. Andreas Vesalius, *De Humani Corporis Fabrica* (Basel: Joannes Oporin, 1543).
5. Alexandre Vanautgaerden (ed.), *Anatomie des Vanités/Anatomie der Ijdelheden* (Turnhout: Brepols, 2008), esp. Jean-Marc Mandosio, 'De la femme démontable à l'art cadavérique', pp. 19–84; Georges Didi-Huberman, *Ouvrir Vénus: nudité, rêve, cruauté* (Paris: Gallimard, 1999); Rafael Mandressi, *Le regard de l'anatomiste: dissections et invention du corps en Occident* (Paris: Seuil, 2003).
6. Damien Hirst, qtd in 'Damien Hirst's Verity, a Statute of a Naked Pregnant Woman, Erected in Devon', *Huffington Post*, 17 October 2012, <https://www.huffingtonpost.co.uk/2012/10/17/damien-hirst-pregnant-woman-erected_n_1972691.html>.

7. Ian Youngs, 'Guerrilla Artist in Statue Stunt', *BBC News Online*, 4 August 2004, <http://news.bbc.co.uk/1/hi/entertainment/3537136.stm>.

8. The structure was cast in gilt bronze and stands 20 feet high. The statue did not stay in place for long because the city council decided to keep it out of public view on the pretext that it could make the toilets under the square unsafe.

9. See Maddalena Spagnolo, *Pasquino in piazza. Una statua a Roma tra arte e vituperio* (Rome: Campisano, 1999).

10. See A. Gloria, *La pietra del vituperio del salone di Padova: Lettera* (Padua: Tipografia Bianchi, 1851).

11. Peter Greenaway, *100 Allegories to Represent the World/100 Allégories pour représenter le monde* (Paris: Adam Biro, USHS, 1998). A similar inspiration can be found in the recent work of the French artist Dany Leriche, proposing the creation of new allegories on the model of Cesare Ripa's *Iconologia* (1593).

12. Greenaway, *100 Allegories*, p. 7.

13. Ibid., p. 225.

14. Ibid., p. 225.

15. Ibid., p. 229.

16. Ibid., p. 233.

17. Ibid., p. 233.

18. Ibid., p. 233.

19. Ibid., p. 271.

20. Craig Owens, 'The Allegorical Impulse: Toward a Theory of the Postmodernism', in Brian Wallis (ed.), *Art After Modernism: Rethinking Representation* (New York: New Museum of Contemporary Art in association with David R. Godine, 1984), pp. 203–53; originally published in *October* 12 (1980), pp. 67–86, and 13 (1980), pp. 59–80.

21. Walter Benjamin, *The Origin of German Tragic Drama* (London: New Left Books, 1977).

22. See Tony Jappy, 'Fond et forme dans l'image allégorique', *Protée* 33, no. 1 (2005), pp. 9–23.

23. Benjamin, *Origin*, pp. 179–80: 'In the allegory, it is the *facies hippocratica* of history that is offered to the viewer's gaze like a petrified primitive landscape. History, in all its untimely, painful, imperfect aspects, is inscribed in the face – no: in a skull. And as true as there is in it no "symbolic" freedom of expression, no classical harmony of form, no humanity, the enigma that is expressed in this figure, the most subject to the empire of nature, is not simply the nature of human existence, but the historicity of individual biography. This is the core of the allegorical vision of the Baroque exhibition of history as the history of the sufferings of the world.'

24. Owens, 'The Allegorical Impulse', pp. 208–9.

25. For a penetrating and well-informed account of this question, see Bernard Vouilloux (ed.), 'Déclins de l'allégorie?', *Modernités*, special issue, 22 (2006), esp. Bernard Vouilloux, 'Introduction. Le retour de l'allégorie', pp. 7–16, and Bernard Vouilloux, 'Entre textes et images. Le tournant moderne de l'allégorie', pp. 17–84.

26. Gotthold Ephraim Lessing, *Laocoön: An Essay upon the Limits of Painting and Poetry*, trans. Ellen Frothingham (1766; Boston: Roberts Brothers, 1887), pp. 69–70.

27. Ivan Gaskell, 'Vermeer, Judgment and Truth', *The Burlington Magazine* 126, no. 978 (1984), pp. 557–61. Gaskell's demonstration, arguing that the woman depicted is a figure of Truth, is intriguing, but it does not restore the ambiguity we believe Vermeer intended. Allegory should not be read as an unequivocal message, and even if the notion of interpretative plurality sometimes gets bad press, it seems futile to decree that an allegorical painting must be read according to a strict iconological code, which, once deciphered, excludes any other rival interpretation.

28. The virtue of Charity can also be the allegorical vector of an institution, and certain allegories of Charity go in this direction.

29. Robert Jacob, *Images de la justice. Essai sur l'iconographie judiciaire du Moyen Âge à l'âge classique* (Paris: Le Léopard d'Or, 1996), pp. 160–4.

30. Laurent de Sutter, *Post-Tribunal. Renzo Piano Building Workshop et l'île de la cité judiciaire* (Paris: Éditions B2, 2018); Christian-Nils Robert, 'Le Tribunal de Paris: piano, piano face à la symbolique judiciaire', *L'Irascible, Revue de l'Institut Rhône-Alpin de Sciences Criminelles* 9 (2022), pp. 155–79.

Bibliography

Works written before 1800

Alciato, Andrea, *Emblemata cum commentariis* (Padua: Tozzi, 1621).

Alciato, Andrea, *Emblematum liber* (Augsburg: Steyner, 1531).

Alciato, Andrea, *Parerga* (Lyon: Jacobus Giuncta, 1539).

Alciato, Andrea, *Parergon iuris libri tres* (Lyon: Simon Vincent & Jean Barbou, 1538).

Argelati, Filippo and Giuseppe Antonio Sassi, *Bibliotheca scriptorum mediolanensium . . .*, vol. 1 (Milan: in aedibus Palatinus, 1745).

Aubéry, Jacques, *Histoire de l'exécution de Cabrières et de Mérindol et d'autres lieux de Provence* (Paris: Cramoisy, 1645; reprinted with notes by Gabriel Audisio, Paris: Les éditions de Paris, 1995).

Augustine, *Expositions of the Psalms, Volume 4: Psalms 73–98*, trans. Maria Boulding (Hyde Park, NY: New City, 2002).

Ayrault, Pierre, *L'ordre, formalité et instruction judiciaire, dont les anciens Grecs et Romains ont usé ès accusations publiques, conféré au style et usage de notre France* (1576; Paris: Laurent Sonnius, 1615).

Bacon, Francis, *The Advancement of Learning* (London: Henrie Tomes, 1605).

Boethius, *De Trinitate*, in *Theological Tractates and the Consolation of Philosophy*, trans. H. F. Stewart, E. K. Rand and S. J. Tester (Cambridge, MA: Harvard University Press, 1918).

Bonifacio, Giovanni, *L'arte de' cenni: con la quale formandosi favela visibile, si tratta della muta eloquenza, che non e' altro che un facondo silentio [. . .]* (Vicenza: Francesco Grossi, 1616).

Buchler, Johann, *Institutio poetica ex R. P. Jacobi Pontani e S. J. libris concinnata* (n.p.: n.d.).

Budé, Guillaume, *Annotationes in Pandectas* (Lyon: Gryphe, 1551).

Bulwer, John, *Chirologia, or The Natural Language of the Hand* (London: Thomas Harper, 1644).

Case, John, *Sphæra Civitatis; Hoc est; Reipublicæ recte ac pie secundum leges administrandæ ratio* (Oxford: Josephus Barnesius, 1588).

Chalvet, Hyacinthe de, *Theologus Ecclesiastes. De quatuor virtutibus cardinalibus*, vol. 8 (Cadomi: Jean le Jeune, 1676).

Chasseneuz, Barthélemy de, *Catalogus Gloriæ Mundi* (Geneva: Pierre Chouet, 1649).

Coke, Sir Edward, *A book of Entries containing perfect and approved presidents of Courts, Declarations . . . and all other matters and proceedings (in effect) concerning the pratick part of the laws of England*, 2nd edn (1610; London: Streeter, 1671).

Combe, Thomas, *The theater of fine devices containing an hundred morall emblems. First penned in French by Guillaume de la Perriere* (London: Richard Field, 1614).

Comenius, John Amos, *Orbis sensualium pictus* (Nuremberg: Michael Endter, 1658).

Comes, Natalis, *Mythologiæ, sive explicationis fabularum libri decem* (Padua: Tozzi, 1616).

Costentin, Eloy, Manuscript of the Poems by 'Eloy du Mont dit Costentin' (1530–1), Bibliothèque nationale de France, manuscrits français 2237.

Court, Benoît Le Court [Benedictus Curtius], *Arresta Amorum* (Lyon: Sébastien Gryphe, 1533).

Court, Benoît Le Court [Benedictus Curtius], *Arresta Amorum* (1533; Lyon: Sébastien Gryphe, 1538).

Coustau, Pierre, *Pegma cum narrationibus philosophicis* (Lyon: Macé Bonhomme, 1555).

Damhouder, Joos [Josse] de, *Praxis rerum criminalium* (Venice: Ioannis Antonium Bertanum, 1572).

Damhouder, Joos [Josse] de, *Opera omnia in quibus Praxis rerum criminalium [. . .] pertractantur* (Antwerp: Petrus Bellerus, 1646).

de Coras, Jean, *Petit discours des parties et office d'un bon et entier Juge* (Lyon: Barthélemy Vincent, 1596).

de La Roche, Flavin Bernard, *Treize livres des parlements de France [. . .]* (Bordeaux: Simon Millanges, 1617).

de Nancel, Nicolas, *Eisodus triomphalis/Triomphes et magnificiences faictes à l'entrée de Monseigneur filz de France et frere unicques du Doyen la ville de Tours, le vingthuictième jour d'aoult 1576*, Bibliothèque nationale de France, Ms. Fr. 848.

de Nesmond, André, 'Neufiesme Remonstrance faicte en Parlement à l'ouverture de la Sainct Martin, l'an 1613: le bandeau ou le diadème de Justice', in *Remonstrances, ouvertures de palais et arrets prononcés en robe rouge* (Poitiers: Antoine Mesnier, 1617), pp. 403–38, <http://gallica.bnf.fr/ark:/12148/bpt6k94691k>.

de Petity, Jean-Raymond, *Le Manuel des artistes et des amateurs, ou Dictionnaire historique et mythologique des emblèmes, allégories, énigmes, devises, attributs et symboles* (Paris: J. P. Costard, 1770).

de Scudéry, Georges, *Discours politiques des Rois, dédiez à Monseigneur le Cardinal Mazarin* (Paris: Augustin Courbé, 1647).

d'Expilly, Claude, *Les Poemes de Messire Claude Expilly, Conseiller du Roy an son Conseil d'Etat & Prezidant au Parlemant de Grenoble* (Grenoble: Pierre Verdier, 1624).

Diderot, Denis, *Salons*, ed. J. Seznec and J. Adhémar (Oxford: Clarendon, 1963).

d'Orléans, Pierre Joseph, *Sermons et instruction chrétienne sur diverses matières* (Paris: Jean Anisson, 1697).

Dubos, Jean-Baptiste, *Réflexions critiques sur la poésie et la peinture* (1719; Utrecht: Étienne Neaulme, 1732).

Duchesne, Léger [Leodegarius a Quercu], *Farrago poematum ex optimis quibusque et antiquioribus et ætatis nostræ poetis selecta*, vol. 2 (Paris: Aegidium Gorbinum, 1560).

d'Urfé, Honoré, *Triomphante Entrée de très illustre dame Mme Magdeleine de la Rochefoucauld [. . .] Faicte en la ville et université de Tournon le dimanche vingt-quatrième du mois d'Avril 1583* (Lyon: Jean Pillehotte, 1583; reprinted as vol. 4 of *Images et témoins de l'âge classique*, ed. Maxime Gaume, Saint-Étienne: Presses de l'Université de Saint-Étienne, 1976).

du Vair, Guillaume, *Les Œuvres du Seigneur Guillaume du Vair* (1617; Geneva: Slatkine, 1970).

Erasmus, *Collected Works of Erasmus*, vol. 66, *Spiritualia: The Handbook of the Christian Soldier*, trans. and annot. Charles Fantazzi (Toronto: University of Toronto Press, 1988).

Erasmus, *Collected Works of Erasmus*, vol. 35, *Adages III iv 1 to IV ii 100*, trans. and annot. D. L. Drysdall, ed. John N. Grant (Toronto: University of Toronto Press, 2005).

Erasmus, *De Copia Verborum ac Rerum*, 1534 edn, in *Collected Works of Erasmus*, vol. 24, *Literary and Educational Writings; 2*, ed. Craig R. Thompson (Toronto: University of Toronto Press, 1978).

Erasmus, *Praise of Folly* (*Encomium Moriæ*) (Basel: Johann Froben, 1515).

Favre, Antoine [Antonius Faber], *Opera omnia* (Lyon: Borde, Arnaud et Rigaud, 1658–61).

Fernel, Jean, *The* Physiologia *of Jean Fernel (1567)*, trans. and annot. J. M. Forrester (Philadelphia, PA: American Philosophical Society, 2003).

Fiera, Battista, *De Justicia Pingenda Fieræ Mantuani Dialogus. Interloquutores Mantynias Momus*, in *Hymni Divini. Sylve Melanisius* (Mantua: Francesco Bruschi, 1515; reprinted as *De iusticia pingenda: On the Painting of Justice: A Dialogue between Mantegna and Momus*, trans., intro. and notes James Wardrop, London: Lion and Unicorn Press, 1957).

Florio, John, *Queen Anna's New World of Words* (1611; Menston: Scolar Press, 1968).

Giraldi, Lilio Gregorio, *De Deis gentium varia et multiplex historia* (Basel: Oporin, 1548).

Gouthière, Jacques, *Tiresias, seu de Cæcitatis & Sapientiæ cognatione* (Paris: Heirs of Nicolas Buon, 1618).

Gruterus, Janus (ed.), *Delitiæ poetarum Germanorum huius superiorisque ævi*, 6 vols (Frankfurt: Nicolaus Hoffmannus, 1612).

Herrenschmid, Jacob, *Osculologia Theologo-Philologica sive De variis variorum Osculis Patriarchum, Prophetarum Impp. Regum, Episcoporum Academicorum, Christianorum, Gentilium, Exoticorum, etc. Commentariolus* (Wittenberg: Heirs of Clément Berget, 1630).

John of Garland, *Liber synonymorum* (1496; Antwerp: T. Martinus, 1507).

Junius, Hadrianus, *Emblemata* (Antwerp: Christophe Plantin, 1565).

Kempius, Martinus, *Opus polyhistoricum dissertationibus XXV de osculis, subnexisque de Judæ ingenio, vita et fine scaris epiphyllidibus* (Frankfurt: M. and A. Hallerword, 1680).

Krantz, Albrecht, *Wandalia in qua de Wandalorum populis, et eorum patrio solo, ac in Italiam, Galliam, Hispanias, Aphricam, et Dalmatiam, migratione* (Coloniæ: Agrippinæ, 1519).

Kretzschmar, Christoph, *De mutuo justitiæ pacisque osculo, ex Psalmo 85,11* (Dresden: J. G. Harpeter, 1755).

Lacombe de Prezel, Honoré, *Dictionnaire iconologique ou introduction à la connoissance des peintures, sculptures, médailles, estampes, pierres gravées, emblèmes, devises [. . .]* (Paris: Hardouin, 1779).

La Justice en son throsne. A tres chrestien Henri IIII Roy de France (Rouen: Jean Petit, 1609).

La Perrière, Guillaume de, *Le Theatre des bons engins* (Paris: Denis Janot, 1544).

Latini, Brunetto, *Li Livres dou Tresor* (1260–7; Paris: Polycarpe Chabaille, Imprimerie Nationale, 1853).

Le Maistre de Sacy, Isaac-Louis, *Les Pseaumes de David, traduits en français avec une explication tirée des Saints Pères et des Auteurs Ecclésiastiques* (Brussels: Henry Fricx, 1710).

Le Rouillé, Guillaume, *De Justitia et injustitia* (Lyon: Jean David, 1529).

Lessing, Gotthold Ephraim, *Laocoön: An Essay upon the Limits of Painting and Poetry*, trans. Ellen Frothingham (1766; Boston: Roberts Brothers, 1887).

Lessing, Gotthold Ephraim, *Laocoön: An Essay on the Limits of Painting and Poetry*, ed. J. M. Bernstein (1766; Cambridge: Cambridge University Press, 2002).

Le Vieux Jérôme, histoire véritable dédiée à M. le marquis d'Armentières, lieutenant général des armées du Roi (Cambrai: Hurez, 1763).

Luther, Martin, *Werke* (Weimar: Böhlau, 1883–1993), WA 1, 357, 6–10; *Luther's Works* (Philadelphia: Fortress; St Louis: Concordia, 1986).

Maran, Guillaume, *Declaration et Manifeste de Maistre Guillaume Maran, Docteur Regent & Doyen des facultez des droicts en l'Université de Tolose, du cinquiesme May 1621* (Toulouse: Veuve de I. Colomiez, 1621).

Marostica, Vincenzo, *Venetia Trionfante* (Venice: Domenica Farri, 1572).

Martianus, Capella, *De Nuptiis Philologiae et Mercurii*, vol. 4 (Leipzig: Adolfus Dick, 1925).

Master Eckhart, *Sermons, traités, poèmes. Les Écrits Allemands*, trans. J. Ancelet-Hustache (Paris: Seuil, 2015).

Meisner, Daniel, *Sciographia Cosmica. Das ist newes Emblematisches Büchlein: darinen in acht Centuriis die Vornembsten Stätt Vestung, Schlosser etc.* (Nuremberg: Paul Fürst, 1638).

Mesarites, Nikolaos, *Description of the Church of the Holy Apostles at Constantinople*, ed. and trans. Glanville Downey (Philadelphia, PA: American Philosophical Society, 1957).

Montaigne, Michel de, 'De l'expérience', in *Essais*, ed. André Tournon, 3 vols (Paris: Imprimerie Nationale, 1998), vol. 3, ch. 13.

Montaigne, Michel de, *Essays of Montaigne*, trans. Charles Cotton (London: Reeves and Turner, 1877).

Montaigne, Michel de, *Journal de voyage en Italie*, ed. M. Rat (Paris: Garnier, 1955).

Nathen, Stephanus, alias Spormächer, *Justitia Vulnerata, Christiane, Iuridice, Politice curate* (Cologne: Iost Kalcoven, 1646).

Oldekop, Justus, *Cautelæ criminales consiliariis, maleficiorum judicibus, advocatis, inquisitoribus et actuariis* (Hildesheim: Heirs of P. Castens, printed by J. Gösselius, 1639).

Oræus, Heinrich, *Aeroplastes Theosophicus, sive Eikones Mysticæ* (Frankfurt: Johann Theodor de Bry, 1620; 2nd edn, 1644).

Oresme, Nicole, French translation of Aristotle's *Nicomachean Ethics*, 1370–5, Bibliothèque Royale de Belgique, Ms. 9505, fol. 89r.

Peacham, Henry, *Three books of emblems*, manuscript written and illustrated by him, prefaced by a letter from Henry Peacham addressed to Henry Frederick, prince of Wales, and based on the *Basilikon Doron* (Royal Gift), James I's book of advice to his son and heir, London, c. 1610, British Library, Royal 12 A LXVI.

Picinelli, Filippo, *Mundus symbolicus, in emblematum universitates formatus, explicatus* (Cologne: Thomas and Heinrich Theodor, 1715).

Pierozzi, Antonino, *Summa sacræ theologiæ, juris pontifices, et cæsare* (Venice: apud Juntas, 1582).

Prangen, Johann Daniel, *Oscula sacra et profana* (Minda: Pilerian, 1688).

Pseudo-Sergius, *Explanationes in artes Donati, Grammatici Latini, ex recensione Henrici Keilii GL*, vol. 4 (Leipzig, 1855–80).

Quellinus, Hubertus, *Architecture, peinture et sculpture de la maison de ville d'Amsterdam, représentée en 109 figures en taille-douce*, vol. 1 (Amsterdam: Gérard Valk, 1719).

Rabelais, François, *Œuvres de François Rabelais*, vol. 4, *Tiers Livre*, ed. Abel Lefranc (Paris: Champion, 1931).

Reusner, Nicolas, *De officiis Magistratus et Subditorum in Republica tam civili quam literaria oratio* (Lavingen: Leonard Reinmichel, 1581).

Reusner, Nicolas, *Elementorum Artis Rhetoricæ libri duo* (Lavingen: Emanuele Salcero, 1571).

Ripa, Cesare, *Iconologia* (Padua: Tozzi, 1611).

Ripa, Cesare, *Iconologia* (Siena: Heirs of Matteo Florini, 1613).

Robinet, Jean-Baptiste, *Dictionnaire universel des sciences morale, économique, politique et diplomatique ou Bibliothèque de l'homme d'état et du citoyen* (London: Libraires associés, 1777).

Scaccia, Sigismondo, *Tractatus de sententia et re iudicata* (Venice: Jacob Scalea, 1629).

Scheifler, Johann Eberhard, *Vita Christi Concionatoria tribus libris comprehensa, primus liber* (Dillingen: Heirs of Joannis Caspari Bencard, 1697).

Schnobel, Joachim, *De pace Germaniae dissertationes quinque* (Rostock: Johannes Haller, 1641).

Senault, Jean-François, *Oraison funèbre de Henriette-Marie de France, reine de la Grande-Bretagne* (Paris: P. Le Petit, 1670).

Spenser, Edmund, *The Faerie Queene: Book Five*, ed. Abraham Stoll (Indianapolis: Hackett, 2006).

Sully, Henry, *Règle artificielle du temps par Henry Sully, nouvelle édition corrigée et augmentée par M. Julien Leroy* (Paris: Grégoire Dupuis, 1737).

Thiéry, Luc-Vincent, *Guide des amateurs et des étrangers voyageurs à Paris ou Description raisonnée de cette Ville [. . .]* (Paris: Hardouin et Gattey, 1787).

Tiraqueau, André, *Semestria in Genialium Dierum Alexandri ab Alexandro Jurisperiti Neapolitano Libri VI* (Lyon: Guillaume Rouillé, 1586).

Toscanus, Ioannes Matthaeus (ed.), *Carmina illustrium poetarum Italorum* (Paris: Gorbinus, 1576).

Valeriano, Pierio, *Hieroglyphica sive De Sacris ægyptiorum aliarumque gentium literis commentarii* (Basel: Isengrin, 1556).

Valeriano, Pierio, *Hieroglyphica sive De Sacris ægyptiorum aliarumque gentium literis commentarii* (1556; Siena, 1616).

Valla, Lorenzo, 'In Bartolemaeum Facium Ligurem invectivæ seu recriminationes', vol. 4 of *Opera* (Basel: Opera, 1540).

Vesalius, Andreas, *De Humani Corporis Fabrica* (Basel: Joannes Oporin, 1543).

Voiture, Vincent, *Hymnus Virginis seu Astrææ. Ad illustrissimum Virum Dominum De Verdun, aequissimum æquissimum Parisiensis Senatus Principem* (Paris: Julliot, 1612).

von Nettesheim, Heinrich Cornelius Agrippa, *Declamatio de nobilitate et præcellentia fœminæ sexus* (On the Nobility and Excellence of the Feminine Sex), trans. Edward Fleetwood (London: Robert Ibbitson, 1652).

Worm, Olav, *Danicorum Monumentum libri sex* (Copenhagen: Joachim Molt-ken, 1643).

Zanetti, Ginevra (ed.), [Irnerius], *Questiones de juris subtilitatibus* (Florence: La Nuova Italia, 1958).

Zetter, Jacob de, *Kosmographia Iconica Moralis* (Frankfurt: Johan Theodor de Bry and Hendrick Laurensz, 1614).

Works written after 1800

Agamben, Giorgio, *Homo Sacer: Sovereign Power and Bare Life*, trans. Daniel Heller-Roazen (Stanford, CT: Stanford University Press, 1998).

Agamben, Giorgio, *Means Without End: Notes on Politics*, trans. Binetti Vin-cenzo and Cesare Casarino (Minneapolis: University of Minnesota Press, 2000).

Alpers, Svetlana, '*Ekphrasis* and Aesthetic Attitudes in Vasari's *Lives*', *Journal of the Warburg and the Courtauld Institutes* 23, no. 3/4 (1960), pp. 190–215.

Andersson, Christiane, 'Harlots and Camp Followers. Swiss Renaissance Draw-ings of Young Women circa 1520', in E. S. Cohen and M. Reeves (eds), *The Youth of Early Modern Women* (Amsterdam: Amsterdam University Press, 2012), pp. 117–34.

Audisio, Gabriel, 'L'affaire Cabrières et Mérindol: de la valeur des témoign-ages (1545–1551)', in Amis de la Méjane (ed.), *Le Parlement de Provence (1501–1790)* (Aix-en-Provence: Presses Universitaires de Provence, 2002), pp. 41–53.

Barasch, Moshe, *Blindness: The History of a Mental Image in Western Thought* (New York: Routledge, 2001).

Barzman, Karen-edis, *The Limits of Identity: Early Modern Venice, Dalmatia, and the Representation of Difference* (Leiden: Brill, 2017).

Baskins, Cristelle L. and Lisa Rosenthal (eds), *Early Modern Visual Allegory: Embodying Meaning* (Aldershot: Ashgate, 2008).

Baudelaire, Charles, *Curiosités esthétiques* (Paris: Michel Lévy frère, 1868).

Baxandall, Michael, *The Limewood Sculptors of Renaissance Germany* (New Haven, CT: Yale University Press, 1980).

Baxandall, Michael, *Giotto and the Orators: Humanist Observers of Painting in Italy and the Discovery of Pictorial Composition 1350–1450* (Oxford: Clarendon, 1971).

Baxandall, Michael, *Painting and Experience in Fifteenth Century Italy: A Primer in the Social History of Pictorial Style*, 2nd edn (Oxford: Oxford University Press, 1988).

Begam, Richard, 'Beckett's Kinetic Aesthetics', *Journal of Beckett Studies*, special issue, 'Transnational Beckett', 16, nos 1 and 2 (2006–7), pp. 46–63.

Behrmann, Carolin, 'Metrics of Justice. A Sundial's Nomological Figuration', *Nuncius* 30 (2015), pp. 161–94.

Belli, Gianluca, 'Un monumento per Cosimo I de' Medici. La Colonna della Giustizia a Firenze', *Annali du architettura. Rivista del Centro internazionale du Studi di Architettura Andrea Palladio di Vicenza* 16 (2004), pp. 57–78.

Belting, Hans, 'Das Bild als Text. Wandmalerei und Literatur im Zeitalter Dantes', in H. Belting and D. Blume (eds), *Malerei und Stadtkultur in der Dantezeit* (Munich: Hirmer Verlag, 1989).

Belting, Hans, *Likeness and Presence: A History of the Image before the Era of Art*, trans. Edmund Jephcott (Chicago: University of Chicago Press, 1994).

Beneduce, Chiara, 'John Buridan on Complexion. Natural Philosophy and Medicine in the Fourteenth Century', in C. Beneduce and D. Vincenti (eds), *Œconomia Corporis: The Body's Normal and Pathological Constitution at the Intersection of Philosophy and Medicine* (Pisa: Edizioni ETS, 2018), pp. 41–9.

Benjamin, Walter, 'The Origin of German Tragic Drama' (1925), in *Schriften*, ed. Theodor Adorno and Gretel Adorno, 2 vols (Frankfurt: Suhrkamp, 1955), vol. 1.

Benjamin, Walter, *The Origin of German Tragic Drama* (London: New Left Books, 1977).

Benveniste, Émile, *Noms d'agent et noms d'action en indo-européen* (Paris: Adrien-Maisonneuve, 1948).

Berman, Joshua, 'The "Sword of Mouths" (Jud. III. 16; Ps. CXLIX, 6; Prov. V 4): A Metaphor and Its Ancient Near Eastern Context', *Vetus Testamentum* 52, no. 3 (2002), pp. 291–303.

Bertelli, Sergio, *Il Re, la vergine, la sposa* (Rome: Donzelli, 2002).

Berthoz, Alain, *Le sens du mouvement* (Paris: Odile Jacob, 1997).

Bjurström, Per, 'Etienne Delaune and the Academy of Poetry and Music', *Master Drawings* 34, no. 4 (1996), pp. 351–64.

Bossuat, André, 'Documents inédits sur l'horloge du Palais et sur les gouverneurs du XVe siècle', *Bulletin de la Société de l'histoire de Paris et de l'Ile-de-France* 56 (1929), pp. 91–102.

Bottici, Chiara, *Imaginal Politics: Images Beyond Imagination and the Imaginary* (New York: Columbia University Press, 2019).

Boucheron, Patrick, *Conjurer la peur: Sienne, 1338. Essai sur la force politique des images* (Paris: Seuil, 2013).

Boucheron, Patrick, '"Tournez les yeux pour admirer, vous qui exercez le pouvoir, celle qui est peinte ici". La fresque du Bon Gouvernement d'Ambrogio Lorenzetti', *Annales. Histoire, Sciences Sociales* (2005–6), pp. 1137–99.

Bragagnolo, Manuela, 'Fisiognomica e profezia nel pensiero giuridico tra Cinque e Seicento. Alcune considerazioni', *Laboratoire Italien* 21 (2018).

Bresc-Bautier, Geneviève, 'Le monument funéraire de Henri II et la Chapelle des Valois à Saint-Denis (1560–1585)', in Dominique Cordellier, assisted by Bernadette Py, exhibition catalogue, *Primatice: Maître de Fontainebleau*, Paris, Musée du Louvre, 22 September 2004–3 January 2005.

Brückner, Wolfgang, *Bildnis und Brauch. Studien zur Bildfunktion der Effigies* (Berlin: Schmidt Erich Verlag, 1986).

Brunier, Isabelle, 'La salle du Conseil, l'apport des sources écrites (XVe–XVIIe siècle)', in Frédéric Elsig and Nicolas Schätti (eds), *Peindre à Genève au XVIe siècle: le décor peint de la salle du conseil d'État à l'Hôtel de Ville* (Geneva: Georg, 2012), pp. 21–38.

Burmeister, Karl Heinz, 'La Justicia de 1559 de Pieter Brueghel el Viejo', *Pensamiento juridico* 24 (2009), pp. 19–37.

Campbell, Peter, *Power and Politics in Old Regime France, 1720–1745* (London: Routledge, 1996).

Carlà, Filippo, *L'oro nella tarda antichità: aspetti economici e sociali* (Turin: Silvio Zamorani Editore, 2009).

Caviness, Madeline H., 'Giving "the Middle Ages" a Bad Name: Blood Punishments in the *Sachsenspiegel* and Town Lawbooks', *Studies in Iconography* 34 (2013), pp. 175–235.

Chabrier, Renaud, 'From Sketches to Morphing: New Geometric Views on the Epistemological Role of Drawing', in Tamar Flash and Alain Berthoz (eds), *Space-Time Geometries for Motion and Perception in the Brain and the Arts* (Cham: Springer, 2021), pp. 151–83.

Changeux, Jean-Pierre, *La beauté dans le cerveau* (Paris: Odile Jacob, 2016).

Chastel, André, *Le geste dans l'art* (Paris: Liana Lévi, 2001).

Cilliers, Louise, 'Vindicianus' *Gynaecia*: Text and Translation of the Codex Monacensis (Clm 4622)', *The Journal of Medieval Latin* 15 (2005), pp. 153–236.

Code Civil des Français (Paris: De l'imprimerie de la République, 1804).

Cowan, Bainard, 'Walter Benjamin's Theory of Allegory', *New German Critique*, special issue on Modernism, 22 (Winter 1981), pp. 109–22.

d'Arco, Carlo, *Delle arti e degli artefici di Mantova*, 2 vols (Mantua: Giovanni Agazzi, 1857).

Darnton, Robert, *The Corpus of Clandestine Literature in France, 1769–1789* (New York: W. W. Norton, 1995).

de Divitiis, Bianca, 'Castel Nuovo and Castel Capuano in Naples: The Transformation of Two Medieval Castles into "all'antica" Residence for the Aragonese Royals', *Zeitschrift für Kunstgeschichte* 76, no. 4 (2013), pp. 441–74.

de Jorio, Andrea, *La mimica degli antichi investigata nel gestire napoletano* (Naples: Dalla stamperia e cartiera del Fibreno, 1832).

Delaborde, Henri, *Marc-Antoine Raimondi; étude historique et critique suivie d'un catalogue raisonné des œuvres du maître* (Paris: Librairie de l'Art, 1888).

D'Elia, Una Roman, *Raphael's Ostrich* (University Park: Pennsylvania State University Press, 2015).

Deonna, Waldemar, 'La Justice à l'Hôtel de Ville de Genève et la fresque des juges aux mains coupées', *Zeitschrift für schweizerische Archäologie und Kunstgeschichte/Revue suisse d'art et d'archéologie* 11 (1950), pp. 144–9.

Deonna, Waldemar, 'Le genou, siège de force et de vie et sa protection magique', *Revue Archéologique* 6th series, 13 (January–June 1939), pp. 224–35.

Derrett, J. Duncan M., 'Rabelais' Legal Learning and the Trial of Bridoye', *Bibliothèque d'Humanisme et Renaissance* 25, no. 1 (1963), pp. 111–71.

Dessi, Rosa Maria, *Les spectres du bon gouvernement* (Paris: Presses Universitaires de France, 2017).

Dessi, Rosa Maria, 'L'invention du "Bon Gouvernement". Pour une histoire des anachronismes dans les fresques d'Ambrogio Lorenzetti (XIVe–XXe siècle)', *Bibliothèque de l'école des chartes* 165, no. 2 (2007), pp. 453–504.

de Sutter, Laurent, *Post-Tribunal. Renzo Piano Building Workshop et l'île de la cité judiciaire* (Paris: Éditions B2, 2018).

de Vandenesse, Jean, *Collection des voyages des souverains des Pays-Bas*, vol. 2 (Brussels: Gachard Louis-Prosper, 1874).

Devijver, Hubert and Frank Van Wonterghem, 'The Funerary Monuments of Equestrian Officers of the Late Republic and Early Empire in Italy (50 B.C.– 100 A.D.)', *Ancient Society* 21 (1990), pp. 59–98.

Didi-Huberman, Georges, 'The Molding Image: Genealogy and the Truth of Resemblance in Pliny's *Natural History*, Book 35, 1–17', in Costas Douzinas and Lynda Nead (eds), *Law and the Image: The Authority of Art and the Aesthetics of Law* (Chicago: University of Chicago Press, 1992), pp. 71–88.

Didi-Huberman, Georges, *Ouvrir Vénus: nudité, rêve, cruauté* (Paris: Gallimard, 1999).

Didron, Ainé, *Annales archéologiques*, vol. 20 (Paris: Librairie archéologique de Victor Didron, 1860).

Donato, Maria Monica, 'Dal "Comune rubato" di Giotto al "Comune sovrano" di Ambrogio Lorenzetti (con una proposta per la "canzone" del Buon Governo)', in A. Carlo Quintavalle (ed.), *Medioevo: Immagine e racconti. Atti del convegno internazionale di studi* (Milan: Parma, 2002).

Douzinas, Costas, 'The Legality of the Image', *The Modern Law Review* 63, no. 6 (2000), pp. 813–30.

Dufey, Pierre Joseph Spyridion, *Œuvres inédites de Michel l'Hospital, Chancelier de France* (Paris: Boulland, 1825).

Durieux, Achille, 'Les artistes cambrésiens du IXe au XIXe siècles et l'école de dessin de Cambrai', in *Mémoires de la Société d'émulation de Cambrai: agriculture, sciences et arts*, Cambrai (16 November 1873), vol. 32, pt 2, pp. 69–70.

Durkheim, Émile, *The Division of Labor in Society* (1893; New York: The Free Press, 1997).

Eberly, Susan S., 'A Thorn among the Lilies: The Hawthorn in Medieval Love Allegory', *Folklore* 100, no. 1 (1989), pp. 41–52.

Eckstein, Friedrich August, 'Bersman, Gregor', in *Allgemeine Deutsche Biographie*, vol. 2 (Leipzig: Duncker & Humblot, 1875), pp. 507–8.

Ehrhardt, Arnold, 'Vir Bonus Quadrato Lapidi Comparatur', *The Harvard Theological Review* 38, no. 3 (1945), pp. 177–93.

Evans, Michael, 'Two Sources for Maimed Justice', *Notes in the History of Art* 2, no. 1 (1982), pp. 12–15.

Ferreira da Cunha, Paulo, *Arqueologias Jurídicas. Ensaios Jurídico-Humanísticos e Jurídico-Políticos* (Porto: Lello, 1996).

Franko, Mark, 'The Conduct of Contemplation and the Gestural Ethics of Interpretation in Walter Benjamin's "Epistemo-Critical Prologue"', *Performance Philosophy* 3, no. 1 (2017).

Freedberg, David, *The Power of Images: Studies in the History and Theory of Response* (Chicago: University of Chicago Press, 1991).

Garapon, Antoine, *Bien juger. Essai sur le rituel judiciaire* (Paris: Odile Jacob, 2001).

Garapon, Antoine, Julie Allard and Frédéric Gros, *Les vertus du juge* (Paris: Dalloz, 2008).

Gaskell, Ivan, 'Vermeer, Judgment and Truth', *The Burlington Magazine* 126, no. 978 (1984), pp. 557–61.

Gatty, Margaret, *The Book of Sun-dials* (London: Bell and Daldy, 1872).

Gibson, Walter S., 'Festive Peasants before Bruegel: Three Case Studies and Their Implications', *Simiolus: Netherlands Quarterly for the History of Art* 21, no. 4 (2004–5), pp. 292–309.

Ginzburg, Carlo, 'Morelli, Freud, and Sherlock Holmes: Clues and Scientific Method', in Umberto Eco and Thomas Sebeck (eds), *The Sign of Three: Dupin, Holmes, Peirce* (Bloomington, IN: Indiana University Press, 1984), pp. 81–118.

Girard, René, *Violence and the Sacred* (Baltimore, MD: Johns Hopkins University Press, 1977).

Gloria, A., *La pietra del vituperio del salone di Padova: Lettera* (Padua: Tipografia Bianchi, 1851).

Goethe, W., *Maximen und Reflexionem. Nach den Handschriften des Goethe-und Schiller-Archivs* (Weimar: Verlag der Goethe Gesellschaft, 1907).

Goldner, George R., Lee Hendrix and Kelly Pask, *European Drawings 2: Catalogue of the Collections* (Los Angeles: Getty Publications, 1992).

Gombrich, E. H., '*Icones Symbolicæ*: The Visual Image in Neo-Platonic Thought', *Journal of the Warburg and Courtauld Institutes* 11 (1948), pp. 178–9.

Gombrich, E. H., 'The Use of Art for the Study of Symbols', *American Psychologist* 20, no. 1 (1965), pp. 34–50.

Gombrich, E. H., 'Ritualized Gesture and Expression in Art', *Philosophical Transactions of the Royal Society of London*, Series B, Biological Sciences, 251, no. 772 (1966), pp. 391–40.

Gombrich, E. H., '*Icones Symbolicæ*', in *Gombrich on the Renaissance, Volume 2: Symbolic Images* (London: Phaidon Press, 1985).

Gombrich, E. H., Review of *Gestures of Despair in Medieval and Early Renaissance Art* by Moshe Barasch, *The Burlington Magazine* 120, no. 908 (1978), pp. 762–3.

González García, José M., *The Eyes of Justice: Blindfolds and Farsightedness, Vision and Blindness in the Aesthetics of the Law* (Frankfurt: Vittorio Klostermann, 2017).

Goodrich, Peter, 'Gynætopia: Feminine Genealogies of Common Law', *Journal of Law and Society* 20, no. 3 (1993), pp. 276–308.

Goodrich, Peter, *OEdipus Lex: Psychoanalysis, History, Law* (Berkeley: University of California Press, 1995).

Goodrich, Peter, *The Laws of Love: A Brief Historical and Practical Manual* (London: Palgrave Macmillan, 2007).

Goodrich, Peter, *Legal Emblems and the Art of Law:* Obiter Depicta *as the Vision of Governance* (Cambridge: Cambridge University Press, 2014).

Goodrich, Peter, *Schreber's Law: Jurisprudence and Judgment in Transition* (Edinburgh: Edinburgh University Press, 2020).

Goodrich, Peter, 'Weird Judgment, Agon, Omniscience and the Absence of an "E"', *Ordine internazionale e diritti humani/International Order and Legal Rights* (2021), pp. 130–9.

Goodrich, Peter and Valérie Hayaert (eds), *Genealogies of Legal Vision* (London: Routledge, 2015).

Gottlieb, Christian Haubold, *Legis judiciariæ utriusque Saxonia regia utitur origines* (Leipzig: ex Officina Walmonia, 1809).

Green, Henry, *Andrea Alciati and His Books of Emblems: A Biographical and Bibliographical Study* (London: Tröner, 1872).

Greenaway, Peter, *100 Allegories to Represent the World/100 Allégories pour représenter le monde* (Paris: Adam Biro, USHS, 1998).

Greene, David M., 'The Identity of the Emblematic Nemesis', *Studies in the Renaissance* 10 (1963), pp. 25–43.

Greenhill, Eleanor Simmons, 'The Child in the Tree: A Study of the Cosmological Tree in Christian Tradition', *Traditio* 10 (1954), pp. 323–71.

Hayaert, Valérie, 'Le Baiser de Justice et de Paix: à propos d'une allégorie politique peinte pour le château de Richelieu par Nicolas Prévost', *Histoire de la Justice* 33, no. 1 (2022), pp. 91–101.

Hayaert, Valérie, 'Le rituel judiciaire d'Ancien régime et ses images face à la mort', in Ilona Hans-Collas, Fabienne Le Bars, Danielle Quéruel, Nathalie Rollet-Bricklin, Yann Sordet and Anne Weber (eds), *Le Livre et la Mort (XIVe–XVIIIe siècles)* (Paris: Bibliothèques Mazarine & Sainte-Geneviève – Éditions des cendres, 2019), pp. 181–204.

Hayaert, Valérie, *'Mens emblematica' et humanisme juridique: le cas du 'Pegma cum narrationibus philosophicis' de Pierre Coustau, 1555* (Geneva: Droz, 2008).

Hayaert, Valérie and Antoine Garapon, *Allégories de justice: la grand'chambre du Parlement de Flandre* (Abbeville: Imprimerie Paillart, 2014).

Heitsch, Ernst, *Die griechischen Dichterfragmente der römischen Kaiserzeit*, vol. 1 (Göttingen: Vandenhoeck & Ruprecht, 1963).

Heraclitus, *Heraclitus: Homeric Problems*, ed. and trans. Donald A. Russell and David Konstan (Atlanta, GA: Society of Biblical Literature, 2005).

Hibbits, Bernard J., 'Making Motions: The Embodiment of Law in Gesture', *Journal of Contemporary Legal Issues* 6 (1995), pp. 51–81.

Hofer, Paul, *Die Kunstdenkmäler des Kantons Bern, Band I, Die Stadt Bern* (Basel: Verlag Birkhäuser, 1952).

Hollstein, F. W. H., *German Engravings, Etchings and Woodcuts c. 1400–1700* (Amsterdam: M. Hertzberger, 1954–).

Hornum, M. B., *Nemesis, the Roman States, and the Games* (Leiden: Brill, 1993).

Houghton, L. B. T., 'Maritime Maro: Virgil in Venice', in *Virgil's Fourth Eclogue in the Italian Renaissance* (Cambridge: Cambridge University Press, 2019), pp. 67–88.

Howard, Peter Francis, *Beyond the Written Word: Preaching and Theology in the Florence of Archbishop of Antoninus 1427–1459* (Florence: Leo S. Olschki Editore, 1995).

Hubach, Hanns, 'Tapestry to Woodcut: Albrecht Dürer's Representation of the Michelfeld-Tapestry (1526)', paper presented at a Study Day on the History of the Textile Image, German Centre for Art History, Paris, 24 June 2010.

Hugo, Victor, 'Le dernier jour d'un condamné' (preface for the 1829 novel), in *Écrits sur la peine de mort*, ed. Marie Salavert (Arles: Actes Sud, 1992).

Husband, Timothy B., Madeline H. Caviness and Marilyn Beaven, 'Monograph Series I: Stained Glass before 1700 in American Collections: Silver-Stained Roundels and Unipartite Panels (Corpus Vitrearum Checklist IV), *Studies in the History of Art* 39 (1991), pp. 3–277.

Husband, Timothy B. and Michael Hoyle, '"Ick Sorgheloose . . ." A Silver-Stained Roundel in the Cloisters', *Metropolitan Museum Journal* 24 (1989), pp. 173–88.

Hüsken, Wim, 'The Michelfeldt Tapestry and Contemporary European Literature. Moral Lessons on the Rule of Deceit', in Dagmar Eichberger and Charles Zika, *Dürer and His Culture* (Cambridge: Cambridge University Press, 1998), pp. 69–92.

Huygebaert, Stefan, Georges Martyn, Vanessa Paumen, Eric Bousmar and Xavier Rousseaux (eds), *The Art of Law: Artistic Representations and Iconography of Law and Justice in Context, from the Middle Ages to the First World War* (Cham: Springer, 2018).

Jacob, Robert, *Images de la justice. Essai sur l'iconographie judiciaire du Moyen Âge à l'âge classique* (Paris: Le Léopard d'Or, 1996).

Jacquart, Danielle, *La médecine médiévale dans le cadre parisien, XIVe–XVe siècles* (Paris: Fayard, 1998).

Jappy, Tony, 'Fond et forme dans l'image allégorique', *Protée* 33, no. 1 (2005), pp. 9–23.

Johnson, Geraldine A., 'Embodying Devotion: Multisensory Encounters with Donatello's Crucifix in S. Croce', *Renaissance Quarterly* 73, no. 4 (2020), pp. 1179–234.

Jornod, Naïma, 'Observations iconographiques', in Frédéric Elsig and Nicolas Schätti (eds), *Peindre à Genève au XVIe siècle: le décor peint de la salle du conseil d'État à l'Hôtel de Ville* (Geneva: Georg, 2012), pp. 97–110.

Judson, J. Richard, 'Jan Gossart North of the Rivers', *Netherlandish Kunsthistorisch Jaarboek* (NKJ)/*Netherlands Yearbook for History of Art* 38 (1987), pp. 128–35.

Kantorowicz, Ernst H., 'ΣΥΝΘΡΟΝΟΣ ΔΙΚΗΙ', *American Journal of Archaeology* 57, no. 2 (1953), pp. 65–70.

Kantorowicz, Ernst Hartwig, *The King's Two Bodies: A Study in Mediaeval Political Theology* (Princeton, NJ: Princeton University Press, 1957).

Kaulbach, Hans-Martin and Reinhart Schleier, *'Der Welt Lauf'. Allegorische Graphikserien des Manierismus*, exhibition catalogue, Stuttgart, 18 October 1997–25 January 1998 and Bochum, 17 May–6 July 1998.

Keith, Thomas R., 'The Fine Art of Horsing Around: A Note on Wordplay in Mesomedes' *Hymn to Nemesis*', *The Classical Quarterly* 64, no. 1 (2014), pp. 428–31.

Kida, Tsuyoshi, 'Appropriation du geste par les étrangers: le cas d'étudiants japonais apprenant le français', unpublished thesis, Université de Provence, 2005.

Kissel, Otto Rudolf, *Die Justitia. Reflexionen über ein Symbol und seine Darstellung in der bildenden Kunst* (Munich: Beck, 1984).

Klibansky, Raymond, Erwin Panofsky and Fritz Saxl, *Saturn and Melancholy: Studies in the History of Natural Philosophy, Religion and Art* (London: Nelson, 1964).

Körner, Hans, *Statuenliebe in St Peter. Rompilger und Romtouristen vor Guglielmo della Portas Grabmal für Papst Paul III* (Düsseldorf: Kreis der Freunde des Seminars für Kunstgeschichte, Heinrich-Heine-Universität Düsseldorf, 1999).

Kroppenberg, Inge, 'Blind Bodies of Justice. Æsthetics and Law in Johann Gottfried Herder's Sculpture', in Werner Gephart and Jure Leko (eds), *Law and the Arts: Elective Affinities and Relationships of Tension* (Frankfurt: Vittorio Klostermann, 2017), pp. 251–70.

Kurth, Betty, 'Zwei unbekantte Fragmente des Michelfeldter Bildteppichs', *Die graphischen Künste* 2 (1937), pp. 27–31.

Landels, J. G., *Music in Ancient Greece and Rome* (London: Routledge, 1999).

Lawrence, D. H., 'The Spirit of Place', in *Selected Literary Criticism*, ed. Anthony Beal (New York: Viking Press, 1966).

Legendre, Pierre, *Leçons VIII. Le crime du caporal Lortie. Traité sur le Père* (Paris: Fayard, 1989).

Lehrmann, Joachim, 'Justus Oldekop (1597 bis 1667). Die Flucht Niedersachsens Streiter wider den Hexenwahn an den Wolfenbütteler Hof', in *Heimatbuch für den Landkreis Wolfenbüttel* (Braunschweig: Oeding, 2005).

Lentes, Thomas, 'Counting Piety in the Late Middle Ages', in Bernhard Jussen (ed.), *Ordering Medieval Society: Perspectives on Intellectual and Practical Modes of Shaping Social Relations*, trans. Pamela Selwyn (Philadelphia: University of Pennsylvania Press, 2001), pp. 55–91.

Leone, Massimo, 'The Frowning Balance: Semiotic Insinuations on the Visual Rhetoric of Justice', *Semiotica* 216 (2017), pp. 41–62.

Liddell, Henry George and Robert Scott, *A Greek–English Lexicon* (Oxford: Clarendon, 1940).

Lindell, Johann, 'Bourdieusian Media Studies: Returning Social Theory to Old and New Media', *Distinktion: Journal of Social Theory* 16 (2015), pp. 362–77.

Lundblad, Kristina, 'The Printer's Mark in Early Modern Sweden', in Anja Wolkenhauer and Bernhard F. Scholz (eds), *Typographorum Emblemata: The Printer's Mark in the Context of Early Modern Culture* (Berlin: De Gruyter, 2018), pp. 227–56.

Lüttenberg, Thomas, 'The Cod-piece – A Renaissance Fashion between Sign and Artefact', *The Medieval History Journal* 8, no. 1 (2005), pp. 49–81.

Maclean, Ian, 'Bourdieu's Field of Cultural Production', *French Cultural Studies* 3 (1993), pp. 283–9.

Maclean, Ian, *Logic, Signs and Nature in the Renaissance: The Case of Learned Medicine* (Cambridge: Cambridge University Press, 2002).

Maclean, Ian, *The Renaissance Notion of Woman: A Study in the Fortunes of Scholasticism and Medical Science in European Intellectual Life* (Cambridge: Cambridge University Press, 1980).

Maguire, Henry, 'Truth and Convention in Byzantine Descriptions of Works of Art', *Dumbarton Oaks Papers* 28 (1974), pp. 111–40.

Manderson, Desmond, *Danse Macabre: Temporalities of Law in the Visual Arts* (Cambridge: Cambridge University Press, 2019).

Manderson, Desmond and Cristina S. Martinez, 'Justice and Art, Face to Face', *Yale Journal of Law & Humanities* 28, no. 2 (2016), pp. 241–63.

Mandressi, Rafael, *Le regard de l'anatomiste: dissections et invention du corps en Occident* (Paris: Seuil, 2003).

Maniscalco, Lorenzo, *Equity in Early Modern Scholarship* (Nijhoff: Brill, 2020).

Mansour, Opher, 'Censure and Censorship in Rome, c. 1600: The visitation of Clement VIII and the Visual Arts', in Marcia B. Hall and Tracy E. Cooper (eds), *The Sensuous in the Counter-Reformation Church* (New York: Cambridge University Press, 2013), pp. 136–60.

Mărgineanu Cârstoiu, Monica, 'Némésis et la coudée. Un édicule votif de Tomis', *Caiete ARA* 2 (2011), pp. 53–68.

Margolin, Jean-Claude, 'Parodie et paradoxe dans l'"Éloge de la Folie" d'Érasme', *Nouvelles de la République des Lettres* 2 (1983), pp. 27–58.

Martens, Didier, 'Ni Hubertus Goltzius, ni Diane de Poitiers: une "Allégorie de l'Infidélité" de Hermann tom Ring à l'Hôtel de Ville de Bruxelles', *Annales d'Histoire de l'Art et d'Archéologie* 18 (1996), pp. 23–34.

Merleau-Ponty, Maurice, *Le visible et l'invisible suivi de Notes de travail*, ed. Claude Lefort (Paris: Gallimard, 1964).

Meuwissen, Daantje D., *Jacob Cornelisz van Oostsanen (ca. 1475–1533): De Renaissance in Amsterdam en Alkmaar* (Zwolle: Waanders Uitgevers, 2014).

Mitchell, William John Thomas, *Iconology: Image, Text, Ideology* (Chicago: University of Chicago Press, 1986).

Moelands, M. A. and J. Th. de Smidt, *Weegschaal & Zwaard. De Verbeelding van Recht en Gerechtigheid in Nederland* (The Hague: Jongbloed Juridische Boekhandel en Uitgeverij, 1999).

Mogens, Herman Hansen, *The Athenian Democracy in the Age of Demosthenes: Structures, Principles and Ideology* (Oxford: Blackwell, 1991).

Müller, Jürgen and Thomas Schauerte (eds), *Die Gottlosen Maler von Nürnberg. Konvention und Subversion in der Druckgrafik der Beham-Brüder* (Emsdetten: Edition Imorde, 2011).

Napier, John Russell, 'The Evolution of the Hand', *Scientific American* 207 (1962), pp. 56–62.

Napier, John Russell, 'The Prehensile Movements of the Human Hand', *Journal of Bone and Joint Surgery* 38-B, no. 4 (1956), pp. 902–13.

North, Helen F., *From Myth to Icon: Reflections on Greek Ethical Doctrine in Literature and Art* (Ithaca, NY: Cornell University Press, 1979).

Onians, Richard Broxton, *The Origins of European Thought about the Body, the Mind, the Soul, the World, Time, and Fate* (Cambridge: Cambridge University Press, 1951).

Owens, Craig, 'The Allegorical Impulse: Toward a Theory of the Postmodernism', in Brian Wallis (ed.), *Art After Modernism: Rethinking Representation* (New York: New Museum of Contemporary Art in association with David R. Godine, 1984), pp. 203–53; originally published in *October* 12 (1980), pp. 67–86, and 13 (1980), pp. 59–80.

Panofsky, Erwin, *A Mythological Painting by Poussin in the Nationalmuseum Stockholm* (Stockholm: Nationalmusei skriftserie, 1960).

Panofsky, Erwin, *Studies in Iconology: Humanistic Themes in the Art of the Renaissance* (New York: Harper Torchbook, 1967).

Pastoureau, Michel, *Les sceaux* (Turnhout: Brepols, 1981).

Perelman, Chaim, *Études de logique juridique* (Brussels: Bruylant, 1966).

Peters, Julie Stone, *Law as Performance: Theatricality, Spectatorship, and the Making of Law in Ancient, Medieval, and Early Modern Europe* (Oxford: Oxford University Press, 2022).

Petey-Girard, Bruno and Alexandre Tarrête (eds), *Guillaume du Vair, parlementaire et écrivain (1556–1621)* (Geneva: Droz, 2005).

Platt, Verity, *Facing the Gods: Epiphany and Representation in Graeco-Roman Art, Literature and Religion* (Cambridge: Cambridge University Press, 2011).

Prosperi, Adriano, *Justice Blindfolded: The Historical Course of an Image* (Leiden: Brill, 2018; first published as *Giustizia bendata. Percorsi storici di un' imagine*, Turin: Einaudi, 2008).

Proust, Marcel, *Remembrance of Things Past: Swann's Way*, trans. C. K. Scott Moncrieff (1913; London: Chatto & Windus, 1920).

Quignard, Pascal, *Le sexe et l'effroi* (Paris: Gallimard, 1994).

Rawls, John, *A Theory of Justice* (Cambridge, MA: Harvard University Press, 1971).

Rawski, C. H. (ed.), *Petrarch's Remedies for Fortune Fair and Foul: A Modern English Translation of De remediis utriusque fortune*, 5 vols (Bloomington: Indiana University Press, 1991).

Redfield, James M., *Nature and Culture in the* Iliad: *The Tragedy of Hector* (Chicago: University of Chicago Press, 1975).

Resnik, Judith and Dennis Curtis, *Representing Justice: Invention, Controversy, and Rights in City-States and Democratic Courtrooms* (New Haven, CT: Yale University Press, 2011).

Resnik, Judith and Dennis E. Curtis, 'The Jayne Lecture: Representing Justice: From Renaissance Iconography to Twenty-First-Century Courthouses', *American Philosophical Society* 151, no. 2 (2007), pp. 139–83.

Richter Sherman, Claire, 'Some Visual Definitions in the Illustrations of Aristotle's *Nicomachean Ethics* and *Politics* in the French Translations of Nicole Oresme', *The Art Bulletin* 59, no. 3 (1977), pp. 320–30.

Ricœur, Paul, *Amour et Justice* (1989; Paris: Seuil, 2008).

Riskin, Jessica, 'Machines in the Garden', in Charlene Villaseñor Black and Mari-Tere Álvarez (eds), *Renaissance Futurities: Science, Art, Invention* (Oakland: University of California Press, 2020), pp. 19–40.

Robert, Christian-Nils, 'Le Tribunal de Paris: piano, piano face à la symbolique judiciaire', *L'Irascible, Revue de l'Institut Rhône-Alpin de Sciences Criminelles*, 9 (2022), pp. 155–79.

Robert, Christian-Nils, 'Naissance d'une image: la balance de l'équité', *Histoire de la Justice* 11 (1998), pp. 85–97.

Robert, Christian-Nils, *Une allégorie parfaite. La Justice: vertu, courtisane et bourreau* (Geneva: Georg Éditeur, 1993).

Roettig, P., *Reformation als Apokalypse: Die Holzschnitte von Matthias Gerung im Codex germanicus 6592* (Bern: der Bayerischen Staatsbibliothek in München, 1991).

Rogister, John, *Louis XV and the Parlement of Paris, 1737–1754* (Cambridge: Cambridge University Press, 1995).

Ronzeaud, Pierre, 'Usages polémiques de l'allégorie en contexte pamphlétaire: les *Mazarinades*', in Marie-Christine Pioffet and Anne-Élisabeth Spica (eds), *S'exprimer autrement: poétiques et enjeux de l'allégorie à l'Âge classique* (Tübingen: Narr, 2016), pp. 215–26.

Rosand, David, *Myths of Venice: The Figuration of a State* (Chapel Hill: University of North Carolina Press, 2005), pp. 67–88.

Rosand, Ellen, *Opera in Seventeenth-Century Venice: The Creation of a Genre* (Berkeley: University of California Press, 2007).

Rowlands, John, *Drawings by German Artists and Artists from German-Speaking Regions of Europe in the Department of Prints and Drawings in the British Museum: The 15thC & 16thC by Artists Born before 1530* (London: British Museum Press, 1993).

Roy, Bruno, 'À propos d'un geste antisémite décrit par Huguccio de Pise', in *Le geste et les gestes au Moyen Âge* (Aix-en-Provence: Presses Universitaires de Provence, 1998), pp. 557–70.

Rubinstein, Nicolai, 'Political Ideas in Sienese Art: The Frescoes by Ambrogio Lorenzetti and Taddeo di Bartolo in the Palazzo Pubblico', *Journal of the Warburg and Courtauld Institutes* 21 (1959), pp. 179–207.

Ruelle, Annette, 'Sacrifice, énonciation et actes de langage en droit romain archaïque (*"agone"*, *lege agere*, *cum populo agere*)', *Revue Internationale des Droits de l'Antiquité* 49, no. 1 (2002), pp. 203–39.

Russell, Daniel, *The Emblem and Device in France* (Lexington, KY: French Forum, 1985).

Russell, Daniel, *Emblematic Structures in Renaissance French Culture* (Toronto: University of Toronto Press, 1995).

Russell, Daniel, Review of Valérie Hayaert, *Mens Emblematica et Humanisme Juridique: Le Cas Du Pegma Cum Narrationibus Philosophicis de Pierre Coustau (1555)*. Travaux d'Humanisme et Renaissance 438. Geneva: Librairie Droz, 2008, *Renaissance Quarterly* 62, no. 1 (2009), pp. 223–4.

Sale, J. Russell, 'Protecting Fertility in Fra Filippo Lippi's *Portrait of a Woman with a Man at a Casement*', *Metropolitan Museum Journal* 51 (2016), pp. 64–83.

Sbriccoli, Mario, 'La triade, le bandeau, le genou. Droit et procès pénal dans les allégories de la Justice du Moyen-âge à l'âge moderne', *Crime, Histoire et Sociétés* 9, no. 1 (2005), pp. 33–78.

Sbriccoli, Mario, *Storia del diritto penale et della Giustizia* (Milan: Giuffrè Editore, 2009).

Schmitt, Jean-Claude, *La raison des gestes dans l'Occident médiéval* (Paris: Gallimard, 1990).

Schneeberger, Ursula, 'Zuo beschirmen die gerechtikeÿtt, [. . .] un wer es allen fürsten leÿtt. Staat, Krieg und Moral im Program der Berner Brunnenfiguren', in André Holenstein (ed.), *Berns mächtige Zeit. Das 16. und 17. Jahrhundert neu entdeckt*, vol. 3 (Bern: Berner Zeiten, 2006), pp. 157–62.

Schwerhoff, Gerd, 'Virtue or Tyranny? Pieter Bruegel, *Justitia* and the Myth of the Inquisition', in Bertram Kaschek, Jürgen Müller and Jessica Buskirk (eds), *Pieter Bruegel the Elder and Religion* (Leiden: Brill, 2018), pp. 79–113.

Seeber, Christine, *Untersuchungen zur Darstellung des Totengerichts im alten Ägypten* (Munich: Deutscher Kunstverlag, 1976).

Simons, Patricia, 'Annibale Carraci's Visual Wit', *Notes in the History of Art* 30, no. 2 (2011), pp. 26–31.

Skinner, Quentin, 'Ambrogio Lorenzetti: "The Artist as political philosopher"', *Proceedings of the British Academy* 72 (1986), pp. 1–56.

Skinner, Quentin, 'Ambrogio Lorenzetti's *Buon Governo* Frescoes: Two Old Questions, Two New Answers', *Journal of the Warburg and Courtauld Institutes* 62 (1999), pp. 1–28.

Spagnolo, Maddalena, *Pasquino in piazza. Una statua a Roma tra arte e vituperio* (Rome: Campisano, 1999).

Stafford, Emma J., '*Nemesis, Hybris* and Violence', in Jean-Marie Bertrand (ed.), *La violence dans les mondes grec et romain* (Paris: Sorbonne: 2005).

Steadman, Philip, *Renaissance Fun: The Machines behind the Scenes* (London: UCL Press, 2021).

Stern, Simon, Maksymilian Del Mar and Bernadette Meyler (eds), *The Oxford Handbook of Law and Humanities* (New York: Oxford University Press, 2020).

Stoichita, Victor I., *Des corps. Anatomies, défenses, fantasmes* (Geneva: Droz, 2019).

Stolleis, Michael, *The Eye of Law: Two Essays on Legal History*, trans. Thomas Dunlap (Abingdon: Birkbeck Law Press, 2008).

Sussman, V., 'Maria mit dem Schutzmantel', *Marburger Jahrbuch für Kunstwissenschaft* 5 (1929), pp. 285–351.

Swann, Julian, *Politics and the Parlement of Paris under Louis XV, 1754–1774* (Cambridge: Cambridge University Press, 1995).

Terpstra, Nicholas (ed.), *The Art of Executing Well: Rituals of Execution in Renaissance Italy* (Kirkville, MO: Truman State University Press, 2008).

Thomas, K., 'Introduction', in J. Bremmer and H. Roodenburg (eds), *A Cultural History of Gesture* (Ithaca, NY: Cornell University Press, 1992), pp. 1–14.

Tournoy-Thoen, Godelieve, 'Le manuscrit 1010 de la "Biblioteca de Cataluna" et l'humanisme italien à la Cour de France vers 1500 (III)', *Humanistica Lovaniensia* 27 (1978), pp. 52–85.

Vanautgaerden, Alexandre (ed.), *Anatomie des Vanités/Anatomie der Ijdelheden* (Turnhout: Brepols, 2008).

Van Kley, Dale K., *The Damiens Affair and the Unraveling of the Ancien Regime, 1750–1770* (Princeton, NJ: Princeton University Press, 1984).

Van Kley, Dale K., *The Jansenists and the Expulsion of the Jesuits* (New Haven, CT: Yale University Press, 1975).

Vecce, Carlo, 'Bernardino Dardano. Un poeta italiano alla corte di Luigi XII', in Gabriella Almanza Ciotti, Sandro Baldoncini and Giulia Mastrangelo Latini (eds), *Studi in memoria di Antonio Carlo Possenti* (Macerata: Istituti editoriali e poligrafici internazionali, 1998), pp. 559–73.

Vercruysse, Jos E., 'Gesetz und Liebe: Die Struktur der "Heidelberger Disputation" Luthers (1518)', *Lutherjahrbuch* 48 (1981), pp. 7–43.

Von Moeller, Ernst, 'Die Augenbinde der Justitia', *Zeitschrift für christliche Kunst* 17 (1905), pp. 107–22, 141–52.

Von Stintzing, Roderich, *Geschichte der deutschen Rechtswissenschaften*, vol. 1 (1880; Leipzig: Wentworth Press, 2018).

Vouilloux, Bernard (ed.), 'Déclins de l'allégorie?', *Modernités*, special issue, 22 (2006).

Wachenheim, Pierre, 'Emblèmes de la Robe: les représentations de la Justice dans l'imagerie pro-parlementaire sous le règne de Louis XV', *Sociétés & Représentations* 18, no. 2 (2004), pp. 233–49.

Wallace, Richard W., 'Salvator Rosa's "Justice Appearing to the Peasants"', *Journal of the Warburg and the Courtauld Institutes* 30 (1967), pp. 431–4.

Walther, Ludwig, 'Die Monodia des Marcus Antonius Muretus zum Tod des Pariser Parlamentspräsidenten Christophe de Thou (1583) – Idealbilder von Humanismus und Gerechtigkeit', in Ivo Volt and Janika Päll (eds), *Quattuor Lustra: Papers Celebrating the 20th Anniversary of the Re-establishment of Classical Studies at the University of Tartu* (Tartu: Tartu University Press, 2012), pp. 273–303.

Warburg, Aby, 'Der Tod des Orpheus', in *Ausgewählte Schriften und Würdigungen*, ed. Dieter Wuttke (Baden-Baden: Verlag Valentin Koerner, 1980).

Warburg, Aby, *Mnemosyne I*, in *Werke in einem Band*, ed. Martin Treml, Sigrid Weigel and Perdita Ladwig (Frankfurt: Surkhamp Verlag, 2010).

Watkins, Renée, 'L.B. Alberti's Emblem, the Winged Eye, and His Name, Leo', *Mittellungen des Kunsthistorischen Institutes in Florenz* 9, nos 3 and 4 (November 1960), pp. 256–8.

Weigel, Sigrid, 'Epistemology of Wandering, Tree and Taxonomy. The System Figuré in Warburg's *Mnemosyne* Project within the History of Cartographic and Encyclopaedic Knowledge', *Images Re-vues*, special issue, 'Survivance d'Aby Warburg', 4 (2013), art. 15.

Werner, Schild, *Bilder von Recht und Gerechtigkeit* (Cologne: DuMont, 1995).

Wirth, Jean, *La jeune fille et la mort. Recherches sur les thèmes macabres dans l'art germanique de la Renaissance* (Geneva: Droz, 1979).

Wixom, William D. (ed.), *Mirror of the Medieval World* (New York: The Metropolitan Museum of Art, 1999).

Wohlfeil, Rainer, 'Pax antwerpiensis. Eine Fallstudie zu Verbildlichungen der Friedensidee im 16. Jahrhundert am Beispiel der Allegorie "Kuss von Gerechtigkeit und Friede"', in Brigitte Tolkemitt and Rainer Wohlfeil (eds), *Historische Bildkunde: Probleme* (Berlin: Duncker & Humbolt, 1991), pp. 211–58.

Wolf, Gerhard, 'Die frau in weiss visuelle strategien und künstlerische argumentation in Ambrogio Lorenzettis fresken in der Sala dei Nove', *Mitteilungen des Kunsthistorischen Institutes in Florenz* 55, no. 1 (2013), pp. 26–53.

Wolfthal, Diane, *Images of Rape: The 'Heroic' Tradition and Its Alternatives* (Cambridge: Cambridge University Press, 1999).

Yates, Frances A., *Astræa: The Imperial Theme in the Sixteenth Century* (London: Routledge, 1975).

Yates, Frances, 'Queen Elizabeth as Astræa', *Journal of the Warburg and Courtauld Institutes* 10 (1947), pp. 27–82.

Young, Alan R., *The English Emblem Tradition, Volume 5: Henry Peacham's Manuscript Emblem Books* (Toronto: University of Toronto Press, 1998).

Zaccaria, Raffaella, 'Dall'Acqua, Aurelio', in *Dizionario Biografico degli Italiani*, vol. 31 (Rome: Istituto della Enciclopedia italiana, 1985).

Zdekauer, Lodovico, *L'idea della giustizia e la sua imagine nelle arti figurative* (Macerata: Bianchini, 1909).

Zeunert, Susanne, 'Bilder in Martin Luthers *Tischreden*. Argumente und Beispiele gegen die Laster Hochmut, Abgötterei und Betrug', unpublished thesis, University of Trier, 2016.

Zschelletzschky, Herbert, *Die 'drei gottlosen Maler' von Nürnberg. Sebald Beham, Barthel Beham und Georg Pencz. Historische Grundlagen und ikonologische Probleme ihrer Graphik zur Reformations- und Bauernkriegszeit* (Leipzig: Seeman Verlag, 1975).

Zupnick, Irving L., 'Appearance and Reality in Bruegel's Virtues', in *Evolution Générale et développements régionaux en histoire de l'art*, Acts of the International Congress of the History of Art, Budapest, 1969, vol. 1 (Budapest: Akadémiai Kiadó, 1972), pp. 745–53.

Index nominum

This index does not contain the names of authors of secondary literature, which appear only in the notes.

Index rerum

EU representative:
Easy Access System Europe
Mustamäe tee 50, 10621 Tallinn, Estonia
Gpsr.requests@easproject.com

www.ingramcontent.com/pod-product-compliance
Lightning Source LLC
Chambersburg PA
CBHW070103290526
45789CB00005B/1898